M000209458

GENES ON THE COUCH

Explorations in evolutionary psychotherapy

GENES ON THE COUCH

Explorations in evolutionary psychotherapy

*Edited by Paul Gilbert and
Kent G. Bailey*

First published 2000
by Brunner-Routledge
27 Church Road, Hove, East Sussex, BN3 2FA

Simultaneously published in the USA and Canada
by Taylor & Francis Inc.
325 Chestnut Street, Suite 800, Philadelphia, PA 19106, USA

© 2000 P. Gilbert and K.G. Bailey (eds.)

Typeset in Times by Keystroke
Printed and bound in the UK by Biddles Ltd, Guildford and King's Lynn

All rights reserved. No part of this book may be reprinted or reproduced
or utilized in any form or by any electronic, mechanical, or other means,
now known or hereafter invented, including photocopying and recording,
or in any information storage or retrieval system, without permission in
writing from the publishers.

British Library Cataloguing in Publication Data
A catalogue record for this book is available
from the British Library

Library of Congress Cataloguing in Publication Data
A catalogue record has been requested for this book

ISBN 1–58391–102–2 (hbk)
ISBN 1–58391–103–0 (pbk)

CONTENTS

CONTENTS

LIST OF CONTRIBUTORS

Nicholas B. Allen, Department of Psychology, University of Melbourne, Parkville VIC 3052, Australia

Kent G. Bailey, Department of Psychology, Virginia Commonwealth University, 806 West Franklin Street, Richmond, VA 23284–2018, USA

Mark T. Erickson, Alaska Psychiatric Institute, 2900 Providence Drive, Anchorage, Alaska 99508, USA

Paul Gilbert, Mental Health Research Unit, Kingsway Hospital, Derby DE22 3LZ, UK

Kalman Glantz, 12 Kinnaird Street, Cambridge, MA 02139, USA

Deborah Greenwald, Department of Counseling, Northeastern University, Boston, MA 02115, USA.

David Harder, Psychology Department, Tufts University, Medford, MA 02155, USA

Daniel Kriegman, 20 Dorcar Road, Newton, MA 02467–3021, USA

Giovanni Liotti, Università Pontificia Salesiana, Roma Scuola di Formazione in Psicoterapia Cognitiva APC, Roma, Italy

Michael T. McGuire, Neuropsychiatric Institute, 760 Westwood Plaza, School of Medicine, University of California at Los Angeles, California 90024, USA

Mary-Beth Moehl, 11 Hillcroft Park, Medford MA 02155, USA

Lynn E. O'Connor, The Wright Institute, 2728 Durant Avenue, Berkeley CA 94704, USA

Natalie Rasgon, Neuropsychiatric Institute, 760 Westwood Plaza, School of Medicine, University of California at Los Angeles, California 90024, USA

Anthony Stevens, Fardel Manor, Fardel, New Ivy Bridge, Plymouth, PL21 GHT, UK

Leon Sloman, Department of Psychiatry, Centre for Addiction and Mental Health, 250 College Street, Toronto, Ontario, M5T 1R8, Canada

Alfonso Troisi, Department of Psychiatry, Universita Tor Vergata, Roma, Italy

ACKNOWLEDGEMENTS

When evolution-informed theories began to be applied to psychology and psychopathology in the 1980s a number of psychotherapists became aware that this might have implications for psychotherapy. Bowlby's pioneering work on attachment theory was one such approach that has had major impact on our understanding of attachment behaviours and psychopathology. In the mid 1980s Russell Gardner at the University of Texas (Galveston) started his newsletter on evolutionary approaches to psychopathology (called ASCP: Across-Species Comparison in Psychopathology). This newsletter not only helped bring people together and share ideas in its pages; he also developed opportunities for small conferences. In 1997 one such was on evolutionary approaches to psychotherapy. We would like to thank Russell for his foresight and leadership.

Over many years, many have aided our thinking on evolutionary ideas and some of these people are presented here. Some are not. Special thanks go to John Price for his pioneering ideas on social rank and depression and to colleagues such as Helen Wood. We must express our deep gratitude to the many patients with whom we have shared ideas and who often gently have pointed out our errors. And of course writing and putting together a volume like this tends to require considerable time away from families. To them we owe much for their understanding, support and love. Last but not least, thanks go to Polly Strauss of Psychology Press who was her usual supportive and encouraging self.

This book represents the beginning of a journey into how the evolved mind creates happiness and misery and how we might help people who are trapped in misery. Twenty years from now things might look very different, but if they do we hope this will be because evolutionary-informed therapy research has identified and corrected errors and succeeded in shedding more light on this many-millions-of-years-old mind of ours.

Section I

THEORY AND PRINCIPLES

1

EVOLUTIONARY PSYCHOTHERAPY

Principles and outline

Paul Gilbert, Kent G. Bailey and Michael T. McGuire

> Our troubles . . . arise from the fact that we do not know what we are and cannot agree on what we want to be. The primary cause of this intellectual failure is ignorance of our origins. We did not arrive on this planet as aliens. Humanity is part of nature, a species that evolved among other species. The more closely we identify ourselves with the rest of life, the more quickly we will be able to discover the sources of humans' sensibility and acquire the knowledge on which an enduring ethic, a sense of preferred direction, can be built.
>
> (E.O. Wilson, 1992: 332)

This opening chapter outlines some of the basic principles of evolutionary approaches to human psychology and psychotherapy. We hope to clarify key concepts and ideas that will reoccur throughout this book and refer readers who wish to follow up on key points and ideas to certain chapters. Our journey begins in the late nineteenth century, where the origins of the 'talking cure' psychoanalysis were rooted in evolutionary theory. Since then there has been the growth of sociobiology, evolutionary psychology, and related fields so that today we stand at the threshold of new models and interventions in psychotherapy based on evolutionary ideas and findings. The aim of this book is to explore some of the directions this new evolutionary psychotherapy may take.

Where we are

Given the high rates of anxiety, depression, violence, and war that plague humanity, one is tempted to view humans as a basically flawed species that carries within itself the seeds of its own destruction (Dixon, 1987). According to this view, our brains are jerry-built devices, cobbled together over millions of years as we plodded the troubled road from DNA sludge to upright primate. Clues as to why we relate to others in the way we do, why we feel certain emotions in certain situations and why we are prone to neurosis, personality disorders and other pathologies, can be found in our evolutionary history. Try as we might to be rational and reasonable in facing our personal, social and ecological problems, our evolved nature can overrule common sense (Bailey, 1987). Good intentions can easily be sacrificed on the altar of innate impulses that place self and kin above others as we struggle with motives and feelings that evolved for matters of survival (of genes) not rationality (Nesse, 1998; McGuire & Troisi, 1998a). Rationality can easily falter in the face of human passion, be it for love, power, sex or revenge.

Psychotherapy is often focused on our passions and emotions (see Plutchick, 1980, 1994). Although different schools may direct therapeutic efforts to change cognitions, behaviours or social relationships, it is the nature of our passions, emotions and motivations that lie behind so much suffering and irrational behaviour. And it is often painful affects that lead us to seek help. This point was grasped by the founders of modern psychotherapy – writing in the immediate post Darwinian era – whose ideas were linked and rooted in the evolutionary theorizing that was rife at the end of the last century. In fact, the birth of psychoanalysis came with various assumptions regarding our animal heritage. These writings represented efforts to illuminate how our evolved, basic natures can be hidden beneath a veneer of socialisation. As Ellenberger (1970: 277) pointed out:

> Psychoanalysis evidently belongs to that 'unmasking' trend, that search for hidden unconscious motivations characteristic of the 1880s and 1890s. In Freud as in Nietzsche, words and deeds are viewed as manifestations of unconscious motivations, mainly of instincts and conflicts of instincts. For both men the unconscious is the realm of the wild, brutish instincts that cannot find permissible outlets, derived from earlier stages of the individual and of mankind, and find expression in passion, dreams, and mental illness.

This was also the age of Dr Jekyll and Mr Hyde, of Frankenstein and renewed interest in Dracula myths. Such explorations in literature showed a cultural fascination for the Platonian 'beast within' – based on some certainty that what nature had prepared us for was little more than a selfish, aggressive, brutish, pleasure seeking, self-promoting life whose deceptions, tricks and illusions know few bounds. Such ideas echo those of religion, such that left to our own devices we are inherently flawed and unregenerate. It is Adam's curse; left unconstrained, we are the Lord of the Flies. Only society and social control can, it is argued, contain our passions from such self-centredness and antisociality.

Exploration of the evolved nature of mind and its machinations in psychological suffering has waxed and waned over this century. Partly because of its implied pessimistic messages and partly because of a poverty of good research paradigms, evolutionary concepts have until recently faired poorly in the human sciences

(Cosmides & Tooby, 1992). Indeed, many students of psychology, psychotherapy and psychiatry do not take courses in evolutionary theory and arrive in the clinic with only the vaguest idea about the evolved mechanisms underpinning needs, anxiety, depression or jealous rage. Lacking an integrating framework for understanding the basic needs and dispositions of human beings, some psychiatrists are apt to see most suffering as 'signs of disease' curable with medications. Faced with epidemics of human misery and need for a rapid turnover of cases, in overworked clinics and crowded hospitals, biopsychiatry searches for drugs that will fine tune biosystems and offer a relatively anxiety- or depression-free existence – regardless of how far the social environment has thwarted evolved needs for care, belonging and status (McGuire & Troisi, 1998a; Troisi & McGuire, Chapter 2, this volume). The less biologically oriented therapist is left to his or her own devices, to chose between suffering as existential crises, distorted thinking, repressed motivations, (early) trauma, or dysfunctional behaviour.

When people are depressed their levels of serotonin may well be depleted, they may well distort the way they think about themselves and others and they may well avoid facing those things that they need to face because fear dictates avoidance. But none of this necessarily points to 'pathology' as such. While happiness and positive moods are related to helpful and beneficial conditions (e.g., good supportive relationships; Buss, 2000; Nesse, 1998), anxiety, depression, low 5-HT and 'distorted thinking' may all suggest (previously) adaptive or evolved defensive responses to a long evolutionary history of harsh and threatening environments (Gilbert, 1998a). As Nesse and Williams (1995) point out, even symptoms like coughing, vomiting and diarrhoea are not diseases, but defensive responses to pathogens. Similarly, Profet (1988, 1992, 1995) outlines a brilliant case for the notion that morning sickness in pregnancy is an evolved adaptive mechanism for avoiding or expelling toxic substances dangerous to the fetus. Further, many cases of suffering can be traced back to thwarted needs for care, love and status, especially when they are replaced in family environments with rejection, abuse and neglect.

To move forward in developing an integrated biopsychosocial approach for our therapies – one that gives due regard to multiple interacting domains (Gilbert, 1995; Hinde, 1987,1989, 1992) – we need to develop a functional analysis of evolved behaviour (Buss, 1991, 1995) and emotions (Nesse, 1998). The starting place of such analysis is to hone down levels of function that give rise to complex systems, whilst preserving the complexity of such systems.

From genes to minds

We begin this aspect of our journey by recognizing that the building blocks of organic forms, from the amoebae to humans, are genes. Genes, both singly and in combination, provide the information to build complex organisms. Genes give rise to adaptive traits that enable organisms to survive and reproduce. Genes help determine the internal structures and functions of the particular organism and external characters such as eye colour, distribution and type of body covering (scales, fur, or hair), and so forth. It was Darwin's great insight that individuals within a species vary as to their exact physical make-up and thus vary in specific traits. Further, he argued that natural selection operates when the environment favours certain traits over others. Understanding the nature of selective pressure offers insights into evolved mental mechanisms (Buss, 1999). There are different types of selective pressure.

Selective pressures

An exploration of the roots of human motives and passions can begin by noting that it is selective pressure that gives rise to various emotional and behavioural predispositions, be these for attachments (Bowlby, 1969), group living (Baumeister & Leary, 1995), or social hierarchies (Gilbert, 1989, 1992; Price, 1972). Evolutionary theory suggests that there are at least three forms of selective pressure that influence which traits are passed from generation to generation:

1   Natural Selection of attributes that give an advantage in survival, e.g., predator avoidance; defences against the cold, and forms of locomotion (e.g., wings and legs).
2   Intersexual Selection, in which one sex chooses and attracts the other for mating, via scents, courting displays, or coerced matings.
3   Intrasexual Selection in which one sex competes with and prevents other members of the same sex from having free access to breeding resources, via ritual agonistic behaviour and other forms of competition.

It is via processes of both natural and sexual selection that the environment favours some traits over others (Ridley, 1994). Generation upon generation, species evolve because the genes governing genotypes (and their phenotypic expression) are undergoing constant selective pressure (e.g., those who are the better attractors of mates will outproduce those who are poor attractors). In recent times, two additional insights have been added to this traditional understanding of selection.

Inclusive fitness

Genes are the building blocks of organisms and gene-traits are primary units of selection (Dawkins, 1976). Thus, following selectionist logic, gene-traits that support their replication into subsequent generations will be advantaged over those that do not. This helps us understand why strategies such as kin altruism have evolved (Hamiliton, 1964). Helping one's kin (genetically related relatives) will result in a higher rate of specific gene replication in subsequent generations compared to organisms who carry genes for (say) non-helping (see Bailey, Chapter 3, this volume). Put another way, caring for one's offspring (and relatives) will aid their survival and reproduction, thus ensuring that familywise genes are passed on to subsequent generations. The term *inclusive fitness* refers to the relative success of particular aggregations of biological kin in doing just that (see Daly Salmon & Wilson 1997; Reeve, 1998 for extensive discussions).

Distal and proximal causes

Complex organisms such as mammals, nonhuman primates, and human beings evolved complex brains selectively honed to do certain things that contributed to fitness (e.g., seek out sexual partners, help allies and kin, and compete with conspecifics and interspecifics). Selective pressures that affect species populations over long expanses of evolutionary time are distal causes and these can be contrasted with proximal causes which operate on individual organisms over their own life span (e.g., Buss, 1999; Hinde, 1992; MacDonald, 1988). The effectiveness and the efficiency of many behaviours (e.g., avoiding threats or seeking partners) is increased when genes build organisms that can internally modify their physiological processes by learning from their environments (see Greenough, Black & Wallace, 1987).

Although both the design of a brain's evolved function and its physiological modifiablity, via external inputs, are undoubtedly influenced by our genes, there remains much controversy on both counts. Exactly what are humans designed to do? And exactly how far can physiological modification go beyond the genes (Mayr, 1977)? To what degree can environmental forces shape brain maturation during development beyond the genes (Greenough *et al.*, 1987; Schore, 1994)? Is 'normality' for a given individual simply a matter of staying within its own species (genetic) bounds, or do human beings have the capacity to 'go beyond' evolved prerogatives (see Bailey, 1987)? Moreover, to what degree are psychiatric disorders, such as manic depression or schizophrenia, fixed in the genes versus being modifiable via environmental inputs? Indeed, how far does the brain's capacity for modifiability allow 'recovery' from injury, emotional traumas or dysfunction and what inputs are required to accomplish it? These are weighty questions, but we agree fundamentally with Hofer (1981: 302) who notes: 'Greater knowledge about the detailed processes of development helps put sociobiology in perspective by casting genes as the conveyors of human potential rather than as modern day equivalents of the Fates' (see also Charlesworth, 1988).

But there is another salient point here. It is not just that human genes build (relatively) flexible and adaptive organisms but that this flexibility now means that behaviours can arise that do not always result in reproductive success. To quote anthropologist Robin Fox (1986: 193):

> ... sociobiology speaks of organisms maximizing their reproductive success or inclusive fitness or whatever. It is not at all clear that this describes the outcome of various of their activity. After all, it is commonplace that animals do not know they are reproducing, much less maximizing, anything. What they are doing is accumulating resources

or power, for which they are proximately motivated. If they get all these right, then maximum reproductive success should follow. But it is these intermediaries they are motivated to achieve, not the success itself. This is no less true of humans. They will strive to accrue resources of all kinds wealth, power, access to sex and normally reproductive success (inclusive fitness) will follow. But it is equally possible that a consideration such as the enormous expense involved in raising offspring to a point where they too can accrue these things might well lead them to limit families . . . Again, there is no real discrepancy here since they are not in this argument motivated to maximize reproductive success *per se*, but those things that will, in the normal course of events, lead to it.

In sum, then, genes are the fundamental building blocks of life and, further, that they shape and (distally) predispose organisms to do certain things. But it is these proximal 'things' in a single individual's life that tells us most about normality and abnormality, joy and sadness, and relief from suffering. The genes may determine the basic structure and function of the ship we humans sail, but there may be some freedom as to where we can go.

Conservation of form and co-opted functions

The Darwinian model builds a compelling picture of how evolution has shaped the design of organisms that exist today, but there is another fundamental principle to the way organisms evolve, known as the conservation of form. Indeed, evolution is slow and for the most part, can only 'tinker' with pre-existing forms and systems. For example, the primate line evolved from previous evolved species reaching back to the stem reptiles that first appeared some 250 million years ago (MacLean, 1990; Bailey, 1987). Most vertebrates have four limbs, heart and lungs and so forth, with the spinal cord along the dorsal surface and the 'brain computer' and sensory organs in the anterior head region (eyes, ears, olfaction and mouth, etc.). These biogrammatical basics (Count, 1973; Tiger & Fox, 1971) find their beginnings in changes occurring in the sea some 400 million years ago. The blueprints of this phylogenetic history remain with us. Evolution allows species to elaborate and extend certain general designs or basic plans (e.g., such as four limbs, pairs of sensory organs, etc. – see Lorenz, 1987 for some fascinating examples), but only so far. Further, having to live within pre-existing structures is not always helpful. For example, not all evolved attributes are necessarily 'adaptive' but can arise as 'side effects' and trade offs of other adaptations (Buss *et al.*, 1998; Nesse & Williams, 1995). A good example is the human skeleton. We have so many back problems because the 'basic plan' of the spinal column first evolved in the sea and was only later retained in land animals. Unfortunately, this retained genetic trait is not well suited for upright locomotion. Clearly, having to accommodate to earlier 'basic plans' in our biology is not without costs. This reasoning holds for brain mechanisms as well. In human beings, various levels of brain structure have their origins at vastly different phylogenetic times. For example, the R-complex or 'reptilian brain' originated over 200 million years ago. The retention of old designs with new requirements and structures (e.g., limbic system and neo-cortex) can cause internal tension and conflict (MacLean, 1990). As Bailey (1987: 63) puts it.

> We must acknowledge that our species possesses the neural hardware and many of the motivational-emotional proclivities . . . of our reptilian ancestors, and, thus our drives, inner subjective feelings, fantasies and thoughts are thoroughly conditioned by emanations from the R-complex. The reptilian carry-overs provide the automatic, compulsive, urgency to much human behavior, where free will steps aside and persons act as they have to act, often despising themselves in the process for their hatreds, prejudices, compulsions, conformity, deceptiveness and guile.

Co-opted functions also work in various other ways. For example, while self-conscious introspections, self-awareness and self-evaluations clearly have adaptive functions in terms of self-control and social manipulation, they carry a serious disadvantage when those same mechanisms lead to feelings of failure and worth-lessness, from which a person can see no escape. Constantly ruminating and reflecting on one's inadequacies acts as an internal negative signal that maintains high stress. Gilbert (Chapter 6, this volume) explores this aspect in terms of how the modern mind allows for unhelpful recursive feedback.

Evolved disadvantages

Not only can adaptive functions come to be used in new, novel and not necessarily helpful ways, some adaptations are a double-edged sword. Although the infant's dependency on early bonds with parents is adaptive it also makes the infant extremely vulnerable to poor parenting (e.g., see Liotti, Chapter 11, this volume). Moreover, humans have become highly manipulable to ideas and beliefs held within groups, and such beliefs can be highly damaging to reproductive success. Barkow (1989) cites the example of how, in some hunter–gather societies, mothers do not feed their babies the colostrum (the pre-milk fluid containing many antibodies) in the mistaken belief it is bad milk and harmful. Some children will die as a result. Similarly, social adaptations help us to seek approval and acceptance from peers and, ultimately, to improve our reproductive fitness, but fear of loss of approval/reputation and shame (Gilbert, 1997; Gilbert & McGuire, 1998) can lead people to behave in shame-avoidant ways that may be detrimental to other aspects of their own self-interests (e.g., violence, taking drugs, risk taking to earn group approval, etc.). Importantly then, adaptations often involve compromises, cost:benefit tradeoffs and need not be 'all good' (Buss et al., 1998; Gilbert, 1998b; Nesse & Willams, 1995).

Building human beings

We see then that selective pressure, operating on gene-trait frequencies result in changes within the morphology of species. Moreover, evolution gives rise to organisms designed to act on their environments in certain ways and whose motivations influence proximal behaviour but not biological fitness as such. Further, we recall that evolution adapts pre-existing designs, retaining features of previous designs – i.e., the brain, is not created *de novo* – and various disadvantages and liabilities ensue from that fact. Thus, we can begin to answer questions of how humans came to be humans (process of selection), what they are evolved to do (e.g., be motivated to engage in acts, such as seeking mates, caring for children, developing alliances) and have further insight into the design of the physiological mechanisms (e.g., brain) that enables them to do it. These underlying factors set the context for our work as therapists, and direct attention to evolved mechanisms for our basic emotions, needs, and social behaviours.

Social strategies

Most forms of mental suffering revolve around the dynamics of social relationships; specifically what people feel others think and feel about them and how they engage their interpersonal environments (Horwitz & Vitkus, 1986). Indeed, it has been the successful navigation of social challenges (namely, those ultimately related to reproductive success) that exerted such a powerful influence on the design of the brain (Nesse, 1990). Put another way, it is now recognized that the evolution of many mental mechanisms was shaped by social challenges (Buss, 1995, 1999; Gilbert, 1989). Humans evolved over millions of years within primate social groups (Baumeister & Leary, 1995; Simpson & Kenrick, 1997) and many of our basic social emotions and behaviours serve the function of enabling individuals to engage others in different types of relationship (e.g., parent–child, friend, sexual, dominant–subordinate, enemy; Buss, 1995; Gilbert, 1989; Nesse, 1990, 1998). Most of these were acted out in small kin-based groups (Bailey, Chapter 3, this volume). Social strategies operate as psychobiological regulators of behaviour and are believed to underpin universal forms of social behaviour (Buss, 1995; Cosmides & Tooby, 1992; McGuire & Troisi, 1998a; Nesse, 1998). For example, social strategies may include mating strategies where men are inclined to mate with younger females, and females to seek out higher status males (Buss, 1989); parent–offspring attachment strategies (Bowlby, 1969, 1980) and a preference for helping kin and in-group individuals over non-kin and out-group individuals, particularly when the cost of helping may be high (Burnstein, Crandall & Kitayama, 1994). Such strategies and motives evolved because they solved social challenges. Such challenges, operating over many millions of years, required a variety of different information-processing strategies and algorithms for attending to, interpreting, and responding to social signals; this process has given rise to the evolution of a wide variety of social motivations and internal processing psychological mechanisms (Buss, 1995;

Gardner, 1988; Gilbert, 1989, 1995). Gilbert (Chapter 6, this volume) explores this aspect of humans having various 'social mentalities'.

Stevens (Chapter 5, this volume) highlights the fact that Jung was one of the first to articulate a theory of how the brain is constructed around specialized, purposeful, internal mechanisms (information-processing systems) for the organization of social inputs and the construction of meaning – which he called archetypes. Stevens outlines how evolutionary archetype theory guides therapeutic insight and responses (Stevens, 1982). There is controversy about the number and form of human social strategies, but there is some agreement that they include the following:

Care eliciting/seeking involves the motivation and behaviours to elicit (and be responsive to) the provision of various resources from others – such as comfort, protection, food, help, support and care. Care-seeking behaviour can also be aimed to control arousal (e.g., getting a cuddle/stroke to be calmed following a threat). These behaviours form the basis of attachment relationships (e.g., Bowlby, 1969) 'inner working models' (Liotti, Chapter 11, this volume) and are often kin-directed (Bailey, 1988; Chapter 3, this volume). One thing we know fairly clearly is that human infants need considerable input from parents/carers. Time and time again therapeutic work focuses on issues of feeling cared for, fears of being deceived about being cared for (Allen & Gilbert, Chapter 7, this volume) and fears of closeness and exploitation-abuse. Without an early 'good enough' experience of caring the brain tends to become threat sensitive and ready to take defensive actions in the form of anxious avoidance or defensive aggression (Gilbert, 1995). A number of authors of this volume (Gilbert; Liotti; Kriegman; O'Connor; Troisi & McGuire) address this issue and the various complexities care-seeking behaviour presents to therapists.

Care giving/providing involves the motivation and behaviours to care, look after and provide resources for others (Fogel, Melson & Mistry, 1986). Such behaviours take account of the cost of providing care and are especially directed at kin and those likely to reciprocate (e.g., Burnstein, Crandall & Kitayama, 1994). Several contributors to this volume (Bailey; Liotti; Sloman; Troisi & McGuire) explore the way in which the kin-related care-seeking–care-giving dynamic shapes the presentation of emotional conflicts and therapeutic response. O'Connor (Chapter 13, this volume) explores some of the adaptive functions of caring behaviour and suggests that care and guilt-based mechanisms can seriously interfere with the maturation of assertiveness and, moreover, that a fear of harming others (for example by being successful) can be a (sometimes unconscious) reason for various self-handicapping behaviours.

Because caring for others is not cost free there is always a 'conflict of interests' between the care seeker and care giver (Trivers, 1985), and this gives rise to various forms of deception (Allen & Gilbert, Chapter 7, this volume). This shows up in the patient–therapist interaction – how much care should/can a therapist provide and how? The inherent difficulties are well articulated by Kriegman (Chapter 4, this volume). For example, the type and quantity of care a client receives is often defined by therapist discretion and not by the client's needs or preferences. Time and time again, we find that clients can recover or find relief when they develop intimate relationships outside of therapy that enable high rates of accessibility (living in close proximity with another), closeness, holding, caressing, cuddling, touching and mirroring. Indeed, we now know that such stimuli, received at a high rate have major physiological effects (see Carter, Lederhendler & Kirkpatrick, 1997; Field, 1998). Miller and Fishkin (1997) have reviewed the evidence on how close adult–adult bonds evolved with physiological regulating impacts on stress and sex hormones, and the immune system (see also Zeifman & Hazan, 1997). The brain evolved to 'need' these signals if it is to mature with a relatively positive disposition. However, we are far from developing therapies that can provide such inputs or substitutes for them and we often are forced to leave our clients enduring pain at a distance where even touching is withheld in case it is perceived as coercive, sexual or abusive (Smith, Clance & Imes, 1998). Once we recognize the importance of social signals on physiological states there may be ways to help clients give *themselves* caring signals rather than hostile ones (Gilbert, Chapter 6, this volume).

Finally, there is a whole area which pertains to how we enable people to be caring of others (Fogel, Melson & Mistry, 1986). There is a range of problems where people follow strategies that are self-enhancing and other-exploiting (Belsky, 1993). We may understand both the evolutionary and developmental origins of such behaviours but when such individuals act as parents, bosses, or policing agents they can do great harm to those around them. Extreme 'psychopathic' and exploitative behaviours may make evolutionary sense (Mealey, 1997), but they are destructive in the modern world. We understand why many psychological therapies and drug companies focus on stopping people from feeling things, for example, stopping or blocking pain, negative thoughts, anxiety and depression – but why is there so little research into drugs for empathy enhancement or the development of prosocial behaviour? How do we help the psychopath take more interest in others, to feel sympathy and compassion, or experience guilt? Is it possible?

Mate selection involves sexual behaviour of attracting, being attracted to, courting, conception (Buss, 1989, 1995) and mate retention (Wilson & Daly, 1992). We now know that men and women are orientated to sexual relationships in different ways (Buss, 1989, Glantz & Moehl, Chapter 8, this volume; Lancaster, 1991). Indeed, Ridley (1994) makes the claim that sexual selection has been responsible for the evolution of numerous psychological systems. Be that as it may, the inherent conflicts in the reproductive strategies of males and females (Buss & Malamuth, 1996) can often show up in marital problems, with men investing less time and energy in their mates or off-spring than women desire, or being extremely jealous and possessive. Similarly, wives may reject or demean husbands who are poor providers, sexually unfaithful, poor fathers, or otherwise 'bad investments'.

An evolutionary explanation for some gender conflicts is given by Wilson and Daly (1992) in their aptly named chapter 'The man who mistook his wife for a chattel'. Historically, men have frequently treated women as property and recruit the psychology of entitlement, ownership and control. There are three central ideas about why this is so: (1) Men (unlike women) cannot guarantee their mate's offspring are their own. Thus, they have to be careful not to invest in a female(s) and her offspring which may actually be sired by someone else, e.g., cuckolded. (2) Human males do invest in their offspring, at least more than many other primates, and females tend to select for (signals of) high rather than low investing males. Thus, being cuckolded could be costly. However, (3) male reproductive interests can be served by cuckolding other males, or at least gaining 'control' over (inseminating) more than one female. There is therefore an inherent motivation to prevent other males from mating with one's partner (via high vigilance and aggression – jealousy) and also to control female sexuality – which through the ages has often been achieved through a process of shaming female sexuality, cloistering of females, and possessiveness. Wilson and Daly (1992: 291) suggest therefore that 'women as property' can easily become a core mindset of men:-

> . . . whose operation can be discerned from numerous phenomena which are culturally diverse in their details but monotonously alike in the abstract. These phenomena include socially recognized marriage, the concept of adultery as a property violation, the valuation of female chastity (and virginity), the equation of the "protection" of women with protection from sexual contact, and the special potency of infidelity as a provocation for violence [brackets added].

Even in contemporary love songs the issues of property and jealousy are often clear. In the Beatles song, 'Run for your life', (from the LP *Rubber Soul*) are the immortal words, 'I'd rather see you dead little girl than to be with another man'.

For women the story is somewhat different. In the first place, sexual acts can be far more costly for females than males and so there is more caution and precision in female choice. Second, the competitive dynamic of female sexuality is often via appearance and attractiveness (Etcoff, 1999). There are now much data on the nature of female physical attractiveness and sexual selection, including posture, hip to waist ratio, youthful looks, healthiness, and hardiness (Barber, 1995). Abed (1998) has suggested that the high rates of eating disorder in females in western societies may be due to female intensified competition with each other to 'look young and nubile', i.e., have high mate value. As Kriegman (Chapter 4, this volume) clarifies, however, this may not reflect either conscious or unconscious motivations to actually be 'a sexual turn on to men' but rather a way of feeling good about the self in general and in the presence of other women in particular. Looking good and feeling good can be strongly related in females (Etcoff, 1999).

Turning to sexual abuse, one thing is clear – sexual abuse of all kinds is deeply damaging (Thornhill, 1996), whether in the home, in the marriage, workplace, or even in psychotherapy (Bates & Brodsky, 1989). Warm and satisfying sexual relations in human beings are conducive to the pair bond itself (Eibl-Eibesfeldt,

1989; Fisher, 1982) and tend to exert positive effects on overall psychological health as well. However, when sex is forced on another as in rape, incest, or sexual harrassment, the victim may suffer a wide range of debilitating effects (Trickett & Putman, 1993). Erickson (Chapter 10, this volume) explores the issue of early incest from an evolutionary perspective and makes a distinction between familial and nonfamilial social relationships. In the former, relations tend to be altruistic (following principles of inclusive fitness) and incestuous behaviour is discouraged, whereas in the latter altruism is at best reciprocal and incestuous slippage is much more probable. However, Erickson proposes that familial relations (namely, among biological kin) may take on the properties of nonfamilial relations when insecure familial attachments are evident. Thus, the family characterized by poor or insecure attachments can be at risk for incest and other sexual pathologies. Clearly, the evolutionary psychotherapist will want to be first sensitive to maladaptive sexual processes in their clients (including early abuse and incest) and second, to aid the client in the restorative process.

Cooperation and the formation of alliances involves aggression inhibition and sharing (Argyle, 1991), affiliation, friendships (de Waal, 1996), group living (Baumeister & Leary, 1995) and reciprocal altruistic behaviour (Trivers, 1985) with the tracking of favours given and received, and cheating (Cosmides, 1989; Cosmides & Tooby, 1992; McGuire & Troisi, 1998a). These social behaviours have a long evolutionary history in mammals and primates. For example, the common chimpanzee forms strong friendships and alliances in the wild (Goodall, 1986), males co-operate in hunting (Goodall, 1971), and in great detail Frans de Waal has discussed chimpanzee politics (1982), coalition and alliance behaviour (Harcourt & de Waal, 1992), social reciprocity (de Waal & Luttrell, 1988; de Waal & Aureli, 1997), and peacemaking behaviour (de Waal, 1989). Indeed, relation-specific affection and voluntary time–space sharing, group-centredness and group dependency, complex social dynamics revolving around kin selection and inclusive fitness, and the body politic are defining characteristics of our closest phylogenetic relatives.

Social ranking behaviour involves direct competition for resources, gaining and maintaining rank/status (dominance/leader), making social comparisons (inferior/ superior; Gilbert, Price & Allan, 1995) and accommodating to those of higher rank (submission/follower; Gilbert, 1992; Price *et al.*, 1994; Sloman, Chapter 12, this volume). In nearly all mammalian and primate groups, social structures are hierarchically organized with dominant animals behaving confidently, engaging in more approach behaviour, defending resources and threatening challengers, whereas subordinates are wary of down-rank attacks, and avoid, escape or submit in the face of stronger opponents. It is not in a subordinate's interests to instigate or escalate conflicts or make claims on resources they cannot win or defend. When subordinates do not obey these rules and social strategies, they elicit attacks that cause injury and have reduced life expectancies (e.g., Higley *et al.*, 1996). In evolutionary terms shame, social anxiety and depression can be seen as reflections of defensive social strategies in individuals who see themselves as subordinate and powerless (Gilbert, 1992, 2000a; Gilbert & Allan, 1998, Gilbert & McGuire, 1998, Price, 1972; Price et al., 1994; Sloman, Chapter 12, this volume). But just as submissive and subordinate behaviour can have adaptive value so can shame (Harder & Greenwald, Chapter 14, this volume).

Although we often talk about dominance hierarchies, it might be more revealing and accurate to speak of subordinance hierarchies. In fact, it is not (only) aggression that determines a hierarchy but also the subordinate behaviours that are elicited. Bernstein (1980: 80–1) put it this way.

> A dominance relationship between two individuals is inferred not because one or both 'assert' their dominance but because one readily submits. If, and only if, the subordinate recognizes the relationship, or 'predicts' the outcome of an agonistic encounter by immediately showing submission, can we assume that a dominance relationship exists. . . . It is . . . the timing and sequencing of submissive signals in an interaction that allows us to infer the existence of a dominance relationship between two individuals.
>
> It is only the submission of subordinates that allows us to argue that dominance may function to partition resources or reduce fighting.

All of this implies internal mechanisms for making these 'predictions'; namely, for working out whether to submit or challenge (see Cummins, 1999). Gilbert (1989, 1992, 2000a) argues that not only are there a variety of different submissive strategies but also many such strategies underpin various forms of psychopathology; that is, the propensity to adopt submissive strategies in social contexts reduces the threshold for shame (Harder & Greenwald, Chapter 14, this volume, Gilbert & McGuire, 1998), social anxiety, and depression (Allan & Gilbert, 1997; Gilbert, 1992; Gilbert & Allan 1998; Price *et al.*, 1994). Be it in seeking care, co-operating or pursuing other types of resource, the issue of the reality of power differentials between individuals plays a key role – in whose interest will the relationship operate? Sloman (Chapter 12, this volume) and O'Connor (Chapter 13, this volume) explore these themes and their implications for therapy, while Kriegman (Chapter 4, this volume) addresses transference and counter-transference aspects of the power differential in therapy.

One of the most salient aspects of *human* competition and rank formation is that it is a social process that depends on the social signals elicited and given. Rarely do humans gain status, group acceptance, or secure mates by aggression alone; they must behave in ways that encourage selection and choice by others. This is experienced as the strong desire to be chosen, be it as a lover, friend, team player, or caretaker. In essence this strategy is one of inducing others to choose in one's favour because there are qualities about one to which others wish to relate or find useful/rewarding. Barkow (1975, 1989) called this 'competing for prestige'.

15

A central and overarching concern in our psychotherapy clients is that they are not sufficiently attractive to have either self-worth or social value to others. They are not just simply afraid of rejection or criticism *per se*, but fear having qualities that are unattractive/undesirable. 'I will be rejected *because* I am ugly, stupid, weak, boring, too demanding, crazy, etc.' or 'I hate myself *because* I am ugly, stupid, weak, boring, too demanding, crazy, etc.'. These negative self-perceptions serve to locate people (in their own minds) as subordinate, inferior and unattractive to others, which then recruits or activates the various psychobiological patterns of, and strategies for, subordinate behaviour. Time and again therapists will engage patients to help them stop such destructive self-devaluation (Gilbert, this Chapter 6, this volume). And time and again shame will be a significant problem to work through (Gilbert 1998c; Gilbert & McGuire, 1998; Harder & Greenwald, Chapter 14, this volume; Kaufman, 1989).

People who are prone to exploit others and/or deficient in shame rarely come for therapy, but they can cause great misery for others. Moreover, when they do enter therapy, they often deflect blame to others for their misfortunes. Family therapists, of course, are well aware that the presenting patient may not be the main source of the problem. For example, co-author Bailey once treated a 'scapegoat child' who presented as normal on interview and psychological tests, but who was labelled as 'sick' and 'mentally disabled' by the parents and siblings, all of whom appeared to have serious psychological problems. The point is that pathologies surrounding the internal and external evaluation of ones rank/status in the family and elsewhere are common – either of feeling and behaving in too subordinate a manner (e.g., the child above), or just the opposite.

Social ranking issues are intimately associated with early developmental experiences, especially in the domain of attachment (Liotti, Chapter 11, this volume, Sloman, Chapter 12, this volume). From the earliest mother–infant bond, parents can instil in their children a sense of value and worth via their approval and love (Kohut, 1977) and set them on track to enter the world with schemas of robust self-esteem, care of others, and capacities for developing stable friendships and pair bonding (Belsky, 1993). Sloman (Chapter 12, this volume) explores these various dynamics and interactions in detail.

Non-logical biases have been adaptive

The information-processing systems that tune attention to certain cues, calculate risks and benefits in particular contexts, and select between alternative strategies are sometimes referred to as *algorithms*. Cognitive therapists (Beck *et al.*, 1979) have been keen on the idea that psychopathology can be understood in terms of various errors and biases in thinking. The evolutionary approach makes clear that biases may not be 'errors' as such but are built into the core of our information-processing systems – algorithms are not rooted in logic (Cosmides, 1989; Gilbert, 1998b). Krebs and Denton (1997) note that many self-serving biases (e.g., seeing ourselves better than others do; or feeling more morally justified than others) and group biases (e.g., positive biases to one's own group over outsiders) may be adaptive. Such common biases include:

Kin biases (care provision) arise from the advantages in being motivated to care for one's own children (rather than any child) and the tendency to favour kin when it comes to caring/helping (Hamiliton,1964; Burnstein, Crandall & Kitayama, 1994) – e.g., to be discriminating in the type and amount of resources (help, support, etc.) one gives and to whom one gives it (e.g., kin and friends).

Kin biases (care seeking) involve the natural tendency to seek parental, kin or friendship care/support. This tendency becomes especially powerful when one's survival is threatened, and may even generalize to nonkin under sufficient stress or deprivation of resources (Bailey, Chapter 3, this volume).

Intersexual attractor biases reflect the tendency to be attracted to (and seek to attract) certain types of sexual partners – with biases towards the young, healthy and/or wealthy rather than the old, sick and poor (Buss, 1989, 1999). As noted above, there are tendencies for males and females to follow somewhat different strategies and be biased to different attractors and behaviours (Buss, 1989; Ridley, 1994) while at the same time both sexes are sensitive to cues and signals of altruism and kindness in potential long-term partners (Jensen-Campbell, Graziano & West (1995) and possibly status (Barkow, 1989).

Intrasexual and competitive biases arise from the tendency to rate self and others in terms of hierarchical relationships, i.e., via social comparisons (stronger–weaker, attractive–unattractive; Gilbert, Price & Allan, 1995). Biases come from either overestimating one's competency in relationship to others (Taylor & Brown, 1988) or underestimating it (Allan & Gilbert, 1997; Hartung, 1987). Social comparison may be one of the earliest types of social cognition because animals that were not able to discern if a conspecific was stronger (and could seriously injure the self) or weaker (and could be challenged) would be at a serious disadvantage (Gilbert, Price & Allan, 1995).

Reciprocal exchange biases arise from the tendency to form reciprocal, co-operative, altruistic relationships with kin and in-group non-kin. Biases arise from the need to detect cheating and monitor exchange and behave in a tit-for-tat manner (Cosmides & Tooby, 1992). Kin and friends, for example, are seen as more reliable or trustworthy in the exchange process than strangers. Biases can also arise from seeing self as giving more than others return (Krebs & Denton, 1997; McGuire & Troisi, 1998a). And issues of exchange and altruism can figure prominently in various psychiatric disorders (McGuire et al., 1994).

Ingroup–outgroup biases include the tendency to distinguish self and others on the basis of group membership (social comparison of same–different, like–unlike;

Gilbert, Price & Allan, 1995). The basis for discrimination may be large (e.g., sex, race, or religion) or small (e.g., preferences in art). Once one has identified with a particular group then there are tendencies to elevate one's own group and see it as superior or more entitled than other groups (van der Dennen, 1986). There is increasing evidence that groups seek to dominate other groups, defend their own interests, attempt to limit subordinate groups' access to resources, and at times attack them. Pratto *et al.* (1994) called this 'social dominance orientation', and explored how people take their self-identities from their own group and set about subordinating other groups. Such biases stand out in paranoia when individuals believe that other groups (or alliances) are ganging up on them and are out to harm, exploit or reveal shameful things about them (the police, the mafia, aliens).

Systematic biases in social reasoning then are built into many of the mind's information-processing systems or algorithms. But there are other biases that pertain to perceived threats and often arise from rapid (Gilbert, 1998a) and 'regressive' brain processing (Bailey, 1987). For example, in threatening situations it can be adaptive to assume the worst and take defensive action rather than to underestimate threats and dangers (Gilbert, 1998a). The nature of biases helps us understand why humans so easily are tipped into xenophobia, jealousy and various interpersonal conflicts, which to an outsider would be so easily settled if only participants would be 'rational, fair and reasonable'.

Mental pain and suffering

The primary focus of the therapist's work is mental pain and suffering, but we must keep in mind that the capacity to feel mental pain (fear, depression, anger) is clearly an adaptation – despite the fact that people in pain may not be able to make best use of the resources around them. Because the capacity to feel aversive states is an adaptation, it does not follow that they work adaptively in all environments (Wakefield, 1999). It is often when they do not serve in the pursuit of goals that therapists may be called in (Troisi & McGuire, Chapter 2, this volume). The evolved function of all painful states is to alert animals of dangers, threats and losses and to take appropriate defensive actions (Gilbert, 1993; McGuire & Troisi, 1998a,b). An evolutionary approach suggests that the more the social environment negatively affects or thwarts inclusive fitness goals (e.g., to form secure attachments, belong to groups, find sexual partners, gain status) the greater the experienced pain or subjective displeasure (see Buss, 2000; Herrnstein, 1977; Wilkinson, 1996). Indeed, McGuire and Troisi (1998b) argue that one of the reasons females experience twice the rates of depression of males is because (modern, patriarchal) social environ-ments more typically thwart female biosocial goals (see also Thornhill, 1996, for a discussion of this issue in regard to rape). This focus on thwarted goals highlights one further factor – that is conflict.

Conflicts arise in nearly all dynamics of life. For example, there is conflict between the amount of investment a child seeks from its parents and the amount the parents are prepared to offer (Trivers, 1985). While it may be in the interests of a dominant to thwart the aspirations of subordinates, it is rarely in the subordinates interests to be thwarted. While coercive sex may be advantageous to an offending male it is certainly not to a female victim (Thornhill, 1996). Cognitive therapists are right to argue that the way we think about such threats can add to or diminish our pain, but this should not be taken to imply that our feelings are always controllable by voluntary control of our thoughts. Evolutionary psychology tells us that outputs in complex organisms occur at emotive, behavioural and cognitive levels, with those in the cognitive domain (e.g., rumination) being the most recent phylogenetically. Although our thinking can be irrational, this is not to encourage victim blaming where the client is viewed as deficient or pathological for 'distorted thinking' or for pursuing (often unconscious) species-normal evolutionary goals (see Gilbert, 2000b; Kriegman, Chapter 4, this volume).

As therapists, we try to help people feel better about themselves and their lives, but this may require swimming against the current of adaptive strategies (Gilbert, 1995). For example, if one has been abused or traumatized it may be adaptive to orientate oneself to the world in a highly defensive and threat-vigilant way, with low 5-HT and high baseline arousal and where anxiety and/or defensive aggression are easily aroused and where low grade depression reduces aspiration and social engagement and thus risks. And this is no voluntary choice but an automatic 'brain selection' of a strategy set for coping with hostile social environments. This raises again the question of just how much therapy input and what type of input is necessary to deactivate such defensive brain states and strategies (Gilbert, 2000b). Do we really believe that one hour a week is going to do this? Given that so many of our borderline personality disorder patients have been sexually abused and traumatized over many years is it any wonder they do so poorly with the poverty of inputs currently on offer? Our conceptualization expands once we give up the notion that these patients have an 'illness' (as opposed to suffering) for which we need to find a cure (see McGuire & Troisi 1998a; Wakefield, 1992, 1999, for discussions). Instead, we can recognize their pain as *adaptive reactions* to specific environments and then proceed to help them switch strategies, from a defensive, mistrusting and emotionally labile set of states/strategies, to a more trusting, confident and stable set. The unstable, lonely and dysphoric borderline patient is a case in point; is his or her relief from extreme suffering going to come from pharmacological agents or highly stylized and at times rejecting forms of treatment, or is there a better way?

Early psychoanalysis made an error in its early evolutionary theories. In adopting Christian-Judaistic ideas about the human fall, the importance of the inhibition of desire, and the repulsiveness of lower animal nature, it absorbed into itself the assumption that beneath the surface of human experience is a realm of wild brutishness – nature red in tooth and claw. It has been this orientation that has lain behind some of the 'stranger' and often erroneous interpretations and ideas of these therapists. In fact what 'lies below the surface' is actually a set of strategies – developmentally and contextually sensitive – where belongingness, emotional needs, compassion, care, friendship and joy in relationship are as much evolved potentials as rape, violence, exploitation, anxiety and depression. The former, as much as the latter, have been successful in gene replication. So a new image of our animal nature emerges. It is one where we may well be adapted to live aggressive, anxious and depressed lives in socially harsh contexts, but yet where the source of our capacity for positive affects, prosocial behaviour and life-enhancing physiological profiles are to be found in the quality of our social relationships (Argyle, 1991; Buss, 2000). Robust immune systems, high 5-HT and low cortisol, are more likely in highly supportive and socially rewarding environments (Uchino, Cacioppo & Kiecolt-Glaser, 1996). Moreover, our attitudes and dispositions to violence or peaceful co-existence are shaped by the social environments in which these behaviours will operate (Overing, 1989).

Evolutionary approaches are not reductionist

We are slowly gaining insight into how evolved dispositions are recruited or limited by the social environment and such insight offers ways to promote human well-being (Buss, 2000) and peacefulness (Overing, 1989). Nonetheless, we suggest that to further our knowledge of psychopathology, we should pay more attention to evolutionary design. There could be no attachment difficulties in a species not adapted for attachment relations; loneliness would not exist in a species adapted for a solitary life; and our sexual proclivities would look very different if we were a species where males rather than females carried the burden of investment in offspring (as in the sea horse). We follow certain social strategies, pursue certain biosocial goals, and are depressed or pleasured by their success or failure, in part at least because we are evolved to be this way. As we noted earlier, our social strategies operate as basic orientating devices to pursue biosocial goals. However, the openness of the human psyche to positive and aversive experiences leaves no doubt that these strategies are flexible and changeable for better or worse. Furthermore, social signals and relationships are powerful biological regulators emanating from the environment (Hofer, 1984; McGuire & Troisi, 1987). Being an evolution-focused therapist necessarily elevates development (history of received social signals) to the forefront, for it is via early experiences that social strategies take the form they do – with all their complex psychobiological interactions (MacDonald, 1988). Indeed, adverse rearing experiences can significantly affect psychobiological maturation and functioning (Hart, Gunnar & Cicchetti, 1996; Rosenblum et al., 1994; Schore, 1994; Trickett & Putman, 1993) – a downside of physiological modifiability. Belsky and colleagues (Belsky, Steinberg & Draper, 1990; Belsky, 1993) used an evolutionary model to postulate a direct link between early rearing environments and subsequent interpersonal behaviour and psychopathology. They argued that early environments act to select which social and reproductive strategies (e.g., affiliative, stable pair bonding and high investment in offspring versus less affiliative, unstable pair bonding and low investment in offspring) become incorporated in affect control and self-systems. Delineating the main factors involved in adverse rearing environments and their influence on physiological maturation, subsequent social behaviour and pathology is one of the challenges for researchers and psychotherapists.

This volume

This volume seeks to bring together a number of therapists whose work has been influenced by evolutionary theory and understanding. There is no one standard approach but rather different therapists tend to shape the therapies they were trained in to accommodate evolutionary considerations. We should add that, as editors, we do not necessarily agree with every view expressed here, but we have encouraged authors to speak for themselves in explicating their conceptual models and providing case illustrations in this budding field of evolutionary psychotherapy.

We hope that what comes through is new insights on old problems. Time and again we will meet the themes of how activation of defensive strategies can make the person difficult to understand or engage; that to help them we must try to understand the meaning and function of these defences not because they are 'sick' or 'disordered' as such but because there are only so many ways one can cope with trauma and thwarted biososocial goals.

Conclusion

All of the major schools of psychotherapy have emerged in the last hundred years. As with so many of the other 'sciences' this century, there has been a rapid diversification and expansion into a plethora of approaches, theories and practices (Troisi & McGuire, Chapter 2, this volume). Yet as we stand at the beginning of a new millennium there are signs that things are coming full circle. We have been through a century when different schools worked to differentiate themselves from each other, but there are now signs for a growing impetus of integration and co-operation (Norcross, 1996; Norcross & Goldfried, 1992). Such efforts will be aided, we believe, by returning to one of the founding paradigms of psychotherapy – that is, the notion that the mind is the product of millions of years of evolution. However, as the authors in this volume attest, the evolutionary focus offers not only integrative possibilities but also important new insight into therapeutic processes. Finally, we acknowledge that understanding and treating pychopathology with evolutionary insights is new and needs to be subjected to formal case studies and treatment trials. Ultimately, it will be research evidence that will inform us of how useful such developments are.

References

Abed, R.T (1998) 'The sexual competition hypothesis of eating disorders', *British Journal of Medical Psychology*, 71: 525–47.

Allan, S. & Gilbert, P. (1997) 'Submissive behaviour and psychopathology', *British Journal of Clinical Psychology* 36: 467–88.

Argyle, M. (1991) *Cooperation: The Basis of Sociability*, London: Routledge.

Bailey, K.G. (1987) *Human Paleopsychology. Applications to Aggression and Pathological Processes*, Hillsdale, NJ: Lawrence Erlbaum Associates Inc.

Bailey, K.G. (1988) 'Psychological kinship: implications for the helping professions', *Psychotherapy* 25: 132–41.

Barber, N. (1995) 'The evolutionary psychology of physical attractiveness: sexual selection and human morphology', *Ethology and Sociobiology* 16: 395–424.

Barkow, J.H. (1975) 'Prestige and culture: a biosocial interpretation', (plus peer review), *Current Anthropology* 16: 533–72.

Barkow, J.H. (1989) *Darwin, Sex and Status*. Toronto: Toronto University Press.

Bates, C. & Brodsky, A.M. (1989) *Sex in the Therapy Hour: A case of professional incest*, New York: Guilford.

Baumeister, R.F. & Leary, M.R. (1995) 'The need to belong: desire for interpersonal attachments as a fundamental human motivation', *Psychological Bulletin* 117: 497–529.

Beck, A.T., Rush, A.J., Shaw, B.F. & Emery, G. (1979) *Cognitive Therapy of Depression*, New York: Wiley.

Belsky, J. (1993) 'Etiology of child maltreatment: A developmental analysis', *Psychological Bulletin* 114: 413–34.

Belsky, J., Steinberg, L. & Draper, P. (1990) 'Childhood experiences, interpersonal development, and reproductive strategy: an evolutionary theory of socialization', *Child Development* 62: 647–70.

Bernstein, I.S. (1980) 'Dominance: a theoretical perspective for ethologists', in D.R. Omark, F.F. Strayer & D.G. Freedman (eds) *Dominance Relations: An Ethological View of Conflict and Social Interaction* (pp. 71–84), New York: Garland Press.

Bowlby, J. (1969) *Attachment: Attachment and Loss*, Vol. 1, London: Hogarth Press.

Bowlby, J. (1973) *Separation, Anxiety and Anger. Attachment and loss*, Vol. 2, London: Hogarth Press.

Bowlby, J. (1980) *Loss: Sadness and Depression. Attachment and Loss*, Vol. 3, London: Hogarth Press.

Burnstein, E., Crandall, C. & Kitayama, S. (1994) 'Some neo-darwinian rules for altruism: weighing cues for inclusive fitness as a function of biological importance of the decision', *Journal of Personality and Social Psychology* 67: 773–807.

Buss, D.M. (1989) 'Sex differences in human mate preference: Evolutionary hypotheses tested in 37 cultures', *Brain and Behavioral Sciences* 12: 1–49.

Buss, D.M. (1991) 'Evolutionary personality psychology', in M.R. Rosenzweig & L.W. Porter (eds) *Annual Review of Psychology*, (Vol. 42), Palo Alto, CA: Annual Reviews.

Buss, D.M. (1995) 'Evolutionary psychology: a new paradigm for psychological science', *Psychological Inquiry* 6: 1–87.

Buss, D.M. (1999) *Evolutionary Psychology: The New Science of the Mind*. Boston, MA: Allyn and Bacon.

Buss, D.M. (2000) 'The evolution of human happiness', *American Psychologist* 55: 15–23.

Buss, D.M. & Malamuth, N.M. (1996) *Sex, Power, Conflict: Evolutionary and Feminist Perspectives*, New York: Oxford University Press.

Buss, D., Haselton, M.G., Shackelford, T.K., Bleske., A.L. & Wakefield, J.C. (1998) 'Adaptations, exaptations and spandels', *American Psychologist* 53: 533–48.

Carter, C.S., Lederhendler, I. & Kirkpatrick, B. (eds) (1997) *The Integrative Neurobiology of Affiliation*, New York: New York Academy of Sciences.

Charlesworth, W. (1988) 'Resources and resource acquisition during ontogeny', in K. MacDonald (ed) *Sociobiological Perspectives on Human Development*, New York: Springer Verlag.

Cosmides, L. (1989) 'The logic of social exchange: has natural selection shaped how humans reason? Studies with the Wason selection task', *Cognition* 31: 187–276.

Cosmides, L. & Tooby, J. (1992) 'Cognitive adaptations for social exchange', in J.H. Barkow, L. Cosmides & J. Tooby (eds) *The Adapted Mind: Evolutionary Psychology and the Generation of Culture* (pp. 193–228), New York: Oxford University Press.

Count, E.W. (1973) *Being and becoming Human: Essays on the Biogram*, New York: Van Nostrand Reinhold.

Cummins, D.D. (1999) 'Cheater detection is modified by social rank: the impact of dominance on the evolution of cognitive functions', *Evolution and Human Behavior* 20: 229–248.

Daly, M., Salmon, C. & Wilson, M.D. (1997) 'Kinship: the conceptual hole in psychological studies of social cognition and close relationships', in J.A Simpson & D.T. Kenrick (eds) *Evolutionary Social Psychology* (pp. 265–296), New Jersey: Lawrence Erlbaum Associates.

Dawkins, R. (1976) *The Selfish Gene*, Oxford: Oxford University Press.

de Waal, F.M.B. (1982) *Chimpanzee Politics*, London: Jonathan Cape.

de Waal, F.M.B. (1989) *Peacemaking Among Primates*, Harmondsworth, UK: Penguin.

de Waal, F.M.B. (1996) *Good Natured: The Origins of Right and Wrong in Humans and Other Animals*, Cambridge, MA: Harvard University Press.

de Waal, F.M.B. & Aureli, F. (1997) 'Conflict resolution and distress alleviation in monkeys and apes', in C.S. Carter, I.I. Lederhendler & B. Kirkpatrick (eds) *The Integrative Neurobiology of Affiliation*, New York: New York Academy of Sciences.

de Waal, F.M.B. & Luttrell, L. (1988) 'Mechanisms of social reciprocity in three primate species: symmetrical relationship characteristics or cognition?', *Ethology and Sociobiology* 9: 101–18.

Dixon, N.F. (1987) *Our Own Worst Enemy*, London: Routledge.

Eibl-Eibesfeldt, I. (1989) *Human Ethology*, New York: Aldine de Gruyter.

Ellenberger, H.F. (1970) *The Discovery of the Unconscious: The History and Evolution of Dynamic Psychiatry*, New York: Basic Books.

Ellis, L. (1989) *Theories of Rape: Inquires into the Causes of Sexual Aggression*, New York: Hemisphere.

Etcoff, N. (1999) *Survival of the Prettiest: The Science of Beauty*, New York: Doubleday.

Field, T.M. (1998) 'Touch therapy effects on development', *International Journal of Behavioral Development* 22: 779–97.

Fisher, H.E. (1982) *The Sex Contract*, New York: William Morrow.

Fogel, A., Melson, G.F. & Mistry, J. (1986) 'Conceptualising the determinants of nurturance: A reassessment of sex differences', in A. Fogel & G.F. Melson (eds), *Origins of Nurturance: Developmental, Biological and Cultural Perspectives on Caregiving*, (pp. 53–67). Hillsdale, NJ: Lawrence Erlbaum Associates Inc.

Fox, R. (1986) 'Fitness by any other name', *Behavioral and Brain Sciences* 9: 192–3.

Gardner, R. (1988) Psychiatric infrastructures for intraspecific communication, in M.R.A. Chance (ed), *Social Fabrics of the Mind*, Hove, UK: Lawrence Erlbaum Associates Ltd.

Gilbert, P. (1989), *Human Nature and Suffering*, Hove, UK: Lawrence Erlbaum Associates Ltd.

Gilbert, P. (1992) *Depression: The Evolution of Powerlessness*, Hove, UK: Psychology Press.

Gilbert, P. (1993) 'Defence and safety: their function in social behaviour and psychopathology', *British Journal of Clinical Psychology* 32: 131–54.

Gilbert, P. (1995) 'Biopsychosocial approaches and evolutionary theory as aids to integration in clinical psychology and psychotherapy', *Clinical Psychology and Psychotherapy* 2: 135–56.

Gilbert, P. (1997) 'The evolution of social attractiveness and its role in shame, humiliation, guilt and therapy', *British Journal of Medical Psychology* 70: 113–47.

Gilbert, P. (1998a) 'The evolved basis and adaptive functions of cognitive distortions', *British Journal of Medical Psychology* 71: 447–64.

Gilbert, P. (1998b) 'Evolutionary psychopathology: Why isn't the mind better designed than it is?', *British Journal of Medical Psychology* 71: 353–73.

Gilbert, P. (1998c) 'Shame and humiliation in complex cases', in N. Tarrier, G. Haddock & A. Wells (eds), *Cognitive Therapy For Complex Cases*, (pp. 241–71), London: Routledge.

Gilbert, P. (2000a) 'Varieties of submissive behaviour', in L. Sloman & P. Gilbert (eds), *Subordination and Defeat: An Evolutionary Approach to Mood Disorders and Their Therapy* (pp. 3–45), Hillsdale, NJ: Lawrence Erlbaum Associates Inc.

Gilbert, P. (2000b) *Counselling for Depression*, 2nd edition, London: Sage.

Gilbert, P. & Allan, S. (1998) 'The role of defeat and entrapment (arrested flight) in depression: an exploration of an evolutionary view', *Psychological Medicine* 28: 584–97.

Gilbert, P. & McGuire, M.T (1998) 'Shame, status and social roles: the psychobiological continuum from monkey to human', in P. Gilbert & B. Andrews (eds), *Shame: Interpersonal Behavior, Psychopathology and Culture*, (pp. 99–125), New York: Oxford University Press.

Gilbert, P., Price, J.S. & Allan, S. (1995) 'Social comparison, social attractiveness and evolution: How might they be related?', *New Ideas in Psychology* 13: 149–65.

Goodall, J. (1971) *In the Shadow of Man*, Boston: Houghton Mifflin.

Goodall, J. (1986) *The Chimpanzees of Gombe: Patterns of Behavior*, Cambridge, MA: Belknap Press.

Greenough, W.T., Black, J.E. & Wallace, C.S. (1987) 'Experiences and brain development', *Child Development* 58: 539–59.

Hamiliton, W.D. (1964) 'The genetical evolution of social behaviour', Parts 1 & 2, *Journal of Theoretical Biology* 7: 1–52.

Harcourt, A.H. & de Waal, F.M.B. (1992) *Coalitions and Alliances in Humans and Other Animals*, Oxford: Oxford University Press.

Hart, J., Gunnar, M. & Cicchetti, D. (1996) 'Altered neuroendocrine activity in maltreated children related to symptoms of depression', *Development and Psychopathology* 8: 201–14.

Hartung, J. (1987) 'Deceiving down: conjectures on the management of subordinate status', in J. Lockard & D. Pulhus (eds), *Self-deceit: An Adaptive Strategy*, (pp. 170–85), Englewood Cliffs, NJ: Prentice-Hall.

Herrnstein, R.J. (1977) 'Doing what comes naturally: A reply to Professor Skinner', *American Psychologist* 32: 1013–16.

Higley, J.D., Mehlman, P.T., Higley, S., Fremald, B., Vickers, J., Lindell, S.G., Taub, D.M., Suomi, S.J. & Linnoila, M. (1996) 'Excessive mortality in young free-ranging male nonhuman primates with low cerebrospinal fluid 5-hydroxyindoleacetic acid concentrations', *Archives of General Psychiatry* 53: 537–43.

Hinde, R.A. (1987) *Individuals, Relationships and Culture. Links Between Ethology and the Social Sciences*, Cambridge: Cambridge University Press.

Hinde, R.A. (1989) 'Relations between levels of complexity in behavioral sciences', *Journal of Nervous and Mental Disease* 177: 655–67.

Hinde, R.A. (1992) 'Developmental psychology in the context of other behavioral sciences', *Developmental Psychology* 28: 1018–29.

Hofer, M.A. (1981) *The Roots of Human Behavior*, San Francisco: W.H. Freeman.

Hofer, M.A. (1984) 'Relationships as regulators: A psychobiologic perspective on bereavement', *Psychosomatic Medicine* 46: 183–97.

Horowitz, L.M. & Vitkus, J. (1986) 'The interpersonal basis of psychiatric symptoms', *Clinical Psychology Review* 6: 443–70.

Jensen-Campbell, L.A., Graziano, W.G. & West, S.G. (1995) 'Dominance, prosocial orientation and female preference: Do nice guys really finish last?', *Journal of Personality and Social Psychology* 68: 427–40.

Kaufman, G. (1989) *The Psychology of Shame*, New York: Springer.

Kohut, H. (1977) *The Restoration of the Self*, New York: International Universities Press.

Krebs, D.L. & Denton, K. (1997) 'Social illusions and self-deception: The evolution of biases in person perception', in J.A. Simpson & D.T. Kenrick (eds), *Evolutionary Social Psychology*, (pp. 21–47), New Jersey: Lawrence Erlbaum Associates Inc.

Lancaster, J.B. (1991) 'A feminist and evolutionary biologist looks at women', *Yearbook of Physical Anthropology* 34: 1–11.

Lorenz, K. (1987) *The Wanning of Humaneness*, London: Unwin.

MacDonald, K. (1988) *Social and Personality Development: An Evolutionary Synthesis*, New York: Springer Verlag.

McGuire, M.T. & Troisi, A. (1987) 'Physiological regulation-disregulation and psychiatric disorders', *Ethology and Sociobiology* 8: 9S–12S.

McGuire, M.T. & Troisi, A. (1998a) *Darwinian Psychiatry*, New York: Oxford Press.

McGuire, M.T. & Troisi, A. (1998b) 'Prevalence differences in depression among males and females: are there evolutionary explanations?', *British Journal of Medical Psychology* 71: 479–92.

McGuire, M.T., Fawzy, F.I., Spar, J.E., Weigel, R.W. & Troisi, A. (1994) 'Altruism and mental disorders', *Ethology and Sociobiology* 15: 299–321.

MacLean, P.D. (1990) *The Triune Brain in Evolution*, New York: Plenum Press.

Mayr, E. (1977) 'Behavioral programs and evolutionary strategies', *American Scientist* 62: 650–59.

Mealey, L. (1997) 'The sociobiology of sociopathy: an intergrated evolutionary model', in S. Baron-Cohen, (ed), *The Maladapted Mind: Classic Readings in Evolutionary Psychopathology*, (pp.133–88), Hove, UK: Psychology Press.

Miller, L.C. & Fishkin, S.A. (1997) 'On the dynamics of human bonding and reproductive success: seeking windows on the adapted-for human-environment interface', in J.A. Simpson & D.T. Kenrick (eds), *Evolutionary Social Psychology*, Mahwah, NJ: Lawrence Erlbaum Associates Inc.

Nesse, R.M. (1990) 'Evolutionary explanations of emotions', *Human Nature* 1: 261–89.

Nesse, R.M. (1998) 'Emotional disorders in evolutionary perspective', *British Journal of Medical Psychology* 71: 397–416.

Nesse, R.M. & Williams, G.C. (1995) *Evolution and Healing: The New Science of Darwinian Medicine*, London: Weidenfeld & Nicolson.

Norcross, J.C. (ed) (1996) 'When (and how) does psychotherapy integration improve clinical effectiveness? A round table', *Journal of Psychotherapy Integration* 6: 295–407 (Special Issue).

Norcross, J.C. & Goldfried, M.R. (eds) (1992) *Handbook of Psychotherapy Integration*, New York: Basic Books.

Overing, J. (1989) 'Styles of manhood: an amazonian contrast in tranquillity and violence', in S. Howell & R. Wills (eds), *Societies at Peace. Anthropological Perspectives*, (pp. 79–99), London: New York.

Plutchik, R. (1980) *Emotions: A Psychoevolutionary Synthesis*, New York: Harper & Row.

Plutchik, R. (1994) *The Psychology and Biology of Emotion*, New York: Harper Collins.

Pratto, F., Sidanius, J., Stallworth, L.M. & Malle, B. (1994) 'Social dominance orientation: a personality variable predicting social and political attitudes', *Journal of Personality and Social Psychology* 67: 741–63.

Price, J.S. (1972) 'Genetic and phylogenetic aspects of mood variations', *International Journal of Mental Health* 1: 124–44.

Price, J., Sloman, L., Gardner, R., Gilbert, P. & Rhode, P. (1994) 'The social competition hypothesis of depression', *British Journal of Psychiatry* 164: 309–15.

Profet, M. (1988) 'The evolution of pregnancy sickness as protection to the embryo against Pleistocene teratogens', *Evolutionary Theory* 8: 177–90.

Profet, M. (1992) 'Pregnancy sickness as an adaptation: a deterrent to maternal ingestion of teratogens', in J. Barkow, L. Cosmides & J. Tooby (eds), *The Adapted Mind*, (pp. 327–65), New York: Oxford University Press.

Profet, M. (1995) *Protecting your Baby-to-be: A Revolutionary New Look at Pregnancy Sickness*, Reading, MA: Addison-Wesley.

Reeve, H.K. (1998) 'Acting for the good of others: kinship and reciprocity with some new twists', in C. Crawford & D. Krebs (eds), *Handbook of Evolutionary Psychology: Ideas, Issues and Applications*, (pp. 43–86), Mahwah, NJ: Lawrence Erlbaum Associates Inc.

Ridley, M. (1994) *The Red Queen: Sex and The Evolution of Human Nature*, London: Penguin.

Rosenblum, L.A., Coplan, J.D., Friedman, S., Bassoff, T., Gorman, J.M. & Andrews, M.W. (1994) 'Adverse early experiences affect noradrenergic and serotonergic functioning in adult primates', *Biological Psychiatry* 35: 221–7.

Schore, A.N. (1994) *Affect Regulation and the Origin of the Self: The Neurobiology of Emotional Development*, Hillsdale, NJ: Lawrence Erlbaum Associates Inc.

Simpson, J.A. & Kenrick, D.T. (1997) 'Why social psychology and evolutionary psychology need one another', in J.A. Simpson & D.T. Kenrick (eds), *Evolutionary Social Psychology*, (pp. 1–20), New Jersey: Lawrence Erlbaum Associates Inc.

Smith, E.W.L., Clance, P.R. & Imes, S. (1998) *Touch in Psychotherapy: Theory, Research and Practice*, New York: Guilford Press.

Stevens, A. (1982) *Archetype: A Natural History of the Self*, London: Routledge.

Taylor, S.E. & Brown, J.D. (1988) 'Illusion and well-being: a social psychological perspective on mental health', *Psychological Bulletin* 103: 193–210.

Thornhill, N. (1996) 'Psychological adaptation to sexual coercion in victims and offenders', in D.M. Buss & N. Malamuth (eds), *Sex, Power, Conflict; Evolutionary and Feminist Perspectives*, (pp. 90–104), New York: Oxford University Press.

Tiger, L. & Fox, R. (1971) *The Imperial Animal*, New York: Holt, Rinehart and Winston.

Trickett, P.K. & Putman, F.W. (1993) 'Impact of child sexual abuse on females: toward a development, psychobiological integration', *Psychological Science* 4: 81–7.

26

Trivers, R. (1985) *Social Evolution*, California: Benjamin/Cummings.

Uchino, B.N., Cacioppo, J.T. & Kiecolt-Glaser, J.K. (1996) 'The relationship between social support and physiological processes: A review with emphasis on underlying mechanisms and implications for health', *Psychological Bulletin* 119: 488–531.

van der Dennen, J.M.G. (1986) 'Ethnocentrism and in-group/out-group differentiation: a review and interpretation of the literature', in V. Reynolds, V. Falger & I. Vine (eds), *The Sociobiology of Ethnocentrism: Evolutionary Dimensions of Xenophobia, Discrimination, Racism and Nationalism*, (pp. 1–47), London: Croom Helm.

Wakefield, J.C. (1992) 'Disorder as harmful dysfunction: A conceptual critique of DSM-111-R's definition of mental disorder', *Psychological Review* 99: 232–47.

Wakefield, J.C. (1999) 'Evolutionary Versus Prototype Analysis of the Concept of Disorder', *Journal of Abnormal Psychology* 108: 400–411.

Wilkinson, R.G. (1996) *Unhealthy Societies: The Afflictions of Inequality*, London: Routledge.

Wilson, E.O. (1992) *The Diversity of Life*, Harmondsworth: Penguin.

Wilson, M. & Daly, M. (1992) 'The man who mistook his wife for a chattel', in J.H. Barkow, L. Cosmides & J. Tooby (eds), *The Adapted Mind: Evolutionary Psychology and the Generation of Culture*, (pp. 289–322), New York: Oxford University Press.

Zeifman D. & Hazan, C. (1997) 'Attachment: the bond in pair-bonds', in J.A. Simpson & D.T. Kenrick (eds), *Evolutionary Social Psychology*, (pp. 237–63), New Jersey: Lawrence Erlbaum Associates Inc.

2

PSYCHOTHERAPY IN THE CONTEXT OF DARWINIAN PSYCHIATRY

Alfonso Troisi and Michael T. McGuire

Introduction

The art of influencing the feelings and behaviour of other human beings has prehistoric roots and the origins of psychotherapy predate the birth of scientific attempts to understand human behaviour (Ehrenwald, 1976). Psychotherapy as a professional activity and form of medical treatment emerged towards the end of the nineteenth century. Since then, psychotherapy has become a remarkably pluralistic and prolific field. In 1959, Harper identified thirty-six distinct systems of psychotherapy. Twenty-seven years later, Karasu (1986) reported a count of more than 400 presumably different schools of psychotherapy.

In this chapter, we discuss psychotherapy within the theoretical framework of Darwinian psychiatry, that is the application of the concepts and methods of evolutionary biology to the study and treatment of mental disorders (McGuire & Troisi, 1998). Our aim is to use evolutionary concepts to develop hypotheses dealing with how psychotherapy works, to discuss its indications relative to other forms of treatment, and to suggest strategies for improving its efficacy. Our objective is *not* to develop a 'new school of psychotherapy' to compete with, or supplant, existing systems. Such an objective would conflict with the current tendency to overcome the ideological barriers that continue to divide schools of psychotherapy (Beitman, Goldfried & Norcross, 1989; Norcross & Goldfried, 1992). In addition, it would ignore the fact that many of the goals and techniques of contemporary psychotherapies already conform, although inadvertently, to the principles of an evolutionary approach to psychological treatment. This does not mean that there are not points of disagreement between the evolutionary approach and current psychotherapy systems. Where these differences are important, they will be mentioned.

The chapter is organized as follows. In order to explain the terms and the concepts used in the chapter, we begin with a brief overview of an evolutionary theory of human behaviour. We then summarise the basic principles that should guide an evolutionary-based psychotherapy. Finally, from an evolutionary perspective, we discuss three problems that are at the centre of the debate on the role of psychotherapy in contemporary psychiatry: how the therapeutic relationship works in bringing about change, the distinction between the 'really sick' and the so-called 'worried well', and predictions of differential responses to psychotherapy and pharmacotherapy.

An evolutionary theory of behaviour

Natural selection is a feedback process that is driven by the differential reproduction of alternative traits (defined as phenotypic characteristics influenced by genetic information which have specific functions). During the course of evolutionary history, natural selection favoured those psychological and behavioural traits that served a specific function more efficiently than did available alternative traits. Therefore, an evolutionary account of the human mind and behaviour is an account of how psychological and behavioural traits function as adaptations and how they vary across persons.

Although adaptations are produced by differential reproduction, studying differential reproduction does not necessarily illuminate adaptations (Williams, 1966). In other words, even though the ultimate function of any evolved trait is to enhance genetic replication, this does not mean that maximizing reproduction is the primary goal of all behaviour. Human beings, like all other organisms, have been designed by natural selection to strive for the achievement of specific goals or experiences, such as acquiring resources, making friends, having high status and reducing the effects of unpleasant emotions. These are the goals that concern humans and that are responsible for most human behaviour (Gilbert, 1989). Focusing on short-term goals facilitates the process of assessing the functional efficiency of individual behaviour. For example, to achieve the ultimate goal of enhancing one's own reproductive success, a person must correctly execute a variety of adaptive behaviours including identifying, selecting and acquiring a mate, accurately interpreting his or her needs and desires, and arousing his or her sexual interest. Each of these activities is a short-term goal that may be primarily rewarding, not simply secondarily rewarding because of its contiguous relationship to the ultimate goal.

Functions and the capacities to carry them out (functional capacities) need to be distinguished. Two persons may have the same short-term goal, yet they may differ in their capacities to achieve the goal. This point brings us to another concept that is central to evolutionary theory, individual variability, or the fact that traits vary across individuals. The variation that exists in a population is the resource with which natural selection works. Natural populations show variation at all levels, from gross morphology to DNA sequences, and new variation is continuously generated by mutation and recombination through sexual reproduction. In addition, because numerous factors (e.g., genetic loading for disorders, developmental insults, adverse upbringing environments) influence trait development, individuals develop variant traits, and some traits are more functional than others. These points have two important implications: most traits can be scaled along a continuum from suboptimal to optimal, when the measure of optimality is taken as the contribution of a trait to achieving short-term goals; and, many enduring features of mental disorders can be characterized in terms of an individual's location at the extremes of trait continua.

Principles of evolutionary psychotherapy

Evolutionary psychotherapy is a theoretical framework, not a technique. Its primary aim is to improve the patient's chances of achieving short-term biological goals. An evolutionary psychotherapy can be based on different combinations of the three therapeutic change agents that are common to all psychotherapies: affective experiencing, cognitive mastery, and behavioural regulation (Karasu, 1986). Although there is no conceptual obstacle to integrating current techniques into an evolutionary psychotherapy, an evolutionary approach introduces important changes into the three basic stages of the therapeutic process: assessment, causal analysis, and intervention.

Assessment

Clinical assessment should focus primarily on functional capacities and person–environment interactions. Like mentally healthy people, individuals with mental disorders act to optimize the achievement of short-term goals and their behaviour reflects interactions between their strategies, their functional capacities, and environmental contingencies. With few exceptions, the motivations and goals of persons with and without mental disorders do not appear to differ. Rather, the difference between the two groups lies in the capacity of enacting efficient strategies to achieve biological goals. *Whatever else they are, most mental disorders are conditions of failed functions.* It follows that an accurate assessment of functional capacities is essential to the development of precise diagnostic evaluation and outcome measurement. A clinical assessment that focuses primarily on signs and symptoms, cognitive distortions, intrapsychic conflicts or inadequate learning, but only secondarily on functional capacities, limits itself to explaining only partial features of mental disorders.

The assessment of functional capacities cannot be properly made without consideration of the environment in which the individual lives. In this regard, the evolutionary approach has much in common with the ecological models of psychopathology (Bailey, 1987). The majority of functions that are of interest to psychiatry are carried out in the social arena. Because features of the social environment change, carrying out the same function often requires the use of different strategies and capacities. Thus, behaviour and its outcomes need to be assessed on a moment-to-moment basis. For example, the efficiency of a social signal is defined in part by the response of the person receiving the signal. When re-examined from such a perspective, the usual methods for functional evaluation in psychiatry and clinical psychology (i.e., global assessments of capacities or inferences about such capacities) are clearly inadequate.

Causal analysis

Evolutionary theory introduces novel approaches to the causal analysis of psychopathology. Prevailing models generally consider psychiatric symptoms as products of one or more underlying dysfunctional processes, such as neurochemical imbalance, intrapsychic conflicts, or learning distortions. Darwinian psychiatry does not contest the validity of these views for explaining some symptoms (e.g., bizarre delusions or melancholic depression), but it also suggests alternative explanations.

In an evolutionary context, symptoms may be seen as reactions to situations associated with negative cost–benefit outcomes. Compromised functional capacities, adverse environments, or a combination of both, are all factors that increase the likelihood of experiencing negative cost–benefit outcomes. From this perspective, much of what is traditionally considered to be the focus of psychotherapeutic efforts should be changed. For example, rather than conceptualizing depression as a mental experience that must be expressed and worked through, it is seen as an evolved warning signal that biological goals have not been or are not being achieved (Nesse, 1991). The therapeutic task, then, is to aid the patient in developing novel strategies that can resolve situations associated with negative cost–benefit outcomes. If the novel strategy is effective, the negative cost–benefit outcomes should be offset and the depressed mood should disappear.

An evolutionary analysis of the pathogenesis of symptoms takes seriously the causative role of the environment because the efficiency of functional capacities is dependent on features of the environment. Adverse environments can compromise the efficiency of optimal capacities, just as favourable environments can offset or mitigate the inefficiency of suboptimal capacities. Moreover, even though the inability to achieve short-term goals is often due to suboptimal capacities, some persons develop symptoms as a reaction to adverse environments that impede the implementation of adaptive behaviour. A feature that often distinguishes healthy people and persons with mental disorders is the incapacity to exit from these environments.

Finally, evolutionary causal analysis suggests that some symptoms and syndromes may serve specific adaptive functions. Individual symptoms may be attempts to minimize the competitive disadvantages that accrue from limited capacities to navigate socially. For example, among some schizophrenic patients, social withdrawal may be an alternative strategy to avoid high costs and low benefits of interacting with others. Further, complexes of symptoms forming a behavioural syndrome may represent evolved strategies such as antisocial and histrionic personality disorders, time-limited anorexia nervosa, and attention deficit hyperactivity

31

disorder (McGuire & Troisi, 1998). For example, a number of investigators have discussed antisocial personality disorder in an evolutionary context. In a society made up primarily of reciprocators, genes for cheaters can enter the population and remain, provided persons with such genes reproduce. Therefore, sociopathy might be the product of evolutionary pressures which, through a complex interaction of environmental and genetic factors, lead some individuals to pursue a high-risk life strategy of manipulative and predatory social interactions (Mealey, 1995).

Intervention strategies

Evolutionary therapy aims at improving the patient's chances of achieving short-term biological goals. Depending on the features of the patient and the factors that cause the symptoms, the therapeutic strategy will include different interventions.

Persons with intact functional capacities who experience dysfunctional states could be helped to identify the environmental and personal constraints that interfere with achieving short-term goals. Therapy should facilitate: (1) the refinement of the capacities to assess cost–benefit outcomes; (2) the development of revised models of the social environment; and (3) the improvement of capacities to selectively enact behaviours associated with goal achievement.

For suboptimal functional capacities that are due to trait variation, therapy should attempt either to refine traits or to foster the use of alternative capacities that improve the likelihood of achieving high priority goals. Altering minimally adaptive capacities is sometimes extremely difficult, however. If the patient is not able to develop and execute novel behavioural strategies, environmental change is usually essential to ensure lasting improvement. Said differently, persons with suboptimal functional capacities should be advised to search actively for environments in which they are most likely to achieve high priority goals. Transient physiological re-regulation (and thus symptom reduction) can be achieved through the therapeutic relationship (see below) and/or the concomitant administration of psychotropic drugs.

Theoretically, conditions that can be adaptive by evolutionary criteria and symptoms that are attempts to adapt should not be treated. In practice, attempts to treat these conditions and symptoms are justified if they are socially undesirable *and* persons with these features run the risk of being ostracized. However, justification does not detract from two important facts: (1) clinical manifestations reflecting evolved adaptive strategies should be distinguished from those that are caused by compromised functional capacities; and (2) treatment of adaptive strategies should be avoided if they do not cause discomfort to the individual or members of the individual's environment.

Clinical case

The description of a clinical case (from McGuire & Troisi, 1998: 270–1, with permission) may be useful to illustrate how an evolutionary approach can be integrated into the different stages of psychotherapy. The full complexity of the individual case history is not addressed here. Rather, the case covers only those features of the patient's past history, current life circumstances and treatment that are relevant to illustrate the clinical use of an evolutionary approach. We use parentheses to allow the reader to link the specific aspects of the case with the general principles discussed above.

The patient was a 37-year-old unmarried female who was unable to bear children because of a constricted uterus. She had begun suffering from depression at age 28. Her depression had remained mild through her early 30s. While she had been able to maintain a job and participate in social relationships, she had avoided close relationships with men because of her fear of rejection should they become aware that she could not have children. At age 36, her depression had worsened and had begun interfering with her capacity to work efficiently. After several warnings about her job performance, she sought therapy.

The patient's symptoms were interpreted as resulting from her having failed to have children (*causal analysis: symptoms as reactions to the failure to achieve biological goals*). The treatment was formulated to address the dysregulating effects of her inability to reproduce (depression) and the compromised capacities that led to her inability to develop novel ways of dealing with her reproductive incapacity (*intervention: planning of alternative strategies*). The specific goal of therapy was to facilitate kin investment.

Combined psychotherapy and pharmacological therapy were used. The psychotherapy focused on the causes of her dissatisfactions. Concurrent antidepressant medication was moderately effective in reducing her symptoms. However, medications did not result in improvement in her job performance (*assessment: distinction between symptoms and adaptive functioning*). During the fifth month of therapy, the patient was encouraged to visit her five siblings, who lived in another part of the country. She took a three-month leave of absence from work and made the visit. While visiting, she experienced a significant decline in her depression and a strong desire to help her siblings raise their children (*causal analysis: regulatory effect of specific social signals*). She returned to therapy and discussed her desire to relocate near her brothers and sisters so that she could assist them with their children. The move was encouraged (*intervention: environmental alteration*). Two months later, the patient moved. Within six months, she had discontinued her medications and was essentially symptom-free. A two-year follow-up revealed that she remained symptom-free, felt that she was a useful family member, and had found a new job.

The therapeutic relationship as a physiological regulator

Many experienced clinicians agree that the therapeutic relationship is an important element in all forms of psychological treatment and that the most powerful determinants of therapeutic success lie in the personal qualities of the patient, the therapist, and the interaction between them. For example, a panel of psychotherapy experts estimated that one-third of treatment outcome is due to the psychotherapist and two-thirds is attributable to the patient; technical variables were thought to have little effect on outcome (Prochaska & Norcross, 1982). In line with these estimates, meta-analytic studies (Smith, Glass & Miller, 1980; Lambert, 1983) have confirmed the limited importance of the particular therapeutic method: only 10–12 per cent of outcome variance is generally accounted for by technique variables.

The evolutionary approach considers the therapeutic relationship a powerful mechanism of change. Indeed, it accords greater importance to the relationship than most schools of psychotherapy. The evolutionary hypothesis of how the therapeutic relationship works is based on the principles of the regulation–dysregulation theory and in particular on its assumption that specific types and frequencies of social interactions are essential for maintaining regulation (McGuire & Troisi, 1987). The term 'regulation' references a state in which psychological and physiological systems are functioning optimally; the term 'dysregulation' references dysfunctional states. The theory offers insights into how events in the social environment influence physiological and behavioural change and trigger the onset of symptoms among persons vulnerable to disorders. *Homo sapiens* is a highly social species that significantly influences and is significantly influenced by the social environment. And, an extensive research literature (reviewed in McGuire & Troisi, 1998) indicates that specific types of social interaction are essential to maintaining central nervous system physiological homeostasis. Taken together, these observations suggest that the key factor for explaining the beneficial effects of the therapeutic relationship is the neurobiological changes initiated by interactions between therapist and patient.

Persons with mental disorders often have suboptimal or dysfunctional capacities to utilize the social environment to regulate themselves physiologically, that is they repeatedly experience negative social interactions and are unable to improve their way of interacting with others. Thus, a spiralling sequence of events is often observed among persons with mental disorders: (1) atypical social signals by the patient lead to others' avoidance of the patient because of the adverse effects of patient's signals on others' physiological and emotional states; (2) others' avoidance causes greater physiological dysregulation in the patient because of the absence of social signals essential to central nervous system homeostasis; (3) dysregulation causes the worsening of symptoms and further impairs patient's social functioning. The therapeutic relationship can break such a vicious circle. If a patient enters a therapeutic environment that is supportive, non-judgemental, minimally demanding socially, and structured, such an environment is one in which the patient is important and the patient's importance is frequently confirmed. An environment with these characteristics is likely to hasten physiological re-regulation and symptom reduction.

As originally formulated, the regulation–dysregulation theory built on data dealing with a variety of human social interactions but it did not address findings from psychotherapy research. Evidence consistent with the theory continues to accumulate although there are as yet few studies of the regulation–dysregulation theory and psychotherapy (see McGuire & Troisi, 1998, Chapter 14, for a notable exception). While more research is required, the regulation–dysregulation hypothesis can serve as the basis for a number of testable predictions.

One prediction is that the benefits of the therapeutic relationship will not be long-lasting unless the patient learns to transfer new ways of interacting from the structured and safe confines of the therapist's office to the real world outside of treatment. Thus, physiological re-regulation induced by the therapist's social signals needs to be complemented by other therapeutic change agents. Because of trait variation, not all patients have the capacity to incorporate novel and more adaptive behavioural strategies into their actions in everyday life. For these patients, the beneficial effects of psychotherapy are likely to be limited to short-lived symptomatic relief and transient physiological re-regulation.

A second prediction is that the beneficial effects of the therapeutic relationship vary with the type of dysregulation experienced by the patient and the type of social signals sent by the therapist. For example, assume that a person seeks therapy for a depressive episode related to a decline in social status (Gilbert, 1992). The regulation–dysregulation theory postulates that dysregulation in this patient involves the psychophysiological system associated with dominance interactions and that only social signals reinforcing the patient's confidence in his or her efforts to be valued and have some status can re-regulate the patient's central nervous system physiology and lead to symptom remission. A psychotherapy which ignores the patient's need for such signals is likely to be unproductive, even if the therapist's attitude towards the patient is empathic and supportive. In this regard, the evolutionary hypothesis contrasts with the view that the relationship between the therapist and the patient is a non-specific therapeutic change agent because the 'healing effects of a benign human relationship' (Strupp & Hadley, 1979: 1135) are common to all forms of psychological treatment.

Finally, an evolutionary analysis of what happens between the therapist and the patient raises the possibility that some forms of psychotherapy may produce harmful effects. This prediction is based on the idea that the role played by non-verbal communication in regulating human interactions is much more important than commonly thought in psychiatry and clinical psychology. For example, the therapeutic setting of classical psychoanalysis (i.e., the patient lies on a couch and talks freely; the therapist speaks rarely and keeps out of sight) may worsen the emotional condition of those patients who rely mostly on visual stimuli and non-verbal signals to monitor others. Or, the reason why psychoanalysis is contraindicated in patients with marked paranoid personality traits (Karasu, 1989) may reside more in the ethological features of the psychoanalytic setting than in the techniques used (e.g., transference interpretations and identification of defence mechanisms). Analytic abstinence and neutrality may also be counterproductive for patients whose interactional capacities are so impaired by depressed mood that they may need active support, even therapeutic 'cheerleading', to balance their deficits (Markowitz, 1994; Michels, 1997).

The idea that psychotherapy is in part a biological intervention is not new: 'It is only in so far as our words produce changes in each other's brain that psychother-apeutic intervention produces changes in patients' minds' (Kandel, 1979: 1037). In addition, recent studies based on brain imaging techniques have begun to identify the anatomical regions where these changes occur (e.g., Schwartz *et al.*, 1996). What remains to be discovered are the specific neurobiological effects of different types of social signals that are exchanged between the patient and the therapist during psychotherapy (see Gilbert, Chapter 6, this volume). Our lack of knowledge in this area is due in part to methodological problems and in part to the absence of a conceptual framework for guiding research. With its emphasis on the complexity and biological relevance of human social behaviour, evolutionary theory has much to contribute to the development of such a framework.

Psychotherapy for whom? The 'worried well' vs. the 'really sick'

Now that we are in the midst of the 'neuroscience revolution' in which the biomedical model dominates psychiatric thinking, the indications for pharma-cotherapy are progressively expanding to include a variety of symptoms and syndromes. Psychological treatment, as a result, runs the risk of being devalued as therapeutically non-specific and marginal. For example, according to Guze (1998) psychotherapy is universal in all personal medical care, consists simply of humanistic and compassionate care by a concerned physician and need not be based on causal hypotheses to be valuable and helpful. He implies that psychiatrists should treat the seriously mentally ill and send patients with 'problems in living' to other mental health professionals, presumably for psychotherapy (Michels, 1998). Similarly, Detre and McDonald (1997) draw a line between seriously and chronically mentally ill patients and the 'worried well' (i.e., those persons who worry but do not have psychiatric disorders) and suggest an analogy between psychotherapy and cosmetic surgery: '. . . the only way to receive treatments that make us feel just a little bit better is to pay for them out of our own pocket, if we can afford it' (Detre & McDonald, 1997: 203).

These opinions about the role of psychotherapy in the practice of contemporary psychiatry rest on a set of explicit or implicit assumptions: (1) psychiatry is a medical speciality which deals with real disorders, not 'problems in living'; (2) real psychiatric disorders are expressions of altered brain functioning; (3) 'problems in living' consist of psychological and behavioural changes in the absence of altered brain functioning; (4) pharmacotherapy effects change through biological mecha-nisms, initiated by the chemical that is administered to the patient; (5) in contrast, psychotherapy brings about change through psychological mechanisms. Except the fourth, all of the above assumptions are questionable when examined from an evolutionary perspective. The hypothesis that psychotherapy may work also through biological mechanisms has been analysed in the previous section and will not be discussed further. Here we focus on the biomedical definition of psychiatric disorder and the distinction between the 'really sick' and the 'worried well'.

Evolutionary reasoning suggests that such a distinction cannot be based on the demonstration of organic pathology because there is no definitive criterion for sorting out altered brain functioning from normal inter- and intra-individual variability, unless we judge a condition in terms of functional consequences. For example, *in vivo* studies of brain functioning based on the use of positron emission tomography have shown that the same neurobiological changes are implicated in the mediation of normal and pathological forms of anxiety (Reiman, 1997). For this reason, the evolutionary concept of health and disease is consequence-oriented: what makes a condition pathological is its maladaptive consequences, not its causes or correlates. The presence of either anatomical or physiological pathology, or both, is not a necessary condition for defining mental disorder (Troisi & McGuire, 1998).

The therapeutic implication of the evolutionary concept of mental disorder is that psychiatric diagnosis and the decision to treat should be based on evidence indicating the presence of compromised functional capacities, not on the severity of symptoms or the demonstration of altered brain functioning. Among the 'worried well' population surely there are persons who are mentally healthy and who do not need psychiatric treatment. However, this population also includes many persons whose behaviour is overtly maladaptive and who deserve the same level of clinical attention and therapeutic concern as that commonly accorded to patients with altered brain functioning and/or major psychiatric symptoms.

From an evolutionary perspective, there is no basis for considering psychotherapy a cosmetic intervention to make worried persons feel just a little better (Detre & McDonald, 1997) or a non-specific intervention limited to humanistic and compassionate care by a concerned physician (Guze, 1998). As conceived of in the context of Darwinian psychiatry, psychotherapy should be based on a pathogenetic theory of symptoms and compromised functional capacities and should set specific treatment goals. As for any other medical therapy, psychotherapy is indicated for some patients but not for others. Hence, the question shifts away from 'Is this individual really sick or just worried well?' towards 'What treatment (psychotherapy, pharmacotherapy or a combination of both) is most effective for this patient?'.

Differential response to psychotherapy and pharmacotherapy

The two major forms of treatment for mental disorders are pharmacotherapy and psychotherapy. Even though over the last three decades hundreds of studies have examined the effectiveness of each of these forms of treatment, the problem of identifying differential predictors of response to pharmacotherapy and psychotherapy remains largely unsolved. A likely explanation is that, to solve the problem, we need not only well-designed empirical studies but also a general theory of the active ingredients and the purported mechanisms by which pharmacotherapy and psychotherapy effect change (Elkin *et al.*, 1988). We believe that evolutionary thinking has much to contribute to the development of such a theory. In particular, it can help to explain some puzzling findings reported in the literature on differential response to pharmacotherapy and psychotherapy.

Several studies of drug response in persons with depressive disorders have reported a seemingly counter-intuitive finding: those patients who are closest to normal controls on a number of clinical measures do not respond to antidepressant therapy. Frank *et al.* (1984) compared the serum cortisol concentration at sleep onset in two groups of depressed patients with different response to drug therapy and found that the hormonal measure was normal in nonresponders and abnormally elevated in responders. Analysing the nonverbal behaviour of depressed patients during pretreatment interviews, Troisi *et al.* (1989) found that a higher frequency of behaviours inviting social interaction and a better capacity to interact with the interviewer were associated with a poorer response to tricyclic treatment. Peselow *et al.* (1992) administered the sociotropy-autonomy scale and an endogenous depression scale to 217 depressed patients to investigate whether these instruments were useful for predicting the response to antidepressant drug treatment. A hierarchical multiple regression analysis performed to determine which factors were predictive of treatment response revealed that higher sociotropy (a measure of interest and concern for social relationships) predicted a poor response to pharmacotherapy whereas endogenous depression scores (a measure of the severity of depressive symptoms) did not do so.

Such a confluence of findings requires an explanation. The explanation based on the biomedical model of disease postulates that, in a subgroup of patients, depressive disorders do not have a sufficient neurobiological basis to be ameliorated by pharmacotherapy (Phillips *et al.*, 1998). Even if correct, this hypothesis does not explain why some patients without neurobiological dysfunction have depressive symptoms virtually identical to those of neurobiologically disturbed patients. As noted (see the section on 'causal analysis'), evolutionary theory suggests a more comprehensive explanation that can incorporate the biomedical hypothesis: *in some depressed patients, symptoms reflect attempts to adapt within the constraints of their disorder.* Having suboptimal capacities for interacting with others, these persons make an excessive use of alternative strategies to alter others' behaviour. If symptoms are understood as an attempt to minimize the competitive disadvantages that accrue from limited capacities to interact socially, there is no reason to expect dramatic improvement in response to drug therapy. By contrast, psychotherapy can be effective, provided that the intervention is successful in teaching the patient new strategies to achieve short-term goals.

Clinical data support the evolutionary hypothesis that psychotherapy should be the preferred modality of treatment in those patients who use symptoms to cope with interpersonal problems and to alter others' behaviour. For example, several studies have shown that women respond more poorly to antidepressant drugs compared with men (Frank, Carpenter & Kupfer, 1988; Kornstein, 1997) whereas the response to psychotherapy does not vary with the gender of the patient (Thase *et al.*, 1994). Frank, Carpenter and Kupfer (1988) have explained this gender difference in response to different modalities of treatment as the result of the fact that, in most cases, the depression of women is more interpersonally based than the depression suffered by men. Nonverbal behaviour data are consistent with such an explanation: during psychiatric interviews depressed women are more socially interactive than depressed men and show higher levels of both affiliative and hostile behaviours (Troisi & Moles, 1999).

Clinicians agree that another group of patients for whom psychotherapy should be preferred over drug therapy is that of persons with somatoform disorders (Bass, 1990). These patients are often resistant to all efforts to modify their patterns of somatization and make somatic illness 'a way of life' (Ford, 1984). Viewed from an evolutionary perspective, their behaviour is an alternative strategy based on a combination of self-deception and deliberate deception of others (Troisi & McGuire, 1991). Patients with somatoform disorders 'need' their symptoms because they lack more adaptive strategies for social interaction.

Conclusion

This chapter has introduced a number of evolutionary views of psychotherapy. While our analysis is neither exhaustive nor conclusive, it suggests new insights into the possible mechanisms whereby psychotherapy effects change and illustrates how evolutionary concepts can improve and refine the intervention strategies used in psychological therapies.

Moreover, evolutionary considerations can cross-fertilise the field of psychotherapy, which has been in search of a scientific perspective since Freud (Akiskal, 1997). The debate on the value and therapeutic significance of psychotherapy is one of the most alarming examples of the opposition between the biomedical and psychosocial models that still plagues current psychiatric thinking. We hope to have interested the reader in the possibility that an evolutionary approach can overcome such an opposition by providing psychotherapy research and practice with a comprehensive theoretical framework that is both biological and anti-reductionistic.

References

Akiskal, H.S. (1997) 'A renaissance of clinical psychiatry through books published during the past decade', *Journal of Clinical Psychiatry* 58: 552–3.

Bailey, K.G. (1987) *Human Paleopsychology*, Hillsdale, NJ: Lawrence Erlbaum Associates Inc.

Bass, C.M. (1990) 'Assessment and management of patients with functional somatic symptoms', in C.M. Bass (ed), *Somatization: Physical Symptoms and Psychological Illness*, (pp. 40–72), Oxford: Blackwell.

Beitman B.D. Goldfried, M.R. & Norcross, J.C. (1989) 'The movement toward integrating the psychotherapies: an overview', *American Journal of Psychiatry* 146: 138–47.

Detre, T. & McDonald, M.C. (1997) 'Managed care and the future of psychiatry', *Archives of General Psychiatry* 54: 201–4.

Ehrenwald, J. (1976) *The History of Psychotherapy: From Healing Magic to Encounter*, New York: Jason Aronson.

Elkin, I., Pilkonis, P.A, Docherty, J.P & Sotsky, S.M. (1988) 'Conceptual and methodological issues in comparative studies of psychotherapy and pharmacotherapy, I: active ingredients and mechanisms of change', *American Journal of Psychiatry* 145: 909–17.

Ford, C.V. (1984) *The Somatizing Disorders. Illness As a Way of Life*, New York: Elsevier.

Frank, E., Carpenter, L.L. & Kupfer, D.J. (1988) 'Sex differences in recurrent depression: are there any that are significant?', *American Journal of Psychiatry* 145: 41–5.

Frank, E., Jarrett, D.B., Kupfer, D.J. & Grochocinski, V.J. (1984) 'Biological and clinical predictors of response in recurrent depression: a preliminary report', *Psychiatry Research* 13: 315–24.

Gilbert, P. (1989) *Human Nature and Suffering*, Hove, UK: Lawrence Erlbaum Associates Ltd.

Gilbert, P. (1992) *Depression: The Evolution of Powerlessness*, Hove, UK: Psychology Press.

Guze, S.B. (1998) 'Psychotherapy and managed care', *Archives of General Psychiatry*, 55: 561–2.

Harper, R.A. (1959) *Psychoanalysis and Psychotherapy: 36 Systems*, Englewood Cliffs, NJ: Prentice-Hall.

Kandel, E.R. (1979) 'Psychotherapy and the single synapse: the impact of psychiatric thought on neurobiological research', *New England Journal of Medicine* 301: 1028–37.

Karasu, T.B.(1989) 'Psychoanalysis and psychoanalytic psychotherapy', in H.I. Kaplan & B.J.O. Sadock (eds), *Comprehensive Textbook of Psychiatry V, Vol. 2, (pp. 1442–61)*, Baltimore: Williams & Wilkins.

Karasu, T.B. (1986) 'The specificity versus nonspecificity dilemma: toward identifying therapeutic change agents', *American Journal of Psychiatry* 143: 687–95.

Kornstein, S.G. (1997) 'Gender differences in depression: implications for treatment', *Journal of Clinical Psychiatry* 58(suppl 15): 12–18.

Lambert, M.J. (1983) *Psychotherapy and Patient Relationships*, Homewood, IL: Dorsey Press.

Markowitz, J.C. (1994) 'Psychotherapy of dysthymia', *American Journal of Psychiatry* 151: 1114–21.

McGuire, M.T. & Troisi, A. (1987) 'Physiological regulation-dysregulation and psychiatric disorders', *Ethology and Sociobiology* 8: 9S–12S

McGuire, M.T. & Troisi, A. (1998) *Darwinian Psychiatry*, New York: Oxford University Press.

Mealey, L. (1995) 'The sociobiology of sociopathy: an integrated evolutionary model', *Behavioral and Brain Science* 18: 523–99.

Michels, R. (1997) 'Psychotherapeutic approaches to the treatment of anxiety and depressive disorders', *Journal of Clinical Psychiatry*, 58(suppl 13): 30–2.

Michels, R. (1998) 'The role of psychotherapy: psychiatry's resistance to managed care', *Archives of General Psychiatry* 55: 564.

Nesse, R.M. (1991) 'What good is feeling bad?', *The Sciences* 31: 30–7.

Norcross, J.C. & Goldfried, M.R.(1992) *Handbook of Psychotherapy Integration*, New York: Basic Books.

Peselow, E.D., Robins, C.J., Sanfilipo, M.P., Block. P. & Fieve, R.R. (1992) 'Sociotropy and autonomy: relationship to antidepressant drug treatment response and endogenous-nonendogenous dichothomy', *Journal of Abnormal Psychology* 101: 479–86.

Phillips, K.A., Gunderson, J.G., Triebwasser, J., Kimble, C.R., Faedda, G., Kyoon Lyoo, I. & Renn, J. (1998) 'Reliability and validity of depressive personality disorder', *American Journal of Psychiatry* 155: 1044–48.

Prochaska, J.O. & Norcross, J.C. (1982) 'The future of psychotherapy: a Delphi poll', *Professional Psychology: Research and Practice* 13: 620–7.

Reiman, E.M. (1997) 'The application of positron emission tomography to the study of normal and pathologic emotions', *Journal of Clinical Psychiatry* 58(suppl 16): 4–12.

Schwartz, J.M., Stoessel, P.W., Baxter, L.R., Martin, K.M. & Phelps, M.E. (1996) 'Systematic changes in cerebral glucose metabolic rate after successful behavior modification treatment of obssessive–compulsive disorder', *Archives of General Psychiatry* 53: 109–13.

Smith, M.L., Glass, G.V. & Miller, T.I. (1980) *The Benefits of Psychotherapy*, Baltimore: Johns Hopkins University Press.

Strupp, H., & Hadley, S.W. (1979) Specific vs. non-specific factors in psychotherapy', *Archives of General Psychiatry* 36: 1125–36.

Thase, M.E., Reynolds, C.F, Frank, E., Simons, A.D., McGeary, J., Fasiczka, A.L., Garamoni, G.G., Jennings, J.R. & Kupfer, D.J. (1994) 'Do depressed men and women respond similarly to cognitive behaviour therapy?', *American Journal of Psychiatry* 151: 500–5.

Troisi, A. & McGuire, M.T. (1991) 'Deception and somatizing disorders', in C.N. Stefanis, A.D. Rabavilas & C.R. Soldatos (eds), *Psychiatry: A World Perspective*, Vol. 3, (pp. 973–8), Amsterdam: Excerpta Medica.

Troisi, A. & McGuire, M.T. (1998) 'Evolution and mental health', in H.S. Friedman (ed), *Encyclopaedia of Mental Health*, Vol. 2, (pp. 173–81), San Diego: Academic Press.

Troisi, A. & Moles, A. (1999) 'Gender differences in depression: an ethological study of non-verbal behavior during interviews', *Journal of Psychiatric Research*, 33: 243–50.

Troisi, A., Pasini, A., Bersani, G., Grispini,. A. & Ciani, N. (1989) 'Ethological predictors of amitriptyline response in depressed outpatients', *Journal of Affective Disorders* 17: 129–36.

Williams, G.C. (1966) *Adaptation and Natural Selection*, Princeton: Princeton University Press.

Acknowledgement

We thank Paul Gilbert and Kent Bailey for useful comments on an earlier version of this chapter.

3

EVOLUTION, KINSHIP, AND PSYCHOTHERAPY

Promoting psychological health through human relationships

Kent G. Bailey

The need to belong is a fundamental and powerful human drive (Baumeister & Leary, 1995) that emanates from the mammalian, primate, and hominid/human ancestry of modern human beings (Mellen, 1981). Ancestral hominid and early human species lived in small, intimate, and often inbred groups typically numbering in the 25–50 range (Lewin, 1993; Service, 1962) but may have numbered up to 70–80 individuals by *Homo habilis* (Dunbar, 1992). Groups might reach 150–200 in later phases of ancestral history and 500 or more in tribal groupings of *Homo sapiens* (see Aiello & Dunbar, 1993), but even then extended in-group relations were intensely intimate relative to out-group relations. Whether in band or tribe, members moved together as a group, exploring and exploiting the environment *en masse*, engaging in communication in the domains of mating, parenting, grooming, food-seeking and food-consumption, and, in general, acting out species scripts in an intricate social ecosystem (Caporael & Baron, 1997).

Over evolutionary time, social togetherness within the group became central to the physical and emotional well-being of the individual (Panksepp, Nelson & Bekkedal, 1997), and real or threatened disruptions of this natural sociality were stressful, aversive, and likely to carry costs in personal and inclusive fitness. In today's world, rejection, devaluation by others, ostracism, and alienation are similarly aversive and stressful (Baumeister & Tice, 1990; Hazan & Shaver, 1994; Weiss, 1979), and such losses or disruptions put one at risk for various forms of both physical and psychological pathology (Baumeister & Leary, 1995; DeLongis, Folkman & Lazarus, 1988; Henderson, 1982; Goodwin, Hunt, Key & Samet, 1987; House, Landis & Umberson, 1988; Lynch, 1979). For example, insecure attachment with early parenting figures can be detrimental to one's physiological functioning (see Carter, Lederhendler & Kirkpatrick, 1997 and Liotti, Chapter 11, this volume), subsequent child rearing practices (see Hazan & Zeifman, 1994), sense of self and self-regulation (Bowlby, 1988; see also Swann & Brown, 1990), internal working models and system of meanings (Simpson & Rholes, 1998), and overall psychological health in adulthood (see Atkinson & Zucker, 1997). It may also be a precursor to family incest (Erickson, 1993; Erickson, Chapter 10, this volume), adult sexual deviance (Sroufe & Fleeson, 1986), sexual promiscuity (Brennan, Shaver & Tobey, 1991), and conflicted dating and mating relationships (Zeifman & Hazan, 1997).

This chapter first addresses kinship psychology from the perspectives of in-group out-group relations, biological and psychological kinship, the problem of the stranger, and the costs and benefits of kinship. The focus will then turn to the implications of natural sociality and kinship for physical and psychological health and well-being, and, finally, all of these currents will converge on evolutionary kinship therapy. Several brief case studies illustrate specific concepts.

Basic principles of kinship psychology

Our kind: their kind

The most fundamental distinction in animals organized into systems of kinship is between our-kind and their-kind, or the in-group versus out-group distinction (Bailey, 1994; Bruner, 1957; Devine, 1989; Gardner, 1994; Krebs & Denton, 1997). Kinship classification in human beings begins with this distinction as well: 'Research in social psychology has revealed that when we encounter other people, we immediately and automatically classify them as in-group or out-group, and this categorization structures our subsequent perceptions of them' (Krebs & Denton, 1997: 21). Once an individual is categorized as within the in-group, then he or she may be further classified as being closer (e.g., brother, sister, mother, father, husband, or wife) or farther from the classifier or ego (e.g., distant in-laws, cousins, and various nonrelatives). How we classify and categorize others determines, in large measure, how we respond to them.

Kinships may be more or less permanent (e.g., as with close biological kinships), or they may be subject to re-classification or even de-classification in extreme instances (see Krebs & Denton, 1997). Hamilton's (1964, 1972) inclusive fitness theory suggests that stability of kinship categories and kin-based altruism are direct functions of genetic relatedness or Wright's coefficient of relatedness r (Daly, Salmon & Wilson, 1997; Reeve, 1998), and, not surprisingly, the mother–infant dyad (Miller & Fishkin, 1997), the male–female mating bond with its shared investment in offspring (Fisher, 1982, 1992; Zeifman & Hazan, 1997) and the core number of close kin or family have probably remained more or less stable since ancestral times (see McGuire & Troisi, 1998). The more reliable kinship categories involve vigorous activation of the attachment, pleasure, and cognitive mechanisms that subserve kinship, with reciprocal deactivation of the mechanisms subserving assessment (see Daly & Wilson, 1988 on kinship assessment), and processes of classification. This pattern is reversed where unfamiliars or weak and indeterminate kin are concerned; inclusive fitness theory would predict that assessment mechanisms would be especially active where potentially threatening strangers are concerned, or where great losses might follow from failure to evaluate correctly the kinship status of an ambiguous object.

Roots of biological and psychological kinship

Our common ancestor and the earliest hominids were certainly capable of making in-group versus out-group distinctions and assessments of relative degrees of in-group closeness, albeit with far less precision and formality than modern human beings. The common ancestor of apes and humans probably lived in semiclosed social networks that were characterized by hostile, male-dominated intergroup relations, exogamous mating with females leaving the group and males remaining more with kin, temporary and variable female alliances within the group (Wrangham, 1987), and significant sexual dimorphism and a gender division of labour within rudimentary hunting and gathering systems (Tanner, 1987; Tooby & DeVore, 1987). This implies a relatively well-developed capacity for rudimentary kin-recognition, classification, and appropriate sex and kin role behaviour within these early groups.

Ancestral bands of hominids and early humans were essentially large extended families that were subdivided into smaller families of parents, children, grand-parents, and close cousins (Mellen, 1981). These smaller families met the formal criteria for *biological kinship* – that is, actual blood relatedness plus the attribution of familiness (Bailey & Wood, 1993) – and their mutual commitment and affection were intense. A few minimally related or even unrelated individuals might be integrated into the family circle on occasion, achieving the status of *psychological kin* (Bailey, 1988; Bailey, Wood & Nava, 1992; see also Shreeve, 1995, on fictive kin in early *Homo sapiens*). Their family obligations and privileges might have been secondary to official biological kin, but they were true kin nevertheless.

Once these adopted individuals were classified as kin or as family, they were further classified in degrees of closeness by established family members (see Buss, 1999). Some family members might consider themselves emotionally closer to the adoptee than some of their biological relatives, whereas others might dislike the adoptee or deny him or her affection and kinship status. However, once the adoptee had enough support within the family, a more or less permanent family status was conferred. The benefits to the adoptee were straightforward in terms of security, resource sharing, and group inclusion, but the established family members stood to gain as well. The adoptee might be a good hunter or gatherer who was willing to share chores and even fight for the group if necessary. There appear to be a number of adaptive advantages to such psychological kinships and 'nonkin social extensions' (Kinzey, 1987).

Development of a few psychological kinships across groups would facilitate intergroup familiarity and increase the likelihood of diplomatic solutions to conflicts and potential hostilities, as well as to open the door to resource exchanges, exogamic exchanges, and political arrangements. Psychological kinships may have developed from accidental meetings, primitive trading, raids and kidnapping, or even between warriors from opposing camps on occasion, but marriage became the most potent means of generating psychological kin and effecting family mergers (Shreeve, 1995). Moreover, the resulting 'new kin' (Fisher, 1992) or nongenetically related affinal kin (e.g., spouses and in-laws) became powerfully attached due to mutual investment in offspring. Spouses of exogamous marriage must forever remain psychological kin, but the spouses and their parents (namely, grandparents) and other close relatives immediately become biological kin with any offspring of the marriage. Formalized marriage is a relatively recent human invention, and would seem to be nature's most reliable cure for the xenophobia that has plagued most of human evolution (see Wrangham & Peterson, 1996).

The special case of friendship

Friendship is second only to marriage as the strongest form of psychological kinship. Moreover, as Tooby and Cosmides (1996) have argued, friendship poses problems for traditional evolutionary explanations. Deep and abiding friendships between nongenetically linked people are not fully explained by either inclusive fitness or reciprocal exchange models; indeed, such nongenetic relations could only affect respective fitnesses indirectly if at all, and precisely balanced reciprocity is often viewed as contrary to true friendship (Shackelford & Buss, 1996). In 'true' versus 'fairweather' friends (Buss, 1999), there is a willingness to incur sometimes serious costs in the absence of probable payback seemingly because the valued other has become 'irreplaceable' in the giver's life (Tooby & Cosmides, 1996). Evolutionarily, having one or more close and irreplaceable nonrelatives would contribute directly to ego's *survival* and perhaps indirectly to ego's *reproductive success* by giving aid and comfort to him or her and close family members. In psychological kinship terms, the category of 'irreplaceable' is another way of saying that the nongenetically related other has been firmly classified as kin and is considered to a be true family member. Moreover, such psychological kinships or 'friend support systems' (Essock-Vitale & Fairbanks, 1979) may be conducive to ego's self-definition and self-esteem (Guisinger & Blatt, 1994), sense of security, and overall levels of health (Baumeister & Leary, 1995; Holmes & Rahe, 1967; Lowenthal & Haven, 1968; Weiss, 1979). Clearly, the evolutionary kinship therapist will encourage these relationships in treatment when feasible and appropriate.

Strangers and more strangers: The mismatch problem

As human biological and cultural evolution proceeded from early ancestral bands to *Homo sapiens* and later through the agricultural, industrial, and technological revolutions, population densities increased dramatically and human within-group and between-group relations became progressively more challenging and complex (Masters, 1989, 1994). With each succeeding generation, biological and psychological kinship aggregations remained essentially stable (as they do today), but the world of strangers was becoming proportionately larger. We humans are ancestrally prepared to relate to the 150 or so people in our modern extended families (Dunbar, 1992), including perhaps a dozen or so psychological kin, but our greatest challenge is to live together in a world that will soon contain six billion people (see Ahern & Bailey, 1997 for discussion). In modern America, strangers in the form of employers, politicians, government agents and functionaries, the various media, internet providers, manufacturers and retailers of desired products, and gatekeepers of all sorts often determine our levels of material comfort, cultural success and even self-perceptions more than do our family or personal support groups. Worse still is the exploitation and violence that comes with extreme nationalism, racial and ethnic conflict, and war, and closer to home for Americans is the omnipresent fear of stranger crime including rape, assault, burglary, kidnapping, and the like.

The modern dilemma of the stranger is a classic nature–culture mismatch problem (on mismatch, see Bailey, 1995; Buss, 1999; Crawford, 1995, 1998; Glantz & Pearce, 1989; Janicki & Krebs, 1998; Nesse & Berridge, 1997; Cosmides & Tooby, 1992). The mismatch is between our ancient, evolved selves and the modern context – that between our natural penchant for small, intimate groupings of biological and psychological kin, and the increasing demands to adjust to thousands upon thousands of interactions between ourselves and persons we hardly know. I suggest that as the gap between the ancestral self and the demands of *traditional culture*, on the one hand, and *technology-based neoculture* on the other progressively widens, tension, frustration, and stress are produced that increase the individual's risk for both physical and psychological pathology (see Figure 3.1 and Bailey, 1995). Reducing levels of mismatch in appropriate ways is thought to have positive health effects for certain medical (Eaton, Shostak & Konner, 1988; Nesse & Williams, 1995) and psychopathological conditions (Bailey, 1997a; Crawford, 1998; Glantz & Pearce, 1989; Nesse & Berridge, 1997). Likewise, reducing anxiety and conflicts surrounding the mismatch stress of the stranger is a major goal of evolutionary kinship therapy (see also Glantz & Pearce, 1989).

The economics of kinship

Like most of human social behaviour, kinship revolves around exchange processes and reciprocity. Once a person is classified as kin, he or she enters into a web of obligation and entitlement that remains in effect for the duration of the kinship (Bailey & Wood, 1998; Maryanski & Turner, 1992). Human beings evolved to favour close kin over more distant kin and nonkin (Hamilton, 1964), and this tendency to discriminate socially on behalf of genetic relatives has made us very effective 'evolved nepotists' (Daly, Salmon & Wilson, 1997) and within-family altruists. Hamilton's (1964) great insight that organisms pursue inclusive fitness (the representation of family genes in future generations) as well as individual fitness (the direct representation of ego's genes in future generations) served to place kinship and family nepotism at the centre of modern biology and evolutionary psychology. Like other animals, human beings are 'obligated' to favour their own

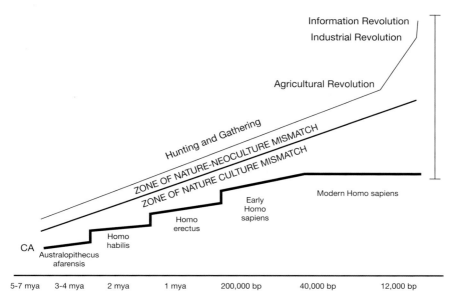

Figure 3.1 Zones of mismatch between biological and cultural evolution. ——, outer limits of neocultural evolution; ——; outer limits of cultural evolution; ▬▬, biological evolution; CA, common ancestor; mya, million years ago; bp, before present.

kind in the sharing of personal and material resources, but each relationship-specific kinship has its own evolved motivational and information-processing devices for coping with the distinctive roles of mother, father, offspring, sibling, grandparent, or mate (Daly, Salmon & Wilson, 1997). Although specific kinships may vary in their patterning of inherent design characteristics and psychological algorithms, all roads nevertheless ultimately lead to inclusive fitness or the representation of family-wise genes in subsequent generations.

Close kinship relations – in their ideal manifestation – tend to be warm, giving, loving, and secure, much like the suite of feelings and behaviours experienced between infant and mother during the process of lactation (see Uvnäs-Moberg, 1997). In ancestral environments, all healthy group members were highly familiar and most if not all were involved in a system of mutual support and shared affection. Ancestral in-group politics were probably less authoritarian and hierarchical and more egalitarian and democratic than is generally true of modern social aggregations, and social order emanated more from evolved social intelligence (Mithen, 1996) than rule of law or enforced cultural conformity. In-group relations were peaceful and tranquil relative to inter-group interactions, although gossip (Barkow, 1992; Dunbar, 1996), sibling rivalry, sexual jealousy, and envy over matters of goods and station were no doubt part of the picture. Certainly, kinship has its dark side, and can sometimes surpass hostile nonkin relations in emotional ambivalence, expressed aggression, and abusiveness; indeed, for some, kinship can be a 'social cage' (Maryanski & Turner, 1992). Nevertheless, warmth, love, acceptance, and sharing of resources are among the defining characteristics of natural kinship.

Just as males are hesitant to share resources when paternity is in doubt, kin interactants are reluctant to engage in obligate giving when kinship status is ambiguous or problematic. Both males with low paternity confidence and other individuals with uncertain kinship status tend to readily activate assessment (Daly & Wilson, 1988) and classification mechanisms (Bailey & Wood, 1998) that seek to clarify the ego–object linkage. Assessment and classification mechanisms are most active under conditions of doubt and uncertainty, and they are progressively relaxed as matters of kinship and degree of genetic closeness are validated. Indeed, 'unconditional love' is predicated on a more or less permanent suspension of concern regarding validity of family status and value as a kinship object.

As Table 3.1 suggests, biological and psychological kinship differ somewhat in their patterns of obligations and entitlements, activation/deactivation of a kinship assessment mechanism, and expressions of love and aggression, but they are theorized to be very similar in patterns of emotional warmth. Kin may direct aggression towards each other, but aggression is not a defining aspect of either biological or psychological kinship as are the dynamics of calculating cost–benefits

Table 3.1 Correlates of kin and nonkin categories

Relations	Obligations	Entitlements	Love	Warmth	Aggression
Kin					
Biological	+++	+++	+++	+++	
Psychological	++	++	++	+++	
Nonkin					
Kin-like				++	
Reciprocal				+	+
Hostile					+++

Note
This table first appeared in Bailey and Wood (1998). All significant human relationships – whether kin or nonkin – probably reflect some particular configuration of activation/deactivation of the above variables. Persons considered *kin* are first cognitively *classified* as within ego's in-group and then he or she is further classified as either biological or psychological kin. Once classified as kin, the individual enters into a more or less formal system of mutual obligations and entitlements which remains in effect for the duration of the classification. In a strong kinship, the classification as kin, associated obligations and entitlements, and related love, warmth, and reduced hostility patterns would be fairly stable.

When an individual is classified as *nonkin* (even though seen as in-group), formal obligations/entitlements and love expressions would be weak or nonexistent, but warmth and aggression would fluctuate depending on the type and quality of relationship. In kin-like relations (highly affiliative but lacking classification as kin), emotional warmth would be high and aggression low, and in nonkin reciprocal relations some warmth might be evident albeit secondary to the exchange process. At the extreme nonkin/kin pole are hostile relations characterized by absence of warmth, aversion and even hatred of the other. Such nonkin relations are especially evident in genocide, war, and ethnic/national conflict where one 'kin' group is set against another.

and expressions of love. In fact, within-family aggression is usually low when frequency of contact is considered (Daly & Wilson, 1988). Emotional warmth *per se* is a cheap commodity (as contrasted with committed love) and may be seen in both kin and nonkin relations.

Nonkin relations are noteworthy in their diminished formal cost–benefit patterns and expressions of love. Thus, kin-like relations may involve activation of warm feelings but in the absence of kinship classification, obligate giving, and love. Reciprocal relations among nonkin may involve a minimum of warmth and/or aggression, but the primary focus is on reciprocal and precisely balanced exchange of material and/or psychological resources (see Trivers, 1985 on reciprocal altruism). Hostility is characterized by enmity, aggression, or avoidance, and is theoretically the farthest from warm and loving kinship relations. Hostility may be seen in any social interaction, but reaches its zenith in out-group interactions, either between individuals, or worse still between antagonistic groups or mobs (Bailey, 1987).

Cost–benefit assessment

The psychological mechanisms subserving cost–benefit assessment in human relations are quite different from those subserving kinship assessment and classification. Cost–benefit assessment characterizes all relationships where potential or actual exchanges are involved, and its function is to detect imbalances, deception, exploitation, and unfairness in a particular relationship's patterns of giving and receiving. Ultimately, the focus of such assessment is on the exchange of *valued goods*, whether they are material objects or desired personal goods (e.g., provision of love, sex, or emotional support). By contrast, the focus of kinship assessment and classification is on the *person* and whether not he or she is classified as in-group/out-group, kin/nonkin, and close/distant within the kinship array. If the person is clearly classified as nonkin at the outset, then kin assessment is relaxed, but cost–benefit assessment will be very active in contexts of trade and other exchanges. However, with reliably classified kin, kinship assessment will be de-activated in proportion to the depth of the relationship, but cost–benefit assessment continues to operate, often quietly in the background. As discussed earlier, close intimates do not expect and are, in fact, often turned off by demands for precise reciprocity (Shackelford & Buss, 1996), and close kin are no doubt resigned to a considerable amount of obligate giving without balanced reciprocation. Nevertheless, even the deepest kinship has its limits, and ongoing cost–benefit assessment keeps each interactant sensitive to unfair or extreme imbalances in the relationship.

Cost–benefit calculations are straightforward among unfamiliars and nonkin, and follow a simple calculus of reciprocity. Strong kinships, however, resonate not only with presses for reciprocity, but with various informal and formal kinds of *obligate giving* and *entitled receiving* as well. Intimate kinships start with baseline expectations that considerable sharing of materials and personal resources is required among family members, and such kin mutuality goes far back into human ancestry. Cost–benefit assessment in strong kinships becomes particularly active with perceptible deviations from baseline expectations regarding giving and receiving; that is, when the kinship is perceived as severely *imbalanced* by one or both members of a kinship dyad.

Balanced and imbalanced kinships

The obligation/entitlement dynamics of particular kinships are very complex – especially over extended time periods – and they resonate with developmental stages, gender, personality, ethnicity, cultural backgound, social status, education, and a host of other variables. Perhaps the most important distinction, however, is whether a given kinship is balanced or imbalanced in its cost–benefit or obligation–entitlement configuration at a given time. As Table 3.2 shows, a balanced configuration is one where the interactants give and receive in a manner considered mutually equitable, whereas an imbalanced one involves excess giving on one person's part and excess receiving for the other. In their comprehensive review of social belongingness, Baumeister and Leary (1995) discuss related concepts including self-interested pseudoaltruism, social loafing (benefiting from the group without assuming any costs), refusal to co-operate or reciprocate, and they say how 'important it is that caring, concern, and affection be mutual and reciprocal' (Baumeister & Leary, 1995: 514).

Although giving and receiving are complex processes (e.g., one person might trade an emotional resource such as affection for a behavioural/material one such

Table 3.2 Balanced and imbalanced kinship relations

Kinship relations	Balanced relationship Obligate giving		Imbalanced relationship Obligate giving	
	Ego	*Other*	*Ego*	*Other*
Biological	strong	strong	strong	weak
	weak	weak	weak	strong
Psychological	strong	strong	strong	weak
	weak	weak	weak	strong

Note
Kinship is fundamentally based on assumption of formal and/or informal obligations with associated presses for obligate giving. Such giving forms the basis of the exchange component of kinship, namely, providing benefits and satisfying entitlements. Balanced kinships occur when obligations and obligate giving are perceived as roughly symmetrical between the two parties in the relationship. That is, a strong sense of obligation in one party is balanced against an analogous strong sense in the other; or, contrariwise, analogous weak senses of obligation would be mutually balanced as well.

Most problematic are imbalanced kinships where strong or weak senses of obligation in one party are in opposition to those of the other. We theorize that imbalanced relationships are associated with feelings of conflict, frustration, and hostility in the giver which increases his/her risk of both physical disease and psychopathology.

50

as money, or a cognitive one such as professions of commitment), the cost–benefit balances and imbalances are discernable to the careful observer.

The sacrificial giver in a severely imbalanced dyad may opt to remain in the relationship indefinitely and suffer the emotional and material costs, or there may be forceful or subtle attempts to induce more equitable patterns of mutual giving and receiving. He or she may make demands, express anger, threaten, manipulate or attempt dominance displays, but coming from the weak partner these strategies may ring hollow. More success is likely to come from inducing guilt or shaming the stronger partner into responding to the sacrificial giver's needs and concerns. Baumeister, Stillwell and Heatherton (1994) present a convincing case that, first, guilt serves adaptive, relationship-enhancing functions within the context of communal relationships, and, second, that guilt helps to minimize inequities in imbalanced relations and enables less powerful partners to assert themselves and redistribute emotional distress. Thus, guilt inducement represents a powerful means by which weaker parties can exert influence over stronger ones, and may have been favoured by natural selection as a means of preventing fitness-reducing forms of exploitation within family aggregations (Trivers, 1985). Survivor guilt and outdoing guilt (see O'Connor, Chapter 13, this volume) refers to the unpleasant emotional state and associated self-recrimination that is experienced when one perceives or believes one has 'won' in surviving an accident where others were killed, being the recipient of good fortune at the expense of another, or just simply by being substantially better off than another. This reasoning implies that perceived interpersonal imbalance, associated guilt feelings, and resulting levelling impulses (Boehm, 1997) can occur in *any* relationship, even between a privileged person and a street beggar, between a lottery winner and corresponding legions of losers, or, more abstractly, between the world's wealthy and starving children in the third world.

Although client concerns about broader social inequities may sometimes enter the picture, evolutionary kinship therapy focuses primarily on imbalanced dyads and family configurations. For example, a client of mine recently precipitated a marital crisis by telling his wife about a brief adulterous affair that had occurred over twenty years ago. The crisis was greatly aggravated by the pre-existing relationship imbalance that had characterized their twenty-seven years of marriage. Although the wife was the more intelligent and resourceful partner in their highly successful family business, the husband was very protective of his role as the titular head of the company. As the wife operated behind the scenes as the heart and soul of the company – while simultaneously raising three children – great resentment was building that spilled over after the infidelity was revealed. The husband was immediately 're-classified' in psychological kinship terms, and, for a time, he became the hated outsider and an enemy. The wife had not given up on him entirely, however, and she put him through several weeks of rather brutal guilt-inducement, fits of screaming and recrimination, and she literally beat him physically several times. His guilt is monumental and he is willing to make any concession, but she has not yet been able to forgive or re-establish the psychological kinship. Given that this is a salvageable marriage, one goal of therapy is to work through her rage and resentment until she is able to re-classify him as 'my closest psychological kin', and, once that is accomplished, a second goal will be to re-establish the marriage on a more realistic and equitable basis.

The kinship-health link

The effects of interpersonal losses, disruptions, imbalances, and mal-attachments on both physical and emotional ill health were discussed earlier, and Liotti (Chapter 11, this volume) discusses the many problems associated with disorganized forms of attachment. Conversely, a wealth of cross-disciplinary research has documented the positive effects of quality of social relationships on overall physical and mental health status (e.g., Antonucci, 1994; Argyle & Martin, 1991; Baumeister & Leary, 1995; House, Landis & Umberson, 1988; Sarason, Sarason & Pierce, 1990; Sperling & Berman, 1994; Zeifman & Hazan, 1997). Warm and fulfilling social relationships are not only pleasurable (Diener, Sandvik & Pavot, 1991) and conducive to subjective feelings of well-being (see Strack, Argyle & Schwarz, 1991), happiness (Argyle, 1987), and life satisfaction (Lewinsohn, Redner & Seely, 1991), they are simply 'good for you' in terms of enhanced immune functioning (Coe, Weiner, Rosenberg & Levine, 1985; Kennedy, Kiecolt-Glaser & Glaser, 1990; Jemmott & Locke, 1984), stress-buffering (Cohen & Williamson, 1991; Cohen & Wills, 1985; Veenhoven, 1991), enhanced mortality and longevity (Berkman & Syme, 1979), resistance to depression (Lewinsohn, Redner & Seely, 1991), and a host of other health-related outcomes. Gilbert (1993) has argued that warm, satisfying social relations involve exchanges of social signals that activate a sense of security and support while simultaneously de-activating defence system processing. The safer and more supported one feels the lower the levels of stress, the lower the levels of internal and external conflict, and the more likely one is to maintain healthy levels of physiological and psychological homeostasis.

Of the various types of intimate relationships, I suggest that biological and psychological kinships that are both balanced and strong *are the most personally satisfying, fulfilling, and conducive to good physical and psychological health in modern human beings*. A strong kinship is one that is high in positive emotionality (warmth), provision of behavioural/material resources (giving), and cognitive commitment to the other (e.g., reliable classification as kin); moreover, when two mutually strong kinships are balanced, then positive social and health outcomes are likely. By contrast, when kinships are balanced but weak in emotionality, helpful actions, and/or commitment, then health benefits may be weak or absent. Strong kinships characterize close, committed biological and psychological kin (as between parents and children or between marital partners), whereas weak ones characterize, for example, distant cousins or old college friends who are classified as kin and as family, but they do not play significant roles in one's daily life.

Imbalanced kin relations are the most interesting and problematic theoretically and clinically. Imbalanced relations may be objectively inequitable or based on distorted attributions regarding self or other, they may reflect unconscious as well as conscious motivation, and they are especially problematic when deception is involved. For example, one interactant may cheat by appearing to be a balanced giver when he or she is really a manipulative taker. Deceptive kinds of non-reciprocation and exploitation have been discussed widely in the fields of ethology (Eibl-Eibesfeldt, 1989), sociobiology (Alexander, 1975; Trivers, 1971, 1985) and evolutionary psychology (Barkow, Cosmides & Tooby, 1992, Dawkins, 1982), and Nesse and Lloyd (1992) outlined how deception and self-deception may be mediated through the Freudian defence mechanisms. In fact, if cheaters can deceive *themselves*, their machinations may be even more effective (Lockard & Paulus, 1988).

Undiscovered and self-deceived cheaters probably suffer little in the way of internal conflict, frustration, or increased health risks, and they may, in fact, prosper and achieve higher levels of reproductive success as long as a pattern of high benefits and low costs can be maintained. By contrast, imbalanced kinships may be very important to the giving party's psychological economy (e.g., caring for an Alzheimer's spouse; Wood, 1998), but they tend to produce high levels of internal conflict, frustration, and disharmony. Like cheaters, sacrificial givers often deceive themselves about the true dynamics of the relationship, and they rely on the Freudian defences to put a rosy face on the underlying imbalances and injustices. It is just this kind of nonmutual relationship that puts the giver at risk for both physical disease and psychological disorders (see Baumeister & Leary, 1995). Anxiety, depression, psychophysiological disorders, and various other inhibition disorders (Bailey, 1997a) are expected for the giver who may stagger under the weight of his or her kinship obligations and demands.

Summary overview

If warm and satisfying relationships are conducive to positive physical and psychological health, and if strong and balanced kinships reflect the deepest and most satisfying patterns of relating, then the evolutionary kinship therapist will want to encourage such patterns where appropriate. Kinship therapists also support their clients through relationship breakups, divorces, death of loved ones, and numerous other negative life experiences, and we strive to help relationship deprived, socially unskilled, and socially alienated clients to effect new and better relationships. Ultimately, however, our goal is to foster strong and balanced kinships that are conducive to good health and optimal quality of life within the limitations of a particular client's life circumstances.

Evolutionary kinship therapy

The central role of togetherness and natural sociality in the ecosettings of human ancestry has led to the evolution of a brain that is more social than technological (Bailey & Wood, 1998; Gilbert, 1989, 1997, Chapter 6, this volume; Kriegman,

Chapter 4, this volume; Mithen, 1996; Ornstein & Sobel, 1987), and Gilbert (Chapter 6, this volume) argues that various evolved *social mentalities* (e.g., information processing strategies and algorithms for care eliciting/seeking, care giving/providing, mate selection, alliance formation, and ranking behaviour) are the foundation stones for concept of self, systems of internal meanings (e.g., inner working models), role-taking behaviour, social signalling, self and other evaluation processes, and a host of other crucial functions. Much like Jung, Gilbert postulates a set of modular-like internal structures (social mentalities) that not only mediate between the individual and the external world, but interact among themselves internally in a dynamic world of mind.

Unfortunately, there are no special evolved social mentalities for being either a therapist or a client in psychotherapy, and we must therefore use or adapt ones that previously evolved for other purposes. Not surprisingly, the evolved social brains of the client and therapist find it difficult to distinguish between older ways of relating and the specific demands of psychotherapy; for example, the client's desire for intimacy or kinship with the therapist may reflect ancient evolved patterns of kinship (Bailey, Wood & Nava, 1992) and the therapist's feelings and countertransference issues may reflect ancient patterns as well (Slavin & Kriegman, 1992). Note that this is a variation of the mismatch problem of reconciling previously evolved adaptations and social mentalities with the demands of current environments (Bailey, 1995; Crawford, 1998).

In therapy, the inclusive fitness domain of the therapist intersects with that of the client throughout treatment, and this has profound implications for the client–therapist relationship, the interventions employed, and the resulting changes in client patterns of achieving biological and cultural success – including improved social relations and enhanced positive health (Bailey, 1997b; see also Kriegman, Chapter 4, this volume). The overlap of client and therapist fitness domains has ethical and moral implications as well, especially when often unconsciously motivated wishes and needs of each member of the therapy dyad come into conflict. Bailey (1988) introduced the idea of a *kinship double standard* in therapy where one set of rules and moral imperatives come into play for the therapist and his or her close relatives, and another for the client. For example, a hardcore sociobiological approach implies that therapist and client are each on inherently selfish and separate fitness tracks, but this dilemma is greatly mitigated when we think of the client in at least kin-like terms (Bailey & Wood, 1998). In the kin-like mode, the warmth component is activated for both client and therapist, and both see each other as family in a metaphorical way – a status significantly less than actual kin but much more than a reciprocal business arrangement between acquaintances (Wood, 1997).

General principles

First, the therapeutic relationship or alliance is central to virtually all forms of psychotherapy (e.g., see Gilbert, Chapter 6, this volume; Glantz & Pearce, 1989; Kriegman, Chapter 4, this volume; Slavin & Kriegman, 1992) and is especially central to kinship therapy (Bailey, 1997b, 1988; Bailey & Wood, 1998; Bailey, Wood & Nava, 1992; Wood, 1997). Glantz and Pearce (1989) refer to the client–therapist relationship as a kind of 'two-person band', and Bailey & Wood (1998: 515) say, 'the practice of psychotherapy involves a deep and profound interaction between two members of species *Homo sapiens*, where one provides a listening ear, empathic understanding, reassurance and advice for living for the other'. Depending on the depth and type of therapy, therapist–client relations may be little more than rapport (emotional warmth) in the context of stylized professionalism, or deeper still, warm, kin-like relations short of kinship, or at the deepest end, actual psychological kinships, as between myself and the borderline client Jennie discussed later. Warm, empathic, kin-like relations seem preferable for most therapeutic encounters (Wood, 1997), which serves to avoid superficiality at the rapport end and the many potential problems of actual kinship with clients at the other. However, the therapist must often confront the fact that clients often *want* a deeper relationship with him or her than is either professionally appropriate or feasible (Bailey, Wood & Nava, 1992). Throughout human evolution, help and support were provided by close family members, medicine men and tribal elders, and others within the extended family and tribal network, so it is no surprise that clients often want to classify us as family in some way. How this 'phylogenetic transference' is addressed in treatment is crucial in fostering trust and a sense of security in the client.

Second, evolutionary kinship therapy focuses on ways of helping clients effectively pursue biosocial goals and adaptive role-taking (see Gilbert, 1989, 1992, Chapter 6, this volume; McGuire & Troisi, 1998). As Bailey and Wood (1998) suggested, effective psychotherapy helps the client become a better functioning member of the species *Homo sapiens* where ancient need systems and biosocial goals are adequately satisfied, but the client is also encouraged and helped in meeting the evolutionarily unique challenges of today's world as well. The final section of McGuire and Troisi's (1998) excellent book on Darwinian Psychiatry addresses treatment in the evolutionary context, and their primary emphasis is on aiding the client in satisfying biological goals through careful functional assessments, altering the functionality of infrastructural systems and algorithms, and optimizing his or her environment while not compromising adaptive capacities (see McGuire & Troisi, 1998: 264).

Third, evolutionary kinship therapy focuses on facilitating biosocial goals and harmonizing social mentalities in the domain of kinship, with special focus on processes of assessment, classification/de-classification, cost–benefit imbalance and resolution, relations with nonkin in the domains of education, work, and other contexts, and the general problem of relationship deprivations, on the one hand, and relationship enmeshments and overloads, on the other. All of this is done with compassion (Gilbert, Chapter 6, this volume), deep empathy (McGuire & Troisi, 1998), and sensitivity to the deeply human concerns of our clients, many of which go back into the dim reaches of phylogeny.

Fourth and finally, evolutionary kinship therapy draws from traditional psychodynamic, behavioural, cognitive, and especially psychotherapy integration models

(Bailey, 1997b; Norcross & Goldfried, 1992) in case conceptualization, treatment planning, and implementing interventions, but preference is for evolutionary models and disciplines including evolutionary psychology (e.g., Barkow, Cosmides & Tooby, 1992; Buss, 1999; Crawford & Krebs, 1998), evolutionary psychopathology (Crawford, 1995, 1998), human paleopsychology (Bailey, 1987), evolutionary psychiatry (Stevens & Price, 1996); Darwinian Psychiatry (McGuire & Troisi, 1998), mismatch theory, and, of course, evolutionary kinship psychology (Daly, Salmon & Wilson, 1997) and psychological kinship theory as described herein. Evolutionary models enrich and extend traditional approaches and provide new insights in approaching the four basic dimensions of psychotherapy: (1) the species dimension, (2) the relationship dimension, (3) the conceptual-procedural dimension, and (4) the moral dimension (Bailey & Wood, 1998).

Case illustrations

Mattie: testing phase and sudden re-classification

Many years ago I worked briefly as a staff psychologist in a federal prison for women. My first hint of 'kinship' in psychotherapy came during a six-week pre-release course of therapy with a 25-year-old African-American inmate named Mattie. She was a large, angry, and intimidating woman who resented authority and greeted me in the first session with the question, 'OK, where are you hiding the damn tape recorder . . . I know you are up to something'. In terms of the initial client–therapist kinship dynamic, we were both low on emotional warmth, high on kinship and cost–benefit assessment of the other, and she appeared roughly to classify me as a hostile 'stranger' whereas my implicit classification of her was that of 'intimidating client'. Certainly, there was not the slightest indication of kinship anywhere in sight. After several sessions, I developed a genuine liking for Mattie after learning that her anger emanated from incidences of egregious white racism in her native state of Louisiana; moreover, I was touched by her love and generosity towards her children and other family members back home. In fact, she made three dollars a day working in the prison laundry, and sent virtually all of it home to her family.

As my feelings of warmth increased towards Mattie, processes of assessment decreased as I more reliably re-classified her into the kin-like category of 'really nice person underneath it all'. However, for more than four weeks Mattie remained cool and distant towards me and would be abusive on occasion. O'Connor (Chapter 13, this volume) discusses the process of *testing* in therapy whereby the client carefully assesses the therapist's reaction to his or her pathogenic beliefs or pathological behaviour. There is a relational version of this as well, where the client will ignore, reject, or provoke the therapist in order to test the limits of the relationship. If the therapist remains thoroughly committed to the relationship under such fire, there is a good chance that a sudden, positive re-classification of the therapist will occur where he or she is now 'family' or at least a nice person. This is exactly what happened in the fifth week with Mattie when she just simply walked in one day and declared, 'You are OK'. From that moment on our relations were relaxed and enjoyable, but even more remarkable was her general improvement in attitude and behaviour in the institution.

The improved client–therapist relationship and Mattie's improved behaviour no doubt reflected changes at the emotional, behavioural and cognitive levels, with cognitive restructuring being, I suspect, the primary change agent. There is a logic to human relationships wherein a single new relationship or a changed older one can reverberate throughout the individual's psychic system and change the entire internal system of meanings about the self, the self-in-relation-to-others, and/or even attributions about the goodness or badness of life in general. In retrospect, I think that once I was 'OK' to Mattie, she said something more or less like this to herself: 'If this young white guy can truly like me after I have treated him so badly, then maybe there is hope for someone like me in the larger world out there'. In any case, Mattie did change positively in the short-run, but lack of follow-up data precludes any conclusions about long-term effects.

John: brief crisis intervention in a kin-like context

John is a 35-year-old African-American man who was brought to the psychology clinic by his mother following suicidal threats and threats of 'hurting' his recently divorced ex-wife. These threats were serious given that John is six feet, seven inches tall, weighs 245 pounds, and is mildly retarded and mildly brain damaged. John was extremely distressed over the wife's abandonment and 'felt he would never find another wife'. The wife was a drug addict who had been married four times before, and apparently married John on a lark. The mother tried to reassure John that he was lucky to get rid of that 'floozy', but he remained heart-broken and potentially violent. The case was assigned to a 40-year-old female social worker who was completing a practicumship in our clinic. The therapist found herself overwhelmed in the first session and called me at home for advice. John was grievously depressed, inconsolable, and fearful of what he might do to himself or to his ex-wife. His mother attended the session, but she was unable to get John under control. I asked to speak to John on the phone, and was surprised at his readiness to open up. A subsequent session was arranged that included John, his mother, the therapist, and myself as co-therapist.

In the session, it was clear that John needed a deeply relational approach to help him through the crisis. Despite differences in race, education, and socioeconomic status, the session developed a kin-like tenor quickly, and both John and his mother expressed appreciation for our sincere concern (we both genuinely liked him and his mother). In kinship terms, there was warm emotion, a minimum of assessment of other, and a mutual attribution of familiness during the session. Moreover, John and his mother were positively affected by the apparent kinship between therapist and supervisor who came across as 'family'. Moreover, all four of us shared similar religious backgrounds, and use of religious metaphor aided communication. The session went extremely well, and both John and his mother left feeling optimistic and hopeful. At the end of the session, it was clear that John's mother wanted to hug both the therapist and me. Moreover, I made a special effort to put my arm around John's shoulder and to give him a hearty handshake.

In a second and final co-therapy session, the primary focus was on case assessment and kinship intervention. Assessment focused on two primary issues: (1) the devastating loss of psychological kinship with his ex-wife, and (2) the availability of other compensating kinship supports in John's life. We concluded that the loss of his wife was a given, and John was probably correct in concerns about future marriage prospects. On the other hand, many other compensating social supports were available in the home (mother and other family), at work (janitor) where John was 'loved' by co-workers, and in the local community. It was difficult for John to confront his great loss, but due to the warm and trusting therapy atmosphere (greatly facilitated by his mother), we were able to do so thoroughly yet nondefensively.

In supervision, we conceptualized the case in terms of kinship loss, severely imbalanced kinship (one loved, the other did not), and nonkin relations at work and in the community, but in therapy our approach was very simple and straightforward. Supportive treatment for John's psychological kinship loss and reinforcement of his solid work ethic were helpful. Further, he learned to more effectively recognize and exploit his excellent existing kinship and nonkin resources. His behaviour stabilized very quickly after two co-therapy sessions and he continued on for a brief time with the student therapist for support and advice-giving.

Jennie: long-term psychological kinship

Some fourteen years ago, a clinical psychologist referred a young woman, Jennie, to me who had just been released from Riverside Psychiatric Hospital in Hampton, Virginia. She was a challenge from the first day. She was abusive, argumentative, appeared to be high on drugs or alcohol, and expressed complete disdain for the counselling process. Nevertheless, at the hour's end, she agreed to come back next week, 'just for the hell of it'.

Jennie had a long history of substance abuse, antisocial behaviour, suicide attempts, and minor brushes with the law. She came from the backwoods of Alabama and her mother had cast her off to relatives as an infant, which initiated a childhood of physical and sexual abuse. Eventually, she was passed on to a kindly aunt and uncle. They cared for her needs, but were extremely rigid, demanding, and affectionless in their parenting approach. When she was in her teens, Jennie ran away and was later informally adopted by a loving, but mentally ill older lady, Wanda. Despite being ill from cancer and suffering from manic-depressive psychosis, Wanda continues to be Jennie's 'true mother' (or closest psychological kin) today.

Early in treatment, Jennie was administered a full battery of psychological tests including a paper and pencil measure of intelligence, the Minnesota Multiphasic Personality Inventory (MMPI), Draw-A-Person Test, Thematic Apperception Test

(TAT), and the Rorschach test. Findings indicated superior intelligence (IQ 123), extreme dyscontrol, depression, anger, distrust, and internal turmoil on the MMPI (e.g., highly elevated *F*, Depression, Psychopathic deviate, Paranoia, and Schizophrenia scales), feelings of alienation, deep longing for love and acceptance on the TAT, and extreme impulsivity and psychological impoverishment on the Rorschach. When her pattern of addiction and suicidality was considered, the data suggested borderline personality of moderate severity.

Aside from Wanda and myself, there were no significant others in Jennie's life, and the client–therapist relationship was pivotal in the early stages of treatment. Wanda lived in another city and had her own problems, and Jennie grabbed on to me as a lifeline. However, her ambivalence was extreme, and each session was loud, boisterous, and painful for both of us as she released her rage and frustration on the only object available. In kinship terms, warm emotionality was low and assessment processes were high for both of us as we struggled to find something to base a relationship on. Kinship classification was equally unclear – she seemed to see me as a potential kinship object and enemy at the same time, and I felt a deep personal and professional obligation towards her but little else. Intuitively, I felt her provocations were a kind of 'test' (see O'Connor, Chapter 13, this volume) of whether I truly cared (as with Mattie above), but there was no theory to draw from at the time. Moreover, it seemed crucial that I be resolute and not give up on her – to do so would be catastrophic. Thus, in this pre-bonding stage, the goal was to hold firm and try to win her trust.

In the fourth of six months of formal treatment, Jennie became angered at my probing questions, and she ran from the room screaming epithets at me and did not return until some twenty minutes later. She appeared very sheepish and subdued and looked at me intensely, apparently trying to assess my reaction to her outburst. At the time, I felt that this was the moment where the relationship would stand or fall. I firmly stated that there was *nothing* she could do to get me to give up on her, so she might as well just knock it off. Surprisingly, she seemed very pleased with that and promised to be back next week. In retrospect, I can now see that this was the very deep 'kinship' affirmation that she had sought all along from others and myself.

Throughout treatment I had noticed that Jennie had spent most of her life trying – without success – to somehow reconstitute her lost family. Now, following our critical incident, it was clear that she had incorporated me into her small family of two (she and her fictive mother). As with Mattie, this new client–therapist bond was effected with dramatic suddenness and it seemed to similarly reflect a general cognitive restructuring and revised view of life and others. Jennie began to dress more attractively, made a few new friends, and found employment; moreover, at post-therapy assessment her elevated MMPI scores had dropped significantly and the other personality measures indicated noteworthy improvement. Unfortunately, she was still borderline clinically, and she has never completely overcome her alcoholism and occasional bouts of depression. However, therapy was successful in bringing her depression under control, in providing her with a new and more positive set of internal meanings, and – most importantly – constraining her downward spiral of self-destructive behaviour.

As luck would have it, Jennie was accepted into the military shortly after cessation of formal therapy, and she eventually became one of three female helicopter mechanics in the United States Army. She served eight years with distinction and eventually achieved the rank of sergeant. Sadly, following a failed marriage she lapsed back into alcoholism and borderline behaviour, and was forced to accept a medical discharge from the Army. She continues to keep in touch with me and my family, and she will occasionally call or come by my home for a visit. She continues to classify not only me but my wife and daughter as 'family', and we see her as something more than a previous therapy client. This is probably the only true psychological kinship I have developed with a client, and I have been willing to accept the obligations and occasional inconveniences that go with it. For obvious reasons, therapy relations typically do not go beyond the kin-like level, but in Jennie's case the psychological kinship seemed to have positive effects that outweighed the risks and obligations.

Conclusion

The need to belong is a fundamental human drive that emanates from the mammalian, primate, and hominid/human ancestry of modern human beings. Secure infant–mother attachment, secure and satisfying family relations, and secure membership in band and tribe are associated with positive physical and psychological health, personal happiness and a sense of subjective well-being, and general life satisfaction. Obversely, real or threatened loss of affection, love, and group membership are extremely aversive subjectively, and disruptions and deprivations in togetherness are associated with a remarkably wide range of negative physical and psychological consequences. Clearly, abandonment, rejection, loneliness, and isolation are not normal conditions for members of the species *Homo sapiens*, and people are highly motivated to avoid breaks in togetherness among those classified as 'our kind'. When such breaks cannot be avoided and re-integration of relations is impossible or problematic, the individual is likely to experience some combination of the following ill effects – increased levels of stress with associated immuno-incompetence, a sense of hopelessness and depression, anger and frustration, lowered self-esteem and self-efficacy, and deep-seated feelings of unhappiness and life dissatisfaction.

The fields of behavioural medicine, health psychology, psychiatry, clinical psychology, and psychotherapy have dwelt on these matters for some time, but a comprehensive theoretical model has been slow to emerge. Following Daly, Salmon and Wilson's (1997) call to arms for a comprehensive kinship psychology, I suggest that an evolutionary kinship psychology is needed to make sense of the power and universality of natural togetherness, and the central role that it plays in both good and poor health and in the heights of happiness and the depths of despair. Kinship is the central and unifying construct in human relationships, and the evolved needs for belongingness, love, and attachment are most clearly expressed in systems of social organization based on kinship (Bailey, 1988; Daly, Salmon & Wilson, 1997). As a working principle, I suggest that kinships that are stable, strong and balanced in mutual giving are the most personally satisfying, fulfilling, and conducive to positive physical and psychological health in human beings, and it follows that kinships that are weak and/or imbalanced in obligations/giving will be associated with either lesser health benefits, no benefits, or negative health consequences.

The general goal of evolutionary kinship therapy is to conceptualize a particular case in terms of patterns of biosocial goal-seeking (see Gilbert, Chapter 6, this volume, and McGuire & Troisi, 1998), mismatch stresses (Bailey, 1995; Crawford, 1998), and kinship deprivations, disruptions, and balances/imbalances, and then to design interventions that aid the client in meeting and/or reconciling species and cultural demands in a manner that optimizes personal happiness and adjustment (Bailey, 1997a). Specifically, evolutionary kinship therapy emphasizes any and all means of encouraging healthy expressions of natural sociality whether in the therapy encounter itself or in the broader contexts of family and community. Empirical evidence is unequivocal that such expressions are conducive to positive physical and mental health, and overall quality of life.

References

Ahern, S. & Bailey, K.G. (1997) *Families-by-Choice: Finding Families in a World of Strangers*, Minneapolis, MN: Fairview Press.

Aiello, L.C. & Dunbar, R.I.M. (1993) 'Neocortex size, group size, and the evolution of language', *Current Anthropology* 34: 184–93.

Alexander, R.D. (1975) 'The search for a general theory of behavior', *Behavioral Sciences* 20: 77–100.

Antonucci, T.C. (1994) 'Attachment in adulthood and aging', in M.B. Sperling & W.H. Berman (eds.), *Attachment in Adults*, (pp. 256–70), New York: Guilford.

Argyle, M. (1987) *The Psychology of Happiness*, London: Methuen.

Argyle, M. & Martin, M. (1991) 'The psychological causes of happiness', in F. Strack, M. Argyle & N. Schwarz (eds), *Subjective Well-Being: An Interdisciplinary Perspective*, (pp. 77–100), New York: Pergamon.

Atkinson, L. & Zucker, K.J. (eds) (1997) *Attachment and Psychopathology*, New York: Guilford.

Bailey, K.G. (1987) *Human Paleopsychology: Applications to Aggression and Pathological Processes*, Hillsdale, NJ: Lawrence Erlbaum Associates Inc.

Bailey, K.G. (1988) 'Psychological kinship: Implications for the helping professions', *Psychotherapy* 25: 132–42.

Bailey, K.G. (1994) 'Our kind-their kind: Response to Gardner's we-they distinction', *ASCAP Newsletter* 7: 5–8.

Bailey, K.G. (1995) *Mismatch Theory and Psychopathology*, Paper presented at the Human Behavior and Evolution Society meeting, June, Santa Barbara, CA.

Bailey, K.G. (1997a) 'Series on mismatch theory and the fourfold model', *ASCAP Newsletter*, February, March, April, and December issues.

Bailey, K.G. (1997b) 'Evolutionary kinship therapy: Merging integrative psychotherapy with the new kinship psychology', Paper presented at the annual meeting of the ASCAP Society, Tucson, AZ.

Bailey, K.G. & Wood, H.E. (1993) 'Psychological kinship theory: Social behavior and clinical practice', Presented at the Human Behavior and Evolution Society Meeting, Binghampton, New York.

Bailey, K.G. & Wood, H.E. (1998) 'Evolutionary kinship therapy: Basic principles and treatment applications', *British Journal of Medical Psychology* 71: 509–23.

Bailey, K.G., Wood, H.E. & Nava, G.R. (1992) 'What do clients want? Role of psychological kinship in professional helping', *Journal of Psychotherapy Integration* 2: 125–47.

Barkow, J.H. (1992) 'Beneath new culture is old psychology: Gossip and social stratification', in J.H. Barkow, L. Cosmides & J. Tooby (eds), *The Adapted Mind* (pp. 627–38), New York: Oxford University Press.

Barkow, J.H., Cosmides, L. & Tooby, J. (eds) (1992) *The Adapted Mind: Evolutionary Psychology and the Generation of Culture*, (pp. 163–228), New York: Oxford University Press.

Baumeister, R.F. & Leary, M.R. (1995) 'The need to belong: Desire for interpersonal attachments as a fundamental human motivation', *Psychological Bulletin* 117: 497–529.

Baumeister, R.F., Stillwell, A.M. & Heatherton, T.F. (1994) 'Guilt: An interpersonal approach', *Psychological Bulletin* 115: 243–67.

Baumeister, R.F. & Tice, D.M. (1990) 'Anxiety and social exclusion', *Journal of Social and Clinical Psychology* 9: 165–95.

Berkman, L.F. & Syme, S.L. (1979) 'Social networks, host resistance, and mortality: A nine-year follow-up study of Alameda county residents', *American Journal of Epidemiology* 109: 186–204.

Boehm, C. (1997) 'The impact of the human egalitarian syndrome on Darwinian selection mechanics', *The American Naturalist* 150: S100–S120.

Bowlby, J. (1988) *A Secure Base: Parent-Child Attachment and Healthy Human Development*, New York: Basic Books.

Brennan, K.A., Shaver, P.R. & Tobey, A.E. (1991) 'Attachment styles, gender, and parental problem drinking', *Journal of Personal and Social Relationships* 8: 451–66.

Bretherton, I. (1985) 'Attachment theory: Retrospect and prospect', in I. Bretherton & E. Waters (eds), 'Growing points of attachment theory and research', *Monographs of the Society for Research in Child Development* 50(1–2, Serial No. 209): 3–35.

Bruner, J.S. (1957) 'On perceptual readiness', *Psychological Review* 64: 123–52.

Buss, D.M. (1999) *Evolutionary Psychology: The New Science of the Mind*, Needham Heights, MA: Allyn & Bacon.

Caporael, L.R. & Baron, R.M. (1997) 'Groups as the mind's natural environment', in J.A. Simpson & D.T. Kenrick (eds), *Evolutionary Social Psychology*, (pp. 317–44), Mahwah, NJ: Lawrence Erlbaum Associates Inc.

Carter, C.S., Lederhendler, I. & Kirkpatrick, B. (eds) (1997) *The Integrative Neurobiology of Affiliation*, New York: New York Academy of Sciences.

Coe, C.L., Weiner, S.G., Rosenberg, L.T. & Levine, S. (1985) 'Endocrine and immune responses to separation and maternal loss in nonhuman primates', in M. Reite & T. Field (eds), *The Psychobiology of Attachment and Separation*, New York: Academic Press.

Cohen, S. & Williamson, G.M. (1991) 'Stress and infectious disease in humans', *Psychological Bulletin* 109: 5–24.

Cohen, S. & Wills, T.A. (1985) 'Stress, social support, and the buffering hypothesis', *Psychological Bulletin* 98: 310–57.

Cosmides, L. & Tooby, J. (1992) 'Cognitive adaptations for social exchange', in J.H. Barkow, L. Cosmides, & J. Tooby (eds), *The Adapted Mind: Evolutionary Psychology and the Generation of Culture*, (pp. 163–228), New York: Oxford University Press.

Crawford, C. (1995) 'The evolutionary significance of true pathologies, pseudopathologies, and pseudonormal conditions', Paper presented at the Annual Meeting of the Human Behavior and Evolution Society, Santa Barbara, CA.

Crawford, C. (1998) 'Environments and adaptations: Then and now', in C. Crawford & D. Krebs (eds), *Handbook of Evolutionary Psychology: Ideas, Issues, and Applications*, (pp. 275–302). Mahwah, NJ: Lawrence Erlbaum Associates Inc.

Crawford, C. & Krebs, D. (eds) (1998) *Handbook of Evolutionary Psychology: Ideas, Issues, and Applications*, Mahwah, NJ: Lawrence Erlbaum Associates Inc.

Daly, M. & Wilson, M. (1988) *Homocide*, New York: Aldine De Gruyter.

Daly, M., Salmon, C. & Wilson, M. (1997) 'Kinship: The conceptual hole in psychological studies of social cognition and close relationships', in J.A. Simpson & D.T. Kenrick (eds), *Evolutionary Social Psychology*, (pp. 265–96), Mahwah, NJ: Lawrence Erlbaum Associates Inc.

Dawkins, R. (1982) *The Extended Phenotype: The Gene as the Unit of Selection*, San Francisco, CA: W.H. Freeman.

DeLongis, A., Folkman, S. & Lazarus, R.S. (1988) 'The impact of daily stress on health and mood: Psychological and social resources as mediators', *Journal of Personality and Social Psychology* 54: 486–95.

Devine, P.G. (1989) 'Stereotypes and prejudice: Their automatic and controlled components', *Journal of Personality and Social Psychology* 56: 5–18.

Diener, E., Sandvik, E. & Pavot, W. (1991) 'Happiness is the frequency, not the intensity, of positive versus negative affect', in F. Strack, M. Argyle, & N. Schwartz (eds), *Subjective Well-Being: An Interdisciplinary Perspective*, (pp. 119–40), New York: Pergamon.

Dunbar, R.I.M. (1992) 'Neocortex size as a constraint on group size in primates', *Journal of Human Evolution* 22: 469–93.

Dunbar, R.I.M. (1996) *Grooming, Gossip, and the Evolution of Language*, Cambridge, MA: Harvard University Press.

Eaton, S. B., Shostak, M. & Konner, M. (1988) *The Paleolithic Prescription*, New York: Harper & Row.

Eibl-Eibesfeldt, I. (1989) *Human Ethology*, New York: Aldine de Gruyter.

Erickson, M.T. (1993) 'Rethinking Oedipus: An evolutionary perspective on incest avoidance', *American Journal of Psychiatry* 150: 411–16.

Essock-Vitale, S.M. & Fairbanks, L. (1979) 'Sociobiological theories of kin selection and reciprocal altruism and their relevance for psychiatry', *Journal of Nervous Mental Disease* 167: 23–28.

Fisher, H.E. (1982) *The Sex Contract: The Evolution of Human Behavior*, New York: William Morrow.

Fisher, H.E. (1992) *Anatomy of Love*, New York: Norton.

Gardner, R. (1994). 'Sociobiology of we-they: Persecutory delusions and proximate causation', *ASCAP Newsletter* 7: 10–13.

Gilbert, P. (1989) *Human Nature and Suffering*, Hove, UK: Lawrence Erlbaum Associates Ltd.

Gilbert, P. (1992) *Depression: The Evolution of Powerlessness*, Hove, UK: Psychology Press.

Gilbert, P. (1993) 'Defense and safety: Their function in social behaviour and psychopathology', *British Journal of Clinical Psychology* 32: 131–54.

Gilbert, P. (1997) 'The Biopsychosociology of meaning', in M. Power & C.R. Brewin (eds), *The Transformation of Meaning: Reconciliation Theory and Therapy in Cognitive, Behaviour and Related Therapies*, (pp. 33–56), New York: Wiley.

Glantz, K. & Pearce, J.K. (1989) *Exiles from Eden*, New York: Norton.

Goodwin, J.S., Hunt, W.C., Key, C.R. & Samet, J.M. (1987) 'The effect of marital status on stage, treatment, and survival of cancer patients', *Journal of American Medical Association* 258: 3125–30.

Guisinger, S. & Blatt, S.J. (1994) 'Individuality and relatedness: Evolution of a fundamental dialectic', *American Psychologist* 49: 104–11.

Hamilton, W.D. (1964) 'The genetical evolution of social behavior. I and II', *Journal of Theoretical Biology* 7: 1–52.

Hamilton, W.D. (1972) 'Altruism and related phenomena, mainly in the social insects', *Annual Review of Ecological Systems* 3: 193–232.

Hazan, C. & Shaver, P.R. (1994) 'Deeper into attachment theory', *Psychological Inquiry* 5: 68–79.

Hazan, C. & Zeifman, D. (1994) 'Sex and the psychological tether', *Advances in Personal Relationships* 5: 151–77.

Henderson, S. (1982) 'The significance of social relationships in the etiology of neurosis', in C. Parks & J. Stevenson-Hinde (eds), *The Place of Attachment in Human Behavior*, (pp. 205–31), New York: Basic Books.

Holmes, T.H. & Rahe, R.H. (1967) 'The social readjustment rating scale', *Journal of Psychosomatic Resarch* 11: 213–18.

House, J.S., Landis, K.R. & Umberson, D. (1988) 'Social relationships and health', *Science* 241: 540–4.

Janicki, M. & Krebs, D. (1998) 'Evolutionary approaches to culture', in C. Crawford & D. Krebs (eds), *Handbook of Evolutionary Psychology: Ideas, Issues, and Applications*, (pp. 163–208), Mahwah, NJ: Lawrence Erlbaum Associates Inc.

Jemmot, J.B. & Locke, S.E. (1984) 'Psychosocial factors, immunologic mediation and human susceptibility to infection: How much do we know?', *Psychological Bulletin* 95: 78–108.

Kennedy, S., Kiecolt-Glaser, J.K. & Glaser, R. (1990) 'Social support, stress, and the immune system', in B.R. Sarason, I.G. Sarason, & G.R. Pierce (eds), *Social Support: An Interactional View*, (pp. 129–49), New York: Wiley.

Kinzey, W.G. (ed.) (1987) *The Evolution of Human Behavior: Primate Models*, Albany, NY: State University of New York Press.

Krebs, D.L. & Denton, K. (1997) 'Social illusions and self-deception: The evolution of biases in person perception', in J.A. Simpson & D.T. Kenrick (eds), *Evolutionary Social Psychology*, (pp. 21–48), Mahwah, NJ: Lawrence Erlbaum Associates Inc.

Lewin, R. (1993) *Human Evolution: An Illustrated Introduction*, Oxford: Blackwell Scientific.

Lewinsohn, P., Redner, J. & Seely, J. (1991) 'The relationship between life satisfaction and psychosocial variables', in F. Strack, M. Argyle, & N. Schwarz (eds), *Subjective Well-being: An Interdisciplinary Perspective*, (pp. 141–72), New York: Pergamon.

Lockard, J.S. & Paulus, D.L. (eds) (1988) *Self-Deception: An Adaptive Mechanism?*, Englewood Cliffs, NJ: Prentice-Hall.

Lowenthal, M.F. & Haven, C. (1968) 'Interaction and adaptation: Intimacy as a critical variable', *American Sociological Review* 33: 20–30.

Lynch, J.J. (1979) *The Broken Heart: The Medical Consequences of Loneliness*, New York: Basic Books.

McGuire, M. & Troisi, A. (1998) *Darwinian Psychiatry*, New York: Oxford University Press.

Maryanski, A. & Turner, J.H. (1992) *The Social Cage: Human Nature and the Evolution of Society*, Stanford, CA: Stanford University Press.

Masters, R.D. (1989) *The Nature of Politics*, New Haven: Yale University Press.

Masters, R.D. (1994) 'The nature of ethnocentrism, nationalism,and xenophobia', Paper presented at the Twelfth Annual Conference of Human Ethology, Toronto, Canada.

Mellen, S.L.W. (1981) *The Evolution of Love*, San Francisco: Freeman.

Miller, L.C. & Fishkin, S.A. (1997) 'On the dynamics of human bonding and reproductive success: Seeking windows on the adapted-for human-environmental interface', in J.A. Simpson & D.T. Kenrick (eds), *Evolutionary Social Psychology*, (pp. 197–236), Mahwah, NJ: Lawrence Erlbaum Associates Inc.

Mithen, S. (1996) *The Prehistory of Mind*, New York: Thames and Hudson.

Nesse, R.M. & Berridge, K.C. (1997) 'Psychoctive drug use in evolutionary perspective', *Science* 278: 63–6.

Nesse, R.M. & Lloyd, A.T. (1992) 'The evolution of psychodynamic mechanisms', in J.H. Barkow, L. Cosmides & J. Tooby (eds), *The Adapted Mind*, (pp. 601–26), New York: Oxford University Press.

Nesse, R.M. & Williams, G.C. (1995) *Why We Get Sick*, New York: Random House.

Norcross, J.C. & Goldfried, M.R. (eds) (1992) *Handbook of Psychotherapy Integration*, New York: Basic Books.

Ornstein, R. & Sobel, D. (1987) *The Healing Brain*, New York: Simon & Schuster.

Panksepp, J., Nelson, E. & Bekkedal, M. (1997) 'Brain systems for the mediation of social separation-distress and social-reward. Evolutionary antecedents and neuropeptide intermediaries', in C.S. Carter, I. Lederhendler & B. Kirkpatrick (eds), *The Integrative Neurobiology of Affiliation*, (pp. 78–100), New York: New York Academy of Sciences.

Reeve, H.K. (1998) 'Acting for the good of others: Kinship and reciprocity with some new twists', in C. Crawford & D. Krebs (eds), *Handbook of Evolutionary Psychology: Ideas, Issues, and Applications*, (pp. 43–86), Mahwah, NJ: Lawrence Erlbaum Associates Inc.

Sarason, B.R., Sarason, I.G. & Pierce G.R. (eds) (1990) *Social Support: An Interactional View*, (pp. 129–49), New York: Wiley.

Service, E.R. (1962) *Primitive Social Organization: An Evolutionary Perspective*, New York: Random House.

Shackelford, T.K. & Buss, D.M. (1996) 'Betrayal in friendships, mateships, and coalitions', *Personality and Social Psychology Bulletin* 22: 1151–64.

Shreeve, J. (1995) *The Neanderthal Enigma*, New York: Avon.

Simpson, J.A. & Rholes, W.S. (eds) (1998) *Attachment Theory and Close Relationships*, New York: Guilford.

Slavin, M.O. & Kriegman, D. (1992) *The Adaptive Design of the Human Psyche*, New York: Guilford.

Sperling, M.B. & Berman, W.H. (eds) (1994) *Attachment in Adults*, New York: Guilford.

Sroufe, A. & Fleeson, J. (1986) 'Attachment and the construction of relationships', in W. Hartup & Z. Rubin (eds), *Relationships and Development*, (pp. 51–71), Hillsdale, NJ: Lawrence Erlbaum Associates Inc.

Stevens, A. & Price, J. (1996) *Evolutionary Psychiatry: A New Beginning*, London: Routledge.

Strack, F., Argyle, M. & Schwartz, N. (eds) (1991) *Subjective Well-Being: An Interdisciplinary Perspective*, New York: Pergamon.

Swann, W.B., Jr., & Brown, J.D. (1990) 'From self to health: Self-verification and identity disruption', in B.R. Sarason, I.G. Sarason, & G.R. Pierce (eds), *Social Support: An Interactional View*, (pp. 150–72), New York: Wiley.

Tanner, N.M. (1987) 'The chimpanzee model revisited and the gathering hypothesis', in W.G. Kinzey (ed.), *The Evolution of Human Behavior: Primate Models*, (pp. 3–27), Albany, NY: State University of New York Press.

Tooby, J. & Cosmides, L. (1996) 'Friendship and the banker's paradox: Other pathways to the evolution of adaptations for altruism', *Proceedings of the British Academy* 88: 119–43.

Tooby, J. & DeVore, I. (1987) 'The reconstruction of hominid behavioral evolution through strategic modeling', in W.G. Kinzey (ed.), *The Evolution of Human Behavior: Primate Models* (pp. 183–238), Albany, NY: State Univerity of New York Press.

Trivers, R.L. (1971) 'The evolution of reciprocal altruism', *Quarterly Review of Biology* 46: 35–57.

Trivers, R.L. (1985) *Social Evolution*, Menlo Park, CA: Benjamin/Cummings.

Uvnäs-Moberg, K. (1997) 'Physiological and endocrine effects of social contact', in C.S. Carter, I.I. Lederhendler & B. Kirkpatrick (eds), *The Integrative Neurobiology of Affiliation*, (pp. 146–63), New York: New York Academy of Sciences.

Veenhoven, R. (1991) 'Questions on happiness: classical topics, modern answers, blind spots', in F. Strack, M. Argyle, & N. Schwartz (eds), *Subjective Well-Being: An Interdisciplinary Perspective*, (pp. 7–26), New York: Pergamon.

Weiss, R.S. (1979) 'The emotional impact of marital separation', in G. Levinger & O.C. Moles (eds.), *Divorce and Separation: Context, Causes, and Consequences*, (pp. 201–10), New York: Basic Books.

Wood, H.E. (1997) 'Staying in the therapy zone: Kinship and the art of therapeutic process', Paper presented at the annual meeting of the ASCAP society, Tucson, Arizona.

Wood, H.E. (1998) *Psychological Kinship, Well-Being, and the Stress of Chronic Caregiving to Dementia Patients*. Unpublished doctoral dissertation, Virginia Commonwealth University.

Wrangham, R.W. (1987) 'The significance of African apes for reconstructing human social evolution', in W.G. Kinzey (ed.), *The Evolution of Human Behavior: Primate Models*, (pp. 51–71), Albany, NY: State University of New York Press.

Wrangham, R.W. & Peterson, D. (1996) *Demonic Males*, Boston: Houghton Mifflin.

Zeifman, D. & Hazan, C. (1997) 'Attachment: The bond in pair-bonds', in J.A. Simpson & D.T. Kenrick (eds), *Evolutionary Social Psychology*, (pp. 237–63), Mahwah, NJ: Lawrence Erlbaum Associates Inc.

Acknowledgements

The author wishes to thank Helen E. Wood and Robin Fox for their help and inspiration in the early phases of psychological kinship theory. I also deeply appreciate Russell Gardner's help in organizing the ASCAP-sponsored Tucson

Conference on evolutionary psychotherapy in 1997 and for his willingness to publish my various commentaries on psychological kinship in the *ASCAP NEWSLETTER*. Lastly, I am especially indebted to Paul Gilbert for helping me shape this chapter to its current form. In the last analysis, however, I must assume responsibility for all errors that remain.

Section II

EVOLUTIONARY
PSYCHOTHERAPIES

4

EVOLUTIONARY PSYCHOANALYSIS

Toward an adaptive, biological perspective on the clinical process in psychoanalytic psychotherapy[1]

Daniel Kriegman

This chapter takes a somewhat provocative position in response to the fact that psychoanalysis has lost much of its popularity with the general public and especially with evolutionary biologists. There are many reasons for this decline. An unfortunate one is the increasing 'medicination' of modern societies' responses to psychological problems. Part of the loss of popularity that psychoanalysis has suffered, however, is well deserved, as psychoanalysts have developed some rather fanciful metapsychological notions that have then been reified (Holt, 1989). Claims that these notions are based on 'objective' clinical 'facts' that only analysts and their patients have access to have contributed to the ridicule that has been directed at psychoanalysis for being unfalsifiable (Popper, 1963) or for having no more of an objective base than religions or the Loch Ness monster (Torrey, 1992; Masson, 1990; Eysenck, 1972; cf. Kriegman & Solomon, 1985b; Bornstein & Masling, 1994). In essence, we are told by such critics that the psychoanalyst is wearing clothes that only the emperor and his court can see. Furthermore, there is evidence of damage that can be caused when analysts insist that their patients don this imaginary clothing.

  Yet, an enormous amount of effort, work, clinical data, and careful study of the human psyche has occurred in the psychoanalytic field. Before we empty the enormous quantity of dirty bathwater, wouldn't we be wise to make a search to see if there is a baby in it? Not only would I suggest that we will find a living baby, I would also suggest that the baby has nearly drowned and is in desperate need of evolutionary biological resuscitation. Let us turn now to look at how evolutionary biology may be applied to psychoanalysis for this purpose. We can do this by first asking the question: how should we act as part of our patient's environment to have maximal impact as a therapeutic agent?

The classical, Freudian model

In the classical psychoanalytic model, Freud envisioned a central organizing agent, the ego, at the heart of a tripartite psychological system. The ego has to manage pressures that cause it to experience three different types of anxiety. These pressures emanate from the other two parts of the psyche, the id (causing instinctual anxiety) and the superego (causing moral anxiety), as well as from reality (causing realistic anxiety). The ego is forced to engage in compromise operations – namely, the defence mechanisms which operate largely unconsciously using repression as their primary tool – in order to manage these powerful, conflicting pressures. The analyst's goal is to make the ego aware of its predicament and its defensive system of compromise operations. Without such awareness (insight), the ego blindly repeats self-destructive and useless actions. If aspects of this system can be brought within the ego's awareness, then new, more productive compromises can be arranged. Because instincts (wishes, desires) conflict with both social pressures and realistic dangers, they must be repressed and thus comprise the largest part of the unconscious forces operating on the ego. The goal is to enable the unconscious instincts to enter consciousness sufficiently so that the ego can better master the compromise solutions it must manage while maximizing the adaptive expression of one's desires and wishes. In treatment, this is accomplished through interpretations in which the analyst – after listening very carefully to the patient's free associations – informs the patient about what is really going on, i.e., what unconscious mental processes and impulses are the true motives and intentions behind the patient's self-deceptive conscious experience. In the Freudian interpretations that evolutionists are fond of ridiculing, patients are told some of the most blatantly absurd things about their psyches, their intentions, and their motives (Daly & Wilson, 1990; Kriegman & Slavin, 1989; cf. Slavin & Kriegman, 1992). But more of this later.

The technique Freud eventually settled upon for uncovering the unconscious was *the basic rule*. The basic rule consists of the patient communicating everything he or she becomes aware of without any form of censorship. Freud then began to notice the tremendous difficulty patients had in acknowledging a whole range of feelings they had about the therapist and certain topics. Some of the most difficult of these were angry critical feelings, shameful sexual and aggressive wishes, disappointment, longings to be cared about, longings to be treated as special, etc. When strongly encouraged to talk about everything including these terribly embarrassing and frightening feelings without censorship in a relationship that consisted of four to five regular meetings every week, the patient began to have a strange experience. The therapist took on a role unlike that of any other person in the patient's life. Given the normal constraints of human life, no one is ever allowed into (or makes the investment of time and attention necessary to enter) another's inner experience to such a great degree. No one – not even our closest relatives and lovers – gets to hear everything. No one gets a chance to come this close to stepping inside of our shoes and seeing what it is really like to have our own unique experience.

The power of a relationship as the therapeutic agent for insight, change, and growth

Freud then noticed that the intense relationship that formed was coloured by unique factors in each patient's circumstances. Each intense relationship that developed was different while each had a reliable internal consistency. As the relationship became the central vehicle of the treatment, the unique colorations and the stable patterns of relating they engendered were termed 'transference'. *Psycho*analysis became *transference* analysis. Since that time, almost all innovations in psychoanalytic theory and technique have been comprised of new theories about human relatedness (Greenberg & Mitchell, 1983). For example, current psychoanalytic theory is far less dominated by symbolic sexual interpretations. There is now far more focus on the meaning of relatedness, the therapist's role in the relationship, and other relational issues. But all too often, psychoanalytic treatment – operating outside of the context of a valid scientific view of human nature – is now dominated by strained, at times untenable, interpretations about relationships.

Evolutionary basis of sociality

We know that humans are extremely social creatures, possibly the most social creatures of all. We know that humans are the most neotanized species with the longest period of childhood dependency in close kin environments. Finally, it is clear that the explosive growth of the human brain had little to do with *technology*; the human brain developed into its current form long before complex technological innovation occurred. The human brain developed as a powerful social 'computer' that evolved to deal with the incredible complexity of kin and reciprocal relatedness and conflict in a relatively reliable tribal web of social connections. This complex task provided the selective pressure that led to the evolution of our empathic capacity (Kriegman, 1988, 1990). An in-depth sense of another's experience gives us a foundation for predicting the other's behaviour (What will they do? Are they reliable?) and for sensing both how and when to try to influence others. Our psyches appear to be complicated social computers designed to comprehend complex mental states (largely through the use of empathic perception) in order to navigate through a complex sea of *intra*tribal conflict and mutuality that occurs in a larger context of *inter*tribal conflict (Kriegman & Kriegman, 1997).

What an irony it is that some academic, behavioural, evolutionary psychologists and biopsychiatrists actually attempt to 'turn off' this marvellous device! Academic psychologists claiming that only their approach safeguards objectivity eschew the attempt to perceive complex mental states through empathy/introspection and try to replace it with complicated, numerical, statistical analyses of isolated bits of behaviour (see Kriegman, 1996a, 1998a for fuller discussions of this problem). Some behaviourists continue to insist that human experience is an epiphenomenon that can be ignored in the study of actions (behaviour). Modern biopsychiatrists not only increasingly question the usefulness of engaging in a long-term empathic exploration of the meaning of another's experience, they can go much further and – sometimes without considering the value or meaning of such experience in an individual's life – attempt to chemically 'adjust' experience by shutting down troublesome parts of it or by 'turning up the volume' on other parts. In their own attempt to ground their new discipline in science and to separate it from the 'touchy-feely', quasi-religious ways in which many view psychotherapy – and especially psychoanalysis, for some of the reasons outlined above – some evolutionary psychologists have relegated these powerful tools (the therapeutic relationship and the empathic immersion in another's experience) to the periphery of psychotherapy. (Although there are other evolutionists who are attempting to integrate empathic understanding with adaptive analyses, e.g., Bailey, Wood & Nava, 1992.)

If the view of the human psyche that I am suggesting is correct, from an evolutionary–psychoanalytic viewpoint, intentionally ignoring the data obtainable through the use of the most sophisticated and exquisite perceptual device ever produced – the human empathic capacity that may be our most impressive evolutionary achievement – seems like a highly misguided strategy. In addition, the failure to tap into the power of the relationship when dealing with such a funda-mentally relational creature is potentially quite limiting. In general, relationships and their quality are central in human psychological functioning. Kohut (1984) referred to the impact of certain crucial elements of human relatedness on the psyche as the equivalent of oxygen's importance to the body. Humans in solitary confinement often go insane. The greatest threat – possibly even greater than death itself – is to be shamed, to be cut off from the tribe. The greatest cause of suicide in physically healthy people is shame and hopelessness about being loved, accepted, and/or respected. Disrespect, as in 'are you dissin' me?' and 'road rage' can often lead to deadly confrontations.

Thus, evolutionary biology suggests that the most powerful tool in shaping and reshaping human experience and behaviour is powerful, intimate, and involving relationships. Unfortunately, most psychotherapies, including some evolutionary approaches, either forgo the exploitation of this potent intervention or try to use its power to manipulate the patient in a manner that the therapist determines is in the patient's best interests. That is, some evolutionary therapists intentionally attempt to ignore the relationship altogether and focus instead on identifying maladaptive patterns of behaviour in order to use an evolutionary understanding to educate and guide the patient. At other times, they intentionally attempt to manipulate the patient using the relationship and the authority the therapist claims for having a truer, more accurate evolutionary understanding of the patient's psychological and social world.

This latter trend is reminiscent of authoritarian psychoanalytic 'treatments' in which 'resistant' patients were told the truth about their psyche by the psychoanalyst who knew what was 'really' going on. If evolutionary biology teaches us anything, however, it should teach us that views of reality are highly likely to represent the actual world accurately only when it is in the best interest of the organism to have such an accurate view, i.e., when a rock is hurtling towards one's head. When we are dealing with social reality, the notion that the human mind is designed to see things accurately is naive indeed (Trivers, 1976; cf. Kriegman, 1996a, 1998a). It is thus extremely dangerous for a therapist of any persuasion to assume that they can see accurately what is best for another better than the other can. After all, the evolved psyche is an 'organ' for representing and promoting one's *own* interests conceptually (knowledge, beliefs), emotionally, and behaviourally. The notion that therapists' psyches (which were designed to view reality in a manner that maximizes their interests) can generally represent patients' interests more accurately than patients' psyches (which were designed to do the same for the patients and their interests) is completely out of sync with an evolutionary view. Evolutionary biology suggests that – unless this outcome is carefully guarded against – judgements of what is best for another are highly likely to be *in the judger's* best interests. This may explain much of the problem that was faced by authoritarian psychoanalysis. It would be a terrible mistake to replace one such flawed system with a new evolutionary 'authority'.

The use of the extraordinary power of an intensive analytic relationship has fallen into disrepute because of what has occurred when psychoanalysts have tried to use it while operating with misleading biological suppositions – suppositions that range from the partially correct, through the naive and wrong, to the absurd – about the aims and goals of human psychological functioning, that is, assumptions about human nature[2]. It is partly in response to the shady history of relationship-focused psychotherapy, that some non-analytic, evolutionary psychotherapies tend to limit the use of the relationship to teaching, advising, manipulating (to convince, inspire, motivate, urge), and suggesting strategies for action, etc. Meanwhile, psychoanalysis has continued to try to utilize the empathic mode of data gathering in order to tap deeply into an unusually involving and powerful human relationship. For some troubled individuals, herein lies both their greatest hope and gravest danger.

Evolutionary biology as a guide to theory and practice

We can apply evolutionary biology to psychoanalysis in two major ways. First, we can use the evolutionary perspective to help us with our *theoretical* understanding of the human psyche. Ideas that are inconsistent with what we know about the evolution of all mammalian behaviour must be questioned at least, and in most cases discarded. Second, and more importantly for clinicians, these evolutionary perspective modifications and clarifications of analytic theory have direct implications for a theory of *clinical practice*, especially if we attempt to construct and enter into the intimate human relationships that may provide the most powerful vehicles for therapeutic change. One overriding principle of evolution is that each of us is designed to operate in the best interest of our own genetic material. Psychoanalysis is a relationship between two unrelated individuals in which, to a great extent, the therapist has enormous power over the patient. Evolutionary theory tells us that it is likely that such power will be used to further the best interests of the one who holds the larger share of power (the therapist) and that the pursuit of such interests may self-deceptively be disguised as being in the best interest of the patient (Kriegman, 1998a; also see Bailey & Wood, 1998).

Proximal versus distal causes

This evolutionary perspective on the inevitable biases in individuals' beliefs, values, and perceptions (Kriegman, 1996a) coupled with the unique understanding of the distinction between *distal* and *proximal* causes that the evolutionary perspective provides (Kriegman, 1998a) together suggest part of a solution to this problem. Distal causes – also known as 'ultimate' causes – are those forces (selective pressures) that shaped a pattern of behaviour, a motivation, or a mental process (conscious or unconscious) over evolutionary time. For example, people eat because if they did not they would die: eating behaviour is adaptive. However, this is the ultimate cause that is distal in the sense that those forces that shaped this behaviour are distant in time from people as acting individuals. The selective pressure (i.e., only those who ate survived to reproduce and pass on their genes, which included the genetically influenced propensity to eat) operated on our ancestors and their compatriots over phylogenetic history. As a general rule, people are not consciously (or unconsciously) motivated to eat in order to live. As people experience it in ontogenetic, personal time, the proximal mechanism that was shaped by the ultimate cause that *now* causes eating behaviour is hunger (or other forms of the desire for food).

Proximal mechanisms include all of the affects people experience: rage, love, fear, anxiety, anger, jealousy, joy, sadness, lust, desire, grief, loneliness, shame, guilt, remorse, compassion, competitiveness, pride, envy, sympathy, and so on. These proximal mechanisms motivate human behaviour and help determine responses by others. The ultimate cause that shaped our affects was the selective reinforcement by the environment of those proximal mechanisms (affects) that made certain behaviours more likely to occur. That is, the affectively motivated propensities to engage in the behaviours that were functional or adaptive (i.e., adaptive in that the individuals who engaged in them had a greater rate of reproductive success) were 'chosen' by the differential outcome in reproductive success (i.e., 'reinforced' by the environment) so that they had a higher frequency in each succeeding generation. The individuals motivated (by proximal mechanisms) to engage in more adaptive behaviours out-reproduced those without such motivations, so that today those who have such proximal motives are the primary form.

As in the example of eating *in order to live* and *hunger*, it quickly becomes clear that the ultimate cause (functional, adaptive aspect of a behaviour) may have little in common with the proximal cause (the mechanism actually motivating the behaviour in the individual). Thus, an organism can be clearly pursuing an adaptive strategy that may be obvious to observers without any awareness or (conscious or unconscious) *intent* to do so. This can lead to major misunderstandings of motivation and may be the ground for some severe critiques of psychoanalysis. For example, consider the classical psychoanalytic understanding of the human preoccupation with sexuality. In men, this seems to be a reflection of reality: anecdote, analytic experience, and empirical studies all conclude that men are in fact preoccupied with sexual thoughts and fantasies (Herman, 1993; Wright, 1994; Buss, 1995). Penis envy is alive and well. However, in my clinical experience, it is primarily found in men who are constantly comparing their size, potency, prowess, status, and so on. Feminists have rightly criticized psychoanalysis for the attempt to characterize female sexuality as a variant of male sexuality.

Let us take a closer look at how confusion between ultimate and proximal causes can cause confusion in psychoanalytic theory and practice. If a female patient's associations do not demonstrate the type of preoccupation that men have with sex, then some analysts assume that such a preoccupation exists in her unconscious. If a female patient dresses in a manner that her male analyst finds sexually provocative, he may conclude that the motive to arouse him exists in her. In fact, the male analyst may be encouraged to explore his inner experience to see what feelings his patient is trying to arouse within him (or what she may be defensively avoiding through projective identification). If she denies any such conscious thought, she is either acting deceptively (lying) or is telling what she believes to be the truth and the true motive is repressed, hidden away in her unconscious but exerting its influence as evidenced in her behaviour.

Yet, males and females of all species may act in a manner that reliably brings about a particular effect without any conscious *or unconscious* motive containing any direct knowledge of the particular functional effect. This is assumed to be so in primitive species in whom the behaviour looks mechanical (reflexive) and higher cortical awareness at either the conscious or unconscious level is assumed to be lacking. People have a harder time accepting their own highly effective mechanisms that govern their emotional life and behaviour without necessitating the use of our higher, uniquely human mental processes. This resistance is a response to the blow to human narcissism that Freud (1917) believed was central to both evolutionary biology and psychoanalysis.

To return to my example of the analytic interpretation of female sexuality: A woman may act enticingly without full awareness of how stimulating she may be to men. An example is the woman who does her best to be attractive, look young, wears make-up, wears stylish clothing designed to 'advertise' her feminine figure by highlighting certain secondary sex characteristics (e.g., enhancing the apparent protrusion of her breasts, buttocks, and hips), and so forth, yet she is genuinely confused (and angry) when she is treated as a sex object. The classical analyst might insist that her behaviour indicates an unconscious wish to be ravished or raped – or to be treated sexually in a manner consistent with male desires – and, in such a view, her anger is part of a reaction formation that helps to maintain the repression of her true motives. The evolutionary psychoanalytic view, however, suggests that such interpretations may be better understood as projections of male wishes mixed with confusions of proximal and ultimate causes. The woman's motive – both consciously *and unconsciously* – in the particular situation[3] may be to be found attractive (e.g., presentable, not ugly, stylish, likeable, someone others would want to be seen with and want as a friend, as well as wanting to be attractive to the opposite sex) without wanting to stimulate fairly intense male lust and desire, as she may report. A repressed wish to drive men to distraction may not be operating even in women whose appearance and behaviour often does.

Am I saying that such female behaviour is unrelated to the male response? Can it be that women spend enormous effort, time, and money to behave in a way that regularly and reliably produces a specific effect and yet the behaviour and the effect are unrelated? It has been well documented in several societies that attractive women marry up the socioeconomic scale: the ability to arouse men has significant adaptive advantages for women (Elder, 1969; Buss, 1992; Ridley, 1993; Fisher, 1992). Women whom men find intensely arousing often have enormous power to select their mate from a large pool of possibilities. Compared with their responses to relatively unattractive women, men will take great risks and make extraordinary efforts to obtain reproductive rights with attractive women. Certainly the vast preoccupation with beauty and the massive industries that arise from its existence and encourage its development cannot be mere accidents. Whether one takes an overly simplistic biological view, a strictly cultural view, or the more reasonable view of a mixture of both biological and experiential factors as shaping human behaviour, one cannot deny the ubiquitousness of women's attempts to enhance their beauty as well as men's preoccupation with it. When women go to such efforts to engage in this behaviour and men are so aroused, how can I say that there may be no conscious or unconscious attempt on the part of women to arouse men sexually?

Although many women do experience the desire to be sexually exciting, there is no evidence that such a motive operates consciously or unconsciously on a minute-to-minute basis (e.g., in the school, on the bus, in the workplace, or in the analytic setting). Even if evidence suggests that most women have such desires at times, the notion that these desires are acting as nearly as ubiquitously, consciously or unconsciously, as the male sexual response suggests may be more accurately seen as a projection. Both the stimulating behaviours and the stimulation exist. Yet, it apparently does not require direct, intentional effort to stimulate fairly intense sexual desire in a sexually preoccupied creature. There may be motives (proximal mechanisms) that generate behaviour that stimulates men without a conscious or unconscious *intent* to produce the male experience. With the distinction between proximal mechanisms (e.g., the motivation to maximize one's 'attractiveness' through various means) and ultimate causes (e.g., the arousal of intense desire on the part of men that enhanced female choice and gave an adaptive [reproductive] advantage to the women in the past who were able to arouse such interest), evolutionary psychologists come to a different conclusion about what may exist in the female psyche today. In this view, the conclusion that stimulating raw, male lust, to the degree that men actually are stimulated to experience it, is the unconscious wish in women may largely be a projection of men's desire.

Yet, as noted, it is often obvious to men (and other women) that there is an enormous advantage to the attractive woman to be so perceived (i.e., women whose appearance and behaviour arouse intense sexual excitement and desire in men are often able to use the male preoccupation with sex to gain numerous advantages, one of which is the extremely valuable ability to exercise a great deal of choice in selecting a mate). The ultimate cause (the enhancement of the self-interest of a woman through maximizing the stimulation of men) is thus obvious from observing the proximal mechanism in action today. However, this does not justify one to take the ultimate cause, meld it with the male experience, and then project it into the female psyche. The result of this confusion of proximal with ultimate causes leads to the presumption of a conscious or unconscious wish in women to produce the male sexual experience. The woman then becomes largely responsible for the man's sexual desire.

Although the crudest form of this projection is repugnant to us all – the rapist's claim that 'she wanted it' because he may have experienced intense arousal in response to her appearance and behaviour – I am, in fact, suggesting that this is only a more extreme version of the same interpersonal process that occurs in analysis. I have heard numerous analysts and analytically trained psychotherapists talk about their 'hysterical' patients in just this manner. As an example, consider Freud's (1905: 28) analysis of Dora. Dora recounted that she was alone with a handsome, married businessman, a friend of the family whom she knew well. Herr K 'suddenly clasped the girl to him and pressed a kiss upon her lips. This was surely just the situation to call up a distinct feeling of sexual excitement in a girl of 14 who had never before been approached'. Freud considered Dora's lack of such a response evidence of hysteria as if the normal feeling in an inexperienced girl of 14 who is suddenly sexually accosted by an adult male friend of the family should be sexual excitement.

From an evolutionary perspective in which sex can be a very costly act for the female and is relatively risk free (with a potential for terrific genetic payoff) for the male (Trivers, 1972), this is an interesting conclusion. No distinction is made between what is a normal response for a male and for a female; the normal female response ought to be like what one might expect from a 14-year-old boy who was suddenly kissed by an attractive adult woman whom he knew well and for whom he presumably had intense sexual desires. This type of assumption – that the analyst has objective knowledge of what is universal and normal (e.g., that the lack of a typical male response in a woman indicates hysterical repression of sexuality) – is a potentially iatrogenic projection that occurs in many forms, not only around sexuality, and I discuss this further shortly when I evaluate the notion of projective identification as it is commonly used.

Another example of the confusion between proximal and distal causes is the simplistic interpretation of altruism as ultimately self-serving. This confusion is found in Freud's (1914, 1915a, 1915b, 1921, 1930) writing as well as in the writing of evolutionists (e.g., Nesse, 1990; cf. Kriegman, 1990). In this view, the adaptive value to the individual of compassion and care for others is used to argue that such concerns are really selfish motivations. Yes, they ultimately are adaptive and thus 'self-serving'. However, this is the ultimate cause – those who cared for others were more reproductively successful than those who did not show concern for others – not the proximal mechanism, which in many cases is a genuine concern for the well-being of others (primary love and compassion). When compassion is considered nothing more than a reaction formation against sadism (Freud, 1915a, 1915b) and parental love is dismissed as born-again, childish narcissism (Freud, 1914), psychoanalytic theory overlooks major points about the basic motivations found in social species, especially those in whom parental care is essential for the survival and well-being of the offspring (Kriegman, 1988, 1990).

Interpretations in which patients are told the 'truth' about their feelings and intentions based on their analyst's subjective responses – responses that may be accurate clues to ultimate, functional aims that shaped the observed behaviours (for the response in others may be one of the effects constituting the selective pressure that shaped the behaviour) – can be abusive to the patient. The interpretation can be iatrogenic even though it may be 'correct', in a sense: the adaptive aims (ultimate causes) of the behaviour of the individual may be correctly identified. For example, women may wear make-up because maximizing their ability to arouse men sexually is their ultimate (adaptive) aim and a person may care for a friend because there are self-serving, adaptive benefits to being seen as a trustworthy ally (Trivers, 1971; Kriegman, 1988, 1990) without these ends existing in their conscious or unconscious motivational system as the primary proximal mechanisms controlling the behaviour in the here and now. Telling patients that their ultimate aims are their proximal motives, even if they are told that the motivating wishes and desires are unconscious, can be experienced as an assault. In such cases, the authority of the analyst (or evolutionary psychotherapist) who knows 'truth' and delivers it to a resistant patient is a dangerous arrangement.

Intentions, projective identifications, and the (evolutionary) psychoanalysis of proximal mechanisms

Although thus far I have critiqued classical (i.e., Freudian) misconceptions caused by a confusion of distal and proximal causes, the same misunderstandings can be found in the relational psychoanalytic approaches. Consider a Fairbairnian interpretation to a 'borderline' patient such as, 'You are enraged. You wish to destroy me because you fear that I am like your father who traumatically disappointed you in the past. You will not allow yourself to be "tricked" and thus you need to destroy your treatment rather than risk being set up for another devastating disappointment'. As the functional meaning of a particular patient's assault on a specific therapist, this interpretation may actually be correct. It may explain the ultimate, adaptive function of Fairbairn's 'antilibidinal ego' (cf. Kriegman & Slavin, 1989). However, it may completely misrepresent and obscure the actual proximal mechanism operating in the patient both consciously and unconsciously. Rather than having any 'wish to destroy' the therapist, which may be how *the therapist* experiences the situation, the patient may be validly sensing some degree of real danger in the limits of the therapist's ability to understand, to be helpful, and commitment not to harm the patient. The protective proximal mechanism serving the interpreted ultimate function (avoidance of retraumatization) may be to be hyper-reactive to the sensed, real danger.

Consciously, then, the patient would certainly not be trying to destroy the treatment to protect against a new trauma. Rather, the patient might simply be trying to express what might be consciously experienced as a reasonable level of frustration or anger at the therapist's real limitations and errors. In addition, even on the unconscious level, the ultimate explanation may have little or no meaning to the patient. The unconscious proximal process may simply be a perceptual or cognitive tendency to exaggerate (distort) the degree of sensed danger with some self-deception about its fit with the actual injury or risk (i.e., to become adaptively hypersensitive after trauma).

Of course, the analyst can point to the maladaptive nature of the over-reaction and the restriction of possibilities that hypersensitivity can cause. However, helping patients see the reasonable, adaptive aspects of a self-protective over-reaction (even if it has debilitating effects) can lead to their feeling safe enough – patients understand that the danger is not being ignored – to put aside the self-protection. By contrast, pointing out the unreasonableness of the over-reaction can lead patients to believe the danger is being minimized and the self-protective function must be clung to more tenaciously. This can lead to regressive spirals in which analysts keep trying to get patients to agree with their supposedly more 'objective' perspective in which such reactions are over-reactions. This, in turn, leads to increased anxiety as patients sense that a real danger to them is being minimized and thus can lead to a louder outcry that in turn is seen by the analyst as a more regressive, infantile, and even psychotically distorted over-reaction, which, of course, leads to patients. . . . Such intractable interactions have been referred to as 'repetition compulsions' (Freud, 1920, 1933), or 'negative therapeutic reactions' (Freud, 1923, 1924, 1937; Glover, 1955, 1956) and 'id-resistance' (Glover, 1955, 1956). Using such conceptualizations, the responsibility for therapeutic impasses can be laid squarely on the patient (cf. Brandchaft, 1983; Kriegman & Slavin, 1989).

A Fairbairnian, relational interpretation may accurately identify the functional meaning of 'what is going on' in the treatment without saying something with any meaning to the patient if the interpretation makes a claim about the patient's conscious or unconscious intention, as if the ultimate aim must be contained in some explicit form in some part of the patient's psyche that is available to direct or indirect observation. The evolutionary perspective suggests that people may be designed to engage in functional actions (such as the interpreted one, in this case) without having any conscious or unconscious 'awareness' of the function.[4]

If an analysis of the proximal mechanism occurs instead (e.g., searching for the danger sensed by the patient and carefully elucidating how the felt danger leads to the rage reaction) after many occurrences its operation may become clear. After a clarifying analysis of the proximal, experience-near process – a process that is seen to have validity and an inherently adaptive function even if it causes enormous problems in its actual operation – most patients are willing to try to understand why they react so forcefully. At such a point, searching for an ultimate explanation (the functional 'why') is often experienced as helpful because it emphasizes the adaptive goal (the healthy aim) of what the patient can then begin to see is an irrational response; understanding the adaptive (ultimate) function of a proximal mechanism can increase the patient's ability to see its distorting, dysfunctional aspects. In this view, the distortion is not seen as pathological with the inevitable shameful association connected to such an appellation. Rather, despite the problems it causes, the distortion is seen as an integral component of a valid, adaptive process. Frequently, therapists find that such patients long to disengage from – what they can see only after repeated analysis of the proximal mechanism – a process of distorting reality. This longing to be free from such over-reactions may occur only after the analysis of the proximal mechanism (as it functions both within and out of treatment) has led to an increased awareness of its existence and nature as well as the difficulties it causes in relationships with others.

Patients then find themselves wishing to alter what has been identified as a formerly (or potentially) functional (but no longer necessary) process because of its troublesome (dysfunctional) effects. The problem with telling patients that they are trying to do something that they may actually be trying to do (in the ultimate sense) is that they often are using proximal mechanisms that may include no conscious or unconscious awareness of their function and thus such interpretations can be experienced as missing the valid, vital meaning of the patient's here-and-now experience (i.e., the proximal mechanism in action). A clear delineation of the difference between proximal mechanisms (including conscious and repressed aims or intentions) and functional meaning may result in a more facilitating mode of clinical communication.

The following clinical example illustrates some of the implications of this evolutionary account of projective identification.

Case example: Sue

Sue was a 'psychotically' depressed woman. During several of her descents into despair, she expressed her distress to me and I struggled to deal with the real danger of suicide. The typical response to Sue – the one she had received all her life – was to try to appeal to her to see the psychotic nature of her despair, i.e., that things were not really the way she experienced them. A long string of children's home attendants, foster parents, adoptive parents, fundamentalist religious counsellors, and mental health professionals had delivered this message to Sue for over forty five years with no beneficial effect. Instead the result was an adult life spent primarily in mental hospitals, over one year in seclusion rooms and mechanical restraints, and an escalation of her suicide attempts that on several occasions included her ending up in a coma. My understanding was that the only options these caregivers thought they had were: (1) to gratify her infantile needs by caring for her in the way she claimed she needed, e.g., to be available to hold her and never leave her whenever her fear and despair were overwhelming; (2) to acknowledge their unwillingness to give her something she may actually need to live, and thus be willing to watch her die because they refused to respond to legitimate needs, or (3) deny the legitimacy of her needs. Despite some abortive attempts, no one was really willing to do the reparenting required by the first option. 'Good, caring' people could never allow themselves to do the second. Thus, the only option left was to deny the legitimacy of her needs, i.e., to tell her that her demands were unreasonable, that things weren't as bad as they seemed, that she could live without what she claimed she needed, or that her bad feelings were caused by her refusal to take Jesus into her heart, or that her psychotic beliefs and feelings were due to the defective brain chemistry that causes schizophrenia and thus could never end if she refused to take her medication (which eventually caused tardive dyskinesia without ever providing any benefit), etc.

Using an evolutionary approach (Trivers, 1974; Slavin & Kriegman, 1992, 1998; see Kriegman, 1996c for a fuller description of this therapy), I realized that there might be a massive conflict of interests between the needs of the caregivers and those of Sue. I felt I needed to find a way to let Sue know that I saw that her needs were legitimate and that this conflict of interests was what led to a lifetime of 'crazymaking' statements by caregivers that had literally induced insanity in her, i.e., a complete inability to feel that any of her feelings and perceptions were real. The degree of distress I experienced and communicated when I tried to deliver this 'interpretation' had a great deal to do with whether she calmed down. If I appeared calm and in control, she often became more agitated and despairing. If I was clearly upset and did not try to hide it, she usually calmed down. My obvious distress made the conflict in our interests palpable: she could directly feel the threat to my well-being (to my interests) that motivated the limits I placed on my investment in her. When my distress was hidden, she experienced me as rejecting and withholding what I could easily give her. This is like Melanie Klein's (Segal, 1964) paranoid–schizoid position, in which the infant believes the mother's depleted breast is not dry; the angry infant believes the mother is withholding the fully available milk she is *unwilling* to give.

Sue often struggled until I more fully grasped her hopelessness and despair. Only when I sensed the massive hopelessness and pain and was moved out of my self-protective ensconcement in a theoretical (therapeutic) cocoon – which helped me to *not* experience her terror, helplessness, and despair – could Sue finally feel truly understood and have the sense that her subjective experience had been grasped. Thus, she struggled until I suffered along with her. She needed to see me sensing her pain and thus suffering myself when I said 'No' to her explicit or implicit expressions of need. Without my suffering, my refusal to care for her seemed like an uncaring, cold rejection, not like the limits of a person with needs and agendas of his own that conflicted with hers.

Some analysts explain such interactions with the notion of projective identification (Klein, 1946). However, in this view I am not confusing intent with cause (cf. Stolorow, Brandchaft & Atwood, 1987). Unlike the traditional way of understanding so-called 'projective identifications', it was not Sue's intent to induce in me a sense of helplessness and thus sadistically (or defensively) project her helplessness into me in order to rid her of the experience. Rather, she fully experienced the helplessness and despair herself; she was not defensively avoiding it through the use of projective identification. She simply could not get the sense of being understood – and thus the isolating struggle with the despair continued and intensified the despair – until I appeared to grasp her horror fully. My real concern for Sue despite my refusal to take care of her could not be sensed by her as long as I appeared to be comfortable in my role as analysing therapist. To paraphrase Sue's complaint:

> How can you make sounds that supposedly indicate an understanding of my ugly, horrifying nonexistence as if you had just seen a poignant motion picture? I have just been exploded by a grenade; my guts are all over your office; my intestines are out and down around my knees; I'm screaming in pain and about to die; and you look at me with a sympathetic look and words that are supposed to indicate that you understand!?! You look as if in a few minutes you'll just say, 'Next', and call in another sufferer to face with sympathetic looks. No, you don't just *look* that way. You really are going to dismiss me and say, 'Next'. You can't possibly understand!

Thus, until therapists seem to be in significant pain themselves, how could such patients believe that the understanding has any depth? The goal is not to rid the patient of pain by projecting it into the analyst. The goal is not to make the analyst feel as hopeless as the patient to act out some vengeful, sadistic fantasy or to change passive trauma into a sense of active mastery. The goal is to be understood, to feel valued, to not be alone. This cannot be experienced until therapists are visibly moved. Furthermore, if what is to be understood is truly horrifying, then the visible movement must be more than a look of concern. Only when therapists appear horrified themselves can such patients believe they are being heard.

Until therapists 'get it', the struggle continues. To imply *intent* to make analysts suffer – which is, in fact, part of what this process was (ultimately) designed to produce – is the same logical error as the ironic saying, 'You always find what you're looking for in the last place you look', as if there is something special about that last place. Or, as if the universe is designed with the intent to make people waste time looking until they have suffered enough and then they are allowed to find the lost item. As in the process misleadingly labelled *projective identification*, once the lost object is found (once the therapist is visibly and powerfully moved), the seeker (patient) can stop looking (stop struggling and claiming the therapist does not 'get it'). Only when the therapist is visibly moved can the patient have the needed experience of being understood. In this analysis, it is true – if the therapist does not get angry or find some way to blame the patient – that once the therapist is filled with despair the patient may feel better. However, the subjective motive (proximal mechanism) on the patient's part was not to hurt the other. Patients do continue to hurt therapists (raising the ante) until they feel understood; their *behaviour* is consistent with that which would be produced if the *intent* were to make therapists suffer. However, it is being understood and valued – not to feel isolated, lost, and alone in despair – that is the patient's urgently experienced (proximal) goal or intent. When this goal is achieved, the process stops spiralling into greater and greater fragmentation and despair on the patient's part. It can appear as if the patient's intent is to bring about the analyst's suffering when, in fact, the patient is struggling to bring about the analyst's palpable understanding and caring, which (unfortunately) cannot be perceived unless the analyst shares some of the patient's discomfort.

The patient often needs to experience the reality of the therapist's struggle with the conflict between the legitimate needs of the patient and those of the therapist that are aroused in treatment in order to use the therapeutic relationship (Slavin & Kriegman, 1998; Kriegman, 1996c). Therapists who manage to deal with their countertransference reactions too well may actually deprive their patients of their genuineness (Myerson, 1973). Havens (1973), in response to this issue, quoted Jaspers (1900: 676), 'Nothing happens until the doctor is touched by the patient'.

Who am I? An evolutionary perspective

Another way to understand the inter-relationship between proximal mechanisms and distal (ultimate) aims comes from considering the meaning of the word 'I'. Kohut's (1971, 1977) attempt to formulate an experience-near conception of the 'self' comes close to the meaning most people intend when they use the word, I: the centre of experience and the source of initiative and action. In this sense in ordinary speaking, one does not say, 'I beat my heart' or 'I grow my hair' or 'I heal my wounds'. I, refers to the experiencing and acting agent, the one who makes meanings, has intentions, wishes, needs, ambitions, values, and goals and, on these bases, acts. Because the processes involved in hair growth, for example, are unconscious bodily events, people can never directly influence them by their thoughts, feelings, or intentions. And, in the normal use of language, people say, 'My hair grows' or 'My heart beats' or 'My wounds heal'.

However, from another way of thinking about the meaning of the word I, this can be thought of as a misperception. In this view, I refers to the entire human organism. And, in this sense, I do beat my heart, grow my hair, and heal my wounds. It is in this sense that it is meaningful to say individuals' aims are the adaptive (ultimate) aims of the human organisms that they are. If an analyst is careful to distinguish between the two meanings of I (the experiencing and acting intentional agent vs. the entire organism), then statements about motives that refer to the design and aims of the entire organism can be meaningful.

This leads to markedly different interpretations that do not confuse proximal and distal mechanisms – or the aims of the 'experiencing I' of intention and initiative (whose unconscious motives can become conscious) and the total 'organismic I' that, in addition, pursues genetic self-interest in myriad ways forever unavailable to direct conscious experience (e.g., motives and behavioural tendencies that were ultimately designed to achieve functional aims without conscious or unconscious intentions to achieve those aims). An interpretation[5] of this sort might run along the following lines when dealing with a common problem that many clinicians have faced (again borderline rage):

> Your acting and feeling self is simply trying (intentionally aiming) to protect your existence, which you sense is threatened. Thus, you are motivated by your fear to state the threat and speak out against how I am affecting you, loudly and angrily. The reason for this is that – as an evolved organism functioning to achieve adaptive, healthy (life-preserving and life-enhancing) ends – you were designed to make sure that threats are recognized and the dangers are not ignored by either you or others. Your fury and rage are a legitimate attempt to protect yourself. Others – who, including myself, are also evolved organisms designed to maximize *their* success – do not want to hear about the danger to you if paying attention to it is more costly to them than ignoring it. Thus, they resist hearing the validity of what you are saying, say you are exaggerating, and try to get you to keep quiet.[6]
>
> You do, in fact, experience the threat as being greater than others believe it is. This is due to a bias: you have a natural inclination to make sure that others cannot minimize the problem and ignore it while it is often in their interests to minimize it. Thus, it is unlikely that either party can see the situation as the other sees it and likely that both tend to bias their perception toward their own interests. A significant part of the process that shapes your view of the situation – in a manner that others call *biased* or *distorted* – operates outside of your awareness, is automatic, and is built into mental processes that you have no access to. In fact, in many situations, you would not act effectively to protect your own interests if you believed that what you are reacting to might not be real (cf. Trivers, 1976); your experience of the world is usually exactly the way you say it is. If I (or others) say it is not so or that you are exaggerating, you feel like I (or you) must be crazy for you see (experience) it exactly as you are saying.
>
> Furthermore, when you sense that the threat may be even more danger-ous if it is ignored, an attempt to convince you of the truth of the other's view of reality compels you to yell louder and then you do make what others experience as extreme statements (e.g., 'You hate me and always have', 'I hate you and wish you were dead', etc.). Although such extreme statements may feel necessary to ensure that your safety is not given short shrift, they, in turn, lead people to label you as 'disturbed' or 'sick' and then to use such labels to dismiss your urgent cries as the distorted statements of someone who is 'mentally ill'. This tends to panic you into speaking even louder and making even more extreme statements. A vicious cycle ensues that can get out of hand and has been the source of enormous problems in your life.

In trying to create a psychoanalytic approach free from the confusion between proximal and distal causes, we should also note that Freud did not use a term like 'the ego', which is a hypothetical, metapsychological construct. In German, Freud's term was *das Ich*, meaning 'the I'. As much as Freud was enamoured with the development of metapsychology, he did not initially set out to understand the metapsychological, experience-distant predicament of a reified psychological construct called an ego. He was trying to understand 'the I's' experience of being-in-the-world. It was James Strachey, in his translation of Freud's work into English, who used the terms 'ego' and 'id' and helped make psychoanalysis more experience-distant with a superficially more objective, scientific, and medicalized (Latinized) aura. To the extent that psychoanalysis has always been an attempt to understand the full meaning of 'the I's' experience of being in the world, psychoanalysis has always been a science of proximal mechanisms, their nature, how we experience them in action, and how we establish meaning in regard to them. If we are careful not to confuse ultimate causes with proximal mechanisms, an understanding of the ultimate function can be helpful in working with our patients, i.e., in working with proximal mechanisms.

Although it may seem obvious, it is nonetheless true – and, I believe, it is enormously important in preventing the type of confusion we have been discussing (in psychoanalysis, other evolutionary therapeutic approaches, as well as in evolutionary psychology in general) – that distal causes *do not exist*; only proximal causes exist. That is, the ultimate cause of any existing phenomenon does not exist in the present although, of course, ultimate causes exist today as evolution is ongoing. By definition, distal/ultimate causes existed long before we have an opportunity to work with what they created, the proximally structured human psyche. Thus, if we avoid talking about distal causes as if they exist, and instead use our understanding of them to explain what does exist (proximal mechanisms, structures, and behaviour patterns), we automatically avoid the confusion between distal and proximal causes. As obvious as this may be, even evolutionists, who clearly know the difference between the two concepts, make this error.

Conclusion

As therapists we all try to wean our patients from destructive and self-defeating beliefs. In the course of doing so, we inevitably try, to some degree, to indoctrinate them into our own belief systems. While this may be inevitable, the evolutionary view I have been presenting suggests that – as frequently necessary and helpful as this may be to our patients – it will as frequently be a way for us to make a comfortable living while affirming our own values, views, and self-esteem, at times, to our patients' detriment (Slavin & Kriegman, 1992, 1998; Kriegman, 1996a, 1998a). The evolutionary perspective can help to correct this detrimental bias, a bias found in all psychotherapeutic approaches and one that has plagued psychoanalysis. It suggests that, rather than being simply guided by a technique or psychological theory, the evolutionary psychoanalyst/psychotherapist must struggle – often *against* his or her own natural impulses (Kriegman, 1996a, 1996c, 1998a; Slavin & Kriegman, 1998) – to help patients find, define, uncover, and develop their own unique configurations of interests, abilities, talents, and beliefs: to develop their own unique identity configurations which – while utilizing universal features of the human psyche – also must tap into features of (and ultimately express) the individual's unique combination of genetic make-up and personal experience. This unique, individual aspect cannot be predicted or found in any psychological theory and will often have to be discovered against the resistance of the analyst or therapist.

References

Bailey, K.G. & Wood, H.E. (1998) 'Evolutionary kinship therapy: Basic principles and treatment implications', *British Journal of Medical Psychology* 71: 509–24.

Bailey, K.G., Wood, H.E. & Nava, G.R. (1992) 'What do clients want? Role of psychological kinship in professional helping', *Journal of Psychotherapy Integration* 2: 125–47.

Bornstein, R.F. & Masling, J.M. (1994) 'From the consulting room to the laboratory: Clinical evidence, empirical evidence, and the heuristic value of object relations theory', in J.M. Masling & R.F. Bornstein (eds), *Empirical Studies of Psychoanalytic Theories*, Vol. 5. *Empirical Perspectives on Object Relations Theory*, (pp. xv–xxvi), Washington, DC: American Psychological Association.

Brandchaft, B. (1983) 'The negativism of the negative therapeutic reaction and the psychology of the self', in A. Goldberg (ed), *The Future of Psychoanalysis*, (pp. 327–51), Madison, CT: International Universities Press.

Breggin, P.R. (1991) *Toxic Psychiatry*, New York: St. Martin's Press.

Breggin, P.R. & Breggin, G.R. (1994) *Talking Back to Prozac*, New York: St. Martin's Press.

Buss, D.M. (1992) 'Mate preference mechanisms: Consequences for partner choice and intrasexual competition', in J.H. Barkow, L. Cosmides & J. Tooby (eds), *The Adapted Mind*, (pp. 249–66), New York: Oxford University Press.

Buss, D.M. (1995) 'Psychological sex differences: Origins through natural selection', *American Psychologist* 50: 164–8.

Daly, M. & Wilson, M. (1990) 'Is parent-offspring conflict sex linked? Freudian and Darwinian models', *Journal of Personality* 58(1): 163–87.

Elder, G.H. (1969) 'Appearance and education in marriage mobility', *American Sociological Review* 34: 519–33.

Eysenck, H.J. (1972) 'The experimental study of Freudian concepts', *Bulletin of the British Psychological Society* 25: 261–74.

Fisher, H.E. (1992) *Anatomy of Love: The Natural History of Monogamy, Adultery, and Divorce*, New York: Norton.

Freud, S. (1905) 'Fragment of an analysis of a case of hysteria', *Standard Edition* 7: 3–124.

Freud, S. (1914) 'On narcissism: an introduction', *Standard Edition* 14: 67–102.

Freud, S. (1915a) 'Instincts and their vicissitudes', *Standard Edition* 14: 117–40.

Freud, S. (1915b) 'Thoughts for the times on war and death', *Standard Edition* 14: 273–302.

Freud, S. (1917) 'A difficulty in the path of psycho-analysis', *Standard Edition* 17: 136–44.

Freud, S. (1920) 'Beyond the pleasure principle', *Standard Edition* 19: 3–64.

Freud, S. (1921) 'Group psychology and the analysis of the ego'. *Standard Edition* 18: 65–143.

Freud, S. (1923) 'The ego and the id', *Standard Edition* 19: 1–66.

Freud, S. (1924) 'The economic problem of masochism', *Standard Edition* 19: 155–70.

Freud, S. (1930) 'Civilization and its discontents', *Standard Edition* 21: 59–145.

Freud, S. (1933) 'New introductory lectures on psycho-analysis', *Standard Edition* 22: 1–182.

Freud, S. (1937) 'Analysis terminable and interminable', *Standard Edition* 23: 216–54.

Glantz, K. & Pearce, J. (1989) *Exiles from Eden*, New York: W.W. Norton.

Glover, E. (1955) *The Technique of Psychoanalysis*, Madison, CT: International Universities Press.

Glover, E. (1956) *On the Early Development of Mind*, Madison, CT: International Universities Press.

Greenberg, J. & Mitchell, S. (1983) *Object Relations and Psychoanalytic Theory*, Cambridge: Harvard University Press.

Havens, L.L. (1973) 'The place of confrontation in modern psychotherapy', in G. Adler & P.G. Myerson (eds), *Confrontation in Psychotherapy*, (pp. 225–48), Northvale, NJ: Jason Aronson.

Herman, H. (1993) 'Question: How often do men think about sex?', *Ladies Home Journal*, March: 96–9.

Holt, R.R. (1989) *Freud Reappraised*, New York: Guilford Press.

Jaspers, K. (1900) *General Psychopathology*, Chicago: University of Chicago Press, Reprinted 1963.

Klein, M. (1946) 'Notes on some schizoid mechanisms', in *Envy and Gratitude and Other Works*. New York: Delacorte Press, Reprinted 1975.

Kohut, H. (1971) *The Analysis of the Self*, Madison, CT: International Universities Press.

Kohut, H. (1977) *The Restoration of the Self*, Madison, CT: International Universities Press.

Kohut, H. (1984) *How does Analysis Cure?* Chicago: University of Chicago Press.

Kriegman, D. (1988) 'Self psychology from the perspective of evolutionary biology: Toward a biological foundation for self psychology', in A. Goldberg (ed), *Progress in Self Psychology*, (Vol. 3), (pp. 253–274), Hillsdale, NJ: The Analytic Press.

Kriegman, D. (1990) 'Compassion and altruism in psychoanalytic theory: An evolutionary analysis of self psychology', *Journal of the American Academy of Psychoanalysis* 18(2): 342–67.

Kriegman, D. (1996a) 'On the existential/subjectivism-scientific/objectivism dialectic in self psychology: A view from evolutionary biology', in A. Goldberg (ed), *Progress in Self Psychology*, (Vol. 12), (pp. 85–119), Hillsdale, NJ: Analytic Press.

Kriegman, D. (1996b) 'The effectiveness of medication: *The Consumer Reports* study', *American Psychologist* 51(10): 881.

Kriegman, D. (1996c) 'Using an experience-near understanding of inherent conflict in the relational world in the treatment of a "psychotic" patient', Paper presented at the 19th Annual Conference on the Psychology of the Self, Washington, D.C., October.

Kriegman, D. (1998a) 'Interpretation, the unconscious, and psychoanalytic authority: Toward an evolutionary, biological integration of the empirical/scientific method with the field-defining, empathic stance', in R.F. Bornstein & J.M. Masling (eds), *Empirical*

Perspectives on the Psychoanalytic Unconscious, (pp. 187–272), Washington, DC: American Psychological Association.

Kriegman, D. (1998b) 'Evolutionary psychoanalysis: An advance in understanding the human psyche or a phylogenetic fantasy', *Contemporary Psychology*, 43(2): 138–9.

Kriegman, D. & Knight, C. (1988) 'Social evolution, psychoanalysis, and human nature', *Social Policy* 19(2): 49–55.

Kriegman, D. & Kriegman, O. (1997) 'War and the evolution of the human propensity to form nations, cults, and religions', Paper presented at the Annual Human Behavior and Evolution Society Conference, Tucson, AZ, June.

Kriegman, D. & Slavin, M.O. (1989) 'The myth of the repetition compulsion and the negative therapeutic reaction: An evolutionary biological analysis', in A. Goldberg (ed), *Progress in Self Psychology*, (Vol. 5), (pp. 209–53), Hillsdale, NJ: Analytic Press.

Kriegman, D. & Slavin, M.O. (1990) 'On the resistance to self psychology: Clues from evolutionary biology', in A. Goldberg (ed), *Progress in Self Psychology*, (Vol. 6), (pp. 217–50), Hillsdale, NJ: Analytic Press.

Kriegman, D. & Solomon, L. (1985a) 'Cult groups and the narcissistic personality: The offer to heal defects in the self', *International Journal of Group Psychotherapy* 35(2): 239–61.

Kriegman, D. & Solomon, L. (1985b) 'Psychotherapy and the "new religions": Are they the same?', *Cultic Studies Journal* 2(1): 2–16.

Langs, R. (1996) *The Evolution of the Emotion-Processing Mind: With an Introduction to Mental Darwinism*, Madison, CT: International Universities Press.

Masson, J.M. (1990) *Final Analysis: The Making and Unmaking of a Psychoanalyst*, Reading, MA: Addison-Wesley.

Myerson, P.G. (1973) 'The meanings of confrontation', in G. Adler & P.G. Myerson (eds), *Confrontation in Psychotherapy*, (pp. 21–38), Northvale, NJ: Jason Aronson.

Nesse, R.M. (1990) 'The evolutionary functions of repression and the ego defenses', *Journal of the American Academy of Psychoanalysis* 18(2): 260–85.

Popper, K.R. (1963) *Conjectures and Refutations: The Growth of Scientific Knowledge*, New York: Harper & Row.

Ridley, M. (1993) *The Red Queen: Sex and the Evolution of Human Nature*. New York: Macmillan.

Segal, H. (1964) *Introduction to the Work of Melanie Klein*, New York: Basic Books.

Slavin, M.O. & Kriegman, D. (1992) *The Adaptive Design of the Human Psyche: Psychoanalysis, Evolutionary Biology, and the Therapeutic Process*, New York: Guilford Press.

Slavin, M.O. & Kriegman, D. (1998) 'Why the analyst needs to change: Toward a theory of conflict, negotiation, and mutual influence in the therapeutic process', *Psychoanalytic Dialogues* 8(2): 247–84.

Stolorow, R., Brandchaft, B. & Atwood, G. (1987) *Psychoanalytic Treatment: An Intersubjective Approach*, Hillsdale, NJ: Analytic Press.

Torrey, F.F. (1992) *Freudian Fraud: The Malignant Effect of Freud's Theory on American Thought and Culture*, New York: Harper Collins.

Trivers, R.L. (1971) 'The evolution of reciprocal altruism', *Quarterly Review of Biology* 46: 35–57.

Trivers, R.L. (1972) 'Parental investment and sexual selection', in B. Campbell (ed), *Sexual Selection and the Descent of Man, 1871–1971*, (pp. 136–79), Chicago: Aldine-Atherton.

Trivers, R. (1974) 'Parent-offspring conflict', *American Zoologist* 14: 249–64.

Trivers, R.L. (1976) Foreword to *The Selfish Gene* by Richard Dawkins. New York: Oxford University Press.

Wright, R. (1994). 'Our cheating hearts', *Time* August 15: 45–52.

Notes

1. An early version of this paper was originally presented at the Human Behavior and Evolution Society conference at Binghamton, NY on 7 August 1993 in the symposium entitled 'Relevance of evolutionary biology to psychotherapy' organized by Leon Sloman.

2. There have been attempts to correct psychoanalytic misconceptions utilizing evolutionary biology, but most such attempts have been by evolutionary psychologists who do not utilize a psychoanalytic approach (e.g., Glantz & Pearce, 1989) or by psychoanalysts who have not developed a clear understanding of modern evolutionary biology (Langs, 1996; cf. Kriegman, 1998b).

3. In another situation, the same woman may indeed have sexual wishes of the type described by classical analytic theory. The point is that the experience created in an observer is an unreliable indicator of the individual's motivations. Is she acting on a conscious or unconscious desire? Or is he projecting his desire? Or is it a mixture of the two? Unlike theories of projective identification and others that recommend the use of countertransference to identify a patient's unconscious (or unstated) motivation, in this view, feelings aroused in the therapist are far more likely to be accurate clues to the therapist's psychic life and, at best, highly biased indicators of the patient's experience and motives. Although feelings in the therapist may indicate what is going on in the patient, they may not. This is why sustained empathic inquiry is necessary: through such a process the analyst's conjectures can be empirically tested against the patient's communicated experience. Again, it is the patient's psyche, the patient's experiential world that must be the ultimate arbiter of the truth, relevance, and value of an interpretation or insight (Kriegman, 1998a).

4. What is being described here includes the phenomenon that has been referred to as narcissistic rage by the self psychologists. However, in contrast to how they understand such anger and aggression – as merely a breakdown product when the self is enfeebled, threatened, or depleted – evolutionary theory also provides a corrective to self psychology's bias. It is fairly clear that angry expressions can have adaptive, functional utility. Therefore, evolutionary theory suggests that such a ubiquitous feature of human interactions is unlikely to be only a reaction of a fragmented self: a fully functional self should be able to utilize anger (even fairly intense anger and destructiveness) when it is adaptive (Kriegman & Slavin, 1990). Thus evolutionary theory provides a corrective to both the extreme relational views focused on interpersonal conflict and destructiveness (e.g., the Kleinian view) as well as to views biased towards harmony and mutuality (e.g., the self psychological view).

5. I am not suggesting the following as a literal interpretation that one might actually say to a patient. Nor am I even suggesting that the content (e.g., the statements about 'evolved organisms') should be said in any direct form; many patients may experience explicitly evolutionary explanations as if an attempt is being made to indoctrinate them into the therapist's religion/belief system. Rather, I am suggesting that the essential, interpersonal, and intrapsychic meaning of the following may be a crucial 'interpretation' in the treatment of a particular patient.

6. The extremes that attempts to keep patients quiet can reach can be seen in the treatment of psychotic patients whose chaotic complaints and outcries (symptoms) are used by others as reasons to take extreme measures to 'shut them down'. Such measures include

drugs, electroconvulsive therapy, and lobotomy. It is unclear to what extent the increasingly common use of drugs for virtually all patients is operating in the self-interest of others besides the patient (Kriegman, 1996b), with evidence of such self-interest being actively suppressed (see Breggin, 1991; Breggin & Breggin, 1994). With healthier patients who can accommodate themselves to others' agendas without psychotic fragmentation, attempts to quiet their complaints can be pursued by becoming more forceful and insistent that the patient accept the analyst's interpretation (Kriegman, 1998a).

7. Portions of this article are based on material that appeared in *Empirical Perspectives on the Psychoanalytic Unconscious*, edited by R.F. Bornstein and J.M. Masling, 1998, Washington, DC: American Psychological Association. Copyright 1998 by the American Psychological Association, Inc. Adapted with permission.

5

JUNGIAN ANALYSIS AND EVOLUTIONARY PSYCHOTHERAPY

An integrative approach

Anthony Stevens

A central concern for all schools of psychotherapy is the question of what has gone wrong for the patient in the first place. The major schools have produced different answers to the same question and different solutions as to how the problem may be resolved. To the classical Freudian the problem is the repressed urges and memories of childhood which need to be made conscious (Freud, 1939); to the object relations theorist it is the formation of a 'false self' at the expense of the 'real self' which the analytic relationship must undo and correct (Gomez, 1997; Greenberg & Mitchell, 1983; Winnicott, 1965); to the attachment theorist it is the pathological development of an internal working model of the self as incapable of receiving and giving love that needs to be readjusted (Bowlby, 1988); to the Jungian it is the frustrated archetypal intent that needs to be liberated so that the patient can achieve his or her full potential (Jung, 1954; Stevens, 1982); to the microbiological psychiatrist it is the absence or excessive presence of some biochemical substance that needs correction (Lader & Herrington, 1990); while to the clinical psychiatrist it is the presence of some pathological process or disease that needs to be diagnosed and treated with medication or electro-convulsive therapy (Grahame-Smith & Aronson, 1992). What the evolutionary perspective can add to these aetiological and therapeutic ideas is a new synthesis capable of integrating as well as transcending them.

Evolutionary psychology offers a new scientific paradigm within which funda-mental questions about human nature can be formulated and answered. It is capable of bringing together the disparate findings of ethology, sociology, psychology, and cross-cultural anthropology within one theoretical perspective – the Darwinian perspective, which promises to become the central conceptual standpoint uniting the behavioural sciences (Wright, 1994). Acceptance of the evolutionary origins of the human mind has now moved so far that it is unlikely that any psychological explanation will prosper if it is incompatible with the Darwinian evolutionary consensus. By allowing us to see beyond the old medical and psychoanalytic models, this wider vision is likely to impact significantly on psychiatric and psychotherapeutic research and practice in the coming years. It could succeed in reconciling the differences between 'biological', 'clinical', and 'social' psychiatry and thus render obsolete the doctrinal squabbles and internecine battles between the classical schools of analysis.

New insights into old mechanisms

By transcending old differences, it does not follow that the knowledge gained during the past century of psychiatric and analytic practice must be lost or negated; rather this information will be absorbed within a more inclusive corpus of scientific understanding. In this chapter, I examine the relevance of this understanding for the integration of Jungian and evolutionary approaches. Already, evolutionary psychotherapy has greatly extended the heuristic and empirical implications of Jung's theory of archetypes. Jung conceived archetypes to be innate structures which unconsciously programme individual members of the species to perceive, respond, and behave in characteristic ways that are adapted to the circumstances prevailing at the time. For its part, evolutionary psychology conceives of entities comparable to archetypes, which it designates 'innate strategies' or 'algorithms', holding them responsible for processing emotional and non-verbal information at a largely unconscious level of experience in accordance with certain specific 'biosocial goals'.

As Gilbert (1989, 1995, 1997) makes clear, there is general agreement that, as a species, we characteristically recognize and invest our resources in our own off-spring; we endeavour to select 'good quality' mates; we recognize and relate to people who are likely to co-operate rather than exploit us; and, when it comes to conflict, we tend to challenge only those whom we stand a fair chance of defeating (see also Buss, 1991, 1995). These characteristics have been listed as such biosocial goals as care-eliciting and care-giving (attachment behaviour), mate-selection (sexual attraction, courtship, conception and mate-retention), alliance formation (co-operation, affiliation, aggression inhibition, friendship, kinship, and reciprocal behaviour) and ranking behaviour (competition for resources, dominance and submissive behaviour, and gaining and maintaining status or rank) (Gilbert, 1995, 1997).

What is particularly interesting is the fact that each of the biosocial goals detected by evolutionary psychologists has historically provided the primary area of concern for the major schools of analysis, namely, care-eliciting, care-giving, and alliance formation (Klein, 1932; Winnicott, 1965; Bowlby, 1969), mate selection and sex (Freud, 1910), and rank behaviour (Adler, 1927), while the whole concept of goal-directed behaviour subserved by the archetypal components of the Self is the key concept of analytical psychology (Jung, 1933). With the unifying perspective that evolutionary psychology offers, the empirical study of the basic programmes running in the unconscious at last becomes a scientific possibility.

Jung, Freud and biology

Jung's ideas about psychopathology and the adaptive nature of psychiatric symptoms, like his theory of archetypes making up the 'collective unconscious' of a phylogenetically endowed psyche, find close parallels in the ideas current in evolutionary psychiatry. Jung was one of the very few psychologists in the twentieth century to reject the *tabula rasa* theory of human psychological development and to replace it with a psychological theory that accepted the profound influence of evolutionary factors on personal development. Jung's (1954) view of dreams as being transparent statements of normal psychic functioning (rather than disguises of repressed wishes as Freud conceived them) have been confirmed by dream researchers of the stature of Hobson (1988). And his insistence on the crucial therapeutic contribution made by establishing a warm, accepting, and reciprocal alliance between analyst and patient (as opposed to Freud's advocacy of a 'surgical' approach to patients characterized by cold objectivity and personal reticence) has been supported by many studies of successful outcome in the practice of psycho-therapy (Aveline & Shapiro,1995; Bergin & Garfield, 1994; Miller, Luborsky, Barber & Docherty, 1993; Roth & Fonagy, 1996).

The major cause of disagreement between Freud and Jung concerned their understanding of the extent to which evolved structures and functions could be held to operate in human psychology. Jung believed that our phylogenetic endowment was much richer and more complex than Freud maintained, holding that the human mind/brain contains within itself much of its own programme for development. It is this position, proposed almost a century before its time, that has been greatly extended by evolutionary psychology.

Whereas Freud insisted that the unconscious mind was entirely personal and peculiar to the individual and made up of repressed wishes and traumatic memories, Jung held that there existed in addition a phylogenetic layer (the 'collective unconscious'), which incorporated the entire psychic potential of humankind. Support for this notion came from Jung's studies of the delusions and hallucina-tions of schizophrenic patients, which contained symbols and images that also occurred in myths, religions, and fairy tales from all over the world (Jung, 1956). He concluded that there exists a dynamic psychic substratum, common to all humanity, on the basis of which each individual builds his or her own experience of life.

Both Freud and Jung shared the highest regard for Charles Darwin and believed that their psychological theories were compatible with Darwinism. Unfortunately, in both cases, theirs was a shaky form of Darwinism, heavily inflected by the ideas of Jean Baptiste Lamarck (that characteristics acquired by one generation could be genetically transmitted to the next) and of Ernst Haeckel (that ontogeny repeats phylogeny). Acceptance of Jung's theory of archetypes, however, like acceptance of 'innate strategies' and 'algorithms', does not require the adoption of a Lamarckian or Haeckelian stance: archetypes can be conceived of as innate neuropsychic structures which evolved by natural selection to accomplish certain specific goals (e.g., to form attachments, seek sexual partners, and form alliances within small groups), and this is compatible with the position that Jung adopted from 1946 onwards (Jung, 1946/1960b).

Due in part to his introverted concern with subjective experience, Jung's approach to psychology has continued to be discounted as 'less scientific' than Freud's. This is doubly unfair: not only have Freud's scientific credentials been seriously impugned (Esterson, 1993; Webster, 1997; Macmillan, 1997; Wilcocks, 1994) but Jung is seldom given recognition for his attempt to ground his own concepts in biology. His model of the psyche is imbued with biological assumptions. Not only did he consider the archetypal structure of the collective unconscious to have an evolutionary origin, but he maintained that the psyche functioned in accordance with the biological principles of adaptation, homeostasis, and epigenesis (Stevens, 1982, 1999).

Where Jung continues to leave many people unconvinced and bewildered, however, is when he goes beyond science to eschew the laws of cause and effect, to embrace a universe in which 'synchronistic' events can transcend the barriers of space and time, as in the phenomena of telepathy, clairvoyance, extrasensory perception, reincarnation, spiritualism, and communication with the dead (Jung, 1960a; 1963). For one of his background and upbringing it is not surprising that he should always have been interested in such phenomena and more than half-inclined to believe in their actuality. The fact that current scientific laws could not account for them was no reason, in his view, for not giving them due consideration or for declining to propose possible hypotheses to account for them. However, one does not have to be convinced by Jung's more esoteric theorizing in order to appreciate the enormous significance of his contribution to our understanding of human nature and to the practice of psychotherapy.

Archetypes of the collective unconscious

Of all Jung's ideas, none has proved more controversial than his theory of a collective unconscious. Yet it is a hypothesis which has been rediscovered and reproposed by specialists in a number of different disciplines (Stevens, 1999). What did Jung mean by it, and how might we understand it today? 'I have chosen the term "collective"', he wrote, 'because this part of the unconscious is not individual but universal; in contrast to the personal psyche, it has contents and modes of behaviour that are more or less the same everywhere and in all individuals' (Jung, 1959a: 3–4).

Jung related this 'common psychic substrate of a suprapersonal nature' to the structure of the brain: 'Every man is born with a brain that is profoundly differentiated, and this makes him capable of very various mental functions, which are neither ontogenetically developed or acquired. . . . This particular circumstance explains, for example, the remarkable analogies presented by the unconscious in the most remotely separated races and peoples' (Jung, 1953: 269–70). It is apparent, he says, in the extraordinary correspondence which exists between the myths, folk tales, religious beliefs and rituals that occur throughout the world. 'The universal similarity of human brains leads us then to admit the existence of a certain psychic function, identical with itself in all individuals; we call it the collective psyche' (Jung, 1953: 270).

This is such a reasonable position to adopt that it is a puzzle to understand why Jung's proposal encountered as much opposition as it did. A major difficulty is the same as the one that has assailed evolutionary psychology, namely, that it subverted the prevailing academic consensus (what has been called the Standard Social Science Model, or SSSM), which eschewed biological thinking altogether and was deeply hostile to the idea that innate structures could have any part to play in human psychology or human social behaviour. In many quarters the SSSM still prevails, although there are signs that its global influence is beginning to wane (see Cosmides & Tooby, 1992, for a discussion of the differences between the SSSM and evolutionary psychology).

Although he remained all his life primarily interested in the psychic aspects of archetypes, Jung nevertheless understood that a strictly scientific approach would make more headway if it concentrated on their behavioural manifestations. As he himself insisted, the archetype 'is not meant to denote an inherited idea, but rather an inherited mode of functioning, corresponding to the inborn way in which the chick emerges from the egg, the bird builds its nest, a certain kind of wasp stings the motor ganglion of the caterpillar, and eels find their way to the Bermudas. In other words, it is a "pattern of behaviour". *This aspect of the archetype, the purely biological one, is the proper concern of scientific psychology*' (Jung, 1977b: 518; italics added). For Jung, archetypes and instincts were inextricably linked, the archetype providing information concerning the meaningful nature of the typical stimulus characteristics by which instinctive energies were activated and towards which they were directed.

Repeatedly, Jung stressed that the archetype was not an arid, intellectual concept but a living, empirical entity, charged not only with meaningfulness but also with feeling. 'It would be an unpardonable sin of omission,' he wrote, 'were we to over-look the *feeling-value* (Jung's italics) of the archetype. This is extremely important both theoretically and therapeutically' (1960b: 209). Psychology, he maintained, is the only science that has to take 'feeling-value' into account, for feeling 'forms the link between psychic events on the one hand, and meaning and life on the other' (Jung, 1977a: 260). In other words, the archetype is 'a piece of life', 'a living system of reactions and aptitudes' (1960b: 157) and it is connected with the living individual by the bridge of emotion' (Jung, 1977a: 257).

In *Archetype: A Natural History of the Self* (Stevens, 1982), I drew attention to the many striking parallels that exist between the concepts of analytical psychology and those of ethology (the branch of behavioural science that studies animals in their natural habitats) and argued that both disciplines were studying the same archetypal phenomena, but from opposite ends. Jungian psychology focused on their introverted psychic manifestations while ethology examined their extraverted behavioural expression. I attempted to demonstrate how these two approaches complemented one another in such fundamental areas as bonding between parents and children, sex and gender differences, courtship and mating, co-operation and hostility between individuals and groups, and the development of the individual through the course of the human life-cycle. I suggested a fruitful interaction between the two disciplines would become more feasible if Jung's terminology were modified: I proposed the term phylogenetic psyche to replace 'collective unconscious' and innate neuropsychic units or potentials to replace 'archetypes'. I went on to argue that if Jungians wished to place analytical psychology on a sound epistemological basis they would do well to draw closer to the ethologists and become aware of the discoveries that were being made not only in the observation of animal behaviour but in the cross-cultural studies of human communities throughout the world (Eibl-Eibesfeldt, 1971). Unfortunately, the majority of Jungians remained indifferent to the epistemological contribution that evolutionary biology could make to analytical psychology, but there are signs that this may be beginning to change (for example, see McDowell, 1999).

Since then, evolutionary psychologists and psychiatrists on both sides of the Atlantic have detected and announced the presence of neuropsychic propensities which are virtually indistinguishable from archetypes. Gilbert (1995), refers to them as 'mentalities', Gardner (1988) as 'master programmes' or 'propensity states', while Wenegrat (1984) borrows the sociobiological term 'genetically transmitted response strategies'. Buss (1995) refers to 'evolved psychological mechanisms', Nesse (1987) to 'prepared tendencies', and Cosmides and Tooby (1989) to 'multiple mental modules'. These response patterns, master programmes, propensity states, response strategies, evolved psychological mechanisms, prepared tendencies, and multiple mental modules are held responsible for crucial, species-specific patterns of behaviour that evolved because they maximized the fitness of the organism to survive and increase the chances of genetic representation in the next generation (technically referred to as inclusive fitness). These strategies are inherently shared by all members of the species, whether they be healthy or ill. As Jung put it, 'the collective unconscious contains the whole spiritual heritage of mankind's evolution, born anew in the brain structure of every individual' (Jung, 1960b: 158). 'Ultimately, every individual life is at the same time the eternal life of the species' (Jung, 1958a: 89).

The reaffirmation of Jung's original insights by contemporary evolutionary psychologists is of great significance for all psychotherapeutic disciplines: a theoretical basis begins to emerge for a science of human development and for a systematic approach to human psychology. Psychopathology can then be understood to occur when 'archetypal' strategies malfunction as a result of environmental insults or deficiencies at critical stages of development. A sound theoretical basis in terms of which hypotheses can be formulated will enable these insults and deficiencies to be empirically investigated and defined. Although Jung is seldom mentioned by evolutionary psychologists, his primacy in introducing the archetypal hypothesis into psychology must be acknowledged: it is one of the truly seminal ideas of the twentieth century.

Jung and evolutionary psychology

Critics of Jung's evolutionary thinking (e.g., Noll, 1994, 1997; McLynn, 1996) have made a great deal of the fact that he was influenced by Ernst Haeckel (1834–1919). Where both Haeckel and Jung adopted a stance at variance with contemporary biology was in the emphasis they placed on Haeckel's 'biogenic law' – the idea that the development of the individual (ontogeny) recapitulates the evolutionary history of the species (phylogeny). That Haeckel's biogenic law does not hold in a number of instances does not invalidate the view that anatomy and psychology share a common basis in evolutionary biology. Nor does the fact that Jung's ideas about psychological development throughout the human life cycle were influenced by Haeckel invalidate Jung's hypothesis of a collective unconscious subject to the laws of Darwinian biology.

What becomes fixed in the genetic structure is the predisposition to the kinds of experience that Jung described as archetypal, not the experiences themselves. Jung eventually acquitted himself of the charge of Lamarckism when he announced, in 1946, a clear theoretical distinction between the deeply unconscious and therefore unknowable archetype-as-such (similar to Kant's *das Ding-an-sich*) and the archetypal images, ideas and behaviours that the archetype-as-such produces (Jung, 1946/1960b: 213). Jung specifically distanced himself from the position which critics have accused him of adopting: 'Again and again', he wrote, 'I encounter the mistaken notion that an archetype is determined in regard to its content, in other words that it is a kind of unconscious idea (if such an expression be permissible). It is necessary to point out once more that archetypes are not determined as to their content, but only as regards their form, and then only to a very limited degree. A primordial image is determined as to its content only when it has become conscious and is therefore filled out with the material of conscious experience' (Jung, 1959b: 79).

Archetypes and complexes

Jung introduced the term complex into psychology as a result of his research using the word-association test while he worked at the Burgholzli Hospital in Zurich in the early 1900s. In this test, originally devised by Francis Galton (1822–1911), a series of words is read out to the subject who is asked to respond to each stimulus word with the first word that comes into his head. Galton found that the responses were automatic expressions of thoughts, feelings, and memories which the subject associated with the stimulus word. Repeating Galton's experiments, Jung realized that these thoughts, feelings, and memories group themselves into dynamic clusters or 'feeling-toned complexes'. He compared these to the 'fragmented' or 'split off personalities' which Pierre Janet (1859–1947), under whom he studied in Paris in the winter of 1902–03, had demonstrated in hypnotized subjects and in patients exhibiting the interesting clinical condition of multiple personality, where two or more apparently separate personalities are revealed in the same person.

Janet linked these 'simultaneous psychological existences' with what he called 'subconscious fixed ideas'. In Jung's view, these were identical with the complexes that he had revealed with his word-association experiments. Eventually, he came to the conclusion that whereas the collective unconscious is made up of archetypes, the personal unconscious is composed of complexes which function as sub-personalities and which 'personate' in dreams and fantasies. Jung recalled that Janet had demonstrated that each fragment of personality had its own peculiar character, its own separate memory, and possessed a high degree of autonomy. Reviewing the complex theory in 1934, Jung commented: 'everyone knows nowadays that people "have complexes". What is not so well known, though far more important theoretically, is that complexes can *have us*' (Jung, 1960b: 96; Jung's italics).

The autonomous power of complexes and their capacity to influence consciousness without our being aware of them is something that Jung drew attention to again and again: 'an active complex puts us momentarily under a state of duress, of compulsive thinking and acting, for which under certain conditions the only appropriate term would be the judicial concept of diminished responsibility. . . . They are the actors in our dreams . . . and the deeper one penetrates into their nature – I might almost say into their biology – the more clearly do they reveal their character as splinter psyches. Dream psychology shows us as plainly as could be wished how complexes appear in personified form when there is no inhibiting consciousness to suppress them, exactly like the hobgoblins of folklore who go crashing about the house at night. We observe the same phenomenon in certain psychoses when the complexes get "loud" and appear as "voices" having a thoroughly personal character' (Jung, 1960b: 96–98).

Complexes are not essentially pathological as is often erroneously supposed. They are as much part of the healthy psyche as they are of the neurotic or psychotic psyche. They are, as Jung makes clear in the above passage, functional units of which the personal psyche is composed. In other words, complexes are archetypes actualized in the mind as well as in behaviour.

How does this process of actualization occur? Jung believed that complex formation proceeded in accordance with two laws of association worked out by academic psychologists at the end of the last century: the law of similarity and the law of contiguity. Normal complexes are formed when both these laws are satisfied. By way of illustration, let us take an archetype which is of great significance during the early years of life: the mother archetype. Jung's interpretation of the Oedipus complex and the incest taboo was quite different from Freud's. In Jung's view (Jung, 1959b, originally published in 1911), a child became attached to his or her mother not because she was the object of incestuous passion, as Freud maintained, but because, like the 'great mother' archetype, she was the provider of love and care – a view which anticipated the theoretical revolution wrought some forty years later by John Bowlby (1969). As Bowlby and his colleagues demonstrated, the neurophysiological structures concerned with the perception and experience of mothering activities, as well as the behavioural repertoire necessary to relate to the figure providing them (usually the mother), gradually mature under the organizing influence of innate 'behavioural systems' (the mother archetype) functioning within the child. Jung proposed that the mother archetype is the vital nucleus of the individual's growing mother complex: originally the archetype-as-such is unconscious; then, as the child matures in close proximity to the mother, so all those behaviours, feelings, and perceptions determined by the mother archetype are activated with the consequent development of the mother complex within the child's psyche and the associated co-ordination of the mother–infant behavioural chain in outer reality.

Thus, a normal mother complex develops when the personal mother is perceived by the child as possessing maternal qualities similar to the anticipations built into the maternal archetype and when she is continuously present, or contiguous throughout the formative years of childhood.

On the other hand, a pathological mother complex would be formed if either of these laws is inadequately satisfied: for example, if the mother's repertoire of maternal behaviours is defective in some important way, or if there should be lengthy periods of mother–child separation. Complexes are thus the bridge between the personal (ontogenetic) psyche and the collective (phylogenetic) psyche: they are the ontogenetic 'flesh' covering the phylogenetic 'skeleton' provided by the archetypes.

An example of an archetype entering the personal psyche as a complex is provided by the evolutionary interpretation of phobic anxiety disorders. To be seized by an attack of phobic anxiety is to experience the power of an autonomous complex operating at an ancient and unconscious level of the brain. Anxiety and fear are adaptive responses to the kinds of dangers humans have been exposed to in the course of their evolution. This is why we fear ancient dangers such as snakes, spiders, high or open places, and not modern dangers such as cars, cigarettes, whisky, and saturated fats, which kill off our contemporaries in infinitely greater numbers (Nesse, 1987; Rachman, 1978; Stevens & Price, 2000). Jung understood this very well and anticipated the evolutionary position by many decades. In a paper, originally published in 1927, he wrote: 'dangerous situations, be they dangers to the body or the soul, arouse affect-laden fantasies, and insofar as such situations typically repeat themselves, they give rise [i.e., through evolution] to archetypes' (Jung, 1960b: 155).

If you suffer from a spider phobia, you may realize how absurdly irrational it is to be terrified of a little spider in the bath, but your higher, recently evolved cerebral capacities are incapable of doing anything to control it. You have to withdraw and leave somebody else to deal with the spider. This is the usual way of coping with a phobia: one does everything possible to avoid proximity to the source of the fear. Being quite unable to control it, one has no option but keep away from everything associated with it. This is the biological 'purpose' of the fear concerned. It is 'designed' to keep one out of harm's way.

In instances such as this, the explanations of Jungian psychology and evolutionary psychiatry overlap and afford a further aspect of Jung's thinking that has well tolerated the passage of time. Reviewing developments in the application of evolutionary concepts to psychiatry, Gilbert (1989) declared that 'the emerging paradigm is that the human mind is a fragmented organization of mixed special purpose processing capabilities, intelligences, talents and so on'. These, he described as relatively 'encapsulated' from one another and 'shaped by experience into emotional schemata and cognitive schemata'. Gilbert commented that 'the greater the degree of aroused affect, the more difficulty there is in using logical reasoning' (1989: 312–13).

'The emerging paradigm', therefore, is Jung's paradigm: Gilbert's 'mixed special purpose processing capabilities' are Jung's complexes and Janet's *idées fixes subconscientes*, which personate in dreams and manifest in phobic symptoms. That reason should be rendered defective by aroused 'emotional schemata' reminds one of Jung's quip that we don't have complexes but complexes have us. The growing accord that the mind-brain is composed of special-purpose units, which Ornstein (1986) calls 'small minds', Fodor (1985) 'modules', Gardner (1985) 'special intelligences', and Gilbert (1995) 'mentalities', affirms Jung's concept of complexes developed through experience on the basis of an archetypal core. The manner in which 'sub-personalities' (Rowan, 1990) are formed out of 'mentalities', and the implications that these forms carry for psychopathology and psychotherapy, are examined by Gilbert, Chapter 6, this volume.

Archetypes, complexes and treatment

The term originally coined by Jung to designate his own theoretical approach was 'complex psychology'. In so far as maternal behaviour may be conducive to later development of psychopathology, the critical factor in the Jungian view is not so much the actual mother's conduct but the mother complex which is formed within the individual's psyche. This complex is no inner reproduction or 'video-recording' of the personal mother-out-there, but a product of her interaction with specific phylogenetic components in the child's maturing psyche. This fact, with all its implications, has to be grasped if success is to be achieved in the psychotherapy of people with dysfunctional parental complexes. For those archetypal components that the personal parents succeed in actualizing in their child may not be as crucial for his individual destiny as those that they fail to actualize. This is a further highly significant contribution that Jungian psychology has to make to the practice of evolutionary psychotherapy.

Theoretically, every archetype possesses a totality: individual parents, however, being human and not gods, are by their very nature imperfect and incomplete; consequently, they can never hope to embody in their own lives all the attributes of a parental archetype. All that any parent can realistically aim to be is 'good enough', to use Winnicott's (1965) phrase, to provide the key that opens the archetypal lock. The parental archetype so released profoundly influences the child's expectations.

Repeatedly, it is found in practice that whatever archetypal characteristics parents may have failed to activate, nevertheless persist as potentials in the child's unconscious psyche and they continue to seek actualization in reality. Indeed, it is this need to actualize unlived potential that brings patients to therapy in the first place. The extent of this unactualized potential is inversely proportional to the parents' effectiveness: the less competent and less available they are, the greater the archetypal potential seeking fulfilment and the greater the 'parental hunger' manifested by the child (hence, for example, the 'clinging' children one encounters in institutions).

This Jungian conception of innate archetypal potential available to be activated to a greater or lesser extent by appropriate figures in the environment is a major theoretical advance beyond object relations and attachment theories. Not only does it provide a unitary explanation of both outer behaviour and inner experience but it also accounts for some of the commonest and most impressive findings in clinical practice.

An example may help to illustrate this: a woman came to see me suffering from a father complex that had blighted much of her life. Her personal father had been a tyrant, who insisted always on having his own way and made terrifying scenes whenever he was thwarted. As a result, the father archetype had been activated in her psyche, but only in the most partial and destructive manner: only the law-giving, authoritarian aspects of the father archetype were built into her father complex, while the loving, protective aspects of the archetype remained in the unconscious as unactivated potential. The result was that throughout her life this woman seemed fated to be drawn into the orbit of bullying, self-righteous men, whom she felt she had no alternative but to placate, appease, and obey. At the same time, there persisted in her an unfulfilled longing for the man who would do none of these things to her but, on the contrary, would give her love, support, and protection. Unfortunately, she could never seem to find him, for she could never get into a relationship with such a man: he was too alien, too essentially unfamiliar to her, and she did not possess the emotional vocabulary necessary to share such love.

In the initial stages of her analysis, her father complex inevitably got into the transference: unconsciously she would project the 'imago' of the tyrannical father on to me, as became clear when she misinterpreted my words or gestures as signs that I was becoming furious with her for not being a better patient! At other times, her dreams, fantasies and behaviour revealed how much she longed for me to bring into living reality the positive father potential that remained unactualized in her unconscious. This was an aspect of the transference that none of the object relations analysts detected because their thinking lacked the archetypal or phylogenetic dimension. There was in the transference not only the father she had, but also the father she never had but longed for.

As the analysis progressed, she was able to become conscious of the destructive influence of her father complex, to find the strength to stand up to the men who bullied and exploited her, and to distance herself from them, integrating some of their authority in her own personality. Gradually, a warm, trusting relationship, largely freed of negative projections, developed between us, and this resulted in activation of enough positive father potential for a much healthier and more supportive father complex to form in her psyche. As a consequence, the capacity to relate to decent men, who were kindly disposed to her, began to improve.

Experience has taught me that the more unconscious a complex the more readily it is projected on to figures in the environment who correspond in certain ways to essential characteristics of the complex. So it was that my patient projected her complex on to men possessing qualities reminiscent of her father and then proceeded to become, much against her will, the victim of their sadistic power. The advantage of Jung's insight into the nature of archetypes and their mode of actualization in the form of complexes is that it provides both an understanding of her condition and the means to help her grow beyond it. The result was that her individuation, which had hitherto been blocked, was now freed to proceed on its way.

An expanded view of the self

In practice, the Jungian analyst, like the evolutionary psychiatrist, looks beyond the personal predicament of the patient and relates it to the story of humankind. Both appreciate that what has traditionally been classified as 'illness' is often a consequence of a potentially healthy organism struggling to meet the demands of life: symptom formation is itself an adaptive process. Both the Jungian and the evolutionary approaches are thus conducive to that priceless commodity, thera-peutic optimism. Instead of forms of futile suffering, symptoms are seen as the growing pains of people struggling to adjust to the demands that life has put on them. The evolutionary view also affirms Jung's insight that every human being is richly endowed with the archetypal potential of the species. This means that however disordered, one-sided, or constricted an individual's psychological development may be, the potential for further growth and better adaptation is nevertheless there, implicit in the psychophysical structure of the organism. As a result, patients may be helped to grow beyond the defective or inadequate form of adjustment that their personal history has permitted.

This perhaps is the most important conceptual contribution that evolutionary psychotherapy has to make: it grants an expanded view of the self. Jung conceived of the Self (preferring to use the initial capital to stress the difference between his concept and the everyday use of the term) as the central nucleus of the entire personality. It contains the archetypal endowment of the individual and co-ordinates and implements the programme for the life cycle from cradle to the grave. The Self is not just the sum total of one's personal life experiences as the object relations theorists and self psychologists maintain, but the product of many millions of years of development. Within each one of us the vast potential of humanity is contained. This provides an added dimension to the individuation process of becoming as complete a human being as one's circumstances allow: it is about integrating ontogeny with phylogeny, uniting one's personal experience with the potential experience of humanity. It means making the most of the mentalities with which natural selection has equipped us and bringing them to fulfilment in our lives.

Success in this endeavour will depend on the therapist's skill in releasing the unused creative potential in the patient's personality. A model for this is provided by classical Jungian analysis, which seeks to mobilize archetypal components of the phylogenetic psyche by encouraging patients to dream, to fantasize, to paint, to open themselves to relationships with new friends, and to find new ways of relating to old ones, as well as becoming conscious of the complexes, strategies and conflicts that have been controlling their lives in the past.

In particular, the evolutionary dimension has re-evoked the central importance of symbol-formation in the therapeutic process. Freud believed symbols to be purely private and pathological, insisting that only repressed material was symbolized. Jung took a wholly different view, maintaining that we possess an innate symbol-forming propensity which exists as a healthy, creative, and integral part of our total psychic equipment. Although possessing a flexible capacity for local and personal variations, this symbolizing ability proceeds on an archetypal basis, which gives rise to characteristic symbolic manifestations (Jung & von Franz, 1964; Kast, 1992; Stevens, 1998a). In adopting this position, Jung again fell foul of the standard social science model, with its *tabula rasa* view of the mind as a general-purpose learning mechanism free of all content other than that which 'culture' put into it. As the SSSM disintegrates, the view is fast gaining ground that the human capacity to use symbols, perceive meanings, and create myths and religions, evolved as the result of selection pressures encountered by our species in the environment of evolutionary adaptedness (Stevens, 1998a). By making use of the essentially adaptive function of symbols arising in the course of an analysis, the skilled therapist can help to mobilize the patient's unlived potential and promote a better adjustment to social reality. This has, in fact, been the main procedure used by classical Jungian analysts since the 1920s. The evolutionary perspective now opens up this richly creative process to a much greater population of therapists from differing backgrounds and traditions.

But it is demanding work, and therapists have to develop their own personality and their own creative abilities if they hope to do much more than patch up their patients and enable them to go on existing. As Jung observed, 'an analyst can help his patient just as far as he himself has gone and not a step further'. It is a heavy responsibility, but it makes the work of a committed therapist one of the most challenging and rewarding professions it is possible to embrace.

Whatever upheavals may be in store for us as a result of theoretical revisions, outcome studies, clinical audits, and research on the biochemistry of the brain, the primary duty of the psychotherapist will remain the same: to put empathy, knowledge, and professional skill at the service of the patient. Above all, the psychotherapeutic quest is a quest for meaning. In the 1930s, Jung wrote: 'About a third of my cases are not suffering from any clearly definable neurosis, but from the senselessness and aimlessness of their lives. I should not object if this were called the general neurosis of our age' (1954: 14). Neurosis, he said, in the nearest he came to a definition, is the suffering of a soul that has not found its meaning. A major factor bringing patients into therapy is a need to make sense of their lives, the need to find meaning. How can the evolutionary perspective serve this quest?

From early childhood a human being is an exploratory organism, forever seeking to impose meaning on events. The development of conscious awareness of ourselves is constructed out of meanings. This is the fundamental datum of the individuation process, for archetypes are meaning-creating imperatives. As a consequence, 'meaning is something that always demonstrates itself and is experienced on its own merits' (Jung, 1958b: 360). Through use of active imagination, dream interpretation, transference interpretation, and, most essentially, the medium of the therapeutic relationship itself, it is the therapist's task to endorse and facilitate the patient's basic need to discover his or her own constellations of meaning.

In the past, biology would have been considered wholly irrelevant to this process. Until very recently, workers in neuroscience and in artificial intelligence have sustained the fantasy that forms of intelligence and language could be devised on the basis of pure logic without having to postulate anything so messy as 'meaning'. The realization has now dawned that this cannot be the case and scientists have begun to accept meaning as a fundamental concept in biology (Bruner, 1990). Meaning, it seems, is something that nature cannot do without, and this may help to explain how it is that dreaming, remembering and consciousness have emerged as the massive biological achievements that they are.

A pretty hopeless case

A case which first brought home to me the heuristic and therapeutic power of the Jungian combined with the evolutionary psychiatric approach was that of a young woman I treated back in the 1970s and first reported under the pseudonym 'Jennifer' in my book, *The Two Million-Year-Old-Self* (Stevens, 1993; 1997). I will summarize the salient details of the case here in the hope that it will clarify the main points that I have been trying to make in this chapter.

Jennifer was 21 years old when she was sent to me by her family doctor: 'A pretty hopeless case, I'm afraid,' he said in his referral letter, 'but you may be able to do something for her'. Although attractive, intelligent, and well-educated, Jennifer had never had a boyfriend or a job. She lived with her father in a large London flat and kept house for him. Her mother had died from injuries in a car crash when Jennifer was six. As I was to discover at our first interview, she was a walking textbook of psychopathology. She still stands in my mind as a vivid witness to the absurdities of the kind of nosological rigour advocated by symptomatic inventories such as the *Diagnostic and Statistical Manual*. To list only the most obvious features of her condition, she was anxious, phobic, depressed, obsessive–compulsive, and schizoid.

She had been a nervous child even before her mother died, afraid of the dark, water, loud noises, animals, strangers, and cripples. After her mother's death, she became frightened of all novel situations. Going to school was a terrifying experience, and by the time she was ten, she had developed full-blown school phobia, with the result that her father took her away from school and arranged private tutoring at home. Although her childhood phobias had subsided by the time she consulted me, she was nevertheless suffering from claustrophobia: she could not use lifts or underground trains or sit comfortably in a room unless the door was open. For the first year of her treatment, my consulting room door had to be held open with a volume of Jung's *Collected Works* as a doorstop.

The diagnosis of depression could be deduced from the fact that she expressed feelings of guilt and worthlessness and wished she could summon up the courage to kill herself. She was disinterested in food and was as thin as a rake. She also woke early every morning in a state of dark despair.

That she was obsessive was abundantly clear. She spent her life cleaning and scrubbing and was terrified that she might in some way contaminate her father's food. She was also afflicted by intrusive thoughts and images over which she could exercise no control. The most common of these were thoughts of stabbing her father and of shrieking obscenities at him. Whenever she left home to do some shopping or post a letter, she spent over an hour checking that the gas taps were turned off, all switches in the off position, all appliances unplugged, all windows shut and locked, all doors bolted and barred.

In addition, she was profoundly introverted and had withdrawn from virtually all contact with people other than her father. She compensated for this social isolation with a rich fantasy life and wrote extraordinary romantic-mythic tales, the composition of which was frequently accompanied by masturbation.

At the end of our first session I concluded that little analytic progress could be made until her symptoms had been reduced in intensity. I therefore prescribed an antidepressant and a tranquilliser and arranged to see her two hours a week for psychotherapy. The antidepressant I chose was Anafranil (clomipramine hydrochloride), a tricyclic which is particularly effective in treating depressions complicated by compulsive symptomatology. At that time the 5HT-reuptake inhibitor fluoxetine, probably more effective than Anafranil, was not available.

When she came for her second session, she arrived four and a half hours late. What had happened was this: on her way to her first appointment with me (which, as she later confessed, she anticipated with a dread amounting to terror), she had counted the number of paces it took her to walk from her father's flat to my consulting room. It took 2,452 paces. On her way to her second visit she knew she had to take exactly the same number of paces. She had arrived with half an hour to spare, but she had taken 2,498 paces. So she had to take a taxi home and start all over again. Next time she took 2,475 paces, so she had to go home once more. It took her four journeys to get it right, and she arrived in a state of extreme agitation.

The critical factors in her history were, I believe, the early loss of her mother and the subsequent development of an exclusive relationship with her father, a brilliantly successful but emotionally unstable lawyer, who was undoubtedly devoted to Jennifer but was also tyrannically possessive and prone to unpredictable bouts of rage, as if possessed by a powerful demon. Jennifer's obsessive rituals were in part acts of propitiation to avert his fury. At the same time, her fears of killing him were a reaction formation against her own murderous feelings towards him. Her depression and sense of personal worthlessness arose because her father made her feel chronically inadequate and incapable of living up to the image of the daughter she believed he wanted her to be.

Her fear of me, and the ritual of counting the number of paces necessary to come to see me, I understood as the result of her transferring the father imago onto me as well as the archetype of the shaman, the medicine man, the healer. The counting ritual had to be gone through as a means of propitiating me and guaranteeing that I would not become incensed with her in the course of her session. The door had to be left open for the same reason: it would guarantee a hurried exit should the demon become operative in me.

For her subsequent appointments, I gave her an hour late in the day so that she would be able to sort out her counting rituals and get to my door in time. She got quite good at this after a while, though she often had to hop the last twenty or thirty paces, much to the astonishment of passers by.

After she had been on Anafranil three weeks, her depression began to lift: and a week later she was able to come to see my by taxi, thus avoiding the need to count her steps. At this point, a conventional psychiatrist would probably have reduced her sessions to once a month. I, on the other hand, increased them to three times a week. With the subsidence of her more incapacitating symptoms, the analysis could begin.

What light could the Jungian archetypal and the evolutionary psychiatric approaches throw on Jennifer's condition? From the Jungian standpoint, the essential issues concerned those archetypal imperatives that had been frustrated in Jennifer's personal history. The age of six is far too early for any child to lose its mother with impunity. This tragedy not only deprived Jennifer of the rich nourishment of a mother's love, but of a female role model to initiate her into womanhood. It also left her with an unresolved Electra complex and an inability to relate to any man except her father.

The absence of an extended family network further emphasized her exclusive dependence on her father. The lack of siblings and peers during childhood had contributed to her schizoid withdrawal, having deprived her of the opportunity which both peer bonding and play bring to the development of emotional spontaneity and the skills of social intercourse. Moreover, she had no contact with animals (her father would not allow them on account of the mess), with nature (she seldom left London), or with religion (her father was an atheist). Her only pleasures were her fantasy life and music (she was a good pianist, and her father had a large record collection).

As a result of these frustrations of archetypal intent, her development had gone seriously awry. The loss of her mother not only predisposed her to depression and impaired her development of what Erik Erikson (1959) called identity formation but effectively imprisoned her in the father–daughter relationship.

Why should her symptoms have become particularly bad as she entered her twenties? This is the archetypal stage of courtship, marriage, achieving social position, and, in the modern world, getting a job. None of these goals had Jennifer achieved or even attempted, but the pressure of the Self towards realization of all this potential was increasing, and something had to give. The result was the emergence of a formidable array of symptoms.

What can evolutionary psychiatry tell us about the meaning of her symptoms? Let us examine each of her symptoms from the evolutionary perspective. These, you will recall, were anxiety, phobia, depression, obsessive–compulsive neurosis, and schizoid withdrawal.

Anxiety is a form of vigilance. To survive in this dangerous world, an organism has to be alert to environmental changes so that it can be prepared to meet whatever emergencies may arise. Vigilance shifts into anxiety when a possible threat or danger has been perceived. The actual experience of anxiety is directly associated with physiological changes that prepare the body for violent action. In the environment of evolutionary adaptedness, vigilance and anxiety were crucial to survival. In the modern world, however, they can seem exaggerated or inappropriate, as they certainly were in Jennifer's case. A crucial question for psychopathology is why a natural psychophysiological response (anxiety) should become exaggerated into a persistent and inappropriate neurotic state (anxiety neurosis).

There have been a number of theoretical approaches to this question. The most influential of these has been the Freudian approach, which sees neuroses as the direct result of traumatic experiences in early childhood. This was certainly true of Jennifer. Life cruelly deprived her of a mother long before she was able to survive happily without one, and life failed to provide her with peers at the time when she most needed them.

As already noted, the psychological consequences of separation from or loss of mother were particularly elucidated by Bowlby (1969). Throughout Bowlby's work one fundamental notion persists – the idea that noncorrespondence between the developing needs of the child and conditions prevailing in its environment contributed to its susceptibility to neurosis. At the time when Jennifer was still in my care, I gave a paper in London comparing Bowlby's approach with Jung's when Bowlby was present. In discussion afterwards he agreed that he accepted the Jungian formulation that neurosis is liable to occur when the archetypal programme unfolding in the psyche of the child is not met by correspondingly appropriate figures and situations in the environment. Essentially, he was in agreement with the proposition that neurotic anxiety results from the frustration of archetypal intent. This, in my view, rather than any specific trauma suffered in infancy, is the cause of psychiatric disturbance in childhood, adolescence, and later life.

Since I have already touched on the evolutionary significance of phobic phenomena, I will confine my observations to the form of phobia which particularly afflicted Jennifer. As is usually the case, this was rich with symbolic meaning. It will be recalled that Jennifer's phobia was of confined spaces. Claustrophobia is evidently an exaggeration of the natural responses shared by all mammals to being trapped in an enclosed area and deprived of all means of escape. It is not surprising, therefore, that it is found in clinical practice that claustrophobia commonly occurs in people who experience home as suffocating and parents as oppressors. Whereas agoraphobics experience the outside world as threatening and feel secure only at home, in claustrophobics it is home that arouses anxiety, and there is a desire to flee from the threatening enclosure that home represents. Characteristically, the clautrophobic flees not only from physical enclosure but also from imprisonment in social roles from which there is no means of escape. As a result, commitments such as marriage and a job are far too dangerous to be risked. This was particularly Jennifer's condition when she entered analysis.

As with anxiety, depression is also a natural and universal experience that human beings share with all mammalian species. The likelihood is, therefore, that it is a biological condition contributing to survival. What can its function be? On the whole, it appears that depression is an adaptive reaction to loss or deprivation. It occurs, for example, in all young mammals when they are forcibly separated from their mothers and in all individuals living in hierarchically organized groups when deprived of rank in the social hierarchy. How can this contribute to survival? Having lost its mother, and after the initial cries of protest are over, the depressed infant lies still, silent and waiting, conserves body energy, and avoids the attention of predators. By this strategy the tiny animal can survive until reunited with its mother or adopted by a surrogate parent moved by its depressed state. Similarly, a depressive reaction to loss of status enables the demoted individual to adopt passively to the lower rank, thus avoiding further attack from the more powerful individual who has displaced him or her. This in turn contributes to peace and social cohesion. Depression, therefore, is linked with the ubiquitous mammalian tactic of submission, while its opposite, mania, is linked with a tactic of dominance (Price, 1967, 1969; Price et al., 1994; Stevens & Price, 2000). Manic-depression is thus inextricably tied into the dominance–submission archetypal system and its linked systems, aggression and defence. In Jennifer's case, her depression was linked to her loss of her mother, her submission to her father's dominance, and to her perceived inability to make her way in the world.

Obsessive–compulsive behaviour such as that manifested by Jennifer is a by-product of the need to control potentially dangerous events, objects, people, thoughts, feelings, impulses, or situations. It is commonly associated with power-ful emotions, particularly fear, anger, and guilt. Guilt, like anxiety, depression or anger, is an emotion to which all social animals are prone. It evolved as an adaptive device designed to maintain social order and homogeneity. Like anxiety it can be exaggerated and become the symptom of neurotic illness.

Guilt is evoked by thoughts, feelings, and actions that offend against whatever moral authority the individual was brought up to respect and which became internalized in the form of the moral complex, that inner patriarch or matriarch which Freud called the superego. Guilt and obsessive–compulsive neurosis are more apparent in people who have internalized their authorities out of fear rather than out of love. Typically, those who have been brought up through fear bear a grudge against authority and wish to defy it, however much they may overtly subscribe to its values. As a result, a conflict rages in them between the desire for defiance and the need to submit. Locked in this conflict, the patient feels compelled to think or do things that are foreign to his or her conscious personality.

In this manner, Jennifer was obsessed by thoughts of murdering her father and felt compelled to engage in all manner of rituals to prevent these thoughts from achieving their objective. Moreover, her condition largely owed its origins and its severity to the fact that her father was himself an obsessive–compulsive personality.

Because of a constant terror that things may get out of hand, obsessive individuals are driven by a compulsion to control events and people. What is intolerable is anything spontaneous, fortuitous, or unpredictable. In his book *Anxiety and Neurosis*, Charles Rycroft (1970) describes the attitude obsessives adopt to their own emotional life and that of people around them as reminiscent of a colonial governor ruling an alien and potentially rebellious population, or like an animal in possession of a territory over which it has established absolute power and mastery. They treat all spontaneous tendencies, all uncensored emotions, as if they were dangerous invaders. That is to say, they go on to the attack either to expel intruders or to force them into submission.

When the intruder is an alienated part of the Self, the attack is recognized by analysts as 'repression'. This formulation helps us to understand why it is that what Jung called 'the shadow personality' (composed of repressed, 'unacceptable' parts of the total personality) is particularly threatening to the obsessive person. The 'shadow' has to be ruthlessly beaten into submission for fear that it might otherwise get out of control. This single fact presented me with the most formidable obstacle to a successful outcome in Jennifer's treatment. I do not believe I could have succeeded were it not for the pharmacological assistance provided by Anafranil.

It is often asserted that schizoid personalities do not become depressed; they are too detached, it is thought, to be depressive. In fact, I have known a number of schizoid people who suffered from depression, and I take this, when it happens, as a positive prognostic sign – they are not so detached from reality as to be unconcerned about what is happening in their lives. This was certainly true of Jennifer.

Why do people become schizoid? In part it is a response to disappointment of basic social needs, but it can also be related to an innate introversion. Schizoid people typically had parents who were either absent for critical periods in their childhood or showed little regard for them as people in their own right (Bowlby, 1969; Stevens, 1982). Such parents seem to overlook the fact that their children have thoughts and feelings of their own; they tend to treat them like dolls to be picked up, put down, packed off to school, or put away in a nursery, as seems most convenient. As a consequence, the child grows up distrusting all human relationships, feeling that its own needs and wishes will never be considered. In these circumstances, the most practical strategy is to opt out from people and retreat into oneself (Laing, 1960).

The schizoid withdrawal from social life into a self-absorbed introversion is thus an appropriate response to repeated frustration of those archetypal imperatives concerned with social development. This is what had happened to Jennifer. Shut up in the isolated citadel of the self, what happens to the archetypes of the collective unconscious? They may remain latent as unconscious potential, they may manifest in dreams and fantasies, or they may be experienced as threatening symptoms – things to be feared and if possible controlled, denied, or repressed. The latter course is the most dangerous, as the repressed archetypal components are projected out onto figures in the environment and that way madness lies. At the beginning of her treatment, I was alarmed to discover that this had begun to occur to Jennifer, and it got into the transference. She reacted with paranoid sensitivity to my most innocent remarks, and there were occasions when she could not bear me to look at her. Just as her claustrophobia prevented her from travelling in underground trains, so her paranoid sensitivity prevented her from riding on buses. She felt people were looking at her, commenting on her, and laughing at her.

This exquisite self-consciousness is common to both schizoid personalities and schizophrenic patients. The fear of being looked at or stared at is the fear of having one's defences penetrated, of being evicted from one's inner citadel. The eye is one of the most common features of schizotypal art. How are we to relate this phenomenon to our evolutionary heritage?

Ethological studies have shown that staring and visual attention are very important in all social mammals (Chance & Jolly, 1970). The higher a dominant animal ranks in the social hierarchy, the more the less-dominant members of the society stare and attend to that one's needs. The dominant animal accepts such attention as rightfully due and is undisturbed by it. But if a subdominant animal is stared at by a dominant animal, the subdominant experiences it as frightening and intimidating. A dominant animal's stare is usually one of reproof and is aggressive in intent (Chance, 1988).

The same is true of human communities. Kings, queens, presidents, prime ministers, television personalities, and pop stars all thrive on being looked at and attended to. Their self-esteem glories in such scrutiny. But a person of low status who is stared at, or one with feelings of low self-esteem, experiences it as threatening and a cause for alarm. For this reason, for a schizoid or a schizophrenic patient whose self-esteem is almost invariably impaired, dislike of being stared at is a normal mammalian response.

In dealing with schizoid patients, the crucial questions are (1) how far has retreat in the citadel proceeded? and (2) to what extent has the ego succeeded in sustaining some kind of relationship to outer reality and at the same time entering into a creative relationship with the Self? Fortunately, Jennifer had not retreated so far as to preclude the formation of a therapeutic relationship. Moreover, her rich fantasy life meant that she was in creative relationship with the Self, and I was able to mobilize this in the service of the analysis. It was not an easy task. No sooner did she begin to trust me than she entered a phase of intense anxious attachment to me. She often experienced difficulty in leaving at the end of sessions. I had to cope with suicide threats on weekends and holidays, and she concocted a series of rituals to go through each time she left my consulting room to ensure that I would still be well disposed to her when she returned on the next occasion.

What was my duty as her doctor-analyst? Essentially, I conceived these to be as follows: (1) to render her symptoms less incapacitating; (2) to become the good father who wanted her to grow up and take on the tasks of adulthood; (3) to mobilize the individuation principle in the Self; and (4) to encourage her to leave home, get a job, become independent of her father, and begin to stand on her own feet. Finally, when these goals had been achieved, I regarded it as essential to refer her to a woman analyst, who could help her to affirm her identity with the feminine principle and to experience herself as a woman.

Was this ambitious therapeutic programme achieved? It is still a source of relief to me – and not a little surprise – to report that, to a greater or lesser extent, it was. It was three years before Jennifer was able to leave her father, set up house on her own, and find a job as a receptionist in a doctor's clinic. A year later, I referred her to a woman analyst, and a year after that she married a publisher. All that is now a long time ago. But when I contacted her in 1992 to request her permission to use her history, suitably disguised, she seemed well and happy. She had two adolescent children, worked for an animal welfare agency, was a vegetarian and a Buddhist, and she was still with the man she had married fifteen years previously.

In the name of clinical honesty I must declare, however, that the successful outcome of this case depended as much on the use of Anafranil as on the analysis. Obsessive–compulsive patients are the hardest to analyse, especially when they are depressed or have a schizoid personality. Without pharmacological help the analysis might have been stillborn, because we would probably have remained bogged down in her appalling symptoms. But if, on the other hand, I had merely played the role of a conventional psychiatrist and contented myself with treating her symptoms, she would in all probability have remained stuck at home with her aged father, and her individuation would have been no further along.

The case of this extraordinarily gifted and afflicted young woman has remained for me a seminal example of how conventional psychopharmacology can be combined with Jungian and evolutionary insights to formulate the details of most complex condition and to facilitate healing and personal growth.

As I hope this example makes clear, to adopt an evolutionary approach is not to espouse a political cause, to submit to biological determinism, or to abandon a proper concern for ethical values. What such an approach does provide is a compass and a new orientation to steer us through the immense complexities of human psychology, its disorders, and their treatment. New psychotherapies continue to appear: new forms, new methods, new theories, new organizations, all offering new trainings, most of them under-researched and under-evaluated. It is likely that all successful psychotherapies are based on a small number of principles which have been known to be effective in bringing psychological relief and personal change for many generations (Stevens, 1993, 1998b). What is needed now is a corpus of informed knowledge about the relationships between individual experience, social influences, and the phylogenetic propensities which guide and inform all human development. This is the programme which Freud and Jung embarked upon at the

113

beginning of the twentieth century. Now, as a new century dawns, we are, perhaps in a better position to bring it to fruition.

References

Adler, A. (1927) *The Practice and Theory of Individual Psychology*, Harcourt: New York.

Aveline, M. & Shapiro, D.A. (eds) (1995) *Research Foundations for Psychotherapy Practice*, New York: Wiley.

Bergin, E. & Garfleld, L. (eds) (1994) *Handbook of Psychotherapy and Behavior Chanac* (4th ed), New York: Wiley.

Bowlby, J. (1969) *Attachment and Loss*, Vol.1, *Attachment*, London: Hogarth Press.

Bowlby, J. (1988) *A Secure Base: Clinical Applications of Attachment Theory*, London: Routledge.

Bruner, J. (1990) *Acts of Meaning*, Cambridge, Mass: Harvard University Press.

Buss, D.M. (1991) 'Evolutionary personality psychology', *Annual Review of Psychology* 42: 459–91.

Buss, D.M. (1995) 'Evolutionary psychology, a new paradigm for psychological science', *Psychological Enquiry* 6: 1–30.

Chance, M.R.A. (1988) 'Introduction', in M.R.A. Chance (ed), *Social Fabrics of the Mind*, Hove, UK: Lawrence Erlbaum Associates Ltd.

Chance, M.R.A. & Jolly, C. (1970) *Social Groups of Monkeys, Apes and Men*. London: Jonathan Cape.

Cosmides, L. & Tooby, J. (1989) 'Evolutionary psychology and the generation of culture. Part 1: case study: a computational theory of social exchange', *Ethology and Sociobiology* 10: 51–97.

Cosmides, L. & Tooby, J. (1992) 'Cognitive adaptations for social exchange', in J.H. Barkow, L. Cosmides & J. Tooby (eds), *The Adapted Mind: Evolutionary Psychology and the Generation of Culture*. New York: Oxford University Press.

Eibl-Eibesfeldt, I. (1971) *Love and Hate*, London: Methuen.

Erikson, E.H. (1959) *Identity and the Life Cycle, Psychological Issues*, (vol. 1, no. 1, monograph 1), New York: International Universities Press.

Esterson, A. (1993) *Seductive Mirage: An Exploration of the Work of Sigmund Freud*, Chicago: Open Court.

Fodor, J.A. (1985) 'Precis of the modularity of mind (plus peer commentary)', *Behavioral and Brain Sciences* 8: 1–42.

Freud, S. (1910) *Five Lectures on Psycho-Analysis* (Vol. 11), London: Hogarth Press and The Institute of Psycho-Analysis.

Freud, S. (1939) *An Outline of Psycho-Analysis* (Vol. 23), London: Hogarth Press and The Institute of Psycho-Analysis.

Freud, S. (1953–74) *The Standard Edition of the Complete Psychological Works of Sigmund Freud*, J. Strachey, (ed.), London: Hogarth Press and The Institute of Psycho-Analysis.

Gardner, H. (1985) *Frames of Mind*. London: Paladin.

Gardner, R. (1988) 'Psychiatric syndromes as infrastructure for intra-specific communication', in M.R.A. Chance (ed.), *Social Fabrics of the Mind*, Hove, UK: Lawrence Erlbaum Associates Ltd.

Gilbert, P. (1989) *Human Nature and Suffering*, Hove, UK: Lawrence Erlbaum Associates Ltd.

Gilbert, P. (1995) 'Biopsychosocial approaches and evolutionary theory as aids to integration in clinical psychology and psychotherapy', *Clinical Psychology and Psychotherapy* 2: 134–56.

Gilbert, P. (1997) 'The biopsychosociology of meaning', in M. Power & C. Brewin (eds), *The Transformation of Mean: Reconciling Theory and Therapy in Cognitive Behaviour and Related Therapies*, (pp. 33–56), Chichester: Wiley.

Gomez, L. (1997) *An Introduction to Object Relations*. London: Free Association Books.

Grahame-Smith, D.G. & Aronson, J.K. (1992) *The Oxford Textbook of Clinical Pharmacology and Drug Therapy*, Oxford: Oxford University Press.

Greenberg, J.R. & Mitchell, S.A. (1983) *Object Relations in Psychoanalytic Theory*, Cambridge, Mass: Harvard University Press.

Hobson, J.A. (1988) *The Dreaming Brain*, New York: Basic Books.

Jung, C.G. (1933) *Modern Man in Search of a Soul*. London: Routledge & Kegan Paul.

Jung, C.G. (1953) 'The structure of the unconscious', *The Collected Works*, Vol. 7, pp. 263–92, London: Routledge & Kegan Paul.

Jung, C.G. (1954) 'The practical use of dream-analysis', *The Collected Works*, Vol. 16, pp. 139–61, London: Routledge & Kegan Paul.

Jung C.G. (1956) 'Symbols of transformation', Foreword to the second Swiss edition. *The Collected Works*, Vol. 5, pp. xxviii–xxix, London: Routledge & Kegan Paul.

Jung, C.G. (1958a) 'Psychology and religion', *The Collected Works*, Vol. 11, pp. 3–105, London: Routledge & Kegan Paul.

Jung, C.G. (1958b) 'Answer to Job', *The Collected Works*, Vol. 11, pp. 357–470, London: Routledge & Kegan Paul.

Jung, C.G. (1959a) 'The concept of the collective unconscious', *The Collected Works*, Vol. 91, pp. 42–53, London: Routledge & Kegan Paul.

Jung, C.G. (1959b) 'Psychological aspects of the mother archetype', *The Collected Works*, Vol. 9i., pp. 75–110, London: Routledge & Kegan Paul.

Jung C.G. (1960a) 'Synchronicity: an acausal connecting principle', *The Collected Works*, Vol. 8, pp. 417–531, London: Routledge & Kegan Paul.

Jung C.G. (1960b) 'On the nature of the psyche', *The Collected Works*, Vol. 8, pp. 159–234, London: Routledge & Kegan Paul. (Originally published 1946)

Jung C.G. (1963) *Memories, Dreams, Reflections,* Recorded and edited by Aniela Jaffe, London: Routledge and Kegan Paul.

Jung, C.G. (1977a) 'Symbols and the interpretation of dreams', *The Collected Works*, Vol. 18, pp. 185–264, London: Routledge & Kegan Paul.

Jung, C.G. (1977b) 'Foreword to Harding: Womens' Mysteries', *The Collected Works*, Vol. 18, pp. 518–20, London: Routledge & Kegan Paul.

Jung, C.G. & von Franz, M.L. (eds) (1964) *Man and His Symbols*, London: Aldus Books.

Kast, V. (1992) *The Dynamics of Symbols: Fundamentals of Jungian Psychotherapy*. (translated by S A. Schwarz). New York: Fromm International.

Klein, M. (1932) *The Psycho-Analysis of Children*, London: Hogarth Press.

Lader, M. & Herrington, R. (1990) *Biological Treatments in Psychiatry*, Oxford: Oxford University Press.

Laing, R.D. (1960) *The Divided Self: A Study of Sanity and Madness*, London: Tavistock Publications.

McDowell, M.J. (1999) 'Relating to the mystery: a biological view of analytical psychology', *Quadrant: Journal of the C.G. Jung Foundation for Analytical Psychology*, New York.

115

McLynn, F. (1996) *Carl Gustav Jung*, New York: Bantam Press.

Macmillan, M. (1997) *Freud Evaluated: The Completed Arc*, Cambridge, Mass: MIT Press.

Miller, N.E., Luborsky, L., Barber, J.P., & Docherty, J.P. (eds) (1993) *Psychodynamic Treatment Research: A Handbook for Clinical Practice*. New York: Basic Books.

Nesse, R.M. (1987) 'An evolutionary perspective on panic disorder and agoraphobia', *Ethology and Sociobiology* 8: 73–84.

Noll, R. (1994) *The Jung Cult: Origins of a Charismatic Movement*, Princeton, NJ: Princeton University Press.

Noll, R. (1997) *The Aryan Christ: The Secret Life of Carl Jung*, New York: Random House.

Ornstein, R. (1986) *Multimind: A New Way of Looking at Human Behavior*, London: Macmillan.

Price, J.S. (1967) 'Hypotheses: the dominance hierarchy and the evolution of mental illness', *Lancet* 2: 243–6.

Price J.S. (1969) 'Neurotic and endogenous depression: a phylogenetic view', *British Journal of Psychiatry* 114: 119–20.

Price, J.S., Sloman, L., Gardner, R., Gilbert, P. & Rohde, P. (1994) 'The social competition hypothesis of depression', *British Journal of Psychiatry* 164: 309–35.

Rachman, S. (1978) *Fear and Courage*, San Francisco: Freeman.

Roth, A. & Fonagy, P. (1996) *What Works For Whom? A Critical Review of Psychotherapy Research*, New York: Guilford Press.

Rowan, J. (1990) *Subpersonalities – The People Inside Us*, London: Routledge.

Rycroft, C. (1970) *Anxiety and Neurosis*, Harmondsworth: Penguin Books.

Stevens, A. (1982) *Archetype: A Natural History of the Self*, London: Routledge & Kegan Paul.

Stevens, A. (1993) *The Two Million-Year-Old Self*, College Station, Texas: The Texas A&M University Press.

Stevens, A. (1997) *The Two Million-Year-Old Self*, New York: International Paperbacks.

Stevens, A. (1998a) *Ariadne's Clue: A Guide to the Symbols of Humankind*, London: Allen Lane.

Stevens, A. (1998b) *An Intelligent Person's Guide to Psychotherapy*, London: Duckworth.

Stevens, A. (1999) *On Jung* (2nd ed), London: Penguin.

Stevens, A. & Price, J. (2000) *Evolutionary Psychiatry: A New Beginning* (2nd edn). London: Routledge.

Webster, R. (1997) *Why Freud Was Wrong: Sin, Science and Psychoanalysis*, London: Harper-Collins.

Wenegrat, B. (1984) *Sociobiology and Mental Disorder*, Menlo Park, California: Addison-Wesley.

Willcocks, R. (1994) *Maelzel's Chess Player: Sigmund Freud and the Rhetoric of Deceit*, Lanham, Maryland: Rowman and Littlefield.

Winnicott, D.W. (1965) *The Maturational Process and the Facilitating Environment*, New York: International Universities Press.

Wright, R. (1994) *The Moral Animal: Evolutionary Psychology and Everyday Life*, London: Little, Brown & Company.

Acknowledgements

The ideas in this chapter are developed in greater depth in the author's *The Two Million-Year-Old Self* (1997) and *An Intelligent Person's Guide to Psychotherapy* (1998).

6

SOCIAL MENTALITIES

Internal 'social' conflict and the role of inner warmth and compassion in cognitive therapy

Paul Gilbert

A popular undergraduate textbook on psychology attempts to stimulate the interest of potential students with the following statement (Coon, 1992: 1).

> You are a universe, a collection of worlds within worlds. Your brain is possibly the most complicated and amazing device in existence. Through its action you are capable of music, art, science, and war. Your potential for love and compassion coexists with your potential for aggression, hatred. . . . Murder?

This focus, on the great variation of potentials *within* an individual (in contrast to variation *between* individuals; Bailey, 1987; Rowan, 1990), is the starting point for many psychotherapies. Most clinicians are familiar with clients describing themselves as having 'different parts', or experiencing 'intense inner conflicts'. And clinicians themselves also view the psyche as made up of different elements that can be labelled in different ways. For Jung there was different archetypes, (Jung, 1954/1993; Stevens, 1982, Chapter 5, this volume) and sub-personalities (Rowan, 1990); for cognitive therapists there are different schema (Young, Beck & Weinberger, 1993) and for evolutionists there are different motivational systems and strategies (Gilbert, 1989; McGuire & Troisi, 1998; Slavin & Kriegman, 1992; Stevens & Price, 1996). Few clinicians see the psyche as a single integrated system but rather view it as made up of various, and often competing, motives, desires, cognitive processes and action tendencies. Conflict and competition are not just operative interpersonally but intrapersonally (Bailey, 1987). We say 'part of me wants to do this (e.g., speak my mind, be assertive, have sex with a neighbour) but part of me worries that this will bring rejection, guilt or shame'.

This chapter suggests that *internal* conflicts arise from evolved strategies (e.g., for caring, attacking, submitting) and can play off against each other. For example, we can get angry with ourselves for failure and call ourselves names (e.g., 'stupid') as if we were trying to derogate a competitor or a subordinate. This anger can act as an internal signal that triggers submissive and defensive strategies leading to feelings of depression when we cannot defend ourselves from our own self-attacks.

To explore internal conflicts, the first section considers the nature of our social evolution and the evolved modules and mentalities that make social meaning and relating possible. It is noted that the brain evolved to be sensitive to *social* signals for deciding what kind of role relationship it is engaged in. Different types of social signal (e.g., friendly–hostile) are analysed with different types of specialized evaluative processes. The second section explores how such evaluative processes (designed for social relating) are the basis for internal self-evaluations and operate through processing systems that evolved for social relating. The third section focuses on the process of therapy by treating self-cognitions *as if* they are social cognitions. Particular attention is given to various therapeutic ways of activating the patient's own *self-directed* inner capacities for caring, compassion and forgiveness.

Evolved social relationships and signal valence

The evolution of many mental mechanisms was shaped by many different social challenges acting over millions of years (Buss, 1995, 1999; Gilbert, 1989, 1998a; Gilbert, Bailey & McGuire, Chapter 1, this volume). These challenges included: finding a mate, conceiving and reproducing, caring for offspring, eliciting support from others, and defending resources from competitors. Such challenges, operating over many millions of years, have given rise to the evolution of a variety of social motivations to create certain types of social role. The social roles in question have been outlined in Chapter 1 and elsewhere (Buss, 1995, 1999; Gilbert, 1989; McGuire & Troisi, 1998) and include ways of relating such as: care eliciting/ seeking; care giving; co-operating; mate selecting and mating; and competing. Many authors in this volume address the inherent internal and interpersonal conflicts that arise from having a mind that seeks such a variety of different social outcomes and can 'play' or enact different roles.

In order successfully to create desired social roles in these various domains (e.g., attachment or sexual relationships, gaining status or subduing competitors and subordinates) individuals need to be competent at the sending and decoding of social signals. Such competency relies on signal detection and analytic systems (sometimes referred to as strategies and algorithms; McGuire & Troisi, 1998). Positive and negative emotions are often elicited by different social signals indicating success or failure in a role (Bailey, 1987; Nesse 1998). For example, a successful enactment of a role (e.g., successful care seeking, co-operation or gaining status) is innately rewarding while their failure is innately aversive. Thus, in the early mother–infant relationship signals of proximity and attunement elicit positive affect while those of separation and misattunement elicit negative affect. In the co-operative domain signals of mutual support and reciprocation elicit positive affect while signals of cheating and rejection elicit negative affect. In the social status domain signals of social respect and approval elicit positive affect while signals of disapproval and being located in an unwanted subordinate position elicit negative affect.

The emotions associated with a social signal depend on the *role meaning* of the signal. For example, behaviours such as eye gaze can have different meanings when exchanged between competitors/enemies, lovers or in the mother–infant dyad. Seeing someone run away from me is aversive if I wish to be sexually attractive to them but rewarding if I wish to compete with them and make them flee the field. When relating to others therefore there can be aversive role mismatches, e.g., a patient wishes to elicit care but the therapist offers sexual advances; a person wishes to form a sexual relationship but the other sees them only 'as a friend'. Thus, the affective tone of social relationships arise from both how we (successfully or not) relate to others in specific roles and how others relate to us (our experience of being related to; Birtchnell, 1993). These are not always congruent and mismatches between what people want out of relationships are common (Gilbert & McGuire, 1998; Liotti, Chapter 11, this volume).

Modules and social mentalities

Modules represent domain-specific ways of processing information (Buss, 1999; Cosmides & Tooby, 1992; Gazzaniga, 1989; Ornstein, 1986). For example, a 'fear of spiders' module orientates the person to spider stimuli, to process rapidly information on (say) dangerous and activate defensive behaviour (e.g., freeze or run away). A sexual module/mentality orientates individuals to sexual stimuli, calculates the cost–benefits of mating, alters arousal and motivation, and on the basis of these instigates certain types of sexual behaviour (e.g., courting behaviour or copulation). Responding to spiders or sexual partners is therefore controlled by different modules making different types of calculation to different stimuli and activating very different responses (Buss, 1999).

A social mentality acts to generate *patterns* of cognition, affect and behaviour into meaningful sequences that allow for the enactment of social roles (Gardner, 1988; Gilbert, 1989, 1995). The two central mentalities we focus on in this chapter are caring and supporting (used for kin-helping and friendship building) versus competitive attacking to control subordinates and derogate competitors. A caregiving mentality involves attention to the object of care (e.g., kin relationships; see Bailey, Chapter 3, this volume), suppression of aggression to the object of care, and in humans may recruit the affects of sympathy, empathy and affection (De Waal, 1996; Fogel, Melson & Mistry, 1986). A hostile competitive mentality utilizes tactics of social undermining involving threats and (in humans) derogation attacks of shaming and put down (Gilbert, 1998a, d). It will be argued that humans can adopt these styles/strategies into their own self-evaluative systems; that is they can be self-nurturing or self-attacking.

The internal organization of mentalities and their integration is shaped during their developmental trajectories via interaction with the social environment. For example, a person's sexual mentalities will be shaped by innate predispositions affecting the timing of sexual interest (e.g., increase in sex hormones at puberty; innate preferences for certain types of partner) interacting with information from the environment. Thus, one person may mature his/her sexuality in a relatively free and open way and be able to commit to, and nurture, a long-term relationship, while another person (perhaps under strict prohibitions from parents or group) may be plagued with inhibitions of guilt and shame that severely limit sexual behaviour. Or a person may have a more exploitative approach to sex with low investment and caring behaviour. Mentalities then, mature both with the innate push towards goals (e.g., sex) but with sensitivity to the social environment (see Belsky, Steinberg & Draper, 1990 for a discussion of how development shapes basic evolved reproductive strategies and interpersonal behaviours). In regard to caring and hostile competitiveness the same principle holds; that is people can mature their caring and hostile competitive strategies and mentalities in different contexts and different ways. Some find it easy to be (self-)nurturing, others do not.

Social signals influence physiological states

One of the key suggestions here is that social signals are crucial to how mentalities work and their affect control. Mentalities are highly attuned to different types of social signal. Indeed individuals are guided to biosocial goals (such as sexual partners, forming alliances/friendships) via the detection, evaluation, and meaning of social signals. Moreover, certain cues/signals trigger psychobiological response patterns that enable the individual to act in role-appropriate ways (Gilbert, 1984). For example, certain sexual signals (sights and smell) can trigger sexual arousal which will involve the release of certain pituitary hormones, changes in bodily states (erection or vaginal lubrication) arouse affect/desire and actions tendencies. Although sex is an obvious example of the linkage between a specific psychobiological response pattern and specific signals there are many others.

The idea that social interactions (involving the exchange of social signals) can have physiological and psychological consequences has been recognized for some time (Bowlby, 1969, 1973; Harlow & Mears, 1979; Hofer, 1984; Troisi & McGuire, Chapter 2, this volume). During the 1960s Harlow demonstrated that the texture of a surrogate mother was a more salient stimulus in calming anxious young monkeys than was a wire surrogate that delivered milk (Harlow & Mears, 1979). Infants require holding, touching, and vocal input (Montagu, 1986). Without such interactions, they become psychologically distraught and physiologically distressed and dysregulated (Hofer, 1984; McGuire & Troisi, 1998; Schore 1994). Indeed we now know that touching and holding have powerful physiological effects (Field, 1998). Infants are motivated to elicit specific types of social signal (to alter and control the frequency and type of others' behaviour), to be calmed or pleasured by the arrival of certain signals, and distressed by their absence. For example, infants are highly attentive to the human face and able to discriminate facial expressions. Research has shown that if a baby smiles and the mother smiles back this *attunement* of facial expressions is innately, positively rewarding and biologically regulating for the infant. Conversely, if the mother presents a blank, expressionless face, this is experienced as aversive and the infant may become distressed, fretful, and turns away (Schore, 1994). This distress is accompanied by sympathetic and parasympathetic arousal and stress hormones such as cortisol. Negative signals from care-givers also affect the maturation of the orbital frontal cortex and various brain areas that come to regulate emotions (Schore, 1994). The fact that mismatches or misattunements in social signalling are innately aversive to the infant is evidence for the power of social signals to exert physiological effects (Tronick, 1989).

It is now well known that people can directly influence each other's physical states. For example, Miller and Fishkin (1997) have reviewed the evidence on how close adult–adult bonds evolved with physiological regulating impacts on stress and sex hormones, and the immune system (see also Zeifman & Hazan, 1997). Gottman and Levenson (1992) found that the way couples interacted at a physiological level predicted whether they stayed together or not. As another example, dominant primates have blood serotonin (5-HT) levels significantly higher than subordinates. The levels are maintained via the submissive signals of subordinates. If, for example, a dominant is removed from a group, so that he can see the group but they cannot see him and thus do not respond to his threat displays, then his 5-HT falls. Contrarily, the threat displays of a dominant are capable of suppressing the 5-HT of subordinates (Raleigh *et al.*, 1984; see also Gilbert & McGuire, 1998; Price *et al.*, 1994 for further examples). And even the interactional style of a social group (e.g., competitive verses co-operative) can affect people's hormone levels (Kemper, 1990). The key point is that social signals are physiologically powerful.

For reasons related to our evolution then, signals operate in the way depicted in Figure 6.1. Eliciting approval and feeling attractive is a central human motivation (Gilbert, 1997a). Caring and supportive signals boost certain brain amines and lower stress hormones. Indeed, there is good evidence for the physiological benefits of care and support (Uchino, Cacioppo & Kiecolt-Glaser, 1996). These in turn promote friendly behaviour. On the other hand signals of aggression will increase stress hormones and (in the event the attack cannot be overcome – it is uncontrollable) lower certain brain amines. Moreover such 'attacks' will trigger evolved defensive behaviour of counter-aggression, flight and/or submission.

The internalization of social signals

There is no doubt then, that external social signals (facial expressions, postures, voice tones and other behaviours) impact on a recipient's physiological and emotional state. A key question is: can certain types of *internally* generated signals have similar impacts on physiology and emotions? To use an extreme example; in so far as people who hear malevolent voices are themselves generating such signals and then becoming distressed by them, and wish to escape or fight back at them, the answer is probably, yes.

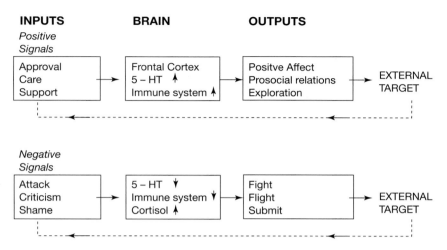

EXTERNAL RELATIONS

Figure 6.1 External signals, brain processes and outputs.

In fact, there is a long history of research showing that the thoughts and images that we create in our minds do indeed impact on physiology and emotional states (see Hackmann, 1997; Frederick & McNeal, 1999 for a review). For example, Beck, Emery and Greenberg (1985) outline how certain types of threat-related thinking can activate various evolved (fight, flight, freeze) responses. Indeed, cognitive therapy rests on this proposition; that the way we think about things and the images we create in our heads activates our emotions which in turn feeds our thoughts and images. That we are able to activate our own sexual arousal by our own fantasies and images is something most discover in adolescence. It is, however, not just emotions that are activated, but complex *patterns* of emotions, thoughts, images and behaviours (mentalities) that have strategic functions. For example, thoughts of threat activate anxiety *and* mobilize flight behaviour (Beck, Emery & Greenberg, 1985); thoughts of loss can activate grief and pining; thoughts of self as inferior, defeated and trapped can activate depressed mood, sleep disturbance and social withdrawal (Gilbert, 1992; Gilbert & Allan, 1998). And in terms of treatment, changing cognitions can have many biological effects (e.g., Joffe, Segal & Singer, 1996)

There is now good evidence that thoughts and memories alone can activate changes in brain functioning. For example, George *et al.* (1995) using positron emission tomography asked subjects to recall happy and sad memories. This simple task resulted in different patterns of brain activity especially in prefrontal cortex and the limbic systems. There have been no studies to my knowledge of what happens in the brain when people engage in positive self-evaluations (self-liking support and caring) and negative self-evaluation (self-criticism and self-attacking). Such studies are urgently needed.

INTERNAL RELATIONS

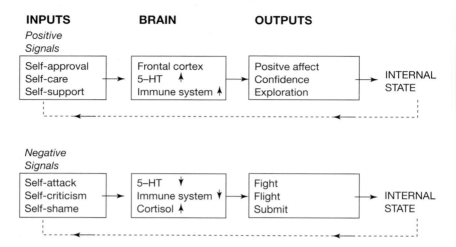

Figure 6.2 Internal signals, brain processes and outputs.

Nonetheless, the proposition is that our own evaluations can (1) act as internal signals which have the same or similar effects as external signals. (2) Negative internal signals (self-criticism) can, under some conditions, activate brain systems that evolved to cope with attacks such as submissive and defeat behaviour. This is depicted in Figure 6.2. As noted later people can certainly feel defeated, shamed and submit to their own internal attack. This is a possible scenario because there are *different* modules and mentalities controlling 'attack' behaviours and the submissive defensives to being attacked. Hopefully future research in brain imaging will be attentive to the possibility of modules (rather than specific emotions) activating and playing off against each other.

It is possible that mild self-criticism may be adaptive to the extent that it aids self-correction, but the types of self-attacking (and lack of self-nurturing) we will explore here do not seem to act this way and people suffering serious psychological problems feel overwhelmed by them and cannot self-correct.

The inner experience of the self

Although there is now general agreement that the mind is essentially designed for social relating, what is less well articulated in the literature is that the nature of internal 'self-talk' is also inherently relational (Gilbert, 1989; Hermans, 1996). My point is that the way we 'talk to' and evaluate ourselves activates and co-ordinates certain patterns of our innate social mentalities. Hence, I suggest that self-evaluations are adapted from evaluative systems originally designed for social relating. The idea that evolution adapts old mechanisms for new ends is well established in evolution theory (Buss, 1999; Bailey, 1987; MacLean, 1990), For example, feathers probably evolved first as thermo-regulation devices but became co-opted for flight (Buss, 1999). Similarly therefore, for the reasons noted above, modules and mentalities for processing social information and orienting social responses have become co-opted for self-evaluations.

The construction of the self via inner relating

There is good evidence now that one way children develop their sense of self-identity is through *internal rehearsal* of roles using role play (e.g., with a doll), self-talk, and imaginary figures (Singer & Singer, 1990; Watkins, 1986). These rehearsals are role-based. In fact, many forms of reasoning about the self are dialogic (Hermans, 1996). Watkins (1986) has given an interesting reflection on the developmental processes of what she called 'imaginal dialogues' and compares and contrasts the work of Piaget, Vygotsky, Mead and object relation theorists on this matter (see also Frederick & McNeal, 1999). For some, the inner dialogue is at the centre of the development and construction of the self. George Herbert Mead was one of the first to articulate how important the human ability for inner dialogue is. He says:

> There is a field, a sort of inner forum, in which we are the only spectators and the only actors. In that field each one of us confers with himself. We carry on something of a drama. If a person retires to a secluded spot, and sits down and thinks, he talks to himself. He asks and answers questions. He develops his ideas and arranges and organizes his ideas as he might in a conversation with someone else. He may prefer talking to himself to talking to somebody else.
>
> (As quoted in Watkins, 1986: 19)

As noted elsewhere (Gilbert, 1989: 324) Mead believed that it was the assuming of roles that led to the emergence of self-consciousness (Farr, 1980, 1987) and that at times, the assuming of these roles took place within the same person. Social roles create meaning via their intended effects on another. Mead, apparently 'saw the origins of language in gesture' (Farr, 1987: 5). Mead believed that:

> Mind emerges naturally out of the conversation of gestures and that this occurred phylogenetically, in the emergence of the species and occurs again, ontogenetically in the development of each individual. Mind arises through communication by a conversation of gestures in a social process or context of experience not communication through Mind.
>
> (Farr 1987: 9)

These ideas have been built on by others (see Hermans, 1996). To assume a role within the self supposes there must be aspects to the self to do the assuming. Hence, the social nature of the internal world gives rise to a plurality of possible selves.

125

The evolutionary view is that this arises because we evolved to enact a plurality of social roles. The ability to play these different roles is because we have specialized modules and mentalities that process information and structure outputs. These are the foundations for 'possible selves or sub-personalities' (Rowan, 1990) which can feel different things and play different parts when we are in different states of mind. In therapy we can even learn to name these different selves and speak with them. We can label them as (for example) the bullying self, the perfectionist self, the vengeful sadist self, the sexual self, the forgiving self, and so on. The sub-personalities are created by the way different modules and mentalities interact in the mind (Gilbert, 1989, 1992).

In a major review of the importance of how different domains of the self can take on different *voices* and emotional textures, Hermans (1996) notes that these inner parts of self can have different voices and can act like 'competing selves' that can agree or disagree with each other, support or attack each other. Hermans (1996: 35) notes that some voices are dominant while others may be dormant and rarely heard, but can 'awake and can cause a transformation in one's views'. In evolutionary terms these inner 'voices' and 'competing selves' are the products of different modules/mentalities which evolved for different role relationships. The point is that the way we inwardly reason about our social roles and interactions, *and form self-constructions* is often in dialogic form.

Hostile and caring sub-selves and their voices

So far I have argued that humans are evolved to be able to assume certain roles. The two key roles focused on have been caring and investing in others, and attacking, with the intent of controlling and/or shaming/derogating competitors and subordinates. Being the recipient of caring signals activates positive affect and pro-social behaviour; being the recipient of aggressive signals can activate fight, desire to escape or submission (see Figure 6.2).

In many cases negative 'self-talk' (Benjamin, 1997) can be re-constructed as forms of an *internal dominant–subordinate relationship*, the inner experience of which is shame (Gilbert, 1998b,d, 2000; Gilbert & McGuire, 1998). Humans can attack themselves and treat themselves as if they are relating to a subordinate, competitor or even an enemy. This mirrors many other approaches that focus on domains of self-punishment (Rehm, 1988), self-criticism (Blatt *et al.*, 1982; Zuroff & Mongrain, 1987), self-attacking (Ellis, 1977; Driscoll, 1988) or conflicts between the ego and superego (Freud, 1917). In this sense the subordinating (punishing) signals are internal and the person may call themselves names (e.g., you are no good, worthless, a failure, etc.). Another way to consider this is that the person seems to have a 'split' where one part (module) of them self-attacks (and feels hostile and angry) and another part (module) experiences the effects of being attacked. Gestalt and emotion therapists label this as topdog–underdog (Greenberg, 1979; Greenberg, Rice & Elliott, 1993). The person is literally enacting hostile-dominance and subordination internally *and continually inwardly rehearsing this interaction*.

Psychosis

Psychosis is a good example of this principle. In psychosis people can hear voices that are hostile to them; that are shaming and/or aggressive (down-rank attacking). The voice is invariably seen as powerful (dominant) and the aspect of self experiencing it as subordinate – although the patient may try to resist the dictates of the voice or believe it is unjust (Chadwick & Birchwood, 1994). Psychosis offers the most vivid insight into the way mentalities, which evolved for external relating, have come to be activated by internally generated signals. That is, the patient may generate a hostile–dominant signal (shaming voice) that then activates defensive strategies – involving defensive aggression (resistance) or efforts to escape or submit (see Figure 6.2). If the patient is unable to defend him or herself against, or escape from, the (inner) attack he or she may feel defeated and become depressed. Why exactly this happens in such a segregated way, such that patients lack aware-ness of their own generation of the hostile voice(s), is unknown. What is known is that people with schizophrenia are highly physiologically sensitive and reactive to others, especially those who are critical (Tarrier, Vaughn, Lader & Leff, 1979), and have problems in attention and reasoning about social information (Penn et al., 1997). Moreover, there is evidence that the generation of voices is associated with patients misidentifying internal signals/speech as external; that is, they are actually talking to themselves but unaware of doing so (McGuire *et al.*, 1996).

Such data point to problems in the *integration* of the modular processes under-pinning self–other cognitions. Cleghorn and Albert (1990) argue that psychosis, and schizophrenia in particular, may be a problem in the *integrated functioning* of internal modular processing systems and coined the phrase *modular disjunction*. Poor modular integration within mentalities (e.g., for social ranking) may arise from the way language evolved. In particular, hostile–dominant affective signals, as may be generated in the right hemisphere, are misidentified by the language system (of the left hemisphere) as 'voices' from outside the self (Crow, 1995). In a way this is like an auto-immune disease when the 'attack' system does not recog-nize itself as itself. Another possibility is that the evolution of self-consciousness has evolved with various 'glitches', such that the rehearsal mechanisms of self-consciousness that allows us to inwardly represent the 'other' in consciousness has somehow become dysfunctional. This is not the place to take these evolutionary speculations further but additional insight can be gleaned from studies of depressive internal self-talk.

Depression

Depression commonly involves problems of feeling beaten down and defeated (Gilbert & Allan, 1998; Price & Sloman, 1987) and is associated with the sub-missive pole of the dominant–submissive interpersonal model (Horowitz & Vitkus, 1986). This can be because life is treating them harshly and they have lost status (Bergner 1988; Gilbert, 1992; Brown, Harris & Hepworth, 1995). But it is common to find that depression-prone people habitually think in social rank terms to give meaning to their place in social relationships. For example, they compare themselves with others – often feeling inferior to others in some domain that is important to them and their social status (Swallow & Kuiper, 1988). And, importantly for the approach taken here, depressed people commonly experience hostile internal (down-rank attack) signals and may judge *themselves* to be worthless, unlovable, or useless. In non-psychotic depression there is not the misidentification of the source of the signal and the person knows it is *self*-dislike and anger at the self that is at issue. But for both the psychotic and depressed person the affective quality of these negative internal messages are usually of them being powerful and hostile. Indeed, recent data from ongoing studies in our unit has found that depressed people do feel dominated and controlled by their (own) self-critical thoughts. Hostile messages that are seen as 'subordinate' or 'weak' or easily dismissed do not cause problems.

Internal role (module) conflict and mismatching

Just as in external relationships one reason for conflict is role mismatching; e.g., I want sex but the other wants a friend; I want a friend but the other wants a dominant relationship. It is similar for the inner world. Modules and mentalities are seeking different things; I want sex but another part of *me* wants to be moral and inhibits this; one part of me wants to be assertive, aggressive and another part of me wants to be dependent and cared for; one part of me strives to be special or superior but another part of me feels unable to live up to this – and so is inwardly attacked (Elliott & Greenberg, 1997).

Internal attacking is often elicited by the failure to obtain certain goals, e.g., to be pretty, competent, talented, esteemed. The *power of the attacks* for such failures can be observed in therapy where patients are encouraged to use two chairs to interact with their hostile–dominant self – or to use a more patient usable term '*internal bully*' (Elliott & Greenberg, 1997 Greenberg, 1979; Gilbert, 1997c). In one chair (the accusing chair) they speak aloud the evaluations of themselves (e.g., you are useless, no good, you don't try hard enough; if only you would diet you would look nice; if only you would work harder you'd get somewhere; if only you would stand up for yourself you wouldn't be so pathetic, etc.). After this they are invited to sit in a facing chair (the feeling chair) and reflect on how they feel when they listen to these critical messages. Two things often happen in depression. First, the person usually agrees that the messages of the bully (from the accusing chair) are accurate; they are useless. Second, when sitting in the feeling chair they often take up a lowered posture, often hunched, with eyes cast down. They may become tearful and feel as if they are getting smaller. *In effect they take up a highly submissive posture to their own attacks.* Greenberg, Elliott and Foerster (1990) point out that it is how a person responds to their own self-criticisms that is often crucial to whether depressed affect occurs. It is when people cannot defend themselves against attacks that depression takes hold. They argued (1990: 170):

. . . depression is much more likely if a person's weak/bad, hopeless, self-organization is triggered, than if the critical self and negative cognitions alone are activated. It is much more the person's response to the negative cognitions and their inability to cope with the self-criticisms, than the cognitions and criticisms alone, that lead to depression. People are unable to counter or combat the negative cognitions when the weak/bad helpless state has been evoked. This is when depressed affect emerges.

In evolution theory, the affects of Greenberg, Elliott and Foerster's (1990) 'weak/bad helpless self' are fuelled by activation of the evolved mechanisms of the brain that co-ordinates behaviour in contexts of defeat and severe down-rank attack (submissive defeat) – made more depressive by thoughts that one is trapped and cannot escape the attacks (Gilbert & Allan, 1998). It can be established then that the way internal signals to self are given structures our affects and biological programmes/strategies (e.g., sexual thoughts/images activate sexual feelings, and hostile thoughts can activate fearful submissive feelings).

As noted above, self-criticism can have adaptive functions. Like shame sensitivity it can entice us to change our behaviour, work harder and so forth (Driscoll, 1988). However, I am making a different point here. This is that self-attacking is using strategies and modules that were deigned to deal with external relationships. Thus, the language and emotional strength of the attacks can be as if the attacked is a non-compliant subordinate, a derogated rival, or at times a hated outsider. In the latter case the person can see part of themselves as highly undesirable and wants to be rid of it – sometimes literally to kill it off.

Overview

It has been suggested that humans evolved to be sensitive, and respond to (in evolutionary meaningful ways) certain signals: for example, stay close to carers, co-operate with allies, submit to threatening, stronger others. Each of these styles of relating are co-ordinated with internal modular-based mentalities that evolved to be sensitive to certain kinds of signal and recruit affects and behaviours accordingly. During the process of human evolution humans became increasing self-conscious, able to think of themselves in these relational ways and internally rehearse them (e.g., we can ruminate on our negative characteristics and failings). Hence, we are able to generate signals that activate our own sexual arousal, or become angry with self over failures and thus generate our own submissive states. Self-attacking recruits inner defensive mechanisms that were designed to deal with outsiders, competitors and non-compliant subordinates.

Psychotherapy

Cognitive psychotherapy and the limits of rationalization

If self-attacking is recruiting modules designed for dealing with competitors and the non-compliant then key questions arise as to how you can turn them off. Cognitive psychotherapy focuses on the consciously available thoughts and beliefs of a person to explore how these contribute to a person's distress (Beck, Emery & Greenberg, 1985; Ellis, 1977). Therapy involves learning to identify negative thoughts (e.g, self-attacking) identify dysfunctional styles of reasoning (e.g., jumping to conclusions, over-generalizing, self-blame); monitor the linkage between thinking/reasoning and feelings and make vigorous efforts to use rational and behavioural techniques to challenge dysfunctional thoughts. The focus is on teaching people how to exert more control over internal processes (Gilbert, 1997c, 2000; Greenberg & Padesky, 1995; Padesky & Greenberg, 1995).

However, there are many who, whilst working within the cognitive paradigm, recognize that an over-reliance on rationality alone can be limited (Emery, 1993; Mahoney, 1991). Indeed, cognitive therapists (and their patients) often find that using logic can have limited effect once affect and moods are *strongly* aroused; i.e., the more depressed or anxious a person the more they may struggle to hold their logical position.

In the last ten years or so there has been increasing recognition that this difficulty may be due to the way information is processed. For example, a distinction has been made between propositional and implicational cognitive systems (Teasdale & Barnard, 1993; Power & Dalgleish, 1997) – which, at the risk of over-simplification, relates to intellectual versus emotional reasoning, respectively. As Teasdale (1997: 146) notes, at the propositional level thoughts such as, 'I am worthless', are simply statements of belief – propositions about properties of self as an object. At the implicational level, however, such a statement represents a rich activation of affect and memories associated with experiences of being rejected or shamed. I would add that implicational thinking of this type taps into evolved heuristics for thinking, e.g., 'take submissive postures if under powerful attack'. Such thoughts are designed to be fast (modular processing) rather than rely on slower rational reasoning (Gilbert, 1998c).

There is increasing evidence that some cognitions operate through very *rapid* information processing systems that are designed for speed rather than accuracy (Epstein, 1994; Epstein, Lipson, Holstein & Huh, 1992) and often have built in biases (see Gilbert, Bailey & McGuire, Chapter 1, this volume). These fast track processing systems (modules) use heuristics, take short cuts to reach conclusions quickly, use crudely integrated information, are reliant on affect and how something feels, are preconscious and possibly rely on earlier experience and conditioned emotional responses (Power & Dalgeish, 1997). Hence, certain emotional and mood states utilize *fast track* modes of functioning and are reliant on more primitive, earlier evolved appraisal-response systems (modules), possibly encoded in limbic and sub-limbic areas (Bailey, 1987; Buck, 1988; MacLean, 1985). We become more irrational in the presence of strong affect because the brain is designed for rapid action when under threat or attack (Gilbert, 1993, 1998c). Hence, trying to enable people to focus 'on the evidence against a negative belief' is in some ways running up against the limitations of basic brain design. Even when people know they are being irrational, and know that if they could focus on the evidence this would be helpful, they may struggle to make it work.

Finally, we can note that recently cognitive therapists have paid more attention to the maturation process in therapy work (Emery, 1993; Mahoney, 1991). The cognitive concept of 'schema', defined as basic core beliefs of self and others can be seen as rather rigid beliefs which change on the basis of evidence and new experiences. Mentalities, on the other hand, have their own internal maturational process requiring different inputs at different times and are integrated in the mind with specific self-organizing preferences and rehearsal routines. In this sense mentalities are like archetypes (Gilbert, 1989; Stevens, Chapter 5, this volume) and change can occur through maturation. This requires therapists to take account of the developmental competencies of a patient (see Emery, 1993; Goncalves & Ivey, 1993) and also needs. One key difference between schema and mentality is that mentalities are innately 'role seeking', aimed at (strategically) engaging others in certain ways and eliciting certain signals (to be cared for and supported; to care and enjoy nurturing others, to have satisfactory sexual relationships, to control subordinates and derogate competitors, etc.) and are innately predisposed to find certain social relationships positive (acceptance, approval status) and others (rejection, disapproval, loss of status) unpleasant (Gilbert, 1989 1997c; Nesse, 1998). As people learn to relate to themselves and others in different ways they will give and receive different social signals (Wagner, Kiesler & Schmidt, 1995) which aid (or hinder) the maturation process of the self (both the internal organization of a mentality and its interaction with other mentalities). Thus, for example, as a person learns to be more caring they may automatically become less competitive and rank focused, and more able to recognize and express emotional needs. In turn others 'warm to them'.

Is it possible then that we can teach a patient to recruit a different mentality (other than rationality) to resolve their inner conflicts and change the quality of self-directed signals? Shortly, I will argue that it is, and that the mentality that can be recruited is one of caring, which was evolved to help kin and friends, and uses the affects of sympathy and compassion. First however, we need to look more closely at *the types* of hostile signal people give themselves.

Internal images of attackers

Taking the idea that the mind is inherently relational, and 'role seeking' it can be useful to ask patients to imagine their inner negative thoughts (and the part that challenges them) as if they were like inner persons or sub-personalities (Rowan, 1990). When I started to do this I was surprised and fascinated by some of the responses.

If one treats these internal dialogues 'as if' they are internal representations of social relationships, they can be *personified* (Benjamin, 1997). Learning to converse with imaginary inner parts of the self is by no means a new therapy technique (Rowan, 1990), and has been used by diverse therapies such as working with inner archetypes (Jung, 1954/1993), and psychosynthesis (Assagioli, 1975). Gestalt therapists have long used techniques of dialoging with parts of the self as if they were separate individuals (Greenberg, 1979; Greenberg & Pascual-Leone, 1997). Frederick and McNeal (1999) give a good overview of such ways of working from an ego strengthening approach. Schwartz (1995) has offered an intriguing development of such ideas calling his therapy approach Internal Family Systems Therapy. This is based on the idea that parts of the self can operate like families, with attackers, victims and helpers, etc. This idea shared by many (Rowan, 1990) also suggests that a therapist can gain 'direct access' to these inner parts of self by inviting them to speak directly to the therapist or an empty chair (Elliott & Greenberg, 1997; Greenberg, Rice & Elliott, 1993). Cognitive therapists also sometimes engage patients in eliciting 'the voice' of a negative schema and dialoguing with it (Bricker, Young & Flanagan, 1993; Gilbert, 2000).

What does an evolutionary approach add to this apart for offering further support to the notion of internal part selves as arising from the evolution of (social) mentalities? First, is the idea that it is the *signal quality* (nonverbal communicative aspects) that the brain is sensitive to not just verbal content (Frederick & McNeal, 1999; Greenberg, Rice & Elliott, 1993; Greenberg & Pascual-Leone, 1997, speak in terms of 'emotional quality'). Hence, it is important to focus specifically on the types of signal quality of these internal dialogues rather than just the content of their communications. That is, an evolutionary approach would specifically focus on the *domains* of the affect – the actual visual and auditory qualities of the signal.

Greenberg, Rice and Elliott (1993) have written an excellent and recommended outline of how to work with the topdog or hostile dominant part of the self. It can simply be added that these internal dialogues probably affect physiological states. Indeed, given the evidence noted above, that hostile signals from a dominant can reduce blood levels of 5-HT in the subordinate, and increase stress hormones, and given that in the two chairs example noted previously a person often adopts a submissive posture to their hostile inner voices, then it is reasonable to suggest that a heightened tendency to engage in hostile internal self-talk will be physiologically disruptive. Indeed, it may well recruit the submissive-defeat profile of lowered 5-HT and increased stress hormones. But on this we lack good data.

Varieties of hostile–dominant inner figures

Hostile attacks can take different forms – from mild verbal rebukes, shaming, rejection through to outright violence. Clearly, the causes of hostile interactions, the level of aggression, the types of aggression and the inhibitors of aggression expression are subject to numerous eliciting and controlling processes. While we have learned something of these processes for *inter*-personal conflict (Archer, 1988; Bailey, 1987; Tedeschi & Felson, 1994) we know rather little about them in *intra*-personal conflict. However, if the intra-personal processes are co-opted from the inter-personal then similar eliciting and control processes may apply. Key questions are therefore what determines the level of self-attacking, the forms it will take, and importantly for the discussion here, what will limit or inhibit it?

Blair (1997) has addressed the issue of aggression inhibition in psychopathic violence and has posited the existence of a violence inhibition mechanism (VIM). This mechanism is normally sensitive to (for example) signals of submission and distress. His research has shown that the psychopath is not affected by cues of distress from others. However, even in non-psychopaths social contexts can affect the extent to which aggression is controlled by submission and distress signals from victims. For example, for some dominant individuals within groups, attacking is ritualized and ceases when there are appropriate submissive signals from the attacked. Furthermore, when conflicts are between groups, persecutors may kill those seen as the enemy or out-group, even though they submit. In other words dominant attacks are not always sensitive to submissive or distress signals. Indeed, human history is littered with atrocities, from mass crucifictions of the enemy to sadistic torture. It would seem possible then that in certain contexts it is not only psychopaths who have innate capacities for such behaviours, where attacks are not inhibited by the distress or submission of the attacked.

This may be an important distinction because when patients enact their hostile self-dialogues and are distressed by them, their internal attacking part may not be deterred by their distress but continues to attack. It is as if three key inhibitors of inter-personal aggression expression (1) responsiveness to submission and distress signals; (2) beliefs about the immorality of attacking others, and (3) fear of counter-attack, are not operating in the intra-personal (self-to-self) domain. A clinical example, from using the two chairs, may help to clarify this idea. When Anita, a person with a borderline personality disorder enacted her self-attacking voice in the two chairs she said to herself, 'You are bad and worthless. You just ruin every-thing around you. You don't deserve to be happy and I am not going to let you'. When asked to sit back in her own (the feeling) chair she became tearful and agreed with the attack she had levelled against herself saying, 'It's true, I am a bad person'. When asked to sit back again in the attacking chair and say how she felt about the other part of self who was submitting and tearful, the attacking part said, 'Oh she is so pathetic and deserves to be punished and destroyed'. The self-attacking part was totally unresponsive to the (inner) distress it was causing; felt justified in (not morally adversed to) delivering this attack and did not fear counter-attack.

It is therefore useful to explore the actual *types of signal* from the critical part of the self. These can vary from aggressive demands to try harder or do differently, through to more sadistic contemptuous attacks (Benjamin, 1997; Elliott & Greenberg, 1997). In the former the patient's mood is usually affected by how well they submit and comply with these standards demanded. If they are hard working, successful and/or comply with demanded standards they do not self-attack.

However, sadistic attacks are more commonly focused on desires to punish and hurt. Just as such desires can be directed to external others so they can be directed to the self. In these cases submission and compliance may not work to stop the attacks. Helping patients recognize the difference between aggressive demands and a sadistic attack can be helpful because people often do not recognize the sadistic nature of their attacks and that submission and agreeing with the attack may not help them.

To distinguish between types of self-attack the therapist can focus on the stimulus qualities of the experienced attack. For example, one can ask the patient to imagine the inner attacking part as a person then ask, 'What does your internal critic/bully *look* like?'. Ask about the size, postures and facial expression. One may also ask, 'What does your internal bully *sound* like?' and 'What do you think is his/her intent?' Invite them to describe the *tone* of the voice. From an evolutionary point of view these are likely to be salient stimulus features that *recruit affect*. Patients may not be fully conscious of these signals but talk about them in terms of 'a powerful presence', or their affective quality. Techniques of guided discovery and imagination, (Padesky & Greenberg, 1995) or amplification (Jung, 1954/1993) can be used – although patients can be highly suggestible, so it is important to clarify that this is a therapy device to aid inner working and thus must 'fit' with their own experience and what is helpful.

It is not uncommon for the person to be able to focus on internal images of their hostile part of self and give descriptions such as 'aggressive', 'powerful', 'big', 'male' with a 'sadistic smile', 'irritated expression' or a 'disgust face', etc. It can be helpful to focus on the typical components of that part of self that can represent the internal bully (which I have argued arises from subordinate control and derogating of competitors' modules) to try to discover the affective quality of the bullying message. Here are some examples.

Kate was a person who became easily disappointed with herself and frustrated by her own limitations. But feelings of disappointment were associated with serious inner shaming/derogating attacks. She would think of herself as stupid and worthless; a waste of space. When asked to personify this inner critical 'voice' she described it as a tall figure, dressed in black, with long nails and an angry, irritated expression. Her face was cold and partly in shadow from a head garment. She felt the figure 'loomed over her and often stood to the side'. This figure was powerful and not easily subdued. When 'this figure' was around she felt powerless to counter-act it, felt easily defeated and subordinated by it, and unable to escape. At these times she felt hopeless and suicidal. In one dialogue she said, 'The only way I can escape her is to kill myself'. When, she tried to rationalize her negative 'self-talk' of being useless she felt that it was mainly from this dark image who told her off for being irrational!

Sam had a strong sense of shame about his sexuality. When asked to describe the image that came to him when he felt ashamed he described it as a stern father-like figure whose face was 'full of disgust'. Aggression was far less evident in this (hostile dominate) bullying figure than for Kate; it was more disgust, contempt and rejection. All Sam wanted to do was hide from it (which he felt was impossible) and felt totally powerless to counteract it.

Jane's visualization of her hostile dominate part was different again. It was not aggressive and all consuming like Kate's. It appeared like a 'prim and proper' teacher – a powerful and intrusive figure who would simply shake her head in disappointment as if to say, 'Oh dear Jane, I expected so much more of you but you just let yourself down all the time. I really don't think it's worth bothering with you'.

These images/thoughts/voices are *dominant* because the person feels unable to escape or counteract them and they are *hostile* because they can be aggressive, sadistic, shaming and/or rejecting – but their exact textures vary. The ego aspect of self usually feels subordinate, less powerful (to counteract) them or even weak in their presence, and unable to escape. My point is then that the strength of the internal *attack* is not simply because of the strength of the belief or a 'must' belief, as in cognitive therapy, but because of the *affective qualities imputed into the internal bully*. The attack may be aggressive, shaming or simply rejecting and ostracizing, but it is usually felt to be dominant and powerful. It is also commonly replayed and rehearsed in consciousness.

It is common to find that patients have felt subordinate to their 'inner bullies' and have spent a long time (rehearsing) trying to placate the inner bully by trying hard to reach certain standards and earn their approval (Greenberg, Rice & Elliott, 1993). In this sense the inner world seems to operate around a central axis of dominant–subordinate that is highly attentive to signals of success–failure and status. This in turn seems to arise from a mismatch between what a person wants to be and what they feel they are. This may be linked with strong beliefs that a person has to prove him or herself and has to *earn* respect and approval. Lapses and failures will be met with social punishment of put down, loss of status and rejection. Just as people can relate to their Gods by trying to live up to the ideals expected (to avoid punishment or rejection) so people try to live up to (subordinate themselves to) their inner relationships as represented by that part of themselves they feel is dominant over them.

When a patient is in the 'attacking' chair, it is possible for the therapist to ask various Socratic questions: e.g., what do you hope to achieve by bullying X (purpose)? When did you first start to bully (origin)? What would convince you that this is not helpful (evidence on the need to reduce attacking)? (Elliott & Greenberg, 1997; Gilbert, 2000).

Having established the salient stimuli/signals (the 'look', 'voice tone' and affective qualities) of the hostile–dominant or bully, which are often fuelled by the effects of disappointment (e.g., when a person fails to reach a desired goal; Gilbert, 1997c), the therapist can then set about exploring ways to cope with these feelings and internal experiences. How do you turn off the hostile–dominant part (modules) of the self?

Challenging the hostile bully

As noted above the three most typical ways that aggression is inhibited is: sensitivity to distress and submission cues; moral beliefs against attacking; and threats of counter-attacking. Each of these can be used to confront self-attacking.

Counter-attack

It is sometimes possible to work with the self-critical thoughts (hostile–dominant part of self) by counter-attacking; a technique not dissimilar to schema attacking (Young, Beck & Weinberger, 1993). It is also possible to use the two chairs technique (Greenberg, Rice & Elliott, 1993) which may enable the patient to deliver counter-aggressive or assertive messages to their self-attacking part as imagined to be sitting in the opposite chair. Or a person may imagine someone who is critical of them and attempt fighting back (e.g., in role play or imagination). The grounds for the counter-attack as those suggested by cognitive therapy such as providing counter-evidence for the attack; e.g., 'You say I am useless but actually I have achieved this, that and the other'. The effect of the counter-attack is encouraged to be forceful and even aggressive. One can call this an attack-attack strategy. Patients, however may worry that they will not be strong enough to subdue their 'inner bully' and it will only attack harder.

Developing (moral) beliefs against attacking

It is not uncommon in depressed and personality disordered people for them to agree with their self-attacks and believe them to be justified. Here the therapist can work to help the patient develop alternative moral beliefs about the value and morality of attacking – be it to self or others. By looking at the evidence for a negative self-attacking set of cognitions the patient may learn to generate alternative beliefs and cognitions that show that the attacks are not justified, are often over-generalized and absolutistic, and, given their harmful effects, immoral (Gilbert, 1997c).

It may also be possible (in mild cases) to soften the hostile part of self with dialogues in the two chairs by, for example, understanding the motives of the bully (e.g., to help the person excel; Greenberg, Rice & Elliott, 1993). However, in some cases, especially those where a person has been abused, the hostile part may be an internalized actual other who was sadistic and/or exploitative and did not have the best interests of the abused at heart. So trying to soften this image may not be that unhelpful. Therapists therefore need to be sensitive to the actual affective (and non-verbal) qualities of the inner bully or hostile, imaginary figure(s).

136

Sensitivity to distress and the role of inner warmth and compassion

The third way attacks can be inhibited is via sensitivity to distress and the activation of caring modules in these contexts. From an evolutionary point of view, counter-attacking may subdue the dominant–hostile part of self but may not do much to move the patient towards (and rehearse) internal role relationships of warmth, compassion and forgiveness – key signals in times of stress and set-backs. As noted elsewhere (Gilbert, 1989, 1997c) warmth, friendship and caring originate in a different evolved mentality to that of attacking. This is not to say that some patients don't find counter-attacking the bully (or learning to be assertive or challenging the logic and evidence of the negative self-cognitions) unhelpful, but therapists need to gain the evidence for this. Even if the patient feels they 'can win' this way it can still leave them feeling empty because there are no internal prosocial signals of support and care.

There is now considerable evidence that caring, supportive and helpful relationships have major physiological benefits (Bailey, Chapter 3, this volume; Field, 1998; Uchino, Cacioppo & Kiecolt-Glaser, 1996). If one takes the evolutionary idea that social signals of care, affection and warmth are biologically potent in activating a sense of safety and well-being (Bowlby, 1969; Gilbert, 1993; Harlow & Mears, 1979) then attention can be given to how these can be internalized. Hence, it is not just counter-attacking, subduing or defending against a hostile part of self that is at issue but to integrate a totally different pattern of mentalities within the self (see Liotti, Chapter 11, this volume). One is seeking to teach the person how to relate to themselves with (and rehearse) inner signals of care/warmth that will have physiological benefits.

Activating care-giving mentalities into the self-system

The innate potential 'to care' has given rise to various psychological competencies such as attention to the needs of self and others, recruitment of emotions such as empathy, sympathy and affection and behaviours that foster development (De Waal, 1996). Fogel, Melson and Mistry (1986: 55) define care giving as: 'The provision of guidance, protection and care for the purpose of fostering developmental change congruent with the expected potential for change of the object of nurturance'. The orientation of caring may be expressed to other humans, animals, plants (one's garden), inanimate objects (e.g., the family car) or the self. It involves the concept of 'looking after'.

Fogel, Melson and Mistry (1986) note four dimensions of caring which include: (1) choice of object (as noted above); (2) expression of caring and nurturant feelings; (3) motivation to care and nurture; and (4) awareness of the role and need for caring. I would also add the ability to forgive (see later), particularly in situations where shame and/or disappointment induce anger. Each of these may require therapeutic attention. A therapist may try to recruit qualities of the care-giving mentality by offering a caring, supportive relationship (Margulies, 1984; Mahoney, 1991; Liotti, Chapter 11, this volume; Schaap, Bennun, Schindler & Hoogduin, 1993), and also by directly teaching patients how to be more caring and empathic to self and others (Frederick & McNeal, 1999). Hence, one way of counteracting a hostile inner module is to try to shift the patient from a social rank (dominate–subordinate) mentality to a care-giving one and to utilize his or her innate dispositions for caring behaviour and responding to being cared for. Sometimes patients have poorly developed caring skills in general while at other times it is primarily the target of caring (e.g., to the self) that is at issue.

Patients often come to therapy with a history of poor early care provision (abuse and neglect) and most therapies have as one of their core aims that of helping patients become more caring to themselves and others. In addition to using the therapeutic relationship, different therapies go about this in different ways, e.g., targeting hostile cognitions (Beck, Emery & Greenberg 1985; Ellis, 1977) and unconscious processes (Greenberg & Mitchell, 1983), altering internal working models of attachment (Safran & Segal, 1990; see Liotti, Chapter 11, this volume), resolving splits using the two chairs or processing split off emotions (Greenberg, Rice & Elliott, 1993), increasing positive reward and reducing self-punishment (Rehm, 1988), de-shaming (Gilbert, 1998d, 2000), and using various fantasy, imagery and hypnotic experiences to recruit care for the self (Frederick & McNeal, 1999). Within Buddhism, a common meditation is that of 'loving kindness' where individuals practise meditation on their own image and directing feelings of 'loving kindness' towards themselves (Dalai Lama, 1993). If one uses this in therapy one might clarify the point of this meditation as helping the person to deliver more positive internal signals to disrupt the cycle of critical attack (from the hostile–dominant part of self) and submissive deflation. I also discuss the possible physiological benefits of this exercise.

Cognitive therapists have begun to move in this direction by using challenges for negative thoughts such as, 'What would you say to a friend in a similar situation?' or 'What would you like someone who cares about you to say?' or 'What would you say to a child to help them overcome this difficulty?' (Greenberg & Padesky, 1995). These kinds of interventions are often couched in the domains of logical challenges but are actually of a quite different type of challenge because they require the person to think of an individual and this makes it a form of relational thinking. Moreover, such interventions seek to internally generate a different type of *emotional* (caring) signal.

The third chair

One way of working with the compassionate self (caring mentalities) is to facilitate the patient to have their hostile dialogue with themselves, moving back and forth between the attacking chair and the attacked. Then invite the patient to sit in a third chair and say, 'Now in this chair I would like you to imagine that you are a compassionate helper, someone who understands the pain of conflicts and would like to heal them. What would you like to say to this chair?' (the chair from which they enacted their bullying dialogues). Then ask, 'and what would you like to say to that part of you that sat in the attacked chair, where you felt beaten down and depressed?'

Different kinds of insight can emerge from this, including gaining insight to self-attacking. For example, one patient suddenly started to cry and said, 'I guess I can see that the bullying part of me is really quite frightened and thinks if I don't make the grade no one will care or love it'. For the first time she saw the bully shrink in size and power. Or you can ask, 'What would it take to heal this bully part of you?' This kind of intervention has moved away from having to subdue or counter-attack the bully and reframed it as an issue of caring and healing. Again this can generate quite strong emotions. It should be collaborative, looking at the benefits and costs of healing one's inner critical self.

When asked to say what she felt (when sitting in the compassionate chair) of the part that felt defeated and tearful this patient said, 'I can see that really this part of me is like a child and has so little power to control the bully. It just wants it to stop attacking, to hide away'. She was able to see then that from the position of the small hurt (subordinate) child she had little chance of dealing with her inner bully.

Visualization

Another way to 'bring on line' the caring mentality and inner caring signals is via visualization. A patient can be asked to imagine an internal carer, helper or compassionate figure (Frederick & McNeal, 1999). In psychosynthesis a person may be asked to imagine a wiser inner spiritual figure (Assagioli, 1975). And for thousands of years prayer has served this function. Discussion with the patient on the properties of care and compassion is important (e.g., as growth enhancing, forgiving, etc.; Gilbert, 1997b,c). It is also useful to check on beliefs about recruiting this aspect of self. Some patients see it as weak or as 'letting the self off the hook' and maintain beliefs that the way to get well is to continually try to placate and live up to the demands of the hostile dominant part of themselves. But if a patient agrees that becoming more compassionate, accepting and less self-attacking would be helpful, then again the focus can be on the affective and non-verbal qualities (e.g., appearance, tone of voice) of this part of self.

What one is attempting here is to help the patient begin to give themselves evolutionary important signals (care and sympathy). To enable this the patient may try creating inner images of a caring other, someone they could be close to, focusing on appearance, facial expression and voice tones. One might ask, 'what might the caring/ compassionate side say when you are down and being very self-critical of yourself?' Sometimes the first images that come up are not particularly useful. For example, in one case, a patient identified a compassionate image of a plumpish woman, covered in pastry and smiling. But when I asked her what this part of her might say to her when she was depressed, her response was, 'she's never there when

I'm depressed. I think she gives up in disgust on me'. Clearly, for this lady, this care giving image could not impact when she was in the depression and her critical side had the upper hand. Eventually, the image of a helper that came to her when she was depressed was that of a fairy-like figure. Practising listening to this figure (who would also give her all of the typical messages of cognitive therapy, e.g., there is little evidence to support this attack) had a helpful impact on her progress. She told me that while she had tried to do the work with writing things down on 'thought forms', she found these difficult to focus on. However, when she imagined herself talking to her fairy-like figure it became much easier and she felt more comforted when she could create a strong image of that figure in her mind. (When I discussed this work at a case conference one of the women said, 'Oh I hate fairies. They are pathetic little things' so one can't proscribe images. The patient has to work to find those that help them.)

Emotional warmth and challenging

The *messages* of the caring compassionate aspect of self, be they enacted in the third chair or through visualization, can be similar to standard cognitive challenges to negative thinking (Gilbert, 1997b; e.g., identifying cognitive distortions; focusing on the evidence against a negative belief) but it is the *emotional* quality of the challenge that can be the key to success.

Challenges to negative beliefs can be taught to be delivered in a warm and friendly way and not as an another instruction, or bullying command (thou shalt be rational – stupid!). Although similar ideas have been described by many cognitive therapists in challenging negative schema (e.g., Bricker, Young & Flanagan, 1993) novice therapists often neglect the focus on this *emotional* warmth aspect of challenging in favour of accuracy and searching for evidence against a negative belief. And they may rarely teach the patient how to have a 'warm voice' when they challenge their own negative beliefs.

One way to do this is to help patients generate alternative thoughts to their self-attacking ones. For example, alternatives might include, 'I am not a bad as I tell myself. My self-attacking is based on ignoring the evidence that I can help others and am able to do X, Y or Z. I am frustrated with myself right now but I probably won't even remember this event in six weeks time'; and so on in standard cognitive therapy ways. When this is done the patient is asked to read through the alternative thoughts but additionally to try to generate a feeling of compassionate understanding and warmth – just like a supporting caring friend might speak to them or they to a friend. This may be practised a number of times and difficulties to doing this explored. Patients may also role play these alternatives in the two chairs. For example, they read out their negative thoughts from the one chair then switch to another chair and deliver the counter-thoughts in a sympathetic, warm voice. This allows the therapist to check on the affective tone of the challenge. Problems in doing this and/or feeling 'emotionally cold' when challenging their self-attacking thoughts can sometimes lead to important areas for work.

The value of generating internal caring 'others' has also been explored in patients suffering from schizophrenia. Thomas (1997), for example, points out that patients who hear hostile voices may try to resist or distract themselves, but with limited success. However, he explores a case in which a lady was able to develop a more friendly compassionate voice to counteract hostile ones. This caring voice had more power to challenge the hostile voices than her ego-self and was distress reducing. It is early days in this kind of work but the potential to generate positive internal signals in the form of inner voices/figures could hold much promise. (For further discussion on the development of inner warmth see also, Frederick & McNeal, 1999.)

Caring and grieving

Beginning a process of internalizing caring signals can activate grief and increase awareness of a sense of painful aloneness. For example, one person who had experienced poor mothering, became emotionally distressed when trying to imagine a caring/compassionate side to herself. She said, 'I can't think of that because it opens up a deep longing and yearning in me as if I will be swamped by sadness and grief'. When she tried to imagine a caring part of herself she felt, 'just an empty void'. It was many months before she felt able to work through her grief and longing to be cared for (and fear of it), and learned how to be more compassionate and 'warm with herself'.

Empathy and sympathy are emotional qualities of the caring giving mentality, and in some situations the compassionate self does not try to reduce pain but empathize with it. Just as a therapist's empathy can be healing when he/she acknowledges the patient's pain and suffering, without necessarily attempting to change it (Margulies, 1984) so too for the caring self. In some ways this is a kind of desensitization where the person learns how to 'bear' or tolerate anxiety, anger, sadness and disappointment. Or in self-psychology terms this might be called self-soothing (Kohut, 1977). One patient found that after working with 'his caring/compassionate self' he was able to tolerate being sad about aspects of his life because he felt there was 'now a part of me that understands it and how awful it was. I don't feel weak now for crying over it'. In this case caring helped to reduce his shame of his need to grieve.

John, who came to see me with a serious depression, had been adopted by an aunt when he was 5 years old after his mother died and father couldn't cope. The aunt was emotionally cold and did not really want him (he felt) but did it out of obligation to her sister. She would often chastise him with ideas of, 'if your mother were here now she'd be very disappointed in you'. John's internal attachment/caring giving figures were thus cold and full of ideas of being a let down and a disappointment. As a child he had thoughts of his mother looking down from heaven and being angry with him. Hence, not surprisingly he had internalized his carers as hostile–dominant ones (aunt) and abandoning (mother and father). These became the template for self-evaluations.

141

We explored ways that he might try to bring some warmth into these internal models of his mother (who he often thought about when depressed) and his own self-evaluative style. We decided to get more data on his mother by him talking to his father about what kind of women she was. It turned out that his father had been very much in love with her and said she was a very warm person and not like her sister (the aunt). John also had an old picture of him sitting on his mother's knee, with both smiling, when he was about four years old. He brought that to therapy and we began imagery work of how sad it was that she had left him, how she would dearly have loved to have been there for him as he grew up, and that maybe, if she were alive today she would empathize with the pain he had felt as a child – and now. Also that when times were hard he could try to imagine her offering loving and supportive messages (the kind he might offer to someone else in pain). This brought out some very moving and tearful sessions (for both patient and therapist) – unblocking profound grief but also helping him internalize a warmer inner mother rather than a critical one. His depression (and negative self-evaluations), for which he had seen other therapists and taken many antidepressants, gradually gave way to a more confident and relaxed individual.

In some types of therapy a therapist may hope that by offering a caring relationship they can re-parent the patient – although there are real dangers in a therapist going too far down this road and believing they can 'love patients back to health' (Frederick & NcNeal, 1999). Nonetheless, patients often say that they can 'hear the voice of the therapist' speaking to them at certain times or recall pictures of helpful scenes from therapy when the therapist was empathic. In other words people *automatically* use images of caring others to help them when things are bad. Indeed, it may be the access to these kinds of images and memories that are particularly healing and soothing because they *evolved to be* soothing signals. There is much anecdotal evidence that when people are separated from loved ones and in times of stress (e.g., in war) they naturally use images of those who care about them to help them cope. In my view it is also sometimes possible to directly create inner compassionate images that a patient will automatically attend to when frustrations and disappointment arise. One of John's therapists had encouraged acknowledging anger to his mother for leaving him. That did not help in this case because it still left a void (no internalized positive signals) in the care-giving mentality.

Inner forgiveness and self-acceptance

An area where the development of the inner compassionate work can be difficult in is in the area of forgiveness. Forgiveness can be related to a quality of caring and compassion that can be important to discuss and develop. When people find forgiveness difficult they often use the concept of 'don't deserve'. Recently, there has been growing attention to the importance of a forgiveness triad (Enright, 1996). The triad involves being able to forgive others rather than ruminate on vengeful and often impotent rage; being able to be helped by receiving the forgiveness of others (e.g. not disqualifying it); and self-forgiveness. Learning to forgive others (i.e., reducing rumination on hostile vengeful thoughts and fantasies – or in evolutionary terms, turning off the desire to act in a hostile–dominant way to others) has been shown to have important therapeutic benefits (Freedman & Enright, 1996; McCullough, Worthington & Rachal, 1997). Forgiveness does not mean one necessarily now likes or wants to associate with the one forgiven, only that one drops the need for vengeance and impotent rage. *Self-forgiveness* in evolutionary terms might be seen as reducing the hostile–dominant – submissive internal relationship. Forgiveness can be over major life events which have caused damage or disappointment to self and/or others, through to common, frequent, mild problems with forgiveness over small, everyday lapses/failures. For some patients small lapses and mistakes generate high levels of anger and self-criticism. Learning the art of the acceptance of human fallibility is a well-articulated rational emotive therapy endeavour (Ellis, 1977; Ellis & Whiteley, 1979). This may be advanced by attention to the affective quality of the signal or dialogue with the self; the process of becoming more accepting of fallibility.

Ellis (1977) suggests that self-acceptance comes from giving up the 'musts' and 'shoulds'. Enright (1996) outlines a number of stages in the process of self-forgiveness which involve: an acknowledgment and uncovering phase of harm done; a decision phase involving commitment to forgive self and avoid self-condemnation; a working through phase involving the acceptance of oneself as fallible and (the Buddhist idea) that disappointment in life is inevitable (Ramaswami & Sheikh, 1996); and, finally, an outcome phase acknowledging the benefits of forgiveness. Learning to foster an inner world of forgiveness creates a different affective structure to the self. At times this is helped by use of caring, compassionate images, and two or three chair work.

The blocks to forgiveness of both self and others often revolve around the evolutionary salient domain of the need to retaliate or coerce. Typical beliefs that inhibit forgiveness of others are, 'I should not let others get away with it. I will be weak if I give up my anger'. Self-forgiveness can be inhibited by beliefs (of the bully) of, 'If I don't criticize myself I will never achieve anything'. These beliefs can be elicited in the normal cognitive way or by directly speaking with the hostile–dominant part of the self. Such beliefs are often fuelled by the needs to gain status, earn approval, respect and feel able to 'hold one's head up'. When individuals are strongly motivated to gain rank and status in the eyes of others (to *prove* themselves worthy) they may look to therapy to help them achieve their goals but often this can serve to placate the bully and does not always help in the tough job of self-acceptance. At these times the therapist may need to advise that the secret of success is in the ability to fail (Gilbert, 1997c).

Conclusion

This chapter has argued that social signals can be hostile, neutral or friendly (Gilbert, 1993). Signal quality evolved to activate specific emotions in recipients. For example, hostile signals will activate fight/flight associated with anger or anxiety, friendly signals can activate feelings of friendship and positive affect, and sexual signals can activate sexual arousal. Importantly, however, these signals can be delivered internally such that we can activate our own fight/flight strategies, our own depressive strategies and even our own sexual strategies. In many mood, personality and psychotic disorders the internal self-dialogues are hostile such that the person experiences an internal critical or attacking signal to which they often feel unable to defend against and thus more defeated or fearfully subordinate.

Since the mind is set up for social relating, it is possible that cognitive therapy can be adapted to utilize the human capacity to personify certain functions. In other words, shape and form can be given to the critical side, to the rational side and to the supportive compassionate side of self. Once these are placed in a relational framework, patients may find it easier to challenge self-attacking and develop more rational and compassionate self-beliefs.

Cognitive therapy tends to see most maladaptive beliefs as originating in early childhood. However, an evolutionary approach suggests that childhood experiences do not create pathology as such but it is how different parts of our (evolved) selves (which reflect underlying evolved strategies) are recruited, mature and are utilized that may cause the disturbance in affect control. If we learn to be intensely self-critical, or become so as we become depressed, then over time, this can activate a submissive, defeated sense of self and activate defensive responses. If we feel trapped with our inner bullies, and beaten into submissive defeat, then this can be particularly depressogenic (Gilbert & Allan, 1998).

Currently, there is little research evidence to show that personifying internal dialogues is more therapeutic than more purely rational approaches (although see Greenberg, Rice & Elliott, 1993). Moreover, some patients have enormous difficulty in developing any sense of inward compassion or caring (Frederick & McNeal, 1999). Even caring signals from a therapist can produce panic (Liotti, Chapter 11, this volume). For example, as a result of past experiences (e.g., abuse) certain types of signal assume very different properties from those they were evolved to provide (e.g., a caring-closeness signal can be seen as a threat). Nonetheless, helping the patient understand the process of developing inner caring (by simply making the distinction between internal friendly and internal hostile signals) can help the patient begin to generate his or her own inner images of caring others and foster a more self-caring, warm emotional tone.

Finally, it should be clarified that these ideas are only adjuncts to other basic therapy techniques. I hope, however, that evolutionary ideas that focus on the evolution of role-creating processes that have certain functions, and which can play off against each other internally, may offer new insights into the healing process of psychotherapy. There is much work still to do before we really understand how these systems and mentalities operate *intra*-personally and how to alter their relationships.

References

Archer, J. (1988) *The Behavioural Biology of Aggression*, Cambridge: Cambridge University Press.

Assagioli, R. (1975) *Psychosynthesis: A Collection of basic writings*, Wellingborough: Turnstone Books.

Bailey, K.G. (1987) *Human Paleopsychology. Applications to Aggression and Pathological Processes*, Hillsdale, NJ: Lawrence Erlbaum Associates Inc.

Beck, A.T., Emery, G. & Greenberg, R.L. (1985) *Anxiety Disorders and Phobias: A Cognitive Approach*, New York: Basic Books.

Belsky, J., Steinberg, L. & Draper, P. (1990) 'Childhood experiences, interpersonal development, and reproductive strategy: An evolutionary theory of socialization', *Child Development* 62: 647–70.

Benjamin, L.S. (1997) 'Human imagination and psychotherapy', *Journal of Psychotherapy Integration* 7: 195–212.

Bergner, R.M. (1988) 'Status dynamic psychotherapy with depressed patients', *Psychotherapy* 25: 266–72.

Birtchnell, J. (1993) *How Humans Relate: A New Interpersonal Theory*, Westport: CT: Praeger.

Blair, R.J.R. (1997) 'A cognitive approach to morality: Investigating the psychopath', in S. Baron-Cohen (ed.), *The Maladapted Mind: Classic Readings in Evolutionary Psychopathology*, (pp. 85–113), Hove, UK: Psychology Press.

Blatt, S.J., Quinlan, D.M., Chevron, E.S., McDonald, C. & Zuroff, D. (1982) 'Dependency and self criticism: psychological dimensions of depression', *Journal of Consulting and Clinical Psychology* 50: 113–24.

Bowlby, J. (1969) *Attachment: Attachment and Loss*, Vol. 1, London: Hogarth Press.

Bowlby, J. (1973). *Separation, Anxiety and Anger. Attachment and Loss*, Vol. 2, London: Hogarth Press.

Bricker, D., Young, J.E. & Flanagan, C.M. (1993) 'Schema-focused cognitive therapy: A framework for characterological problems', in K.T. Kuehlwein & H. Rosen (eds.), *Cognitive Therapies in Action: Evolving Innovative Practice*, (pp. 88–125), San Francisco: Jossey-Bass.

Brown, G.W., Harris, T.O. & Hepworth C. (1995) 'Loss, humiliation and entrapment among women developing depression: A patient and non-patient comparison', *Psychological Medicine* 25: 7–21.

Buck, R. (1988) *Human Motivation and Emotion*, New York: Wiley.

Buss, D.M. (1995) 'Evolutionary psychology: A new paradigm for psychological science', *Psychological Inquiry* 6: 1–87.

Buss, D.M. (1999) *Evolutionary Psychology: The New Science of Mind*, Boston: Allyn & Bacon

Chadwick, P. & Birchwood, M. (1994) The omnipotence of voices: A cognitive approach to auditory hallucinations. *British Journal of Psychiatry* 164: 190–201.

Cleghorn, J.M. & Albert, M.L. (1990) 'Modular disjunction in schizophrenia: A framework for a pathological psychophysiology', in A. Kales, C.N. Stefanis & J.A. Talbott (eds.), *Recent Advances in Schizophrenia*, (pp. 59–80), New York: Springer-Verlag.

Coon, D. (1992) *Introduction to Psychology: Exploration and Application: Sixth Edition*, New York: West Publishing Company.

Cosmides, L. & Tooby, J. (1992) 'Cognitive adaptations for social exchange', in J.H. Barkow, L. Cosmides & J. Tooby (eds.), *The Adapted Mind: Evolutionary Psychology and the Generation of Culture*, (pp. 163–228) New York: Oxford University Press.

Crow, T.J. (1995) 'A Darwinian approach to the origins of psychosis', *British Journal of Psychiatry* 167: 12–25.

Dalai Lama (1993) *Power of Compassion*: Wembley Lectures (Audio cassettes available from: Tibet Foundation, 10 Bloomsbury Way, London, WC1A 2SH).

De Waal, F. (1996) *Good Natured: The Origins of Right and Wrong in Humans and other Animals*, Harvard: Harvard University Press

Driscoll, R. (1988) 'Self-condemnation: A conceptual framework for assessment and treatment', *Psychotherapy* 26: 104–11.

Elliott, R. & Greenberg, L.S. (1997) 'Multiple voices in process-experimental therapy: Dialogues between aspects of self', *Journal of Psychotherapy Integration* 7: 225–40.

Ellis, A. (1977) 'Psychotherapy and the value of a human being', in A. Ellis & R. Grieger (eds.), *Handbook of Rational Emotive Therapy*, New York: Springer.

Ellis, A. & Whiteley, J.M. (eds.) (1979) *Theoretical and Empirical Foundations of Rational Emotive Therapy*, California: Brooks-Cole.

Emery, G. (1993) 'Radical cognitive therapy', in K.T. Kuehlwein & H. Rosen (eds.), *Cognitive Therapies in Action: Evolving Innovative Practice*, (pp. 301–25), San Francisco: Jossey-Bass.

Enright, R.D. (1996) 'Counselling within the forgiveness triad: On forgiving, receiving forgiveness, and self-forgiveness', *Counselling and Values* 40: 107–26

Epstein, S. (1994) 'Integration of the cognitive and the psychodynamic unconscious', *American Psychologist* 49: 709–24.

Epstein, S., Lipson, A., Holstein, C. & Huh, E. (1992) 'Irrational reactions to negative outcomes: Evidence for two conceptual systems', *Journal of Personality and Social Psychology* 62: 328–39.

Farr, R. (1980) 'Homo socia-psychologicus', in A.J. Chapman & D.M. Jones (eds.), *Models of Man*, Leicester: The British Psychological Society.

Farr, R. (1987) 'The science of mental life', *Bulletin of the British Psychology Society* 40: 2–17.

Field, T.M. (1998) 'Touch therapy effects on development', *International Journal of Behavioral Development* 22: 779–97.

Fogel, A., Melson, G.F. & Mistry, J. (1986) 'Conceptualising the determinants of nurturance: A reassessment of sex differences', in A. Fogel & G.F. Melson (eds.), *Origins of Nurturance: Developmental, Biological and Cultural Perspectives on Caregiving*, (pp. 53–68), Hillsdale, NJ: Lawrence Erlbaum Associates Inc.

Frederick, C. & McNeal, S. (1999) *Inner Strengths: Contemporary Psychotherapy and Hypnosis for Ego Strengthening*, Mahwah, NJ: Lawrence Erlbaum Associates Inc.

Freedman, S.R. & Enright, R.D. (1996) 'Forgiveness as an intervention goal with incest survivors', *Journal of Consulting and Clinical Psychology* 64: 983–92.

Freud, S. (1917) 'Mourning and melancholia', in J. Strachey, (transl. and ed.), *Completed Psychological Works*, Vol. 14, (standard ed.), London: Hogarth Press.

Gardner, R. (1988) 'Psychiatric infrastructures for intraspecific communication', in M.R.A. Chance (ed.), *Social Fabrics of the Mind*, Hove, UK: Lawrence Erlbaum Associates Ltd.

Gazzaniga, M.S. (1989) 'Organization of the human brain', *Science* 245: 947–52.

George, M.S., Ketter, T.A., Parekh, P.I., Horwitz, B., Hercovitch, P. & Post, R.M. (1995)

'Brain activity during transient sadness and happiness in healthy women', *American Journal of Psychiatry* 152: 341–51.

Gilbert, P. (1984) *Depression: From Psychology to Brain State*, Hove, UK: Lawrence Erlbaum Associates Ltd.

Gilbert, P. (1989) *Human Nature and Suffering*, Hove, UK: Lawrence Erlbaum Associates Ltd.

Gilbert, P. (1992) *Depression: The Evolution of Powerlessness*, Hove, UK: Psychology Press.

Gilbert, P. (1993) 'Defence and safety: Their function in social behaviour and psychopathology', *British Journal of Clinical Psychology* 32: 131–54.

Gilbert, P. (1995) 'Biopsychosocial approaches and evolutionary theory as aids to integration in clinical psychology and psychotherapy', *Clinical Psychology and Psychotherapy* 2: 135–56.

Gilbert, P. (1997a) 'The evolution of social attractiveness and its role in shame, humiliation, guilt and therapy', *British Journal of Medical Psychology* 70: 113–47.

Gilbert, P. (1997b) 'The biopsychosociology of meaning', in M. Power & C. Brewin (eds.), *The Transformation of Meaning: Reconciling Theory and Therapy in Cognitive, Behaviour and Related Therapies*, (pp. 33–56), Chichester: Wiley.

Gilbert, P. (1997c) *Overcoming Depression: A Self-Guide Using Cognitive Behavioral Techniques*, London: Robinsons and New York: Oxford University Press.

Gilbert, P. (1998a) 'Evolutionary psychopathology: Why isn't the mind better designed than it is?', *British Journal of Medical Psychology* 71: 353–73.

Gilbert, P. (1998b) 'What is shame? Some core issues and controversies', in P. Gilbert & B. Andrews (eds.), *Shame: Interpersonal Behavior, Psychopathology and Culture*, (pp. 3–36), New York: Oxford University Press.

Gilbert, P. (1998c) 'The evolved basis and adaptive functions of cognitive distortions', *British Journal of Medical Psychology*, 71.

Gilbert, P. (1998d) 'Shame and humiliation in complex cases', in N. Tarrier, G. Haddock & A. Wells (eds.), *Cognitive Therapy For Complex Cases*, (pp. 241–71), London: Routledge.

Gilbert, P. (2000) *Counselling for Depression, 2nd edition*, London: Sage.

Gilbert, P. & Allan, S. (1998) 'The role of defeat and entrapment (arrested flight) in depression: An exploration of an evolutionary view', *Psychological Medicine* 28: 584–97.

Gilbert, P. & McGuire, M. (1998) 'Shame status and social roles: The psychobiological continuum from monkeys to humans', in P. Gilbert & B. Andrews (eds.), *Shame: Interpersonal Behavior, Psychopathology and Culture*, (pp. 99–125), New York: Oxford University Press.

Goncalves, O. & Ivey, A.E. (1993) 'Developmental therapy: Clinical implications', in K.T. Kuehlwein & H. Rosen (eds.), *Cognitive Therapies in Action: Evolving Innovative Practice*, (pp. 326–52), San Francisco: Jossey-Bass.

Gottman J.M. & Levenson, R.W. (1992) 'Toward a typology of marriage based on affective behavior: Preliminary differences in behavior, physiology, health and risk of dissolution', *Journal of Personality and Social Psychology* 57: 47–52.

Greenberg, J.R. & Mitchell, S.A. (1983) *Object Relations in Psychoanalytic Theory*, Cambridge MA: Harvard University Press.

Greenberg, L.S. (1979) 'Resolving splits: Use of the two-chair technique', *Psychotherapy, Theory, Research and Practice* 16: 316–24.

Greenberg, L.S. & Pascual-Leone, J. (1997) 'Emotion in the creation of personal meaning', in M. Power & C. Brewin (eds.), *The Transformation of Meaning: Reconciling Theory and Therapy in Cognitive, Behaviour and Related Therapies*, (pp. 157–73) Chichester: Wiley.

Greenberg, L.S., Elliott, R.K. & Foerster, F.S. (1990) 'Experiential processes in the psychotherapeutic treatment of depression', in C.D. McCann & N.S. Endler (eds.), *Depression: New Directions in Theory, Research and Practice*, (pp. 157–85), Toronto: Wall & Emerson.

Greenberg, L.S., Rice, L.N. & Elliott, R. (1993) *Facilitating Emotional Change: The Moment-by-Moment Process*, New York: Guilford Press.

Greenberg, P. & Padesky, C.A. (1995) *Mind Over Mood: A Cognitive Therapy Treatment Manual For Clients*, New York: Guilford Press.

Hackman, A. (1997) 'The transformation of meaning in cognitive therapy', in M. Power & C. Brewin, (eds.), *The Transformation of Meaning in Psychological Therapies*, (pp. 125–40), Chichester: Wiley.

Harlow, H.F. & Mears, C. (1979) *The Human Model: Primate Perspectives*, New York: Winston & Sons.

Hermans, H.J. (1996) 'Voicing the self: From information processing to dialogical interchange', *Psychological Bulletin* 119: 31–50.

Hofer, M.A. (1984) 'Relationships as regulators: A psychobiologic perspective on bereavement', *Psychosomatic Medicine* 46: 183–97.

Horowitz, L.M. & Vitkus, J. (1986) 'The interpersonal basis of psychiatric symptoms', *Clinical Psychology Review* 6: 443–70.

Joffe, R., Segal, Z. & Singer, W. (1996) 'Change in thyroid hormone levels following response to cognitive therapy for major depression', *American Journal of Psychiatry* 153: 411–15.

Jung, C.G. (1954/1993) *The Practice of Psychotherapy*, (2nd Edition), London: Routledge.

Kemper, T.D. (1990) *Social Structure and Testosterone: Explorations of the Socio-Bio-Social Chain*, New Brunswick: Rutgers University Press.

Kohut, H. (1977) *The Restoration of the Self*, New York: International Universities Press.

McCullough, M.E., Worthington, E.L. Jr. & Rachal, K.C. (1997) 'Interpersonal forgiving in close relationships', *Journal of Personality and Social Psychology* 73: 321–36.

McGuire, M.T. & Troisi, A. (1998) *Darwinian Psychiatry*, New York: Oxford University Press.

McGuire, P.K., Silversweig, D.A., Wright, I., Murray, R.M., Frackowiak, R.S.J. & Frith, C.D (1996) 'The neural correlates of inner speech and auditory verbal imagery in schizophrenia: Relationship to auditory verbal hallucinations', *British Journal of Psychiatry* 169: 148–59.

MacLean, P.D. (1985) 'Brain evolution relating to family, play and the separation call', *Archives of General Psychiatry* 42: 405–17.

MacLean, P.D. (1990) *The Triune Brain in Evolution*, New York: Plenum Press.

Mahoney, M.J. (1991) *Human Change Processes: The Scientific Foundations of Psychotherapy*, New York: Basic Books.

Margulies, A. (1984) 'Toward empathy: The uses of wonder', *American Journal of Psychiatry* 141: 1025–33.

Miller, L.C. & Fishkin, S.A. (1997) 'On the dynamics of human bonding and reproductive success: Seeking windows on the adapted-for-human-environment interface', in

J. Simpson & D.T. Kenrick (eds.), *Evolutionary Social Psychology*, (pp. 197–235), Mahwah, NJ: Lawrence Erlbaum Associates Inc.

Montagu, A. (1986) *Touching: The Human Significance of the Skin*, (3rd edition), New York: Harper and Row.

Nesse, R. (1998) 'Emotional disorders in evolutionary perspective', *British Journal Of Medical Psychology* 71: 397–416.

Ornstein, R. (1986) *Multimind: A New Way of Looking at Human Beings*, London: Macmillan.

Padesky, C.A. & Greenberg, D. (1995) *Clinician's Guide to Mind Over Mood*, New York: Guilford Press.

Penn, D.L., Corrigan, P.W., Bentall, R.P., Racenstein, J.M. & Newman, L. (1997) 'Social cognition in schizophrenia', *Psychological Bulletin* 121: 114–32.

Power, M. & Dalgleish, T. (1997) *Cognition and Emotion: From Order to Disorder*, Hove, UK: Psychology Press.

Price, J.S. & Sloman, L. (1987) 'Depression as yielding behavior: An animal model based on Schjelderup-Ebbe's pecking order', *Ethology and Sociobiology* 8: 85–98.

Price, J.S., Sloman, R., Gardner, R., Gilbert, P. & Rhode, P. (1994) 'The social competition hypothesis of depression', *British Journal of Psychiatry* 164: 309–15

Raleigh, M.J., McGuire, M.T., Brammer, G.L. & Yuwiler, A. (1984) 'Social and environmental influences on blood 5-HT concentrations in monkeys', *Archives of General Psychiatry* 41: 405–10.

Ramaswami, S. & Sheikh, A.A. (1996) 'Buddhist psychology: Implications for healing', in A.A. Sheikh & K.S. Sheikh (eds.), *Healing East & West: Ancient Wisdom and Modern Psychology*, (pp. 91–123), Chichester: Wiley.

Rehm, L.P. (1988) 'Self-management and cognitive processes in depression', in L.B. Alloy (ed.), *Cognitive Processes in Depression*, (pp. 143–76), New York: Guilford.

Rowan, J. (1990) *Subpersonalities: The People Inside Us*, London: Routledge.

Safran, J.D. & Segal, Z.V. (1990) *Interpersonal Process in Cognitive Therapy*, New York: Basic Books.

Schaap, C., Bennun, I., Schindler, L. & Hoogduin, K. (1993) *The Therapeutic Relationship in Behavioural Psychotherapy*, Chichester: Wiley.

Schore, A.N. (1994) *Affect Regulation and the Origin of the Self: The Neurobiology of Emotional Development*, Hillsdale, NJ: Lawrence Erlbaum Associates Inc.

Schwartz, R.C. (1995) *Internal Family Systems Therapy*, New York: Guilford.

Singer, D.G. & Singer, J.L. (1990) *The House of Make-Believe: Play and the Developing Imagination*, Massachusetts: Harvard University Press.

Slavin, M.O. & Kreigman, D. (1992) *The Adaptive Design of the Human Psyche: Psychoanalysis, Evolutionary Biology, and the Therapeutic Process*, New York: Guilford.

Stevens, A. (1982) *Archetype: A Natural History of the Self*, London: Routledge & Kegan Paul.

Stevens, A. & Price J.P. (1996) *Evolutionary Psychiatry*, London: Routledge.

Swallow, S.R. & Kuiper, N.A. (1988) 'Social comparison and negative self evaluation: An application to depression', *Clinical Psychology Review* 8: 55–76.

Tarrier, N., Vaughn, C., Lader, M.H. & Leff, J.P. (1979) 'Bodily reactions to people and events in schizophrenics', *Archives of General Psychiatry* 36: 311–15.

Teasdale, J.D. (1997) 'The transformation of meaning: The interacting cognitive subsystems approach', in M. Power & C.R. Brewin (eds.) *The Transformation of*

Meaning in Psychological Therapies: Integrating Theory and Practice, (pp. 141–56), Chichester: Wiley.

Teasdale J.D. & Barnard, P.J. (1993) *Affect, Cognition and Change: Remodelling Depressive Affect*, Hove, UK: Lawrence Erlbaum Associates Ltd.

Tedeschi, J.T. & Felson, R.B. (1994) *Violence, Aggression and Coercive Actions*, Washington, DC: American Psychological Association.

Thomas, P. (1997) *The Dialectics of Schizophrenia*, London: Free Association Books.

Tronick, E.Z. (1989) 'Emotions and emotional communication in infants', *American Psychologist* 44: 112–19.

Uchino, B.N., Cacioppo, J.T. & Kiecolt-Glaser, J.K. (1996) 'The relationship between social support and physiological processes: A review with emphasis on underlying mechanisms and implications for health', *Psychological Bulletin* 119: 488–531.

Wagner, C.C., Kiesler, D.J. & Schmidt, J.A. (1995) 'Assessing the interpersonal transaction cycle: Convergence of action and the reaction interpersonal circumplex measures', *Journal of Personality and Social Psychology* 69: 938–49.

Watkins, M. (1986) *Invisible guests, The Development of Imaginal Dialogues*, Hillsdale, NJ: Lawrence Erlbaum Associates Inc.

Young, J.E., Beck, A.T. & Weinberger, A. (1993) 'Depression', in H.D. Barlow (ed.), *Clinical Handbook of Psychological Disorders*, (pp. 240–77), New York: Guilford.

Zeifman, D. & Hazan, C. (1997) 'Attachment: The bond in pair-bonds', in J. Simpson & D.T. Kenrick (eds.), *Evolutionary Social Psychology*, (pp. 237–63), Mahwah, NJ: Lawrence Erlbaum Associates Inc.

Zuroff, D.C. & Mongrain, M. (1987) 'Dependency and self criticism: Vulnerability factors for depressive affective states', *Journal of Abnormal Psychology* 96: 14–22.

Acknowledgements

Patient details have been changed to avoid identification.

The author would like to acknowledge the helpful comments and suggestions of Kent Bailey, Michael McGuire, Hilary Howell and Ken Goss and many patients during the preparation of this chapter. Patients who have used some of the techniques outlined have suggested they have found they offered insight and useful ways to cope; and they have also offered many helpful insights into what would help them further.

7

SOCIAL INTELLIGENCE, DECEPTION, AND PSYCHOPATHOLOGY

A challenge for cognitive therapy?

Nicholas B. Allen and Paul Gilbert

> A man who cannot live in society, or who has no need to do so because he is self-sufficient, is either a beast or a god; he is not part of the state. All human beings, then, are endowed by nature with the social instinct.
>
> *Aristotle: 'Politics'*

In his review of a handbook of contemporary behaviour therapy, Alan Ross (1991) called for the future development of psychological treatment to be based on integrating new scientific ideas and principles, not simply applying current methods in new areas. He stated (1991: 743):

> One thing is for certain: The field has grown but it has not progressed. The growth has taken the form of moving into new areas of application. Progress would have meant applying additional psychological principles in old and new areas, supplementing those of conditioning and learning with which the field began. What is being applied is whatever promises to work. Conceptual source and empirical support seem irrelevant.

A new conceptual source that holds much promise for our understanding of psychopathology and its therapy is evolutionary psychology. In fact the theory of evolution by natural selection is one of the most important principles in modern science, and has recently been successfully applied to a host of psychological issues (Buss, 1999). Indeed, as calls to make cognitive science more 'evolutionarily rigorous' are increasingly heeded (Cosmides & Tooby, 1994), it will be important that *clinical* cognitive science, and the psychotherapies associated with it, do likewise.

This chapter outlines how recent models of the evolution of social cognitive abilities in primates and humans are based on a certain degree of self- and other-deception. Cognitive therapists are yet to fully appreciate this or explore the implications for cognitive and interpersonal assessments, and interventions (Gilbert, 1998). This chapter begins this effort to integrate evolutionary ideas and reflect on possible implications for therapy.

The social domain

Most forms of psychopathology are focused on the social domain in one way or another (Horowitz & Vitkus, 1986). The socially anxious patient fears what others think of him or her and the potential for rejection; the depressed person sees him or herself as a failure or defeated, unable to control desired social resources; the paranoid person thinks others are against him or her and out to do harm, and marked problems in interpersonal cognition and behaviour are a hallmark of most personality disorders. While cognitive therapists see these problems as rooted in styles of information processing, and in particular consciously available cognitive distortions (Beck, 1987; Beck *et al.*, 1979), an evolutionary approach can reframe these difficulties in a new way. Basically, it suggests that we are set up to detect certain threats (those which damage our reproductive interests) and be vigilant to the possibility of deception. These inner information-processing systems for monitoring and responding to threats did not evolve via logical reasoning but adaptive heuristics (Cosmides & Tooby, 1994; Gilbert, 1998). The essence of the evolutionary approach is that social behaviour and cognition evolved to serve the reproductive interests of individuals such that we are able to exploit the social environments in self-serving ways (Gilbert, Bailey & McGuire, Chapter 1, this volume; Krebs & Denton, 1997).

One way of doing this is via social communications that impact on others so that the actors are able to exert control over the emotions and behaviours of those with whom they interact. For example, sexual attraction depends on sending signals to a potential mate that are attractive and arousing; reducing threats from another involves sending submissive signals that act to terminate or reduce attacks; care eliciting signals are designed to elicit support or help from others. All of these signals are efforts at social manipulations and none of them requires that the actor is necessarily sending 'truthful' signals (Dawkins & Krebs, 1978; Krebs & Denton, 1997). Acts of social communication can involve a good deal of bluff and deceit. For example, a male can deceive a female into believing that he will be more investing than he is likely to be; a submissive signal may be used to deceive another of the actor's 'true' long-term intentions for status acquisition, a care-eliciting signal may deceive the other into giving resources that are in the best interest of the receiver but at cost to the provider. Understanding the manipulative aspects of social communication opens up new ways of thinking about many of the social and personal cognitions that plague individuals when they suffer aversive states.

Adaptive problems

Social relationships are a critical means of solving adaptive problems in group-living species. Cosmides, Tooby and Barkow (1992: 8) have defined an 'adaptive problem' as a 'problem whose solution can affect reproduction, however distally'. Human groups contain concentrations of particular reproductive resources, including potential mates, kin to whom altruism can be directed, and non-kin with whom to exchange resources. As such, the effect of social exclusion on adaptive tasks can be considerable (Buss, 1990). In the Pleistocene period, social exclusion/rejection may have threatened one's survival by excluding the individual from the benefits of group foraging, protection from predators, or simply being able to engage in profitable reciprocal relations. It is then understandable that a considerable amount of theory and research has shown that humans are strongly motivated to avoid social exclusion (e.g., Baumeister & Leary, 1995; Baumeister & Tice, 1990; Leary & Downs, 1995), and rejection (Sloman, Chapter 12, this volume), and that social exclusion is associated with aversive emotional reactions (Leary, 1990). Under threat of social exclusion/rejection, or loss of control over social resources (such as losing rank) it would be very important to reduce the likelihood of further damage to social relationships, however minor or temporary.

In order to do this humans have to calculate a number of social outcomes. For example, humans have evolved a sophisticated capacity to judge their value to others; their attractiveness, talents, skills, and resources, *as judged by* others. It is via being seen as attractive in some way that humans are often chosen for certain advantageous relationships (e.g., as a sexual partner, friend or leader; Gilbert 1989, 1997a). But they must also calculate their potential for shame and rejection (Gilbert & McGuire, 1998) as well as their potential burden on others (i.e., the cost, *as perceived by others*, of their participation in the group or dyad). If, in social contexts that were important to fitness (which can include close attachment relationships, collaborative relationships and coalitions, or relationships based on status and authority; Haslam, 1997), an individual's attractiveness/value to others dropped to a level that approached their burden on others, they were in danger of status loss and exclusion (e.g., rejection, ostracism). In such circumstances minimizing the risk of further losses in their social value could be more adaptive than status enhancement. And indeed it would seem that people with high self-esteem use self-enhancement strategies while those with low self-esteem use damage limitation strategies (e.g., Baumeister, Tice & Hutton, 1989). One way of viewing social anxiety and depression is that they reflect defensive strategies that seek to reduce the risk of (further) damage to social relationships by adjusting social–perceptual processes so that they become vigilant for indications of rejection, subordination, and ostracism. In the area of social behaviour, these mechanisms affect both communicative behaviour (signalling in order to reduce threats *and* to elicit safe forms of support/acceptance), and resource acquisition behaviours that might bring about social conflict (via a general reduction in acquisitive behaviours). To put this another way, there are alternative strategies for coping with possible social exclusion/rejection according to how attractive or how much of a burden on others one perceives oneself to be. But as we shall argue later, both strategies may also involve various degrees of self- and other-deception.

Many models of psychopathology focus explicitly on aversive social circumstances. For instance, with respect to depression these include the attachment-loss (Bowlby, 1980; Ingram, Miranda & Segal, 1998), status-loss (Gilbert, 1992; Price, 1972; Price *et al.*, 1994), and social-risk (Allen & Gilbert, 2000) models. All these models see various behaviours associated with psychopathology, in part, as a form of social manipulation that is designed to improve the individual's circumstances by creating certain states of mind in others (e.g., concern, appeasement) and/or limiting damaging threats.

Crucially, the eliciting circumstances for these behaviours require judgements about the mental states of others, and the 'true intents' of others towards the self. This is especially so in the social risk model (Allen & Gilbert, 2000). This posits that anxious and dysphoric states can be elicited by circumstances that merely threaten loss. One key area where a loss is threatened is if one is victim to deception (Gilbert, 1989, 1998). Hence, people can become anxious or dysphoric when they think that others' pleasant behaviours towards them are deceptive, e.g., 'I know she says she likes me, but she only says that because it makes her seem like a good person' or 'I know Billy says he loves me but that is only so he can sleep with me'. The consequences of being victim to deception can be very serious, and the victim of it will either have to confront the other and risk rejection, or break off the relationship and risk the losses that a complete breakdown in the relationship will bring. We will look at this more closely later. For the moment we note that the role of deception and trust are so central to much psychopathology and psychotherapy that it is timely to recognize the considerable complexity of these mechanisms, including the way that the human psyche may well have evolved with 'glitches' and problems in these information-processing systems. In fact mechanisms for detecting deception and deceiving others are the cornerstone of social intelligence – the very thing that has made humans one of the dominant species.

The evolution of social intelligence, self-awareness, and theory of mind

The idea that the social environment has presented the most critical adaptive challenges shaping the evolution of primate intelligence can be traced back to a variety of sources. For instance, Michael Chance and Allan Mead (1953) proposed a link between primate social complexity and neocortical enlargement, especially with respect to the extended sexual receptivity of female primates and the consequent increased likelihood of conflict situations between males. Chance and Mead (1953) proposed that the need to keep track of both the receptive females and the competing males, as part of the reproductive efforts of the primate species, posed a significant cognitive challenge for primate males. Although the idea that sexual conflict is the most critical form of social interaction in primate societies is no longer accepted (de Waal, 1989; Cords, 1997), Chance and Mead's idea did presage more recent proposals regarding the relationship of social complexity to brain evolution (e.g., Dunbar, 1995), and the social origins of primate intelligence.

In 1966, Alison Jolly noted that the lemurs of Madagascar, while performing more poorly than other primates on standardized tests of intelligence, lived in similar-sized social groups to various other monkey species. Also, they appeared to display comparably sophisticated social behaviours, such as long chains of social interactions. This led Jolly (1966: 504) to suggest that:

> The social use of intelligence is of crucial importance to all social primates. As the young develop, they depend on the troop for protection and for instruction in their role in life. Since their dependence on the troop both demands social learning and makes it possible, social integration and intelligence probably evolved together, reinforcing each other in an ever-increasing spiral.

Jolly's conjecture led to two ideas. First, social intelligence and non-social intelligence (i.e., intelligence about dealing with objects, food and other species), might be somewhat differentiable and compartmentalized; second, social contexts that may have arisen without need for high levels of social intelligence, will subsequently select for social intelligence. Nicholas Humphrey (1976) came to similar conclusions when he noted that primates appear to have 'surplus' intelligence when one considers the relative simplicity of the physical challenges posed by their way of life in nature. He suggested that the reason for such extended intellectual abilities might lie in the social rather than the physical world. In particular, group living, while providing significant benefits, also provided individuals with the challenge of how to extract greater levels of benefit than other group members. Social manipulations towards other group members had to be achieved, however, without disrupting one's membership of the group. Therefore there is a need to deceive others about their losses. Humphrey argued that such circumstances favoured intelligence as a trait, and, as these contingencies applied to all members of the group, an evolutionary 'arms race' for higher levels of intelligence is set up within group-living species.

This proposal has been formulated into what is known as the 'Machiavellian intelligence hypothesis' (Byrne & Whiten, 1988; Whiten & Byrne, 1997), which states broadly that 'possession of the cognitive capabilities we call "intelligence" is linked with social living and the problems of complexity it can pose' (Byrne & Whiten, 1997: 1). The name 'Machiavellian' is given because the hypothesis conjec- tures that primate intelligence evolved primarily to perform social manipulations, especially deception and 'cunning co-operation' (Byrne & Whiten, 1997), which result in benefits to individual fitness at the cost of other group members. Although 'social complexity' is not a well-specified idea (Gigerenzer, 1997), many authors have emphasized the fluid and interactive nature of relationships as being crucial to the complexity of the social domain. Humphrey (1976: 312) states:

Any social transaction is by its nature a developing process and the development is bound to have a degree of indeterminacy to it. Neither of the social agents involved in the transaction can be certain of the future behaviour of the other; as in Alice's game of croquet with the Queen of Hearts, both balls and hoops are always on the move. Someone embarking on such a transaction must therefore be prepared for the problem itself to alter as a consequence of his attempts to solve it – in the very act of interpreting the social world he changes it. Like Alice he may well be tempted to complain, 'You've no idea how confusing it is, all the things being alive'.

Social manipulation in non-human primates

If social intelligence evolved in response to this kind of social complexity, and if one of its fullest expressions is the deception of conspecifics, then we would expect there to be instances of the intelligent use of deception in the interactions of socially living primates. Indeed, examples of deceptive behaviour are common-place throughout nature (e.g., mimicry and camouflage). Primatologists have also provided anecdotal reports of deception amongst primates (e.g., Goodall, 1971; de Waal, 1982). However, a critical distinction must be made between deceptive behaviour that is a relatively instinctual part of a species' behavioural repertoire, and deceptive behaviour that is based on advanced social intelligence. Byrne (1995) proposes that such a distinction can be provided by focusing on examples of 'tactical deception', which are defined as instances where an animal uses part of its normal behavioural repertoire in a unique context, resulting in other individuals being manipulated to that animal's advantage.

Byrne and Whiten (1985) provided an example of tactical deception where a young male baboon was being threatened by a group of older males. The young baboon suddenly stopped, stood up on his hind legs, and scanned the horizon; a behaviour that usually signals the approach of a predator. Despite the fact that no predator was present, this behaviour was successful in convincing the older baboons to abandon their hostile approach in order to scan the horizon as well. After attempts to compile a carefully validated record of incidental observations of tactical deception by primatologists, Byrne and Whiten (1990) noted that although examples of such behaviour were present in most primate species, some species appeared to use deception more often than others. In particular, chimpanzees and baboons appear to use tactical deception more often than other non-human primates. Furthermore, when the frequency of instances of tactical deception in a species was correlated with that species' typical 'neocortical ratio' (the ratio of neocortex size to the rest of the brain), there is a highly significant correlation of 0.77 (Byrne, 1995). This suggests that species with a greater proportion of neocortex in their brains (implying that the species has a greater capacity for conducting complex cognitive operations) also make greater use of tactical deception.

Despite these fascinating findings many researchers still felt that observational reports were not enough to support the strongest version of the hypothesis; i.e., that when animals behaved this way they were doing so on the basis of an understanding of the other animals' mental states, not just their behaviour (Premack, 1988). The answer to this dilemma was to conduct experiments that were specifically designed to assess understanding of mental processes in others, and it is to this literature that we shall now turn.

Self-recognition and self-awareness in primates

One of the most critical experimental methods for studying self-concept in primates arose from Gordon Gallup's (1970) observations that humans and chimpanzees were capable of recognizing themselves in mirrors, whereas various species of monkeys were not. In order to make a more direct test of the notion that chimpanzees were recognizing the image in the mirror as their own, Gallup anaesthetized chimpanzees and marked them with a bright red dye, undetectable by smell or touch, on their upper eyebrow ridge and ear. Upon wakening the chimpanzees they were observed for a period without a mirror present, during which they rarely touched the red dye marks. However, after the mirror was introduced and the chimpanzees were able to inspect their reflection, they invariably reached up to touch the otherwise invisible marks on their *own* head – not their reflection's head. This technique has therefore provided clear evidence that chimpanzees do recognize their reflection in the mirror as their own, and this has been replicated many times with both chimpanzees and orangutans, but not reliably in gorillas (Povinelli & Prince, 1998). Perhaps more interesting from an evolutionary point of view is the *lack* of such compelling evidence of self-recognition in primate species outside the great ape/human group, or within non-primate animals (Gallup, 1994; Povinelli & Prince, 1998).

What is the psychological significance of this apparently qualitative psychological difference between humans and great apes versus other species? Gallup (1977) proposed that in order to recognize the image in the mirror as their own, the chimpanzees must have some sort of self-concept. Later, he further speculated that the presence of a self-concept might also confer the ability to introspect about one's own mental states in chimpanzees, and that this might in turn lead to an understanding of the mental states of others (Gallup, 1982). These ideas led to the predictions that the common ancestors of the great apes and humans had a uniquely developed psychological system that allowed them to reason about their own, and others', mental states. Such a psychological system has been referred to as a 'theory of mind' (Premack & Woodruff, 1978). This system was referred to as a 'theory' because it concerned states that were not directly observable, yet was used to make predictions about the behaviour of others.

'Theory of mind' in non-human primates

In contrast to humans, strong tests of the ability to reason about the mental states of others have not been extensively conducted with non-human primates (Povinelli & Prince, 1998). However, one area where such investigations have been conducted concerns the understanding that 'seeing' is the behavioural concomitant of the mental state of attention. In other words, these studies have attempted to establish whether non-human primates understand that when another animal looks at an object, this results in them *attending* to the object in such a way as to change their *knowledge or beliefs*. This tests the notion that primates have a theory of mind because it addresses their ability to utilize knowledge of others' mental states (e.g., attention, knowledge, beliefs).

Instances of chimpanzees and other primates following each other's lines of sight have been described in naturalistic observations (e.g., Byrne & Whiten, 1985), and these have been interpreted as instances of 'joint attention', reflecting the fact that chimpanzees understand the intentional states associated with seeing (Baron-Cohen, 1997). However, recent experimental tests of chimpanzees' understanding of 'seeing-as-knowing' have concluded that there is little compelling evidence that chimpanzees understand these or other mental states in the way implied by the theory of mind model (see Povinelli & Prince, 1998, for a review). In an illustrative study Povinelli and Preuss (1995) presented chimpanzees that had previously been trained to use a begging gesture to ask human experimenters for food, with two experimenters. Due to the use of a blindfold one of these experimenters could see the chimpanzee subjects and the other could not. The chimpanzees did not show any tendency to favour the experimenter who was visually in contact with them in their efforts to beg for food, suggesting that they did not understand that only one of the experimenters was visually aware of their efforts.

Although scientific work on the extent of mental state attribution (i.e., theory of mind) in non-human primates is ongoing, the current state of knowledge suggests that while some apes may have a well-developed sense of self-awareness, their capacity to reason about the mental states of others (as suggested by the conjectures of Gallup, 1982, and Premack & Woodruff, 1978) has yet to receive clear support. This is despite the fact that chimpanzees, in particular, appear to *act* as if they understand mental states such as intention, knowledge, and belief (Povinelli, 1994). By contrast, in the case of humans, developmental studies have documented the emergence of a wide variety of theory of mind abilities over the first few years of life.

The development of 'theory of mind' in humans

Human babies demonstrate a sensitivity to eyes and faces from at least 2 months of age when they will fixate longer on figures that contain faces, especially those containing eyes. Such behaviour has major implications for affect development (Schore, 1994). Despite this, a full understanding of the fact that seeing is associated with attention does not emerge until around the middle of the second year of life (Schore, 1994). Baldwin and her colleagues (Baldwin, 1991, 1993; Baldwin & Moses, 1994) have demonstrated that by 19 months, child subjects were able to identify an object by the name that an experimenter gave it while they were looking at the object (out of sight to the child) in a bucket. This suggests that these children can understand that, when looking into the bucket, the experimenter's speech must have been referring to what they were 'seeing', and therefore attending to. By about 2½ years of age, children understand that seeing with the eyes is what connects people to the external (visual) world, and by 4 years of age, they understand that visual perception leads to internal states of knowledge (e.g., Flavell et al., 1981; Wimmer, Hogrefe & Perner, 1988). For instance, 3-year-olds usually do not understand that when a person looks into a box, they know what is inside, whereas such inferences are usually automatic by 4–5 years old.

Interestingly, recent research on autism has demonstrated that autistic children have a deficit in 'theory of mind' abilities, as is evidenced by their poor performance on the 'false belief test' (Baron-Cohen, 1995, 1997; Baron-Cohen, Leslie & Frith, 1985). In this test, a child is presented with a scenario where Sally puts her marble in one place, and then, while she is absent, Anne moves the marble to another hiding place. In order to accurately answer the question, 'Where will Sally look for her marble when she returns?', the child must understand that Sally (due to her absence) is not *aware* of the marble's new hiding place (i.e., she has a *false belief* about its whereabouts). The fact that autistic children show a specific deficit on this, and other tests of theory of mind abilities, has been interpreted as evidence that these abilities reflect the function of a specific mental module, designed by evolution to solve a specific adaptive problem (Baron-Cohen, 1995).

Conclusions regarding the evolution of social intelligence, self-awareness, and theory of mind

The research work conducted thus far in developmental and comparative psychology, as well as primatology, does provide some insights into the evolution of these critical social-cognitive abilities. Perhaps most important is the finding that although members of the great ape group, especially chimpanzees, and orangutans, do show striking evidence of self-awareness and tactical deception, such abilities seem to be relatively absent amongst monkeys and non-primate species. Furthermore, despite the fact that naturalistic observations of ape behaviour have suggested that they do reason about the mental states of others (Byrne, 1995), experimental evidence of theory of mind abilities has been more equivocal (Povinelli, 1994; Povinelli & Prince, 1998). What these findings suggest is that something specific to the evolution of the great ape/human clade has selected for these particular kinds of advanced social cognitive abilities.

By contrast, 'theory of mind' abilities are well documented amongst humans, and there is evidence to suggest that the evolution of these abilities may have continued throughout the course of human evolution, specifically. Steven Mithen (1996) has proposed that the archaeological records suggest that the early humans of the Lower and Middle Palaeolithic period, despite having some advanced social-cognitive skills, were unable to bring these skills to bear on non-social tasks due to their relatively rigid, domain-specific nature. By contrast, the humans of the Upper Palaeolithic and Mesolithic periods were able to use their social intelligence to achieve social co-ordination of activities across a wide range of domains (e.g., natural environment, technical, language), and this resulted in much more complex and effective patterns of social behaviour.

Theory of mind abilities may have been the impetus behind the evolution of self-awareness and in particular capabilities for self-evaluation. This implies that self-evaluation serves strategic functions of enabling individuals to co-ordinate their behaviour according to social contexts (Gilbert, Chapter 6, this volume). In other words, self-evaluation cannot be separated from the social behaviours that flow from it. As we shall argue shortly, positive and negative self-evaluation may therefore reflect the operation of social strategies which may in part serve deceptive and manipulative ends (e.g., deceiving up and deceiving down) and/or reflect strategies for dealing with others' possible deceptions.

Theory of mind, self-deception and psychopathology

Whatever the particular evolutionary path that has led to the establishment of the ability to reason about the mental states of ourselves and others, it is clear that this is a highly evolved, species-typical (although perhaps not species-specific), capacity amongst humans. Such capacities, however, once established in a species, bring their own burdens. For instance, these capacities confer the ability to deceive as well as the ability to detect deception (i.e., to attribute a deceitful or dishonest state of mind to others). As many authors have noted, animal communication is not designed for conveying the truth, but for conveying whatever message will be most adaptive for the sender (Byrne & Whiten, 1990; Dawkins & Krebs, 1978; Hauser, 1997). As the 'social brain' has evolved, the psychological mechanisms for detecting deception have become ever more sensitive (Cosmides, 1989; Mealey, Daood & Krage, 1996). In this environment there is likely to be an 'arms race' between the evolution of psychological mechanisms for detecting deception and socially manipulative (i.e., deceptive) signals, whereby these deceptive signals need to become increasingly 'genuine' in appearance in order to be successful.

It has been speculated that this 'arms race' will bring about the evolution of *self-deceit* in order to achieve more reliable deceit of others (Alexander, 1975; Hartung, 1988; Krebs & Denton, 1997; Lockard, 1980). For instance, the most 'genuine' displays of need (i.e., those that are most likely to elicit help from others), are those that result from the individual's conviction that they genuinely need help. Evolution, therefore, had to produce a 'design compromise' between the capacity for self-deception about one's own mental states (in order to achieve more effective social manipulation), and the need to manipulate the social environment to reduce threats and elicit care at times of social loss and danger.

This compromise, however, can create a 'glitch' in the system. In order for signals regarding (for example) subordinate status to be effective (in defusing aggression from others) they must be credible. In other words, they must be able to overcome the deception–detection mechanisms of others. If a dominant thinks that a subordinate is 'only pretending to submit' and is not 'really' deferential then attacks may continue until he or she is convinced. In self-aware species, this may require that individuals sending such signals (e.g., the subordinate) are convinced of their credibility. Thus, in humans, to 'play' the subordinate strategy successfully may mean that one must be personally convinced one is subordinate or inferior – even if at times one is not (Hartung, 1988). Given, however, that the dysphoric mood states that are generating these signals are often controlled by internal, as well as external, signals of status and power, such self-deception has the potential to further activate these mood states. Thus as people become depressed they become more convinced that they *are* failures and inferior. This creates a positive feedback loop whereby (say) depressive behaviour can be maintained or exacerbated by the very changes (and their consequences) activated by the depressed strategy (see Gilbert, Chapter 6, this volume). This is not to deny possible early learning (schema) of such labels, but it may throw light on why people without aversive histories can also become depressed and generate powerful negative self-cognitions – cognitions that are believed to be true (often) despite evidence to the contrary.

Thus, in the context of a self-aware species with capacity for theory of mind, depressive behaviours can become a risky gamble. There is a conflict between the goal of the strategy in the ultimate evolutionary sense (e.g., to avoid direct confrontation with up rank individuals, and also allow social resources to rise beyond critical levels without further loss) and the positive feedback loop described above. In some cases (perhaps the majority of instances of mildly depressed mood) the strategy is successful in that low mood elicits signals of care and support, reduces signals of threat, and is deactivated accordingly. In other cases, however, it becomes a spiral of escalating negative self-assessment, social withdrawal and psycho-biological retardation (see Gilbert, Chapter 6, this volume; Sloman, Chapter 12, this volume).

Cognitive therapy and deception

Before we proceed to explore how *beliefs about deception* and *beliefs* that are *themselves deceptions* (e.g., believing one is more inferior or dependent than one is) emerge in a variety of psychopathologies, it is useful to say a few words on cognitive therapy. Cognitive therapy is primarily aimed at the beliefs and information-processing strategies people use to make sense of their world. Depending on the exact definition of the term 'cognition', this could include nearly all psychotherapeutic approaches, but we focus on the explicitly cognitive approach to psychotherapy as described by Beck and his colleagues (Beck *et al.*, 1979). Beck describes cognition as 'any ideation with verbal or pictorial content' (Beck *et al.*, 1979) or as 'stream-of-consciousness or automatic thoughts that tend to be in an individual's awareness' (Beck, Epstein & Harrison, 1983). Clearly, these are exactly the kind of phenomena that the evolutionary views of social intelligence and self-deception suggest will be manipulated in order to ensure the credibility of social signals. Dobson and Block (1988) suggest that cognitive therapies share three basic propositions: (1) cognitive activity affects behaviour, (2) cognitive activity may be monitored and altered, and (3) desired behavioural change is achievable through cognitive change. Cognitive therapy, therefore, achieves therapeutic change by focusing on exactly the phenomena that we propose may be at the heart of the evolutionary 'design-compromise' that has rendered humans vulnerable to escalation of dysphoric mood states and other psychopathological phenomena.

The aims of the techniques utilized in cognitive therapy are twofold. The first is to reduce distress by teaching skills to recognize, evaluate and change relevant cognitive processes. Second, in later phases, the therapy attempts to engender an understanding of themes in maladaptive cognitions. This should help to modify the enduring sets of attitudes and beliefs that are the basis of the client's vulnerability. The approach involves the following steps: eliciting automatic thoughts, testing their accuracy and viability, developing realistic alternatives, and identifying and challenging underlying maladaptive schemata (Allen, 1996; Beck et al., 1979; Gilbert, 1997b). According to the cognitive model, three types of cognitive phenomena determine pyschopathology: automatic thoughts, cognitive distortions, and schema. Automatic thoughts, the 'surface level' of cognition, are the transitory verbal and pictorial experiences that maintain abnormal mood states. They are automatic in as much as they emerge spontaneously, and are often difficult to resist. Despite the ubiquitous nature of automatic thoughts, many people are unaware of them, and need help to develop the skill of 'thought catching' before further therapy proceeds. Cognitive distortions refer to misinterpretations of reality that reinforce negative conclusions. Beck (1967) describes specific kinds of cognitive distortions, including overgeneralizing (a single instance is taken as an example of a wide range of situations), dichotomous thinking (only extreme points of view are considered), selective abstraction (attending solely to negative aspects of a situation), personalizing (assuming oneself is the cause of an event or of another's actions), 'should' statements (absolute imperatives are applied to one's own or another's behaviour), 'catastrophizing' and minimizing (emphasizing negative and down-playing positive outcomes).

Information about oneself and one's environment is perceived, stored, and recalled through schema, which are assumed to develop during repeated experiences. Schema help a person to recognize consistencies so that novel information is linked to current knowledge efficiently. Since a bias towards schema-congruent information occurs, psychopathological states result from schema that facilitate interpretation of situations in terms of threats to the self, such as loss, failure, rejection and danger. These schema are sometimes not accessible without considerable introspection. Although it is possible to describe them in verbal terms such as: 'If I am a good person, bad things will not happen to me', it is not expected that they exert their influence necessarily through verbal conscious processes. In other words, the nature of these schema is usually deduced on the basis of recurrent cognitive distortions and automatic thoughts. Once a schema is activated by a congruent mood state or event, it dominates perceptions of current and future situations.

The evolutionary angle on schema however, suggests that they serve strategic ends. For example, Belsky, Steinberg and Draper (1991; Belsky, 1993), using an evolutionary model, suggested a direct link between early rearing environments and subsequent interpersonal behaviour and psychopathology. They argued that early environments act to select which social and reproductive strategies (e.g., affiliative, stable pair bonding and high investment in offspring versus less affiliative, unstable pair bonding and low investment in offspring) individuals may adopt. Thus, self–other cognitions (e.g., others as trustworthy, self as caring) reflect str?tgetic choices – choices that may not be available to consciousness. And in so far as one attempts to change schema then one is also trying to modify strategic choices that are coded in psychobiobiological and gene-neural interfaces. This may help to explain why some people need (for example) repeated experiences (signals) of (say) being cared for before they can change, because what is at stake is switching strategies.

Concepts of 'schema' and adaptive strategies are both seen as strongly influenced by ontogenetic development (Gilbert *et al.*, Chapter 1, this volume; Ingram, Miranda & Segal, 1998), which can create further variations in each individual's vulnerability to experience serious psychopathology. But the distortions in thinking and feeling that arise from these schema are not errors as such. Nowhere is this more apparent than in the study of deception – for as we have seen this has been a fulcrum for the evolution of many of our social cognitive abilities.

Cognition and deception

While cognitive therapy tends to focus on consciously available beliefs, the idea that we may not be fully conscious of the motives behind our thinking processes has a long history, and was of course a cornerstone of early psychoanalysis (Ellenberger, 1970). However, the lack of knowledge of inner processes can have various sources. First, there is no need for animals to be conscious of any ultimate (evolutionary) motives, such as seeking reproductive success. Indeed, humans are not simply 'inclusive fitness maximizers', but rather are motivated by the biosocial goals that lead to it, such as seeking sexual partners, caring for offspring, and so forth (Buss, 1999; Gilbert *et al.*, Chapter 1, this volume). Thus, deceptions in the service of genetic reproductive interests are not really part of the human psyche, but deceiving self and others of the proximate motives that lead to it are. Second is the question of whether some of the motives behind some deceptive behaviour have ever been (in our evolution) conscious, or whether information is processed in the brain in such a way that there are limitations on access to such information if this is detrimental to reproductive interests. Krebs and Denton (1997) have explored this possibility by noting differences in hemispheric information processing and conscious access.

Third is the level at which information *could be* conscious, but is kept out because it would seriously disrupt the pursued strategies (e.g., presenting self as attractive, or needy, or of high or low status) if fully conscious. This bears on issues of defence mechanisms such as denial and repression – a subject well covered elsewhere (Nesse & Lloyd, 1992). Fourth is the fact that deceptions give rise to biases in information processing that are often self-serving (for example see Gilbert *et al.*, Chapter 1, this volume; Krebs & Denton, 1997) and although these are often positive and self- (or group-) enhancing there may be times when negative biases could be adaptive (Hartung, 1988). For example, as individuals have to change strategies (e.g., a high status person loses status and falls in the hierarchy), a new strategy (of say acting in a subordinate manner) necessitates he or she focuses on his or her limitations and not a self-serving positive bias. In essence he or she must switch from positive self-deception to negative self-deception. The latter is important both to attune to new threats in the situation, and to send signals to others of his or her changed (non-challenging, needy) state. Negative biases in processing self-relevant information can arise therefore for reasons other than punitive early experiences.

These elements of the evolutionary approach described above have implications for cognitive therapy. The evolutionary model posits that the 'schema' associated with strong emotions may reflect adaptive (or previously adaptive) strategies in species-typical design. These strategies are role serving, aimed to secure biosocial goals, and to be sensitive to threats along the way. Unlike standard cognitive therapy, we suggest it is important to consider the (possible) adaptive (strategic) significance of certain types of beliefs, and not view them as simply errors in reasoning (Gilbert, 1998). Thus, a belief like 'I am a failure' or 'I am unlovable', may have some defensive function (e.g., to reduce aspirations in a threatening environment, or alert the person to potential damage from bonding) – even if this is not immediately obvious.

Social cognition and beliefs of being deceived

The issue of trust and fear of being deceived is one of the most common issues in therapy, but few theorists approach this from the point of view of there being innate cheater detection systems arising from the fact that deception is common and has been adaptive over millions of years (Cosmides & Tooby, 1994). Consider social anxiety. As we noted above, many psychological problems revolve around social cognitions and beliefs about what others think of the self, whether they can be trusted, and if not, what one should do. In some cases, such as social anxiety, the person automatically assumes that others will reject them if they make social errors. Even in situations where this is a rare outcome, they may persist with this belief. When a belief does not respond to clear evidence to the contrary, evolutionary therapists often suspect the operation of some evolved heuristic strategy. In this case, it may be to *assume the worse*. In some situations it can be better to assume the worse and survive than underestimate danger and suffer the consequences (Gilbert, 1998). Evolutionary therapists may therefore explore these beliefs in that light. In fact, we have often found that some socially anxious people believe that others are behaving deceptively, i.e., 'they may act friendly, but they are still thinking I am stupid or unattractive'. This is not to say that such patients may not have had past traumatic experiences of rejection, only that the fear of deception is crucial to the maintenance of these beliefs. Few cognitive models of social phobia address this issue (fear of deception). Sometimes it can be helpful to discuss the possibility that their 'cheater detection system' is over-active – and how they could test this out. It is not so much that people are making errors in social reasoning rather it is that using certain types of social reasoning modules in certain contexts may not be helpful. It may also help to explore the actual dangers to the patient, even if others are being deceptive (Gilbert, 1997b).

When the consequences of deception are high, the probability of fear of, and vigilance to, deception increases. This is particularly true in sexual relationships where jealousy can cause such havoc. The consequence of deception in sexual relationships can be very serious from an evolutionary point of view (e.g., a man is deceived into caring for an offspring that is not his own, or a women is deceived into having sex with a man who will subsequently abandon her). For this reason the mind set of some people (males in particular) tends towards ownership and high sexual guarding (Wilson & Daly, 1992). Conversely, women may fear that 'he is only being nice to me because he wants to get me in bed'. From an evolutionary point of view the high intensity emotions in jealousy or sexual coyness/avoidance are related to the costs of deception (Glantz & Moehl, Chapter 8, this volume). These may not be easily quelled with rational arguments. Nor may others (including therapists) recognize that their thinking is guided by reproductive strategies that are self-protective and for self-interests (Kriegman, Chapter 4, this volume).

Self-deception about others' deception and avoidance of conflict

Individuals who fear they are being deceived (rightly or wrongly) have to face a dilemma. On the one hand, detecting deception activates strong hostile feelings to retaliate. Such action evolved because, in the past, retaliation has been adaptive in reducing deceptions. But detecting deceptions and subsequent retaliation is not cost free (Krebs & Denton, 1997). For example, if one is in a subordinate position, then such actions may result in a complete breakdown of the relationship with further major losses. The other may angrily protest his or her innocence, or the evidence may not be clear enough to convince the other that one can prove the deception. (After all deceivers will normally be motivated to hide and deny it to others and to themselves.) Another option is just to leave the relationship – but again this can involve further major losses.

Self-blame and deception

Something similar has been outlined by Bowlby (1980) in his notion of defensive exclusion. A parent is harsh and critical of the child, but tells the child they are doing this in the child's best interests, or that it is the child's fault. Challenging this obvious deception on the parent's part is impossible for the child because this would lead to further trouble, and the child is certainly not able to leave the parent. The only thing the child can do is to deceive him- or herself into believing he or she really is the one at fault. That the parent is deceiving the child of their own (as parents) bad behaviour would be apparent to any outside observer. As a result the child grows up fearful of revealing deceptions involved in others' harsh or unfair treatment. Sometimes they are just not able to recognize others' exploitations and deceptions. This information is excluded from conscious processing (Bowlby, 1980) and self-blame is used as a way of reducing possible retaliation-anger and maintaining bonds. Self-blame can be part of a submissive strategy – but it is highly unlikely that the person has insight into this for then the submission might not be credible. There is a need for more research into what situations and mechanisms might promote deceptive or strategic self-blame. However, Andrews and Brewin (1990) found that women living with abusive males often blamed themselves for the violence, but changed their attributional style when they moved away, i.e., when it was safe to do so. Gilbert (1992) suggested this may be an example of a defensive cognitive strategy.

The therapeutic implications are that the therapist can clarify in whose interests the harsh treatment was, the advantages and disadvantages of self-blame and explore how the patient's own deceptive strategies (of not acknowledging unfair treatment) may be a defensive/submissive strategy that may have worked during childhood, or when escape from an abusive other was not possible, but may now need altering. The evolutionary therapist works with the themes of self-interest and adaptive value of such 'self-deception'. A similar case can be made for sexual abuse where the therapist clarifies in whose interest the abuse took place. Once a patient understands that an abuse was not in their interests but that of the perpetrator (Erkison, Chapter 10, this volume) they may then more easily deal with issues of responsibility.

The basic idea, then, is that when retaliating against a deception or exploitation is costly (e.g., one is in a highly subordinate position), there are likely to be motivational reasons why individuals may deceive themselves into not recognizing others' deception or exploitation, but rather engage in self-blame. Self-blame can also be a form of 'deceiving down'; that is seeing oneself as more subordinate/ inferior than is actually the case.

A variation on this theme has been offered by Hartung (1988). In some situations it would be more costly to acknowledge one's strengths and abilities if this lead to serious conflicts and abandonment by others. This may be especially so for women who, in many societies, are often in subordinate and dependent positions. It may be more adaptive to deceive oneself into believing that one is less able than (say) one's husband, if this maintains the stability of the bond and protects his status. As the social structure reduces female dependence (on say husbands) this strategy may become less adaptive and change. Again, however, we suggest that if there is an evolved strategy at work in deception then it may not yield easily to logical arguments, and insight into its adaptive functions may be necessary.

On being a fake

Deception, faking, bluffing and lying are salient social behaviours that run from the deeply unconscious to conscious cynical manipulations with various defence mechanisms along the way (Nesse & Lloyd, 1992). We can fake good and see ourselves as better than others see us (Taylor & Brown, 1994), fake bad and see ourselves as worse than we are (Hartung, 1988) and we can miss-attribute others' negative behaviours in order to avoid conflicts (e.g., defensive exclusion, see earlier). In this section we raise an issue that is again common in therapy. This concerns beliefs that one is acting deceptively and is at risk of discovery.

If others can be deceptive to oneself, then we in turn may act deceptively to others. Awareness of deception can cause numerous problems of shame and guilt in relationships (Gilbert, 1989). One reason for this is that guilt evolved to prevent us from exploiting others and suffering their consequent retaliation (Crook, 1980). Also inner awareness of deceptions makes them more risky and easily detected. For example, men and women may have (evolutionary understandable) fantasies and desires to have sex with people other than their spouse. But to acknowledge this openly could be painful to both parties. Consider Jane. She was the more sexually active in her relationship but felt her husband was a rather insecure man who needed her to 'love and desire' him. However, she had powerful fantasies of having sex with high status men during intercourse and sometimes faked her orgasms with him. Instead of acknowledging the evolutionary reasons for these fantasies she saw them as something bad about her. As her guilt and shame at her deceptions increased her depression she came for therapy. Understanding the evolutionary meaning of these desires – that they were the result of adaptations in human psychology – helped to depersonalize them and reduce her guilt and depression. There can be a host of moral dilemmas that bubble up in these kinds of situations (e.g., whether to reveal or not) but we raise it to underline the problems that can ensue by awareness of deception.

Of course 'keeping things secret' for fear of shame, guilt or rejection has a long history in psychotherapy, (and studies of the confessional) but recent research has shown that certain types of conscious deception (keeping certain types of secrets) is bad for one's mental and physical health and causes problems in social behaviour. While some successful conscious deceptions are helpful (e.g., in a poker game) others are not (Pennebaker, 1997). Moreover, as O'Connor (Chapter 13, this volume) discusses there are times when therapists must see through a patient's deceptive behaviour and explore it. Not to do so lets patients believe that the therapist is easily fooled and therefore no good.

James (1997) has drawn attention to the increasing number of people who seem to be highly competent but are convinced they are useless and failures and become depressed. Such individuals have been described in many ways, including perfectionist and achievement orientated. However, the key question is, why are they riddled with a fear of being a fake – of deceiving others of their competency? One answer to this is that deceiving others has been costly (if discovered), and although enhancing one's reputation through deception has been evolutionarily advantageous, we are also motivated to avoid excess (i.e., non-credible) self-enhancement (Krebs & Denton, 1997).

Carol came from a high achieving and demanding family. She had to be number one. Even when she did well though, her parents thought she could do better. It was in her parents' interest to push her as far as they could. However, Carol had serious doubts about her abilities, and was constantly fearful of falling short of the mark. The fear of her parents' rebuke (and withdrawal of love) gave some substance to a deception on the part of her parents. They would say, 'We love you regardless of how well you do,' but Carol *experienced* them as following the rule of 'we only love you if you do well'. So she learnt that others are deceptive. As a child she could not challenge this as a possible deception. Living in the fear that she 'would not be good enough' caused her constantly to monitor her performance. Consequently, instead of focusing on her *actual* abilities, she focused on her ability to convince *others* of her ability.

Carol had been forced to adopt a high-rank competitive strategy when she should have been developing peer relationships, looking to her parents to provide resources, learning from and accepting mistakes and inferiorities/limits, and having fun. Her behaviour was high- or up-ranking also because she had to convince those higher in the rank than her of her talents (not just her peers) – her teachers and (critical) parents. This excessive, competitive up-rank strategy also had the effect of seriously disturbing her interest in, and her ability to form, peer-group relationships. Her social world was filled with higher ranking individuals, whom she had to appease, and who could add or subtract from her status. Once the strategy was channelled into convincing others of her (doubted) abilities she developed a heightened fear of being exposed as a fake. If she made a mistake at work she would (she believed) suffer not only the criticism of making a mistake, but also the shame of being exposed as having deceived others of her abilities. In fact, as she progressed into early adulthood, her whole orientation to her social relationships was filtered through this fear of being a fake and deceiving others, including her intimate partners, and others deceiving her. Even when she became depressed she worried if she were faking her illness to get sympathy! – and if the therapist was faking 'kindness' because he was paid to.

There are many complexities to a case like this, including her enormous difficulty in assuming that anything positive said to her could be genuine. However, her fear of exposure also triggered a subordinate strategy that made her highly vigilant to attacks (for fooling others and being caught out), anxious and depression prone. An empathic response to her fear of deception (and not being up to others' expectations of her), with agreement that given her background that was *a sensible adaptive stance*, plus an evolutionary rationale, helped build a therapeutic alliance. Challenging cognitive distortions head-on did not seem helpful, but having a discussion about the adaptive value of her mistrust and depression (as a submissive damage limitation strategy) seemed to be.

It is sometimes said that depressives have more realism. Perhaps. We would prefer to suggest that many psychopathologies represent a heightened sensitivity to deception – by both self and others – which is sometimes adaptive and sometimes not. And although therapists will often try to offer experiences of genuine caring, patients can easily dismiss this as 'not genuine' and as Kreigman (Chapter 4, this volume) notes, we should also be aware of our own self-deceptions in the endeavour. A therapist who is over-motivated to promote themselves as genuine and caring may be a liability to patients who do not easily trust.

Faking up

Finally we should mention one common personality disorder where faking up can cause serious problems. Although self-serving biases are common (Krebs & Denton, 1997; Taylor & Brown, 1994) excessive forms are seen in disorders like narcissistic personality disorder. Narcissists tend to be grandiose, arrogant and feel they deserve better treatment than others. Their anger at criticism, or lack of the admiration they seek, acts as a strategy of intimidation towards others to treat them as up-rank – people of status and talent (Gilbert, 1989). The thing that strikes most therapists is not only their exploitativeness but also their self-deceptions and illusions of grandeur. The narcissist him- or herself however may have little insight into this and will often doggedly hold beliefs that it is others who are treating them unjustly or with insufficient admiration. Undoubtedly beliefs in one's own ability and in being deserving of high rank status can have great pays-offs if successful. Not least because these people take on the confidence of a high rank individual. If they do gain insight that their up-rank orientation is more bluster than real they can be at risk of collapse into depression. It is often when they cannot manage their deceptions that they may come for therapy. In such cases they will often engage the therapist in competitive manoeuvres, rarely acknowledging a need for being cared for but rather to be admired.

Our social deceptions can work to give us a sense of entitlement in many ways. We may believe that we give more to others than others give to us; that is, we are more co-operative, sharing and caring than we are (McGuire & Troisi, 1998); we can believe we are more up-rank (more attractive, talented and clever) and deserving of the rewards of rank than others see us as deserving. But when these deceptions become excessive or fail to elicit the desired social benefits, pathologies and dysfunctions result. Insufficient modesty, exploitativeness and insufficient sharing (meanness) leads to rejection. The cognitive therapy implications are again to focus on the potential adaptive function of narcissism, to recognize that some degree of positive self-illusion is adaptive (Taylor & Brown, 1994) and that a supportive therapeutic relationship is crucial to help those whose deceptions are out of control to cope with (small) falls from grace.

Conclusion

We have outlined how deception and social manipulation have played a salient role in the evolution of our social intelligence and forms of social behaviour. And we have argued that people fear deception and 'Machiavellian' strategies being used against them, as well as fearing that their own deceptions and 'Machiavellian' strategies will be detected. A further complication is that there are some situations where individuals may be motivated to maintain *another's* deception (particularly in dominant/subordinate relationships). Despite this, few therapies recognize the extraordinary complexities of deception, and the strategies used to detect and avoid it. Yet many people come to therapy with concerns about being deceived or deceiving others, or are not able to recognize deceptions, so it would seem pertinent to explore the strategies and algorithms for deception in psychopathology.

There is no doubt that cognitive therapy is effective because it teaches self-awareness and self-management skills (DeRubeis & Feeley, 1990). Numerous outcome studies have shown cognitive therapy to be a highly effective treatment of (for example) non-psychotic unipolar depression, and that it is at least as effective as pharmacotherapy and other recognized psychotherapies in dealing with acute episodes (Dobson, 1989; Hollon, Shelton & Loosen, 1991; Robinson, Berman & Neimeyer, 1990). More interesting is the mounting evidence that cognitive therapy is specifically effective in reducing relapse. Hollon, DeRubeis and Seligman (1992) suggest that depressed patients treated with cognitive therapy may be at less than half the risk of relapse than are patients treated with pharmacotherapy alone. This raises the question of how cognitive therapy achieves these effects, and whether an evolutionary perspective is helpful in understanding and enhancing the process of cognitive therapy. We believe that patients can benefit further when their thinking is seen as a reflection of adaptive (although not necessarily happiness-promoting) strategies. We have some way to go before we fully understand how the dynamics of deception operate in psychopathologies and the powerful emotions that support them. But cognitive therapy, like other therapies, may gain greatly by incorporating new insights from evolutionary cognitive science into its theory and therapy.

The evolutionary perspective is compatible with the literature on cognitive therapies that suggests that a critical ingredient of therapy is a focus on developing concrete skills for managing cognitive symptoms (e.g., DeRubeis & Feeley, 1990). It also extends the standard cognitive therapy models by suggesting that the origin of various psychopathologies is likely to be in the adaptations for manipulation of the social environment that are a distinctive part of primate (especially human) evolution. It therefore provides a basis for further exploration of the links between cognitive and interpersonal approaches to psychotherapy (e.g., Safran & Segal, 1990), and to a richer understanding of the way in which psychopathological phenomena arise from evolved strategies interacting with the modern social ecology.

References

Alexander, R.D. (1975) 'The search for a general theory of behavior', *Behavioral Science* 20: 77–100.

Allen, N.B. (1996) 'Cognitive psychotherapy', in S. Bloch (ed), *Introduction to the Psychotherapies* (3rd edition), Oxford: Oxford University Press.

Allen, N.B. & Gilbert, P. (2000) 'Social risk and depression: Evolutionary, psychosocial, and neurobiological perspectives', Manuscript submitted for publication.

Andrews, B. & Brewin, C.R. (1990) 'Attributions of blame for marital violence: A study of antecedents and consequences', *Journal of Family and Marriage* 52: 757–67.

Baldwin, D.A. (1991) 'Infants' contribution to the achievement of joint reference', *Child Development* 63: 875–90.

Baldwin, D.A. (1993) 'Early referential understanding: Infants' ability to recognize referential acts for what they are', *Developmental Psychology* 29: 832–43.

Baldwin, D.A. & Moses, L.J. (1994) 'Early understanding of referential intent and attentional focus: Evidence from language and emotion', in C. Lewis & P. Mitchell (eds), *Children's Early Understanding of Mind*, Hove, UK: Lawrence Erlbaum Associates Ltd.

Baron-Cohen, S. (1995) *Mindblindness: An Essay on Autism and Theory of Mind*, Cambridge, MA: MIT Press.

Baron-Cohen, S. (1997) 'How to build a baby that can read minds: Cognitive mechanisms in mindreading', in S. Baron-Cohen (ed), *The Maladapted Mind: Classic Readings in Evolutionary Psychopathology*, Hove, UK: Psychology Press.

Baron-Cohen, S., Leslie, A. & Frith, U. (1985) 'Does the autistic child have a "theory of mind"?', *Cognition* 21: 37–46.

Baumeister, R.F. & Leary, M.R. (1995) 'The need to belong: Desire for interpersonal attachments as a fundamental human motivation', *Psychological Bulletin* 117: 497–529.

Baumeister, R.F. & Tice, D.M. (1990) 'Anxiety and social exclusion', *Journal of Social and Clinical Psychology* 9: 165–95.

Baumeister, R.F., Tice, D.M. & Hutton, D.G. (1989) 'Self-presentational motivational differences in self-esteem', *Journal of Personality* 57: 547–79.

Beck, A.T. (1967) *Depression: Clinical, Experimental and Theoretical Aspects*, New York: Harper and Row.

Beck, A.T. (1987) 'Cognitive models of depression', *Journal of Cognitive Psychotherapy: An International Quarterly* 1: 5–38.

Beck, A.T., Epstein, N. & Harrison, R. (1983) 'Cognitions, attitudes and personality dimensions in depression', *British Journal of Cognitive Psychotherapy* 1: 1–16.

Beck, A.T., Rush, A.J., Shaw, B.F. & Emery, G. (1979) *Cognitive Therapy of Depression*, New York: Guilford Press.

Belsky, J. (1993) 'Etiology of child maltreatment: A developmental analysis', *Psychological Bulletin* 114: 413–34.

Belsky, J., Steinberg, L. & Draper, P. (1991) 'Childhood experiences, interpersonal development, and reproductive strategy: An evolutionary theory of socialization', *Child Development* 62: 647–70.

Bowlby, J. (1980) *Depression: Vol 3 Attachment and Loss*, London: Hogarth Press.

Buss, D.M. (1990) 'The evolution of anxiety and social exclusion', *Journal of Social and Clinical Psychology* 9: 196–201.

Buss, D.M. (1999) *Evolutionary Psychology: The New Science of the Mind*, New York: Allyn & Bacon.

Byrne, R. (1995) *The Thinking Ape*, New York: Oxford University Press.

Byrne, R.W. & Whiten, A. (1985) 'Tactical deception of familiar individuals in baboons (*Papio ursinus*)', *Animal Behaviour* 33: 669–73.

Byrne, R.W. & Whiten, A. (1988) *Machiavellian Intelligence: Social Expertise and the*

171

Evolution of Intellect in Monkeys, Apes, and Humans, Oxford: Oxford University Press.

Byrne, R.W. & Whiten, A. (1990) 'Tactical deception in primates: The 1990 database', *Primate Report* 27: 1–101.

Byrne, R.W. & Whiten, A. (1997) 'Machiavellian intelligence', in A. Whiten & R.W. Byrne (eds), *Machiavellian Intelligence II: Extensions and Evaluations*, Cambridge: Cambridge University Press.

Chance, M.R.A. & Mead, A.P. (1953) 'Social behaviour and primate evolution', *Symposia of the Society of Experimental Biology Evolution* 7: 395–439.

Cords, M. (1997) 'Friendships, alliances, reciprocity and repair', in A. Whiten & R.W. Byrne (eds), *Machiavellian Intelligence II: Extensions and Evaluations*, Cambridge: Cambridge University Press.

Cosmides, L. (1989) 'The logic of social exchange: Has natural selection shaped how humans reason?', *Cognition* 31: 169–93.

Cosmides, L. & Tooby, J. (1994) 'Beyond intuition and instinct blindness: toward an evolutionarily rigorous cognitive science', *Cognition* 50: 41–77.

Cosmides, L., Tooby, J. & Barkow, J.H. (1992) 'Introduction: Evolutionary psychology and conceptual integration', in J.H. Barkow, L. Cosmides & J. Tooby (eds), *The Adapted Mind: Evolutionary Psychology and the Generation of Culture*, (pp. 3–15), Oxford: Oxford University Press.

Crook, J.H. (1980) *The Evolution of Human Consciousness*, Oxford: Oxford University Press.

Dawkins, R. & Krebs, J.R. (1978) 'Animal signals: Information or manipulation', in J.R. Krebs & N.B. Davies (eds), *Behavioral Ecology: An Evolutionary Approach*, Oxford: Blackwell Scientific Publications.

de Waal, F. (1982) *Chimpanzee Politics: Power and Sex Among Apes*, New York: Harper & Row.

de Waal, F.M.B. (1989) *Peacemaking Among Apes*, New York: Penguin.

DeRubeis, R.J. & Feeley, M. (1990) 'Determinants of change in cognitive therapy for depression', *Cognitive Therapy and Research* 14: 469–82.

Dobson, K.S. (1989) 'A meta-analysis of the efficacy of cognitive therapy for depression', *Journal of Consulting and Clinical Psychology* 57: 414–19.

Dobson, K.S. & Block, L. (1988) 'Historical and philosophical bases of the cognitive behaviour therapies', in K.S. Dobson (ed), *Handbook of Cognitive-Behavioural Therapies*, London: Hutchinson.

Dunbar, R.I.M. (1995) 'Neocortex size and group size in primates: A test of the hypothesis', *Journal of Human Evolution* 28: 287–96.

Ellenberger, H.F. (1970) *The Discovery of the Unconscious. The History and Evolution of Dynamic Psychiatry*, New York: Basic Books.

Flavell, J.H., Everett, B.A., Croft, K. & Flavell, E.R. (1981) 'Young children's knowledge about visual perception: Further evidence for the level 1-level 2 distinction', *Developmental Psychology* 17: 99–103.

Gallup, G.G., Jr. (1970) 'Chimpanzees: Self-recognition', *Science* 167: 86–7.

Gallup, G.G., Jr. (1977) 'Absence of self-recognition in a monkey (*macaca fascicularis*) following prolonged exposure to a mirror', *Developmental Psychobiology* 10: 281–4.

Gallup, G.G., Jr. (1982) 'Self-awareness and the emergence of mind in primates', *American Journal of Primatology* 2: 237–48.

Gallup, G.G., Jr. (1994) 'Self-recognition: Research strategies and experimental design', in

S. Parter, R. Mitchell & M. Boccia (eds), *Self-Awareness in Animals and Humans*, Cambridge: Cambridge University Press.

Gigerenzer, G. (1997) 'The modularity of social intelligence', in A. Whiten & R.W. Byrne (eds), *Machiavellian Intelligence II: Extensions and Evaluations*, Cambridge: Cambridge University Press.

Gilbert, P. (1989) *Human Nature and Suffering*, Hove, UK: Lawrence Erlbaum Associates Ltd.

Gilbert, P. (1992) *Depression: The Evolution of Powerlessness*, Hove, UK: Psychology Press.

Gilbert, P. (1997a) 'The evolution of social attractiveness and its role in shame, humiliation, guilt and therapy', *British Journal of Medical Psychology* 70: 13–147.

Gilbert, P. (1997b) *Overcoming Depression: A Self-Help Guide Using Cognitive Behavioral Techniques*, London: Robinsons/New York: Oxford University Press.

Gilbert, P. (1998) 'The evolved basis and adaptive functions of cognitive distortions', *British Journal of Medical Psychology* 71: 447–63.

Gilbert, P. & McGuire, M.T. (1998) 'Shame, status and social roles: The psychobiological continuum from monkey to human', in P. Gilbert & B. Andrews (eds), *Shame: Interpersonal Behavior, Psychopathology and Culture*, (pp 99–124), New York: Oxford University Press.

Goodall, J. (1971) *In the Shadow of Man*, Boston: Houghton Mifflin.

Hartung, J. (1988) 'Deceiving down: Conjectures on the management of subordinate status', in J.S. Lockard & D.L. Paulhus (eds), *Self Deception: An Adaptive Mechanism*, New York: Prentice-Hall.

Haslam, N. (1997) 'Four grammars for primate social relations', in J.A. Simpson & D.T. Kenrick (eds), *Evolutionary Social Psychology*, Mahwah, NJ: Lawrence Erlbaum Associates Inc.

Hauser, M.D. (1997) 'Minding the behavior of deception', in A. Whiten & R.W. Byrne (eds), *Machiavellian Intelligence II: Extensions and Evaluations*, Cambridge, MA: Cambridge University Press.

Hollon, S.D., DeRubeis, R.J. & Seligman, M.E.P. (1992) 'Cognitive therapy and the prevention of depression', *Applied and Preventative Psychology* 1: 89–95.

Hollon, S.D., Shelton, R.C. & Loosen, P.T. (1991) 'Cognitive therapy and pharmacotherapy for depression', *Journal of Consulting and Clinical Psychology* 59: 88–99.

Horowitz, L.M. & Vitkus, J. (1986) 'The interpersonal basis of psychiatric symptoms', *Clinical Psychology Review* 6: 443–70.

Humphrey, N.K. (1976) 'The social function of intellect', in P.P.G. Bateson & R.A. Hinde (eds), *Growing Points in Ethology*, Cambridge: Cambridge University Press.

Ingram, R.E., Miranda, J. & Segal, Z.V. (1998) *Cognitive Vulnerability to Depression*, New York: Guilford Press.

James, O. (1997) *Britain on the Couch: A Treatment for the Low Serotonin Society*, London: Century.

Jolly, A. (1966) 'Lemur social intelligence and primate intelligence', *Science* 153: 501–6.

Krebs, D.L. & Denton, K. (1997) 'Social illusions and self deception: The evolution of biases in person perception', in J.A. Simpson & D.T. Kenrick (eds), *Evolutionary Social Psychology*, Mahwah, NJ: Lawrence Erlbaum Associates Inc.

Leary, M.R. (1990) 'Responses to social exclusion: Social anxiety, jealousy, loneliness, depression, and low self esteem', *Journal of Social and Clinical Psychology* 9: 221–9.

Leary, M.R. & Downs, D.L. (1995) 'Interpersonal functions of the self esteem motive: The self esteem system as a sociometer', in M.H. Kernis (ed), *Efficacy, Agency, and Self-Esteem*, New York: Plenum Press.

Lockard, J.S. (1980) 'Speculations on the adaptive significance of self-deception', in J.S. Lockard (ed), *The Evolution of Human Social Behavior*, New York: Elsevier.

McGuire, M.T. & Troisi, A. (1998) *Darwinian Psychiatry*, New York: Oxford University Press.

Mealey, L., Daood, C. & Krage, M. (1996) 'Enhanced memory for faces of cheaters', *Ethology and Sociobiology* 17: 119–28.

Mithen, S. (1996) 'The early prehistory of human social behaviour: Issues of archaeological inference and cognitive evolution', in W.G. Runciman, J. Maynard Smith & R.I.M. Dunbar (eds), *Evolution of Social Behaviour Patterns in Primates and Man*, Oxford: Oxford University Press.

Nesse, R.M & Lloyd, A.T. (1992) 'The evolution of psychodynamic mechanims', in J.H. Barkow, L. Cosmides & J. Tooby (eds), *The Adapted Mind: Evolutionary Psychology and the Generation of Culture*, (pp. 601–24), Oxford: Oxford University Press.

Pennebaker. J.W. (1997) *Opening Up: The Healing Power of Expressing Emotions*, New York: Guilford.

Povinelli, D.J. (1994) 'What chimpanzees (might) know about the mind', in R.W. Wrangham, W.C. McGrew, F.B.M. de Waal & P.G. Heltne (eds), *Chimpanzee Cultures*, Cambridge, MA: Harvard University Press.

Povinelli, D.J. & Preuss, T.M. (1995) 'Theory of mind: Evolutionary history of a cognitive specialization', *Trends in Neurosciences* 18: 418–24.

Povinelli, D.J. & Prince, C.G. (1998) 'When self met other', in M. Ferrari & R.J. Sternberg (eds), *Self-Awareness: Its Nature and Development*, New York: Guilford Press.

Premack, D. (1988) 'Does the chimpanzee have a theory of mind, revisited', in R. Byrne & A. Whiten (eds), *Machiavellian Intelligence*, New York: Oxford University Press.

Premack, D. & Woodruff, G. (1978) 'Does the chimpanzee have a theory of mind?', *Behavioural and Brain Sciences* 1: 515–26.

Price, J.S. (1972) 'Genetic and phylogenetic aspects of mood variations', *International Journal of Mental Health* 1: 124–44.

Price, J., Sloman, L., Gardner, R., Gilbert, P. & Rhode, P. (1994) 'The social competition hypothesis of depression', *British Journal of Psychiatry* 164: 309–15.

Robinson, L.A., Berman, J.S., & Neimeyer, R.A. (1990) 'Psychotherapy for the treatment of depression: A comprehensive review of controlled outcome research', *Psychological Bulletin* 108: 30–49.

Ross, A. (1991) 'Growth without progress', *Contemporary Psychology* 36: 743–4.

Safran, J.D. & Segal, Z.V. (1990) *Interpersonal Process in Cognitive Therapy*, New York: Basic Books.

Schore, A.N. (1994) *Affect Regulation and the Origin of the Self: The Neurobiology of Emotional Development*, Hillsdale, NJ: Lawrence Erlbaum Associates Inc.

Taylor, S. & Brown, J. (1994) 'Positive illusions and well-being revisited: Separating fact from fiction', *Psychological Bulletin* 116(1): 21–7.

Whiten, A. & Byrne, R.W. (1997) *Machiavellian Intelligence II: Extensions and Evaluations*, Cambridge: Cambridge University Press.

Wilson, M. & Daly, M. (1992) 'The man who mistook his wife for a chattel', in J.H. Barkow, L. Cosmides & J. Tooby (eds), *The Adapted Mind: Evolutionary Psychology and the Generation of Culture*, (pp. 289–322), New York: Oxford University Press.

Wimmer, H., Hogrefe, G-J. & Perner, J. (1988) 'Children's understanding of informational access as a source of knowledge', *Child Development* 59: 386–96.

8

RELUCTANT MALES

Evolutionary perspectives on male psychology in couples therapy

Kalman Glantz and Mary-Beth Moehl

Introduction

It is now well recognized that there are important differences in the relating styles of men and women (Winstead, Derlega & Rose, 1997). These differences can produce problems for psychotherapists, most notably that men can be very reluctant to engage in therapy and easily alienated if they do. In this chapter we argue that what men and women bring to their relationships reflect variations *in evolved reproductive strategies* as well as in socialization processes (see Rasgon, McGuire & Troisi, Chapter 9, this volume). It is important to consider these variations in male and female reproductive strategies if we are to understand relational conflicts between the sexes.

Sex and gender have exerted powerful selective influences on the psychology of the genders for hundreds of millions of years (Batten 1994; Blum, 1997; Buss, 1999; Crawford & Krebs, 1998; Daly & Wilson, 1983; Fisher, 1982, 1992; Forsyth, 1993; Margulis & Sagan, 1991; Maxwell, 1994; Morbeck, Galloway & Zihlman, 1997; Wilson, 1983; Wrangham & Peterson, 1996). Evolutionary approaches emphasize the notion that selective processes have designed into every man and woman predispositions to form assumptions about (1) reality; (2) concepts of the opposite sex; (3) notions about motivation; and (4) sex-typical emotional responses to environmental cues (see Buss, 1999; Pinker 1997). These ancient elements of mind can influence how each client behaves in therapy and thus how each therapist looks at client problems. Some of the major sex differences in male and female psychology include:

- Men and women have different sexual strategies which show up in mate preferences, fantasies and behaviours (e.g., Buss, 1989).
- The brains of men and women are organized somewhat differently (Blum, 1997).
- Men and women use language differently (cf. Tannen 1990/1991).

- Men and women are interested in different things; sex-typical attitudes towards sex, intimacy, sports and shopping are especially noteworthy.
- Men and women have different responses to the same environmental cues (e.g., the silhouette of the opposite sex; the sight of a newborn baby).
- Men and women want some of the same things from their partners but, as noted below, men and women also want different things.

Because of such wide-ranging differences, there are inherent conflicts between men and women – conflicts that have, often mistakenly, been attributed to individual pathology. When the therapist understands the nature of these conflicts and is able to explain them to both sides, it can help to defuse tension and encourage problem resolution. Unless therapists specifically educate themselves in the language, interests, desires and needs of *both* sexes, they may unwittingly favour one gender over the other and limit their effectiveness.

From reports by clients who have previously seen other therapists, and through discussing cases with therapists who are treating one or another member of a couple we are seeing, we have come to the conclusion that therapists often fail to recognize core male needs. For example, some of the fundamental principles of therapy – communication, connection, and sharing feelings – tend to reflect desires, needs and wants that are more commonly found among females than among males. Male clients in such an environment run the risk of being misunderstood, confused, and even shamed for not feeling what they are 'supposed to feel'. Shame often triggers defensive behaviour of withdrawal and aggression (Gilbert, 1998).

One way to organize information about male–female differences is through the concept of 'reproductive strategy'. We will discuss the basic elements of this concept and then go on to see how a grasp of the notion of male and female reproductive strategies can help therapists to deal more successfully with reluctant males.

The origins of reproductive strategies

Sexual variations in reproductive strategies revolve around five major patterns of behaviour: (1) ways the sexes compete between themselves for sexual access and opportunity; (2) ways that males and females attract each other; (3) ways that males and females seek to maintain or reduce post-sexual contact; (4) ways that males and females contribute to care of offspring, and in humans; (5) ways that males and females relate and express emotional needs over the long term.

Every species has a typical suite of reproductive strategies – ways the members of the species go about ensuring survival and reproduction (Batten, 1994). For example, part of the 'strategy' of many male mammals is to grow larger than the females of the species. This is especially so in mammals where females invest heavily in offspring and males compete with each other for sexual access or to provision females and their offspring. These processes are particularly striking in species characterized by strong *sexual selection*, and Crawford (1998) concludes that humans are a 'moderately sexually selected species' where men are about 7 per cent larger than women, men are more prone to aggression and risk-taking, and men die off faster than women at all ages. Evolved strategies are the product of confronting and solving various problems (Buss, 1999) and the problems differ between the sexes.

The female problem

Females are limited in their reproduction by live birth following a long gestation period and subsequent need to provision offspring in the form of milk, food, warmth and protection. Compared to males, females have severe limitations on the number of offspring they can produce in a lifetime.

The characteristic reproductive pattern of mammals includes internal fertilization, live birth, and production of milk – characteristics that are absent, for example, in birds and reptiles. The ability to produce milk gives the mother a special role in child care (Wilson, 1975). Milk has another consequence: it limits the need for a contribution from another parent. If a female can nourish her young on her own, she has less need of a male to help in parenting offspring. She needs good genes from the male (sperm) and may benefit from the male's protection, but the mammalian male's role is likely to be peripheral in most other ways. Thus, many mammalian males usually play a minimal role in rearing the young. They exhibit little 'parental investment', even after the birth of the offspring. This is in contrast to birds, for example, where males often invest as much as females (apart from production of the egg). However, as will be noted later, human males do invest in their offspring to varying degrees. And this has consequences on the emotional disposition to relating and mating.

The male problem

Males on the other hand can increase their reproductive success through multiple matings and relatively lower investment in offspring and many mammalian males have little in the way of intimate relationships with the opposite sex, although in some primate (monkey and ape) species, something akin to friendship does develop (Strum, 1987). They are free to pursue their genetic interests, i.e., multiple mating opportunities with little or no long-term social involvement. Much depends on the species as to whether males live in groups or follow a more solitary existence. But the simple fact of variation in potential numbers of offspring is one major difference between the sexes. Whereas females know that their offspring carry 50 per cent of their genes, males can be virtually obsessed about matters of paternity and cuckolding.

Intra-sexual competition

Although females do compete with each other for access to desirable sexual partners, the process is more vigorous for males. The basic female strategy is to *choose* well to assure reproductive success, but the male must *compete* against other males for mating opportunities if his genes are to be represented in future generations. Such competition can take many forms, including threats, ritualized behaviour and actual fighting (Eibl-Eibesfeldt, 1989). In species where fighting is important, the biggest, strongest and most aggressive males will have most of the mating opportunities (Ellis, 1995).

But mock fighting (ritual agonistic display) is equally important. In mock fighting, animals test themselves against each other to see which would likely win if fighting did occur. Once that is settled the weaker opponent backs down, leaves the field and concedes the females to the other. Mock fighting has a great advantage over real fighting: no one gets hurt. Even the winner in a real fight could sustain serious injuries.

In mock fighting, and indeed in many competitive interactions, bluffing is often extremely important. For example, many animals fluff themselves up to make themselves look bigger or find ways to make themselves look fierce (Wilson, 1975). Showing a willingness to fight can also be a good form of bluffing. If one can intimidate an opponent, one does not have to fight or flee.

Attracting strategies

Males and females are attracted to different signals of reproductive potential. A fascinating account of such differences can be found in Helena Cronin's book *The Ant and the Peacock* (1991), where she describes display tactics such as the peacock's fabulous tail and genital colouring by females to indicate sexual receptivity. In humans, males tend to be attracted to women with a certain hip to waist ratio who are relatively youthful and have clear skin. These are some of the indicators of good health. Males are less attracted by signs of high status. Women, on the other hand, while also attracted to signs of health, respond strongly to signals of status. Note though that there are also similarities. In choosing a long-term partner, both sexes are attracted by dependability, faithfulness and kindness (Barber, 1995; Buss, 1999).

Maintaining relationships

In species where alliances and inter-sexual relationships are important females are oriented to signals that males are committed to the relationship and will invest in them and their offspring. In humans, this is expressed in dependability, kindness and positive interactions with offspring. By contrast, males are attracted to two types of matings; short-term and long-term. Short-term implies relatively quick copulation with little subsequent development of relationship. Long-term relationships, however, are dependent on signals of faithfulness and competency for mothering and frequent sexual access.

Investment in offspring

In humans both partners invest in offspring but in different ways. For the most part, particularly during the early phase of development of the infant, it is the mother who remains in close proximity, feeds and protects the infant while the father tends to provisioning and protecting the family.

Individual variations

Within any population there will be variations in the vigour and type of sexual strategy of either sex. Although males tend to seek multiple matings and minimize their investments in their selected cohorts, there is enormous variation among individuals. For example, dominant male baboons seem to be of two basic types. Some are affiliative, spending much time with their offspring and in close liaisons with females. These are reasonably relaxed individuals who can be aggressive if threatened but do not typically initiate fights once established in their rank. Some are basically loners who form opportunistic alliances with other males, are often aggressive, threaten females and are coercive, rarely spend time with offspring, and generate high levels of stress in those individuals around them. When considering male psychology, it is therefore important to recognize that there are variations within males in their affiliative/aggressive strategies.

The human condition

In the transition to *Homo sapiens*, as some of our ancestors foraged on the savannas and began to rely more heavily on meat, a sexual division of labour came about, drastically increasing the level of male–female interdependence and the necessity for co-ordinated activity. Males began to hunt and, while females continued to forage for vegetable foods, these now were gathered and brought back to a home base. Food sharing, bartering and rudimentary exchange processes came into effect, often where males exchanged meat for the foods gathered by the females. Over time, females increasingly selected males who were willing to invest (Jensen-Campbell, Graziano & West, 1995). The resulting interdependence, the hallmark of the hunter–gatherer way of life, has remained central to human life ever since (Bailey, 1987; Fisher, 1982, 1992; Kinzey, 1987; Tooby & DeVore, 1987).

A male's provision of meat, protection, and support became especially important to the overall health and biological fitness of his mate and offspring; a slightly more mutual investment in progeny was now the norm (Hill & Kaplan, 1988). Mothers needed fathers for more than their sperm and became 'dependent' on men in a way that ancestral females may not have been. Something like a sex contract (Fisher, 1982, 1992) or marriage arose and women began to value men for their reliability and competence as well as their good genes.

Over millions of years, a variety of evolutionary pressures have led to the development of more committed male/female relationships than appear in most

180

other primate species. For example, with the evolution of intelligence, there has been substantial pressure on giving birth to large(r) brained infants (Zeifman & Hazan, 1997). This, in turn, has meant a high risk of death in childbirth. If males did not provide some investment in their offspring, then the death of the mother at some point early in her reproductive cycle would result in the loss of those offspring already born. Therefore, there has been a selective pressure for males to invest more in their existing families.

It remains true, however, that human females have greater certainty of biological parenthood than human males, and that human females cannot increase their reproductive success simply by mating with additional males. As a result, women are more oriented toward maximizing investment in existing offspring than human males, which means they tend to put a higher priority on commitment. These different (genetic) priorities contribute to the conflicts that exist in marriage. As Zeifman and Hazan (1997) note, males and females tend to follow different strategies for mate maintenance. For males relationship maintenance is based on sending signals of continued ability to provide resources, competency for gaining and maintaining status within same-sex groups and being an important ally in times of conflict. Males are particularly attentive to signals of rejection on these counts and possible female defection (thus being cuckolded). Female sexual relationship maintenance on the other hand is orientated to continuing to attract the male (trying to stay young and attractive) but more importantly maintaining signals from the male that he is emotionally invested in that relationship.

Despite these strides in co-operation and affiliation between the sexes, males and females continued to differ greatly in their sexual strategies and social styles within existing hunting and gathering economies. The fact remained that males could always vastly out-produce females if they could gain access to multiple partners, whereas female reproductive success required heavy parental investment in a few precious offspring.

New tensions and new conflicts

Once the hunting–gathering way of life emerged, ancestral men and women were more inclined to bond in close-knit groups, a desire that remains powerful today (Baumeister & Leary, 1995). This helped men and women to maintain relatively stable relationships and to co-operate in the raising of children. Neither gender was as free as before to engage in sex exactly when desired. The era of 'adjustment' had begun. As males began to increase their parental investment in offspring they were reasonably sure were theirs, women had to develop a capacity to adjust to the psychological peculiarities of males (and vice versa).

As men became more reliable mates and parents, they became more valuable resources for women. Consequently, there was pressure for women to compete for males and their resources. With the formation of a male–female bond, infidelity became a bigger issue, especially for the male who, more likely to invest in one female, deeply feared being cuckolded. Similarly, females deeply feared loss of emotional commitment of their mate to another, and males were thus required to exhibit commitment and put limits on their promiscuity. Pursuing additional mating opportunities would grievously offend his mate and might compromise the survival of their existing children. In this complex situation, the 'best' reproductive strategy became unclear and elusive.

Changes were happening, but males and females nevertheless retained elements of their original mammalian and primate heritage. Men today continue to pursue multiple mating opportunities within limits, while women continue to be more choosy about mates. The invention of agriculture some 12,000 years ago and the rise of civilization only made relationships between men and women more complex. This was because in competing with other males, the disparity in resources that any one male, or small group of males, could control, increased. That created huge variations between the haves, have nots and have lots. The conflict between good genes (as indicated by physical attractiveness) and parental investment was drastically complicated by the invention of money, accumulated wealth, and cultural rules of inheritance. Men, even if they were weak, and/or physically unattractive, could nevertheless attract desirable women if they had resources. All but the most fortunate women now were faced with a choice between excitement, on the one hand, and security and resources/status on the other.

The contemporary scene

In the last few hundred years, industrialization and the market economy have added significantly to the complexity of sexual relationships. The decline of the hunting and gathering sexual division of labour, labour-saving devices and birth control, and the increasing competitiveness of society have accentuated natural sexual tensions. Moreover, the vast wealth and seemingly limitless opportunities that characterize the world's developed countries adds even more fuel to the fire. Who wants to stay down on the farm with a loyal spouse when the world is there for the taking?

Developments over the last 30 years have further confused male–female relationships. Behaviourism and the 'standard social sciences model' (see Tooby & Cosmides, 1992) have been teaching that there are no essential differences between women and men. This notion leads people to believe that men should reveal their emotions, talk about the relationship, and put their weaknesses and fears on display – i.e., to be like women (see, for example, Shem & Surrey, 1998).

It is true that women like to communicate in this way with each other. But can men follow suit so easily? These notions rub up against men's deeply evolved feelings and anxieties. For example, the concealment of emotion is the essence of bluffing in intra-sexual competition. To reveal fear is to risk losing. If one loses the bluffing contest, one will either have to fight or abandon the mating opportunity. Hence there is strong selection on the ability to conceal emotion. This theme of *emotion concealment* may be culturally amplified into 'big boys don't cry' and suggests there are different processes in emotion expression for males and females. Female displays of vulnerability are due to their evolved need for protection. Hence,

182

self-disclosure and expressions of feelings of insecurity have very different meanings for men and for women. Moreover, observations indicate that women are not attracted to men who show emotions indicative of anxiety and insecurity (weakness). Women prefer males who are of high rather than low status, who display confidence, who indicate the ability to gain and maintain status, and who signal the ability to protect a mate from (amongst other things) other males (Buss, 1989, 1999). Indeed, women compete with each other to attract males with these traits and this has become more vigorous and acute in the modern world of make-up, fashion clothes and lifestyle magazines (Abed, 1998). Competing for a youthful and clear-skinned appearance is also a female–female competitive strategy.

It then becomes easy to see why women might be disposed to seek out high(er) status males and then to maximize the investment from them, while simultaneously constraining the male's penchant for multiple matings. It is also understandable why males, on the other hand, seek to display and elevate their status/strengths to other males (McCarthy, 1994), and try to avoid being cuckolded by controlling female sexual behaviour (Wilson & Daly, 1992). Should we be surprised that men also want access to other women for mating opportunities that might ultimately increase their inclusive fitness? These themes are consistent for men and women cross-culturally (Gilmore, 1990) although the structure of the social group plays a significant role in the way these gender relationships are expressed (Overing, 1989).

Reaching back to the biblical Genesis, women have long suffered from the shaming of their sexuality, but increasingly, men are also being subjected to shaming and confusing messages. For example, men are being told they should not care about the physical appearance of women; we often encounter young men who 'confess' that it *does* affect them and who seek help for this 'shameful defect of character'. Men are further told that they should not want multiple mating opportunities: 'If you love your wife why would you want sex outside of marriage?' While this isn't really new – some religions have been sending this message for two millennia – now the message is coming through secular channels as well. Additionally, men are being told that their competitiveness and desire for status, their most basic survival and reproductive strategies, are destructive and bad. Lastly, men are being told that their natural mode of communication is unacceptable (e.g., Shem & Surrey, 1998) despite the fact that biologically and socially they have not been equipped to so easily share complex and confusing feelings as are women (Miedzian, 1992). When men hear, or think they hear, messages like these in therapy, they do not expect to be either liked or understood.

Complicating matters further is the question of status. Men don't like to feel subordinate. Going to therapy may feel like giving in to the dominant position of the therapist. Therapists who understand these feelings and attitudes and their deeply evolved origins will find themselves better able to deal with the reluctant male.

Core therapy issues

Our approach was developed in part as a result of recognition of the powerful role sexual strategies can play on behaviour, especially differences in sexual strategies and gender typic behaviours (see Gilbert, Bailey & McGuire, Chapter 1, this volume, for a discussion of basic evolutionary principles). Our clinical experience has been heavily coloured by evolutionary principles in both practice and theory (Bernhard & Glantz, 1991; Glantz & Pearce, 1989) and has inspired a basic set of propositions: (1) male–female differences in attitudes toward therapy reflect fundamental differences in evolved mating strategies; (2) these differences show up as variations in the desires, preferences and needs of men and women; (3) acknowledging these differences can be a powerful way to establish an alliance with a man; (4) status is often a crucial variable for men. Many men in today's society feel they are weak, not strong. Hence, (5) protecting and even generating feelings of increased status can be a useful therapeutic tool; (6) interventions oriented towards reluctant male clients can be productively framed in terms of *costs, benefits and advantage* to the man, rather than being framed as 'better'. For example, 'It is to your advantage to respond empathically. You'll get a better result'. And, finally, (7) increases in communication in and of itself may be counter-productive in some couples.

Among the core issues dealt with in couples therapy, one would have to include control, communication, commitment, respect/appreciation, and sex. In the following section, we discuss how these problem areas relate to the evolutionary themes discussed so far, with special emphasis on the needs of males in treatment.

Control issues

One of the most frequent complaints voiced by women is that men try to control them. There is truth in this assertion and it is partly based in male evolved psychology (Wilson & Daly, 1992) but the therapist must avoid simply shaming or deploring it. Men can be virtually obsessed with avoiding being cuckolded, or worse still, spending a lifetime of their resources on another man's genetic offspring. As a result, men often respond aggressively and defensively to confrontation or challenges and they tend to be possessive and jealous in their relations with mates. Some men are more prone to these reactions than others; indeed, some men are more domineering, and more prone to aggression, violence, and jealousy than other men (Winstead, Derlega & Rose, 1997). Note that extreme cases of this type will probably not respond well to couples therapy.

We have found it counter-productive to accuse men of misusing their power, of being bullies, and in general of being bad. This is experienced as shaming and often activates unhelpful aggressive or withdrawal defences. In fact, we generally take a much more roundabout approach. We reframe inappropriately aggressive reactions to a woman as weakness. To begin the reframing, we explain the purpose and function of competition among males. It is necessary to take time doing this, so that the man can increase his awareness of male sexual strategies. We explain the natural context of such behaviour (e.g., the rigours of the African savannas), and the ongoing need for men to stand up to other men when necessary. The therapist can then introduce this intervention: 'So if your strength is designed to help you compete with other men, why would you use it at home?' This helps the man think more deeply about what threatens him and what he hopes to achieve via aggression, and prepares him to accept the idea that using his strength or intimidation against a woman is a misuse of his power that will be counter-productive if he wants his partner to be a loyal ally (Gilbert, 1989).

Caution must be exercised in this approach. The therapist must not appear to be recommending that a man simply give in to his partner. This will generally destroy any chance for a therapeutic alliance with a male. The idea is to help men see that there are appropriate ways to maintain their integrity and pursue their interests while attending to the needs of their mate. Once this goal is achieved, the therapist can then use standard therapeutic techniques (e.g., assertiveness training) to give proper guidance in negotiating conflicts and maintaining standards of fair play. Each intervention is aimed to counter beliefs that it is simply a matter of the strongest wins – and if you don't win you are a failure and loser.

Not surprisingly, women in therapy tend to be threatened by the size and aggressiveness of the males in their lives, and they are often puzzled and turned off by macho bravado and risk-taking. By the same token, men can be puzzled as to why women do not respect the very things that raise them in the eyes of other men.

Women listening to these kinds of interventions can also learn something of importance. They learn that if they are also pulled into a 'the strongest wins' mentality or 'my needs are more important, reasonable or right than yours' or if shaming becomes a tactic of control, they will never resolve conflicts. This tends to put the man in a better light for each can see how they are 'locking horns' in understandable but unproductive ways.

Communication

Problems in communication go right to the core of couples therapy. Perhaps the most common contemporary communication problem is the one made famous by Deborah Tannen in her book *You Just Don't Understand* (1990–91). The *Ur* miscommunication described in her book is one in which the woman wants to talk about her problems, and the man, instead, offers advice. The woman, irritated and fed up, says something like, 'He keeps trying to control me' whereas the confused man responds with, 'I don't understand. I was just trying to be helpful'.

This is a point in therapy where the man often feels criticized and shamed. It is important for the couples therapist to understand that legitimate and conflicting needs are in play here. Men are designed to want to solve problems. Men form their bonds around activities (e.g., hunting, sport or work) where solutions to problems and overcoming obstacles produce mutually enjoyable emotions (see Nardi, 1992). If a man talks to another man about a problem, he is probably looking for a solution.

He isn't simply expressing himself or cementing a relationship. Thus, in trying to help his spouse, he is simply doing what comes naturally.

Why do women find this behaviour so difficult and unhelpful? Isn't the biological argument that women want a strong man to protect them? But if so, why would they not want advice and assistance? Recall that in the hunter–gatherer environment, men and women had separate spheres of competence and activities. They spent most of their time with members of the same gender and did not compete across genders for status and resources. In today's world, separate spheres rarely exist and the sexes often do compete against each other in the workplace, so it is easy for a man's helpfulness and advice-giving to be seen as competitive and intrusive. When we suggest that the best response is, 'Oh, my, that's really awful' or 'Come to think of it, I once had a similar problem', men are often amazed: 'But that's terribly condescending. I can't talk to my wife that way. It would be like ignoring her.' They cannot see the point in sharing feelings – it doesn't solve anything. Most men we have dealt with in therapy are at first afraid to even try to give this 'empathic' response, because they believe their wives will feel demeaned. The couples therapist needs to validate the male's behaviour as well as carefully explain why this behaviour can work in the intimate male–female environment. We have found that the phrase 'helpful is not supportive' is an eye-opener for men. Until the issue is presented to them in that way, they have trouble grasping the difference in the way men and women think.

Perhaps the most important point we can make in this section is that more communication is not necessarily always for the best without concern of how and what to communicate. First, communicating more, if the spouses do not understand each other, may only make matters worse. It will increase the incidence of painful, destructive interactions. Second, increasing communication is often what the woman wants and what the man may fear. Third, one spouse may be harbouring thoughts and feelings that would be destructive if communicated. Many married men (and of course women) are living lives of drastically reduced expectations. They may not desire their spouses any more but they don't want to abandon their children. A man in this situation may hunker down and suppress his feelings. 'Hey, I do what I have to do', is a typical statement. They meet their responsibilities. They act like men. When they come home, they try to avoid the pitfalls and traps that arise when they have to 'talk about the relationship'. One commonly reads that men neglect their relationships because they bury themselves in their jobs. The reverse can be just as often true. Men can bury themselves in their jobs in order to save the relationship. Men may tolerate such a life if they don't have to think too much about what they are giving up. Bringing these feelings to the surface may break up the relationship.

Here's an extreme example. Janet came to therapy complaining that her husband rarely made love to her any more. They were very compatible and were terrific partners, but she wanted more sex and he refused to talk about it. He simply avoided the topic or denied that there was a problem. The husband finally consented to come to therapy. When it came time for him to talk, he visibly girded himself as for an ordeal. He solemnly turned in her direction and revealed: 'I'm just not interested in you that way any more.' The horrifying impact of this revelation ultimately led to divorce for this couple. Clearly, the couples therapist needs to understand the destructive potential of full disclosure.

Confiding weaknesses

Many women today say that they want their mate to confide in them and reveal his weaknesses. However, in our experience women, in private, frequently complain about weaknesses of various sorts in their men. Here are some typical complaints: he's tentative, never makes a decision, never suggests we do anything, never takes initiative; he complains about his boss, about not being respected enough, about not being paid what he's worth, but never does anything about it; he lets himself be pushed around, doesn't ask for what's rightly his; he doesn't make enough money (the modern version of 'he doesn't bring home enough meat'), he always asks me what I want, never says what he wants; he follows me around like a puppy dog; he kind of begs for sex, he doesn't ever just take me; he keeps asking me if he's pleasing me.

Men seem instinctively to sense that women do not like weakness or dependence. Hence many men will not be comfortable if asked to talk about their weaknesses in therapy. Encouraging men to listen and respond empathetically to their wives' concerns is a relatively safe and effective procedure, but encouraging men to open up about their concerns, self-doubt, feelings of failure, and other aspects of weakness, may be destructive of relationships. Male self-disclosure does not always have these negative effects, but therapists would be well advised to consider this possibility.

Men and women utilize therapy in different ways. It is sometimes better to help a man become more assertive in a relationship than to get him to talk about his insecurities. Men are more likely to change if change is framed as learning to be a better provider–leader. With leadership as a goal, the passive man may begin to take initiative and the weak-appearing man may begin to exhibit his hidden strengths. More generally, men will respond if something is presented to them as being to their advantage. For example, instead of presenting communication as a goal, a therapist could stress the advantages of having a partner who feels understood. Interventions need to be framed with such gender-specific traits in mind.

Commitment

Any discussion of commitment must, of necessity, begin with the fact that men have inherited a tendency to seek multiple mating opportunities and are more willing than women to desert their marriages, even if it means leaving children behind. Thus, therapeutic techniques based either on condemning or shaming this aspect of the male psyche, or treating it like a disease, are not helpful. If one really wants to know what men feel, then one has to face up to a disturbing fact: one of the things men can feel is a desire to escape commitment and play the field. Indeed, men can exist in a state of 'mild torment' because of their desire for sexual variety and multiple partners (Singer, 1985a,b). In general, some men who have not had 'their share' of attractive women can feel deprived, envious, and quite often inferior.

Commitment is what women more commonly seek in recent times, although how much this relates to who controls resources is unclear in this world of increasing single mothers. Nonetheless, couples therapists must understand that in promoting commitment, they may be *ipso facto* promoting female interests, i.e., a goal dictated by the female reproductive strategy. So how does one help couples to stay together if staying together is not necessarily in the (genetic) interests of one party? The answer partly lies in the nature of reproductive strategies. Reproductive strategies are designed to promote reproductive success, not happiness. It is in a man's *genetic* interest to mate with many women, but doing so will not necessarily make him happy. Ever since hunter–gatherer times, men have also been endowed with a desire for a family, children and emotional bonds as well as for multiple mating opportunities. Consequently, in men, phylogenetically older and newer reproductive strategies are in eternal conflict.

For example, Barry came to therapy because he was having trouble deciding whether to get married or not. He was engaged to a woman who he loved but did not find sexually exciting. He constantly fantasized about other women, and when the opportunity arose, he had an affair with a beautiful young woman. However, he wanted a family and did not want to give up his fiancée. These two conflicting desires were agonizing: the part that wanted a family he saw as frightened and weak and the part that wanted excitement he saw as morally corrupt. Through an intellectual understanding of reproductive strategies, he eventually was able, not to eliminate either one of his desires, but rather to make peace with the fact that he had conflicts. Interestingly enough, he subsequently chose to marry the woman he loved and had less trouble with the issue of her physical appeal.

The security of marriage comes at a cost for both men and women, but the genetic costs of fidelity are higher for men. It is, therefore, not helpful for a therapist simply to ask men to suppress their feelings about commitment, even though that is the socially appropriate course of action. Promoting full understanding of the nature of the trade-offs is more respectful of the needs of males. It is better if the woman involved can accept a man's true feelings, without thinking this means there is anything wrong with her. However, given the religious and political ideologies that dominate Western society today, such acceptance is difficult to come by. For that reason, much of the work of helping a man come to terms with his inner conflicts (see Gilbert, Chapter 6, this volume) over commitment is better done individually, in what has been called one-person family therapy.

Sexual jealousy

Before birth control, and for untold thousands of years, the infidelity of a wife has had, potentially, far more severe genetic consequences than the infidelity of a husband. An unfaithful wife exposes her husband to the risk of spending his life raising offspring that are not his. This would seriously reduce his inclusive fitness (Gilbert, Bailey & McGuire, Chapter 1, this volume). A husband who strays does not expose his wife to this risk. What she has to lose from sexual defections (from an evolutionary point of view) are resources and protection if he should abandon her for another woman. For both parties, sexual defection carries psychological costs, and is therefore painful for both males and females. But because the genetic costs are higher for males, they are more prone to extremes of sexual guarding and sexual jealousy (Wilson & Daly, 1992).

Jealousy can operate in another way too. Because women are usually the sole providers of food (milk) and protection to their infants they will shift their investment to their offspring at time of birth. For some males this shift can be difficult as they are not receiving sufficient signals of being valued and wanted and feel they may have little role to play at this time. It is a sad but true fact that violence and conflict can increase at this time and males can feel jealous of the attention doted on their offspring.

Lack of appreciation

This is a particularly complex issue to analyse, because it does not map directly to evolutionary themes (although see Gilbert, 1997). Indeed, men and women fail to appreciate each other for all sorts of reasons. However, there is at least one dimension to lack of appreciation that does yield profitably to an evolutionary analysis. That dimension is reciprocity (reciprocal altruism, to use the technical term). The issue of balance in the give and take of kinship relations (Bailey, Chapter 3, this volume; Cory, 1999) and in social relations in general (Baumeister & Leary, 1995) is relevant.

Reciprocity is the human tendency to return a favour – or to take revenge. It is a deeply rooted genetic trait (Trivers, 1971), supported by a variety of emotions, including guilt, gratitude and moral outrage. The 'golden rule' of the Judeo-Christian tradition is but a restatement of the genetic principle of reciprocity. Reciprocity plays an especially significant role in marriage. Unfortunately for peace and harmony, men and women tend to disagree about who owes what to whom. With the exception of people for whom guilt is a severe problem, men and women both tend to overvalue what they give and undervalue what they receive.

Only part of this disparity is due to gender differences, but gender differences do figure in the equation. One could say that husbands and wives tend to want to get paid in different 'currencies'. For example, most husbands like being looked up to. They might appreciate being left alone for a while. Most wives want to feel loved, valued, looked upon as a partner. They would like more intimate conversation. These distinctions are subtle and the 'currencies' are not mutually exclusive. The emphasis is what tends to differ from gender to gender. As a result, the exchange of goods and services that characterizes marriage is often fraught with misunderstandings and dissatisfaction. Yet in most cases, men and women are not conscious that they are calculating reciprocity at all, much less that they are calculating it differently from one another.

One major area of dispute is the value of 'work' and here the male perspective is often not well understood by therapists. Most men feel that if they go out into the world of work, make a living, and provide for their children, they have made their contribution to the family and are now owed something in return (dinner, some time to unwind, rest, sex, etc.). Most homemakers, on the other hand, feel that when a husband comes home from his day away from the drudgery she experiences, he should do something for the family (i.e., *he* owes *her*). Many marriages are consumed by this acid. 'Every time I try to explain to him/her how I feel, s/he experiences it as an attack. I can't even express my point of view any more'. Such simmering standoffs can easily destroy love, sex, and mutual respect.

Having a wife who works outside the home does not really change how men feel about this. They can understand intellectually that a working woman has the same needs for rest and recreation, but they may 'feel' cheated at the unconscious level, which is where reciprocity operates. And if their wife earns more than they do they can feel this as an attack on their status and adequacy. Men do not want to be paid for their work in money (a wife's earnings). They want to be paid in leisure and respect. And men do not want to pay for a wife's work in child care or extra work around the house. The couples therapist must (1) recognize these problems for what they are; (2) find the currencies each gender wants to be paid in; and (3) find a language that permits each side to express feelings without causing the other side to feel unheard and cheated.

Sexual conflicts

Much of the sexual maladjustment that plagues our species is due to the differing reproductive strategies of men and women (Buss, 1994; Singer, 1985a,b). In brief, men reach orgasm quickly because it is in their *genetic* interests to do so. Male mammals are designed to spread their genes. They can increase their reproductive success any time they manage to inseminate a female, and to do that requires that they ejaculate. If they can do so quickly and without effort, they can move on to the next female and continue the pattern. Hence, the phenomenon of 'premature ejaculation'. Because of their reproductive strategy, men also want to achieve penetration as soon as possible. Hence they are less interested than women in foreplay, intimacy, or prolonging the sex act.

Women, being the choosy gender, have mechanisms that impel them to delay or withhold intercourse (see Baker, 1996). Not getting aroused too quickly gives them time to think about what they are doing; to have or not have sex. Furthermore, withholding orgasm decreases the likelihood of conception (Baker & Bellis, 1993; see also Ridley, 1994) and this gives a woman another bit of choice with regards to the offspring she will bear. If she chooses a bad risk to have sex with, she can still avoid having to carry his genes to term.

Sex therapy contains a set of techniques, usually known as sensory focus, designed to overcome these disparities by making sex slower and more sensual. These techniques help people to (1) increase the amount of time dedicated to foreplay; (2) focus on areas of the body other than the genitals; and (3) engage in pleasurable activities other than in-and-out thrusting (see Kaplan, 1974 for details). In essence, these techniques teach men to make love more like women and in a way (most) women like. But men who successfully master the techniques generally benefit from an increase in sexual satisfaction and from the appreciation of their partners.

Unfortunately, the power of sensory focus is not unlimited. Some men find it unpleasant to slow down: 'It's completely artificial. My mind wanders. I can't concentrate on sex at all.' It is possible that such men are unable to focus on their usual arousal scenario (fantasy). At any rate, they may lose their erection and be unable to continue. Men who have this kind of problem generally require a lot of support and extensive individual therapy in order to help them understand that it is to their advantage to make love in this way.

Another important male–female difference has to do with the relationship between sex and 'connection'. Most women want sex to flow out of connection with their partner. The feeling of connection is hard to define, but among its main elements most people would include talking, sharing feelings, doing things together, and feeling understood and 'in tune'. For many men, sex *is* the connection. The notion that talking to one's wife about the problems she had with the children, or listening to her complaints about the drudgery of housework, or actually doing some housework, could serve as a prelude to sex, is absolutely incomprehensible. Most men have to *ignore* those concerns to even start thinking about sex. A therapist who understands this can help men to provide the connection that women crave.

Another problem area for many men (and women, but for different reasons) is sexual boredom. To understand this phenomenon it helps to be aware of something called the Coolidge effect (Buss, 1994; Glantz & Pearce, 1989). The Coolidge effect, named after the former United States President, is a simple phenomenon with grave consequences. If one introduces a new female to a male mammal who is sexually sated, the male will get aroused again. In other words, mammal males tend to get bored with any individual sex partner, but interest is rekindled with a new partner.

The Coolidge effect goes far to explain the sexual unhappiness that undermines so many marriages. The man starts to lose interest in sex with his wife. She responds by losing interest in her husband. But other women begin to flash like strobe lights in his peripheral vision. If he is a 'nice' man and loves his wife, and especially if he has children, he may experience this sexual disinterest in his wife as a terrible failure. Moreover, the loss of his sexual interest, not to mention capability, is shaming and he may well start avoiding sex to hide from his shame. His partner begins to feel shut out, unloved. She may leave him alone for a while, then she begins to question him, to look for reassurance. He withdraws, unable to tell her the truth. In time, she loses sexual interest in him, or becomes depressed by his withdrawal, and the marriage spins out of control.

Therapists who do not understand this dynamic are helpless to intervene. They will not be able to elicit the relevant information from the man, who may want desperately not to have to deal with this defeat. Worse, they may well contribute to unrealistic expectations that will doom both spouses to a life of dissatisfaction. The Coolidge effect helps to explain the decline of sex over the course of a marriage, and it is not generally reversible, except briefly, as in a second honeymoon. Therapists should not encourage people to think that the passion of youth can somehow magically be restored.

Nevertheless, therapists can indeed help couples to overcome some of the obstacles to sex. Anger over past dissatisfactions can be reduced. Hopelessness resulting from frequent disappointments can be overcome. New modes of relating can be developed. Spouses can learn, for example, to pleasure each other in turn without making demands, and to take pleasure in the other's pleasure. But these results can be achieved only if realistic expectations are generated.

Overview

It is at the very least understandable why men, especially those whose nature it is to be swayed by the ancient mammalian and primate reproductive strategies of our ancestors, are often reluctant participants in psychotherapy. The impulse to bluff and bluster, the tight control of emotion, the secret desire for multiple mating opportunities, the inadmissible sexual boredom, the drive to compete, the obsession with status, the nagging fear that other males are similarly inclined, all contribute to making conventional psychotherapy a confusing and often threatening milieu.

In attempting to establish an alliance with such men, it helps to have a set of concepts that men can relate to intuitively. In our experience, evolutionary biology provides an effective tool for understanding and communicating with men who are otherwise likely to be resistant. Men feel more comfortable when male–female differences are acknowledged and male preferences and desires are acknowledged as legitimate. The concept of reproductive strategy explains why differences exist. Defining therapy as a process of discovering ways of dealing with difference clears away any implication that one gender is right and the other wrong.

The value of the evolutionary approach to couples therapy lies in its usefulness, not in its theoretical correctness. Each case is different. We find that we have to pick and choose among these concepts, depending on circumstance and the level of sophistication of the client. We only introduce a concept when it is clear that clients are struggling with a relevant issue. If the concept doesn't quickly produce a clearing of the air, we drop it. As is the case with all therapeutic theories, there is no substitute for clinical intuition and careful attention to the characteristics of each individual.

References

Abed, R.T. (1998) 'The sexual competition hypothesis of eating disorders', *British Journal of Medical Psychology* 71: 525–47.

Bailey, K.G. (1987) *Human Paleopsychology: Applications to Aggression and Pathological Processes*, Hillsdale, NJ: Lawrence Erlbaum Associates Inc.

Baker, R. & Bellis, M. (1993) 'Human sperm competition: ejaculation manipulation by females and a function for the female orgasm', *Animal Behaviour* 46: 887–909.

Barber, N. (1995) 'The evolutionary psychology of physical attractiveness: Sexual selection and human morphology', *Ethology and Sociobiology* 16: 395–424.

Batten, M. (1994) *Sexual Strategies: How Females Choose their Mates*, New York: Putnam.

Baumeister, R.F. & Leary, M.R. (1995) 'The need to belong: Desire for interpersonal attachments as a fundamental human motivation', *Psychological Bulletin* 117: 497–529.

Bernhard, J.G. & Glantz, K. (1991) Management theory, in M. Maxwell (ed), *The Sociobiological Imagination*, (pp. 53–70), New York: State University of New York Press.

Blum, D. (1997) *Sex on the Brain: The Biological Differences between Men and Women*, New York: Viking (Penguin).

Buss, D.M. (1989) 'Sex differences in human mate preferences: Evolutionary hypotheses testing in 37 cultures', *Behavioral and Brain Sciences* 12: 1–49.

Buss, D.M. (1994) *The Evolution of Desire*, New York: Basic Books.

Buss, D.M. (1999) *Evolutionary Psychology: The New Science of the Mind*, Boston: Allyn & Bacon.

Cory, G.A., Jr. (1999) *The Reciprocal Modular Brain in Economics and Politics*, New York: Kluwer Academic/ Plenum Publishers.

Crawford, C. (1998) 'The theory of evolution in the study of human behavior: An introduction and overview', in C. Crawford & D.L. Krebs (eds), *Handbook of Evolutionary Psychology: Ideas, Issues, and Applications*, (pp. 3–42), Mahwah, NJ: Lawrence Erlbaum Associates Inc.

Crawford, C. & Krebs, D.L. (eds) (1998) *Handbook of Evolutionary Psychology: Ideas, Issues, and Applications*, (pp. 3–42), Mahwah, NJ: Lawrence Erlbaum Associates Inc.

Cronin, H. (1991) *The Ant and the Peacock. Altruism and Sexual Selection from Darwin to Today*, Cambridge: Press Syndicate of University of Cambridge.

Daly, M. & Wilson, M. (1983) *Sex, Evolution, and Behavior* (2nd edition), Boston, MA: Willard Grant.

Derlega, V.J., Hendrick, S.S., Winstead, B.A. & Berg, J.H. (eds) (1991) *Psychotherapy as a Personal Relationship*, New York: Guilford.

Eibl-Eibesfeldt, I. (1989) *Human Ethology*, Hawthorne, NY: Aldine de Gruyter.

Ellis, L. (1995) 'Dominance and reproductive success among nonhuman animals', *Ethology and Sociobiology* 16: 257–333.

Fisher, H.E. (1982) *The Sex Contract*, New York: William Morrow.

Fisher, H.E. (1992) *The Anatomy of Love*, New York: W.W. Norton.

Forsyth, A. (1993) *A Natural History of Sex*, Shelburne, VT: Chapters Publishing.

Gilbert, P. (1989) *Human Nature and Suffering*, Hove, UK: Lawrence Erlbaum Associates Ltd.

Gilbert, P. (1997) 'The evolution of social attractiveness and its role in shame, humiliation, guilt and therapy', *British Journal of Medical Psychology* 70: 113–47.

Gilbert, P. (1998) 'What is Shame? Some core issues and controversies', in P. Gilbert & B. Andrews (eds), *Shame: Interpersonal Behavior, Psychopathology and Culture*, (pp. 3–36), New York: Oxford University Press.

Gilmore, D.D. (1990) *Manhood in the Making: Cultural Concepts of Masculinity*, New Haven, CT: Yale University Press.

Glantz, K. & Pearce, J.K. (1989) *Exiles From Eden: Psychotherapy from an Evolutionary Perspective*, New York: Norton.

Hill, K. & Kaplan, H. (1988) 'Tradeoffs in male and female reproductive strategies among the Ache', in L. Betzig, M. Borgerhoff Mulder & P. Turke (eds), *Human Reproductive Behavior*, (pp. 277–306), New York: Cambridge University Press.

Jensen-Campbell, L.A., Graziano, W.G. & West, S.G. (1995) 'Dominance, prosocial orientation and female preference: Do nice guys really finish last?', *Journal of Personality and Social Psychology* 68: 427–40.

Kaplan, H.S. (1974) *The New Sex Therapy*, New York: Brunner/Mazel.

Kinzey, W.G. (ed) (1987) *The Evolution of Human Behavior: Primate Models*, Albany, NY: State University of New York Press.

McCarthy, B. (1994) 'Warrior Values: A socio-historical survey', in J. Archer (ed), *Male Violence*, London: Routledge.

Margulis, L. & Sagan, D. (1991) *Mystery Dance: On the Evolution of Human Sexuality*, New York: Summit Books.

Maxwell, K. (1994) *The Sexual Imperative*, New York: Plenum.

Miedzian, M. (1992) *Boys Will Be Boys: Breaking The Link Between Masculinity and Violence*, London: Virago.

Morbeck, M.E., Galloway, A. & Zihlman, A.L. (eds) (1997) *The Evolving Female: A Life-History Perspective*, Princeton, NJ: Princeton University Press.

Nardi, P.M. (1992) *Men's Friendships*, London: Sage.

Overing, J. (1989) 'Styles of manhood: An Amazonian contrast in tranquillity and violence', in S. Howell & Wills (eds), *Societies at Peace. Anthropological Perspectives*, (pp. 79–99), London: New York.

Pinker, S. (1997) *How The Mind Works*, New York: Norton.

Ridley, M. (1994) *The Red Queen: Sex and the Evolution of Human Nature*, New York: Macmillan.

Shem, S. & Surrey, J. (1998) *We Have To Talk*, New York: Basic Books.

Singer, B. (1985a) 'A comparison of evolutionary and environmental theories of erotic response. Part I: Structural features', *Journal of Sex Research* 21: 229–57.

Singer, B. (1985b) 'A comparison of evolutionary and environmental theories of erotic response. Part II: Empirical arenas', *Journal of Sex Research* 21: 345–74.

Strum, S. (1987) *Almost Human. A Journey into the World of Baboons*, New York: Random House.

Tannen, D. (1990/1991) *You Just Don't Understand*, New York: Ballantine Books.

Tooby, J. & Cosmides, L. (1992) 'The psychological foundations of culture', in Barkow, J., Cosmides, L. & Tooby, J. (eds), *The Adapted Mind. Evolutionary Psychology and the Generation of Culture*, (pp. 19–136), New York: Oxford University Press.

Tooby, J. & DeVore, I. (1987) 'The reconstruction of hominid behavioral evolution through strategic modeling', in W.G. Kinzey (ed), *The Evolution of Human Behavior: Primate Models*, (pp. 183–238), Albany, NY: State University of New York Press.

Trivers, R. (1971) 'The evolution of reciprocal altruism', *Quarterly Review of Biology* 46: 35–57.

Wilson, E.O. (1975) *Sociobiology: The New Synthesis*, Cambridge, MA: Harvard University Press.

Wilson, G. (1983) *Love and Instinct*, New York: Quill.

Wilson, M. & Daly, M. (1992) 'The man who mistook his wife for a chattel', in J.H. Barkow, L. Cosmides & J. Tooby (eds), *The Adapted Mind: Evolutionary Psychology and the Generation of Culture*, (pp. 289–322), New York: Oxford University Press.

Winstead, B.A., Derlega, V.J. & Rose, S. (1997) *Gender and Close Relationships*, New York: Sage.

Wrangham, R. & Peterson, D. (1996) *Demonic Males*, Boston: Houghton Mifflin.

Zeifman, D. & Hazan, C. (1997) 'Attachment: The bond in pair-bonds', in J.A. Simpson & D.T. Kenrick (eds), *Evolutionary Social Psychology*, (pp. 237–63), Hillsdale, NJ: Lawrence Erlbaum Associates Inc.

9

GENDER AND PSYCHOTHERAPY

An evolutionary perspective

Natalie Rasgon, Michael T. McGuire and Alfonso Troisi

Introduction

Although the few reported studies of gender–psychotherapy interactions have failed to establish clearly that females and males respond differently to psychotherapy, there are good psychological, clinical, social, and evolutionary reasons for expecting that they do (e.g., Pajer, 1995; Shear, 1997; McGuire & Troisi, 1998b; Rasgon, McGuire & Troisi, in press; Godfroid, 1999; Glantz & Moehl, Chapter 8, this volume). This chapter addresses the topic of gender–psychotherapy interactions. It begins with a sampling of clinical experience. Selected research and theoretical findings are then reviewed, followed by a discussion of reasons for expecting gender-specific responses to psychotherapy. The chapter closes with a set of predictions based on evolutionary models.

Clinical experience

In the process of writing this chapter, the authors asked clinicians about those female–male differences they believed influenced psychotherapy outcome. The majority of those queried agreed on the following points. Compared to males, females are: (1) more verbal; (2) value emotional support more; (3) connect with their feelings more rapidly; (4) develop 'transferences' earlier; (5) somatize their feelings more; (6) use less alcohol and other substances to cope with adverse emotional states; (7) stay in psychotherapy longer; (8) more easily accept the idea of therapy; (9) are less stigmatized by therapy; (10) less often organize their sense of worth around personal autonomy; (11) more often use self-blame as a submissive and non-aggressive strategy; (12) more often seek out supportive others during periods of stress; (13) more often reflect on and seek out therapy for feelings of vulnerability, lack of affection, and lack of closeness; (14) more often co-operate in groups and build networks outside the therapy sessions; (15) more often present with self-harming and self-attacking behaviours rather than outward aggression; (16) more often reveal shame. Reports addressing many of these points can be found in the clinical and social psychology literature (e.g., Barnett & Gotlib, 1988; Brown & Harris, 1978; Surtees, 1980).

The preceding points are consistent with the view that there are female–male differences in response to psychotherapy. For example, because females are more verbal than males, have quicker access to their feelings, and accept psychotherapy more readily, a reasonable expectation is that, on average, females will have a higher percentage of successful therapeutic outcomes compared to males (see Troisi & McGuire, Chapter 2, this volume).

Research findings and hypotheses

The literature addressing psychiatrically relevant female–male differences and mental disorders has focused primarily on issues of disorder prevalence, disorder presentation, and disorder-contributing factors. Far less has been written on differential responses to psychotherapy. For example, studies consistently document great prevalence differences among women for disorders such as depression, anorexia nervosa, bulimia, and attention deficit disorder (e.g., Kessler *et al.*, 1994). Such differences suggest sex-related predispositions and vulnerabilities for different disorders. Psychosocial factors (e.g., stress, poverty, discrimination), their possible differential impact on females, and their influence on therapy have been studied by a number of investigators (e.g., Brown & Harris, 1978; Krawitz & Watson, 1997; Rasgon, McGuire & Troisi, 2000; Godfroid, 1999). A consistent theme among these studies is that adverse life events impact females more severely than males and, in turn, influence disorder prevalence. Abuse is also a factor. Whiffen and Clark (1997) found that childhood sexual abuse, which occurs more often among females, accounts for a significant proportion of the prevalence differences in depression. Bebbington (1996), who has written a comprehensive review of gender differences and depression, expresses a similar view in arguing that biological factors, while influential in the emergence of depression, do not account for prevalence differences. Rather, evidence points to psychosocial factors as the major contributor.

Disorder presentation also differs. In a study of chronic major depression, women were found to have higher scores on the Hamilton Rating Scale for Depression, the Beck Depression Inventory, and the Clinical Global Impression assessment instrument. Depressed women are reported to show greater degrees of psychomotor retardation and functional impairment than males (Kornstein *et al.*, 1995), more socially interactive behaviours than depressed males and, in patient–therapist interactions, higher levels of nonverbal hostility and submissive and affiliative behaviours (Troisi & Moles, 1999). Males and females also differ in the presentation of substance abuse disorders with males having more alcohol-related problems and females having more co-morbid diagnoses (Brady, Grice, Dustan & Randall, 1993).

Yet other factors influence prevalence rates and disorder presentation. In a study of monozygotic twins and seasonal mood disorders, males and females differed significantly in the heritability of disorders irrespective of additive genetic factors

(Jang, Lam, Livesley & Vernon, 1997). Shear (1997) has suggested that differences in the male and female brains are likely contributing factors to both prevalence and outcome differences although such differences and their associated effects remain to be demonstrated. Ethnicity can also be a factor both in diagnosis and response to treatment (e.g., Kosch, Burg & Podikuju, 1998) and therapist gender has been implicated in therapeutic outcome (e.g., Waller & Katzman, 1998; Fowers, Applegate, Tredinnick & Slusher, 1996).

Psychological studies of male–female differences among normal populations consistently report sex-related differences in a variety of behaviours, many of which seem likely to influence psychotherapy. For example, women's sociality is oriented toward dyadic close relationships, whereas men's sociality is oriented towards a larger group (Baumeister & Sommer, 1997). Emotional responses also differ. In studies of undergraduates' responses to emotional films, women are more expressive of their emotions and demonstrate different patterns of skin response conductance (Kring & Gordon, 1998). Links between the body, self-perceived attractiveness, and self-esteem also distinguish men and women with studies showing links for women's attractiveness but not for men's (Wade & Cooper, 1999). A meta-analysis of the literature (Feingold, 1994) finds that males are more assertive and have slightly higher self-esteem than females while females have higher measures of extraversion, trust, anxiety, and tender-mindedness.

Turning to intervention outcome, Pajer (1995) has suggested that there are four factors that may contribute to the greater longitudinal course of depression among females. These include (1) sex differences in pharmacokinetics and responsiveness to medications, (2) higher rates of disorder co-morbidity among females, (3) normal female hormone changes possibly serving as 'triggers' for mental disorders among genetically vulnerable females, and (4) the possibility that females are subject to unique psychosocial stressors that impede recovery. Mann et al. (1996) have noted that when male and female alcoholics are treated with group psychotherapy, females have a better response to treatment as measured by the Giessen test (a test assessing psychosocial features of personality). Zlotnick et al. (1996) conducted a naturalistic follow-up study involving a large number of both depressed males and females in which the authors investigated possible gender interactions with (1) type of treatment received, (2) dysfunctional attitudes, (3) life events, and (4) social support. In addition, psychosocial factors (e.g., need for approval) that were thought to be more important among females than males were evaluated to determine if they had a different impact on symptoms of depression and treatment outcome. Over the 18-month study they were *unable* to identify any main effects for gender or any significant interactions involving any of the variables of interest. Findings from this and related studies (e.g., Yanovski, Menduke & Albertson, 1995) raise obvious questions about gender–psychotherapy interactions.

At best, the preceding review is suggestive of possible gender–psychotherapy interactions; at worst it suggests that such interactions are either absent or so minimal that they will elude detection.

What does psychotherapy do or, how does it work?

The focus of this chapter invites the question, 'Are there features of psychotherapy that lead to differential female–male responses?' Despite an extensive literature on the mechanics of psychotherapy, there appears to be little agreement about how psychotherapy works. It would be prohibitive to review this literature. Thus, for this chapter we have picked five generally agreed upon points and looked at their potential implications for gender–psychotherapy interactions. (1) Patients learn new ways of perceiving social events and understanding their own and others' behaviour. (2) Patients learn that unpleasant emotions can be understood and mastered. (3) Patients take the knowledge gained in therapy and utilize it in their social interactions. (4) Patient–therapist relationships have greater influence on outcome than technical differences (Orlinsky & Howard, 1986). And (5), physiological changes occur in parallel with psychological and behavioural changes (e.g., Baxter *et al.*, 1992). Point (2) is compatible with the idea that females will more often experience successful psychotherapy outcomes than males, with differential access to emotions being a key contributing factor. Point (4) invites the hypothesis that females may be better therapists for females and males may be better therapists for males due to similarities in orientation. Point (5) has interesting implications. There are well-documented physiological differences among females and males (reviewed in Nyborg, 1994). There are also well-documented instances in which verbal interactions influence physiological states. When these points are combined, a reasonable postulate is that the same verbal input from a therapist will affect male and female physiology differently. In turn, outcome may be influenced.

An evolutionary perspective

Can an evolutionary perspective serve as the source of research questions relevant to sex-related response differences in psychotherapy? As noted, there are few empirical studies in the literature addressing this question. Thus, it is not possible to test evolutionary-based hypotheses against empirical data. What is possible is to use an evolutionary perspective to make specific predictions about response differences.

As a way of introducing the evolutionary perspective, a second look at the Zlotnick *et al.* (1996) study will be helpful. This study did not demonstrate gender-specific differences in response to psychotherapy. A possible reason is that the investigators grouped study subjects by disorder type (e.g., depression) rather than by specific stressors that may elicit disorders (e.g., reproductive failure). From an evolutionary perspective, some stressors can be ameliorated by a therapist who is aware of their adaptive importance (reviewed in McGuire & Troisi, 1998a) while others cannot be ameliorated regardless of a patient's skills in using the tools of psychotherapy or a therapist's skills or sex. This view derives from an evolutionary analysis of the aetiology of disorders and implies that future studies of differential psychotherapy responses should address gender-specific vulnerabilities to different stressors that have adaptive relevance.

Evolutionary theory not only recognizes anatomical and physiological differences among males and females, but it also recognizes motivational, behavioural, and functional differences with respect to reproductive function, investment in offspring, mate selection, type and intensity of bonding, and cross- and within-sex interactions. For example, females are more likely to invest more time and energy in raising offspring and developing and maintaining kin networks.

Because of the importance of reproduction to both females and males, reproduction provides a convenient focus for illustrating how hypotheses addressing therapy outcome can be derived from evolutionary theory. Crawford and Johnston (1999) have developed a useful model in which they divide sex differences into three categories applicable to both males and females: (1) residual reproductive value, (2) value to the opposite sex, and (3) costs to each sex for mating and reproduction. The differences are considerable. For example, for females, their residual reproductive value is tied to youth, health, status, intelligence, physical appearance and available resources. For males, it is tied to health, danger to life (e.g., war, predators), status, controlled resources, youth and physical prowess. Behavioural strategies adopted by males and females as well as the priorities associated with residual values reflect themselves in characteristic sex-related behaviours and responses to events. Males search for physically attractive and healthy females who will not engage in extra-relationship sexual encounters and who will be good mothers, while females search for males with resources or who signal capacities to obtain resources. Other authors add hierarchy or status as an important within-relationship variable (e.g., Price, 1967; Gilbert, 1984, 1989, 1992; McGuire & Troisi, 1998b).

Bonding preferences and their associated behaviours are also critical to the evolutionary perspective. For example, compared to males, females bond with greater intensity and are more vulnerable to bond disruptions (McGuire & Troisi, 1998b). With peers, females tend to form supportive peer groups rather than hierarchies (Savin-Williams, 1987). Males bond less intensely with peers and form spontaneous hierarchies among non-kin groups (Savin-Williams, 1987). Males are more overtly competitive with each other compared to females and they are more likely to engage in aggression to settle status disputes (reviewed in McGuire & Troisi, 1998b). Two other reproduction-related factors can be added to these points, male paternity uncertainty and female maternity certainty. These differences not only influence how males and females bond with offspring but also their degree and intensity of investment.

All this is not to suggest that evolutionary theory can serve as a 100-percent-certain guide to the conduct of psychotherapy or to predict its outcome in individual cases. Evolutionary theory is in part about genetically influenced behavioural predispostions or tendencies and in part about how predispositions are influenced by development, culture, experience, and the current social environment. These 'non-genetic' factors can be as important in everyday behaviour and therapy as the behaviours that are strongly influenced genetically (e.g., Loewenthal et al., 1995). Further, 'conflicts' between predispositions and, for example, learned social roles are often at the very centre of psychotherapy and the substance and intensity of conflicts will differ from patient to patient. (See Archer, 1996, for a comparison of the explanatory power of evolutionary theory versus social role theory; McGuire & Troisi, 1998a, and Mealey, 1995 for examples of evolutionary models explaining female–male disorder prevalence differences.)

This brings us to examples of how an evolutionary perspective can be used to predict female–male outcome differences in psychotherapy.

Physical attractiveness

Will self-perceived physical unattractiveness result in different psychotherapy outcomes among males and females? *Yes.* Females are more likely to focus on and be sensitive to physically attractive traits than are males (Buss, 1985, 1987, 1988, 1989, 1994). Further, links between self-perceived attractiveness and self-esteem have been shown to be greater in females than in males (Wade & Cooper, 1999). From an evolutionary perspective, physical attractiveness and self-perceived reproductive potential positively correlate, e.g., the more beautiful a female, the more she will interest males, and the more mating options she will have. Physical unattractiveness thus is more often likely to be a concern of females than males seeking psychotherapy and in situations in which cross-sex unattractiveness is roughly equivalent, males would be expected to experience a higher frequency of successful psychotherapy outcomes.

Infertility

Will infertility result in different psychotherapy outcomes among males and females? *Yes.* Considering disorder prevalence, studies demonstrate that knowledge of infertility is significantly more likely to be associated with a mental disorder among females than among males (e.g., McEwan, Costello & Taylor, 1987). From an evolutionary perspective, the fact that women invest more than males in both the process of reproduction and in the upbringing of offspring easily translates to the view that reproduction and upbringing are more valued and more meaningful events to females than males. Further, males may engage in greater degrees of self-denial when they are the cause of infertility. Successful psychotherapy for infertility among females thus is likely to require therapy designed to provide insights into a patient's somatic condition and her response to lost reproductive options as well as a suitable substitute for reproduction (e.g., increased investment in non-offspring kin). For males, a diversion of energy into nonparental activities may be sufficient to ameliorate an adverse response.

Suboptimal offspring

Will suboptimal offspring result in different psychotherapy outcomes among males and females? *Yes.* Compared to males, females invest more in offspring, are more closely bonded to offspring, and are more responsive to offspring's needs, successes, and failures. Clinically, degree of investment does not appear to differ among females as a function of degree of offspring optimality – indeed, there may be an inverse correlation between suboptimality and investment. Female certainty of offspring and male paternity uncertainty are also relevant here. One consequence of paternity uncertainty appears to be a reduced influence on responses such as self-esteem, guilt, and 'sense of responsibility' in association with suboptimal offspring. To be successful, psychotherapy with females may require a more intense focus on bonding and interactions with offspring as well as attempts to uncouple bonding and investment from the mother's self-view.

Failed social relationships

Will failed heterosexual relationships result in different psychotherapy outcomes among males and females? *Yes.* From an evolutionary perspective, females are more likely to trade sex for resources and are more protective of sexual access (Buss, 1994). Males, on the other hand, are more likely to trade resources for sex and they are more oriented towards casual sex. Further, compared to males, females are more likely to accept dependence on a high resource provider without damage to self-image while males have greater difficulty accepting dependence on females. The reasons for males and females seeking psychotherapy because of failed relationships thus are likely to differ. When the reasons for seeking psychotherapy are roughly equivalent (e.g., abrupt and unexpected discontinuation of a relationship by another), females would be expected to gain greater insight into their responses compared to males and, as a result, be less vulnerable in similar situations in the future.

Loss of social status

Will loss of social status result in different psychotherapy outcomes among males and females? *Yes.* Compared to females, males are more invested in obtaining status in the social arena, more inclined to spontaneously develop all-male hier-archies, more inclined to compete with other males over status and access to females, and more inclined to suffer from loss of status, which, at times, leads to social ostracism, substance abuse, and suicide (McGuire & Troisi, 1998a,b). In contrast, females appear to be more invested in peer groups, providing group members with support, and avoiding status confrontations (Savin-Williams, 1987). When competing, females are more likely to compete with the same sex non-aggressively by displaying signals of high resource value. Moreover, females are less likely to externalize or blame others because of the potential damaging effects on reproductive success. Psychotherapy due to status loss thus is likely to focus on different issues among males and females, to address different motivational intensities, different responses to social variables, and different views of the self in the social arena.

Poverty

Will poverty result in different psychotherapy outcomes among males and females? *Yes* and *No*. If there are offspring, females are more likely to be affected by poverty because of its adverse effects on offspring development. To the degree that psychotherapy does not lead to alterations in a patient's poverty state, it is unlikely to be effective – in such situations depression is not so much a disorder as it is an unavoidable response to a chronically stressful social condition. With increasing age, when reproduction is no longer a possibility for women and unlikely for men, it is unclear if males and females will be affected differently. As they grow older, males and females appear to be able to make significant adjustments to declines in resource availability. Thus, it is during reproductive years when offspring are present that cross-sex differential psychotherapy outcomes in response to poverty are most likely.

Loss of spouse

Will loss of spouse result in different psychotherapy outcomes among males and females? *Yes*. Clinically, compared to males, females suffer greater adverse effects from the loss of a spouse to which they have bonded. Their response may reflect different bonding intensities, the resource-related considerations of daily living, decline in social status (if status was primarily contingent on the spouse's social status), and the consequences of increased management of offspring (if applicable). Migration may also be a factor. Following the loss of a spouse, males are more likely to migrate and join new groups than females. Psychotherapy of females thus would require dealing with loss of spouse, social readjustment, and practical features of daily living. For males, loss itself is likely to be the most important factor.

Physical abuse by one's spouse

Will physical abuse by one's spouse result in different psychotherapy outcomes among males and females? *Yes*. Like rape, physical abuse impacts women differently than men and a key factor in understanding these differences has to do with the impact of abuse on a women's perception of her reproductive potential (Thornhill & Thornhill, 1990a,b). Further, males as well as other members of a social group, often view sexually abused women as 'tarnished'. Women also appear to be more vulnerable to overt signs of physical damage than males in that physically abused males are less often viewed as having compromised reproductive potential. The requirements for successful psychotherapy thus would be predicted to be more complex for females, to address a broader range of psychological issues, and to take longer.

Excessive life events

Will an excessive number of life events that are not closely linked to reproduction (e.g., moving, change of jobs) result in different psychotherapy outcomes among males and females? *Uncertain.* There is no clear prediction from evolutionary theory to this question. In part, the absence of an answer is due to the fact that different life events impact males and females differently. Even when the life event(s) is postulated to be the same (e.g., moving) the answer remains unclear because of the different implications of the event, e.g., males may move because of resource opportunities while spouses may have to deal with the effects of introducing children into new social and school environments and establish new social networks. As noted, life events that link to reproduction such as rape and sexual abuse are another matter.

Death of offspring/death of close genetic kin

Will death of offspring or of close genetic kin result in different psychotherapy outcomes among males and females? *Yes.* Different types and intensities of bonding among males and females and paternity uncertainty are important factors here. Psychotherapy of females would be predicted to require a more intense focus on the impact of loss and the realization that one's reproductive and child-raising investment will not result in expected genetic replication.

Age

Will age result in different psychotherapy outcomes among males and females? *Yes.* Female certainty of genetic relatives and male uncertainty are relevant here, as is the tendency of grandmothers to be more invested in their grand-offspring through their daughters compared to grandfathers. Thus, females who are unable to invest in offspring or grand-offspring or whose investment capacities are compromised are likely to require a more intensive and broader-based psychotherapy.

Conclusion

Available data do not strongly support the view that there are differential gender-specific responses to psychotherapy. This fact conflicts with clinical intuition, which is consistent with the idea of cross-sex response differences. We have argued that the introduction of an evolutionary perspective will help resolve gender-related psychotherapy related questions.

References

Archer, J. (1996) 'Sex differences in social behavior', *American Psychologist* 51: 909–17.

Barnett, P.A. & Gotlib, I.H. (1988) 'Psychosocial functioning and depression: distinguishing among antecedents, concomitants, and consequences', *Psychological Bulletin* 104:97–126.

Baumeister, R.F. & Sommer, K.L. (1997) 'What do men want? Gender differences and two spheres of belongingness: Comment on Cross and Madison (1997)', *Psychological Bulletin* 122:38–44.

Baxter, L.R., Schwartz, J.M., Bergman, K.S., Szuba, M.P., Guze, B.H., Mazziotta, J.C., Alazaki, A., Selin, C.E., Ferng, H., Munford, P. & Phelps, M.E. (1992) 'Caudate glucose metabolic rate changes with both drug and behavior therapy for obsessive–compulsive disorder', *Archives of General Psychiatry* 49:681–9.

Bebbington, P. (1996) 'The origins of sex differences in depressive disorder: bridging the gap', *International Review of Psychiatry* 8:295–332.

Brady, K.T., Grice, D.E., Dustan, L. & Randall, C. (1993) 'Gender differences in substance use disorders', *American Journal of Psychiatry* 150: 1707–11.

Brown, G.W. & Harris, T. (1978) *Social Origins of Depression*, London: Tavistock.

Brown, G.W., Adler, Z. & Bifulco, A. (1980) 'Life events, difficulty and recovery from chronic depression', *British Journal of Psychiatry* 152:487–98.

Buss, D.W. (1985) 'Human mate selection', *American Scientist* 73:47–51.

Buss, D.W. (1987) 'Sex differences in human mate selection criteria: An evolutionary perspective', in C. Crawford, M. Smith & D. Krebs (eds.), *Sociobiology and Psychology: Ideas, Issues, and Applications*, (pp. 335–51), Hillsdale, NJ: Lawrence Erlbaum Associates Inc.

Buss, D.W. (1988) 'The evolution of human intrasexual competition: Tactics of mate attraction', *Journal of Personality and Social Psychology* 54:616–28.

Buss, D.W. (1989) 'Sex differences in human mate preferences: Evolutionary hypotheses tested in 37 cultures', *Behavioral Brain Sciences* 12:1–49.

Buss, D.W. (1994) *The Evolution of Desire*, New York: Basic Books.

Crawford, C.C. & Johnston, M.A. (1999) 'An evolutionary model of courtship and mating as social exchange: Implications for rape law reform', *Jurimetrics* 39:181–200.

Feingold, A. (1994) 'Gender differences in personality: A meta-analysis', *Psychological Bulletin* 116:429–56.

Fowers, B.J., Applegate, B., Tredinnick, M. & Slusher, J. (1996) 'His and her individualisms? Sex bias and individualism in psychologists' responses to case vignettes', *Journal of Psychology* 130:159–74.

Gilbert, P. (1984) *Depression: From Psychology to Brain State*, Hove, UK: Lawrence Erlbaum Associates Ltd.

Gilbert, P. (1989) *Human Nature and Suffering*, Hove, UK: Lawrence Erlbaum Associates Ltd.

Gilbert, P. (1992) *Depression: The Evolution of Powerlessness*, Hove, UK: Psychology Press.

Godfroid, I.O. (1999) 'Sex differences relating to psychiatric treatment', *Canadian Journal of Psychiatry* 44:362–7.

Jang, K.L., Lam, R.W., Livesley, W.J. & Vernon, P.A. (1997) 'Gender differences in the heritability of seasonal mood change', *Psychiatric Research* 70:145–54.

Kessler, R.C., McGonagle, K.A., Zhao, S., Nelson, C.B., Hughes, M., Eshelman, S., Wittchen, H.-U. & Kendler, K.S. (1994) 'Lifetime and 12-month prevalence of DSM-III-R psychiatric disorders in the United States', *Archives of General Psychiatry* 51:8–19.

Kornstein, S.G., Schatzberg, A.F., Yonkers, K.A., Thase, M.E., Keitner, G.I., Ryan, C.E. & Schlager, D. (1995) 'Gender differences in presentation of chronic major depression', *Psychopharmacology Bulletin* 31:711–18.

Kosch, S.G., Burg, M.A. & Podikuju, S. (1998) 'Patient ethnicity and diagnosis of emotional disorders in women', *Family Medicine* 30:215–19.

Krawitz, R. & Watson, C. (1997) 'Gender, race and poverty: bringing the sociopolitical into psychotherapy', *Australian and New Zealand Journal of Psychiatry* 31:474–9.

Kring, A.M. & Gordon, A.H. (1998) 'Sex differences in emotion: Expression, experience, and physiology', *Journal of Personality and Social Psychology* 74:686–703.

Loewenthal, K., Goldblatt, V., Gorton, T., Lubitsch, G., Bicknell, H., Fellows, D. & Sowden, A. (1995) 'Gender and depression in Anglo-Jewry', *Psychological Medicine* 25:1051–63.

Mann, K., Ackermann, K., Gunthner, A., Jung, M. & Mundle, G. (1996) 'Changes in the self-concept of alcohol dependent women and men during inpatient psychotherapy', *Psychotherapie, Psychosomatik, Medizinische Psychologie* 49(9–10):350–5.

McEwan, K.L., Costello, C.G. & Taylor, P.J. (1987) 'Adjustment to infertility', *Journal of Abnormal Psychology* 96:108–16.

McGuire, M.T. & Troisi, A. (1998a) *Darwinian Psychiatry*, New York. Oxford.

McGuire, M.T. & Troisi, A. (1998b) 'Prevalence differences in depression among males and females: Are there evolutionary explanations?', *British Journal of Medical Psychology* 71:479-91.

Mealey, L. (1995) 'The sociobiology of sociopathy: An integrated evolutionary model', *Behavioral and Brain Sciences* 18:523–9.

Nyborg, H. (1994) *Hormones, Sex, and Society*, Westport, CT: Praeger.

Orlinsky, D.E. & Howard, K.I. (1986) 'The psychological interior of psychotherapy: Explorations with the Therapy Session Report', in L.S. Greenberg & W.M Pinsof (eds.) *The Psychotherapeutic Process: A Research Handbook*, (pp. 477–502), New York: Guilford.

Pajer, K. (1995) 'New strategies in the treatment of depression in women', *Journal of Clinical Psychiatry* 56(Suppl. 2):30–7.

Price, J. (1967) 'The dominance hierarchy and the evolution of mental illness', *Lancet* 7502:243–6.

Rasgon, N.L., McGuire, M.T. & Troisi, A. (2000) 'Evolutionary concepts of gender differences in depressive disorders'. In K. Yonkers & M. Skeiner (eds), *Mood Disorders in Women*, (pp. 35–45), New York: Raven Press.

Savin-Williams, R.C. (1987) *Adolescence: An Ethological Perspective*, New York: Springer-Verlag.

Shear, M.K. (1997) 'Anxiety disorders in women: Gender-related modulation of neuro-biology and behavior', *Seminars in Reproductive Endocrinology* 15:69–76.

Surtees, P.G. (1980) 'Social support, residual adversity and depressive outcome', *Social Psychiatry* 15:71–80.

Thornhill, N.W. & Thornhill, R. (1990a) 'An evolutionary analysis of psychological pain following rape: 2. The effects of stranger, friend, and family-member offenders', *Ethology and Sociobiology* 11:177–93.

Thornhill, N.W. & Thornhill, R. (1990b) 'An evolutionary analysis of psychological pain following rape: 3. The effects of force and violence', *Aggressive Behavior* 16:297–320.

Troisi, A. & Moles, A. (1999) 'Gender differences in depression: an ethological study of nonverbal behavior during interviews', *Journal of Psychiatric Research* 33:243–50.

Wade, T.J. & Cooper, M. (1999) 'Sex differences in the links between attractiveness, self-esteem and the body', *Personality and Individual Differences* 29:1047–56.

Waller, G. & Katzman, M.A. (1998) 'Female or male therapists for women with eating disorders? A pilot study of experts' opinions', *International Journal of Eating Disorders* 23:117–23.

Whiffen, V.E. & Clark, S.E. (1997) 'Does victimization account for sex differences in depressive symptoms?', *British Journal of Clinical Psychology* 36(Pt 2):185–93.

Yanovski, A., Menduke, H. & Albertson, M.G. (1995) 'Analysis of gender and visual imagery reactivity of conventional and imagery Rorschach', *Perceptual and Motor Skills* 80:1319–40.

Zlotnick, C., Shea, M.T., Pikonis, P.A., Elkin, I. & Ryan, C. (1996) 'Gender, type of treatment, dysfunctional attitudes, social support, life events, and depressive symptoms over naturalistic follow-up', *American Journal of Psychiatry* 153:1021–7.

Notes

The authors thank Paul Gilbert, Kent Bailey, and Nancy Brown for their helpful suggestions in preparing this manuscript.

Section III

SPECIAL ISSUES

10

THE EVOLUTION OF INCEST AVOIDANCE

Oedipus and the psychopathologies of kinship

Mark T. Erickson

Understanding the nature of human kinship has been a virtual obsession of many of the twentieth century's most prominent social scientists (Bailey, Chapter 3, this volume). In this pursuit, Sigmund Freud (1953/1913), Claude Levi-Strauss (1969), and others maintained that a cultural rule, the incest taboo, was the cornerstone of kinship. Without this cultural mandate, incest would be common and bonds of kinship would rupture. Culture would disintegrate. The incest taboo was the essential element defining humanity (Levi-Strauss, 1969; White, 1948).

This sweeping view of human nature rested on the critical but unsupported assumption that incest was common in non-human species. Freud (1953/1913) took this assumption one step further by postulating that humans inherit an incestuous impulse which, in contrast to other species, is repressed. He hypothesized that repression of incestuous impulses creates a universal neurosis unique to our species. Freud called this neurosis the Oedipus complex.

In contrast to earlier beliefs, research now shows that incest is, in fact, rare throughout nature. Moreover, it is now abundantly clear that humans, like other species, inherit an incest avoidance adaptation (Shepher 1971; Wolf 1970, 1995). Ironically, as we have discovered a biology of incest avoidance we have also found that incest is more common in humans than was earlier thought. Additionally, we now know that incest is linked to an increased frequency of depression, anxiety disorders, substance abuse, somatoform disorder, dissociative disorders and borderline personality disorder in victims (Chu & Dill, 1990; Courtois, 1979; Gelinas, 1983; Herman, 1981; Kluft, 1985; Meiselman, 1978; Morrison, 1989; Putnam, 1989; Schetky, 1990; Shearer, Peters, Quaytman & Ogden, 1990; Stone, 1990; Summit & Kryso, 1978).

One purpose of this chapter is to show how understanding the biology of incest avoidance provides insight into why incestuous behaviour occurs (Erickson, 1989, 1993, 1999; Wolf, 1993, 1995). A second, and broader purpose of this chapter is to revisit kinship from a contemporary evolutionary perspective. Contemporary findings indicate that Freud was correct to some extent; understanding kinship is essential to explain key adaptive functions of the unconscious mind and how these adaptations can go awry. To this end, the first section of this chapter looks at kinship *vis-a-vis* the incest avoidance findings. The second and third sections discuss, respectively, how the psychological boundary between familial and sexual forms of affiliation is established, and how it may be disrupted with resultant psychopathology. In section four, the conceptual value of the evolutionary perspective for interpreting a patient's life story is examined. I will draw from Freud's self-analysis, as revealed through his letters to Wilhelm Fleiss, as a case example.

Evolution and incest avoidance

Incest avoidance is, currently, the category of human behaviour which offers the fullest test of an evolutionary hypothesis (Wilson, 1998). The first major insight came just over a century ago from the Finnish anthropologist, Edward Westermarck (1922/1889). Westermarck was aware of the harmful effects of close inbreeding and believed that an adaptation for incest avoidance had evolved. Specifically, he proposed that an aversion to sexual intercourse develops naturally between individuals living in close proximity from early childhood. Because children are raised in close proximity to their family, in virtually all traditional cultures, his hypothesis was plausible. Widely rejected during his lifetime, Westermarck's hypothesis is now recognized as the fundamental theoretical contribution to our understanding of incest avoidance (Demarest, 1977; Erickson, 1983,1989,1993; Fox, 1980; Murray & Smith, 1983; Parker & Parker, 1986; Shepher, 1971; van den Berghe, 1980; Wolf, 1970,1993,1995).

Biologists have verified that close inbreeding increases expression of deleterious recessive genes and reduces heterozygotic vigour (Bateson, 1983; Packer, 1979), effecting a marked increase in mortality and morbidity in humans (Adams & Neel, 1967; Carter, 1967; Seemanova, 1971) and other species (Packer, 1979; Ralls & Ballou, 1982a, b). Incest avoidance should, therefore, be naturally selected.

Incest avoidance in non-humans

Because of the long-held belief that incest was common in nature, early researchers openly voiced their surprise at finding mother–son incest to be rare in rhesus monkeys (Sade, 1968: 19):

> the rarity of mother–son mating is even more remarkable when the fact is considered that behavior such as grooming, body contact, and mutual defense occur frequently between mother and some mature sons during the mating seasons as well as the non-mating seasons. One would expect by extension that mating would occur most commonly between mother and son, but in fact the reverse is true.

Subsequent studies have shown that incest is avoided in other primates, other mammals, avian, and even insect species (Agren, 1984; Amos, Schlotterer & Tautz, 1993; Burda, 1995; Enmoto, 1978; Evans, 1986; Gavish, Hofman & Getz, 1984; Goodall, 1986; Hoogland, 1982; Keller & Passera, 1993; Koenig & Pitelka, 1979; Murray & Smith, 1980; Packer, 1979; Paul & Kuester, 1985; Pereira & Weiss, 1991; Piper & Slater, 1993; Pusey, 1980; Scott, 1984; Smuts, 1985; Tokuda, 1961; Tutin, 1979; Woolfenden & Fitzpatrick, 1978). Completely reversing earlier belief, it now appears, with few exceptions (e.g., Sherman, Jarvis & Braude, 1992), that incest is avoided throughout the animal kingdom (Bischof, 1975; Murray & Smith, 1983).

A remarkable example of incest avoidance can be found in the pilot whale (Amos, Schlotterer, & Tautz, 1993). Adult males of this species reside within the same group or 'pod' as their mother and sisters. Notwithstanding this exceptional degree of proximity, genetic analysis shows that incestuous mating is virtually nonexistent in pilot whales. Males mate with females of other pods but consistently avoid mating with close kin.

Close proximity to immediate kin, in early life, is critical for establishing incest avoidance in nonhuman species, just as Westermarck had predicted for humans (Agren, 1984; Burda, 1995; Gavish, Hoffman & Getz, 1984, Yamazaki et al., 1988). The prairie vole, for example, rarely mates with biological siblings when reared naturally. However, if siblings are experimentally separated at birth and placed in foster litters, as adults they sexually avoid unrelated foster sibs but readily mate with their unfamiliar biological kin (Gavish, Hoffman & Getz, 1984). These data are strikingly similar to human anthropological and clinical findings suggesting that the biological processes underlying incest avoidance have been conserved during evolutionary history.

Given the importance of infantile sexuality in psychoanalytic theory, it is worth noting that early sexual play is observed in other primate species. An infant male Japanese macaque, for example, may mount his mother or siblings (Hanby & Brown, 1974). Such play is accepted impassively and disappears as maturity approaches. Similar behaviour is seen in infant male chimpanzees (Tutin, 1979).

Incest avoidance in humans

An exceptionally important finding in anthropology, in recent decades, has been the discovery of an innate incest avoidance adaptation in humans. Two important lines of research, one on communal farms (kibbutzim) in Israel, and the other in rural Taiwan, have provided particularly convincing support for an evolutionary explanation of incest avoidance (see also Bevc & Silverman, 1993, and McCabe, 1983).

Kibbutz peers in Israel

Until recent years, children living on communal farms in Israel were raised in a unique way. Not long after birth, parents placed their infants in a communal 'children's house'. In this setting, children of similar age and of different families were raised by nurses in relatively stable 'peer groups' through high school graduation. Peers lived in nearly continuous association, playing together, eating together, bathing together, and so forth. The only regular contact with parents occurred during evening visits home.

Under these circumstances, Westermarck's hypothesis predicts that, upon reaching adolescence, kibbutz peers should avoid one another sexually. The results of all relevant studies are supportive (Bettelheim, 1969; Shepher, 1971; Spiro, 1965; Talmon, 1964). Shepher's (1971) study is the most extensive. Following the premarital sexual preferences of 65 adolescents of a single kibbutz, Shepher detected no sexual affiliations between peers who had been cosocialized from early childhood (0–6 years).

Shepher (1971) also analysed marriages of individuals raised on a kibbutzim. In a large study (n=2,169) he found not a single marriage in which the couple had also been associated within the same peer group throughout early childhood (0–6 years). By contrast, eight marriages were found in which couples had been together in the same peer group for most of late childhood (6–12 years) and nine marriages where couples were together during most of adolescence (12–18 years). Shepher and many other writers (cf. Spiro, 1965) have interpreted the kibbutz findings as supportive of Westermarck's hypothesis.

Simpua marriage in Taiwan

Since 1957, Stanford anthropologist, Arthur Wolf, has studied an unusual type of marriage found in Taiwan. In simpua, or minor marriage, couples are typically betrothed in infancy by parental arrangement. The 'child bride' or simpua moves into the home of her future husband, usually in early childhood, to be raised by his family. Couples grow up in continuous association throughout childhood, as do siblings. They are married in their mid to late teens in a ceremony often followed by an extreme reluctance of the couple to consummate their relationship (Wolf, 1970).

Wolf recognized that simpua marriage presented a nearly ideal test of Westermarck's hypothesis. There exists continuous proximity between couples from early childhood. Furthermore, not only is there no taboo against sexual relations, to the contrary, the couple is strongly urged to procreate. If Westermarck were right, simpua couples should experience a mutual sexual aversion despite countervailing cultural pressures. Exploring government records, Wolf found that the divorce rate for simpua couples was much higher than for other arranged marriages. Through interviews, marital infidelity was found to be almost three times more frequent among simpua brides brought together with their husband in early childhood, than with brides brought together at age 4 years or later. Birth records revealed that the birth rate, per year of marriage, was at least 30 per cent lower for simpua couples than other arranged marriages. Wolf believes that the fecundity of simpua couples would have been even less were it not for the intense parental pressure to produce offspring. Remarkably, a number of simpua couples confessed to having never consummated their relationship despite years of marriage. They explained that their children were the products of extramarital affairs and were recorded as their own (Wolf, 1970,1995). Wolf (1995) has studied over 14,000 simpua couples. After submitting his findings to numerous alternative explanations he concludes that Westermarck's evolutionary hypothesis provides the most plausible interpretation.

Of enormous clinical importance is Wolf's (1995) finding that the first 2½ years of childhood seem to be a critical period for the development of incest avoidance. Wolf has found that sexual avoidance is pronounced if association starts before that age. However, if simpua couples are first brought together at the age of 3, or later, they do not show the sexual aversion evident in those with earlier association.

Clinically, incest is seen as a boundary violation in which sexual behaviour impinges on what should be a nonsexual, familial relationship. Until recently, however, there existed no coherent explanation of the source of this familial–sexual boundary. Is it biological or cultural? When and how does this boundary develop? Wolf's research indicates that a psychological boundary does exist between familial and sexual forms of relatedness, that it is a biological adaptation, and that this boundary has a defined developmental time line.

The gene, kin recognition, and familial bonds

Hamilton and the gene

The current revolution in evolutionary psychology was given birth in the 1960s by the British biologist, W.D. Hamilton (1964). An intuitively useful summation of his argument is that natural selection maximizes the abilities of individual organisms, not species, to gain genetic representation in future generations (Williams & Nesse, 1991). Hamilton realized that this shift in frame of reference, from the species to the individual organism, had profound significance for understanding the evolution of social behaviour; particularly kin-directed behaviour. This is so because identical copies of genes are much more likely to be carried by kin than non-kin. Hence, organisms that favour kin in particular situations, would be more proficient in gaining genetic representation in future generations and would therefore be at a great selective advantage.

A general prediction of Hamilton's 'inclusive fitness' hypothesis is that altruistic behaviours, e.g., warning calls, providing food, providing shelter, etc., should occur almost exclusively between close kin. This prediction is supported by research showing that virtually all instances of altruism in nature occur between closely related individuals, usually between immediate kin (e.g., Arnold *et al.*, 1996; Axelrod & Hamilton, 1981; Vogel, 1985). To give one example, the Belding ground squirrel is known to give out a warning call if a predator is sighted. As predicted, Paul Sherman (1977) at Cornell found that giving a warning call (which may be dangerous to the caller because it draws the attention of a predator) is more likely to occur if close kin are nearby, and who are likely to benefit, than if unrelated conspecifics are in proximity.

A second general prediction is that attachment behaviours of the young will be directed primarily to kin because kin are most likely to be responsive (altruistic) to attachment needs. This prediction is supported by the observations of Bowlby (1969) who found that attachment behaviours are directed primarily to close kin, across cultures.

Traditional Freudian psychology assumed that kinship was a largely cultural, and hence uniquely human phenomenon. The research which followed W.D. Hamilton's (1964) theoretical advance has demonstrated, to the contrary, that kinship is a basic organizing principle of all social species, from invertebrates to humans.

Kin recognition

To behave adaptively organisms must in some, presumably unconscious way, 'recognize' their kin. This process is called 'kin recognition' by animal behaviourists. Kin recognition can be defined as 'the differential treatment of conspecifics as a function of their genetic relatedness' (Holmes & Sherman, 1982). Kin recognition is inferred by the observation of behaviours such as kin-directed attachment, kin-directed altruism, and incest avoidance.

There are several different adaptations by which organisms learn to recognize kin. A review of these adaptations is beyond the scope of this paper (see Holmes & Sherman, 1982; Pfennig & Sherman, 1995; for reviews). The most common mechanism of kin recognition is called association. Association depends, quite simply, on proximity to kin during a critical period of life. Incest avoidance, a measure of kin recognition, is dependent on association in humans (Shepher, 1971; Wolf, 1995), and other species (e.g., see Agren, 1984; Burda, 1995; Gavish, Hofman & Getz, 1984; Yamazaki *et al.*, 1988).

A tacit assumption in much kin recognition research is that a single kin recognition adaptation integrates all kin-directed behaviours. Rather than supposing there are separate kin recognition adaptations for incest avoidance, altruistic behaviours, and attachment behaviour, I will likewise assume that a single kin-recognition adaptation integrates self-kin behaviours.

It follows that the critical period for incest avoidance (0–2½ years) may be, more broadly, a critical period for biologically based kin recognition in humans. Social bonds formed when at least one member of a dyad is within this critical period should then develop as familial bonds in which incest avoidance, attachment behaviours, and altruistic behaviours are prominent features. Social bonds formed after this critical period would generally be non-familial and quite possibly sexual in nature. This notion is consistent with attachment research in which the critical period for attachment is estimated to be somewhat more than 2 years (Rutter, 1995). This is earlier than traditional Oedipal psychology in which the development of incest avoidance is estimated to occur between 2½ and 6 years of age (Brenner, 1955).

It is important to note that incest avoidance develops at an unconscious level. No one on Israeli kibbutzim anticipated that peers would become sexually avoidant because of their early proximity. Recognizing this effect was due to serendipitous observation as second generation peers began to reach maturity. Likewise, when Arthur Wolf (1995) began his research on simpua couples in rural Taiwan villages he did not anticipate his findings of reduced fecundity in simpua marriage. Wolf did not go to Taiwan to study Westermarck's hypothesis. His research turned in this direction only because he vaguely recollected Westermarck's hypothesis from graduate studies and saw that simpua marriage presented a test case. For therapists, recognizing the important effects of this critical period can lead to a different conceptualization of a patient's life story as will be illustrated at the conclusion of this chapter.

Critical periods and a similar phenomenon, imprinting in birds, are widely observed in species with much simpler nervous systems (see Bateson, 1979; Lorenz, 1937). These adaptations are evolutionarily ancient mechanisms designed to canalize social behaviour. Their function is controlled by primitive parts of our brain. Humans can, to a significant extent, consciously override this evolved system and develop 'kin-like' relationships with persons first encountered outside the critical period (see Bailey, 1988; Bailey, Chapter 3, this volume; Bailey & Nava, 1989; Bailey, Wood & Nava, 1992; Bailey & Wood, 1998). For example, a stepfather may develop a 'psychological kinship' with his stepdaughter without any overt sexual component. Nevertheless, the effects of this critical period in our species are profound, as demonstrated by the kibbutz and simpua marriage findings and by clinical research that I will shortly review.

Familial bonding

The term kin-recognition is used primarily by zoologists in the study of discrete behaviours. It does not adequately convey a sense of the developmental history or the enduring quality of the social bonds which underlie kin-recognition. For this reason I will use the term 'familial bond' to refer to bonds formed within the critical period (0–2½ years) described by Wolf (1995). This term generally refers to child-to-parent, parent-to-child, and sib-to-sib bonds. However, as the incest avoidance research has shown, it is early proximity, not genetic relatedness *per se*, that creates a familial bond. Kibbutz peers and simpua couples are examples of non-kin who, by an accident of fate, are linked by familial bonds. The term 'familial bond hypothesis' will be used to refer to the complete hypothesis being presented (Erickson, 1989, 1993).

For familial bonds to be fully adaptive they must be reciprocal. Incest avoidance, for example, needs to develop not only from parent to child, but also between siblings and, at least eventually, from child to parent. Reciprocal incest avoidance develops in non-human species and there is no reason to believe that humans are different. The kibbutz peer study shows reciprocal sexual avoidance developing between individuals who are both within the critical period when first associated. Simpua couples, by contrast, may be years apart in age. Although the data is less extensive, incest avoidance still seems to develop in simpua couples, of very different ages, as long as one of the individuals is within the critical period when they come together (Wolf, 1998). It appears that for humans, as in other species, there is some quality in the very young that evokes a nonsexual bond in those who are older, whether they be parents, older siblings, or a simpua bride or groom.

Once a familial bond has developed it imparts a sense of kinship. Kibbutz peers and simpua couples are fully conscious that they are not biological kin, yet sexual aversion develops nevertheless. When asked why they are not sexually attracted both kibbutz peers and simpua couples commonly state that they experience each other as a brother or sister. The one kibbutz-raised individual that I have known described her peers as more 'kin-like' than her biological siblings. In using such terms to describe their relationship, kibbutz peers and simpua couples may be unconsciously illustrating how language describes biologically distinct categories of social affiliation, e.g., familial vs. sexual.

Reciprocal familial bonds start forming very early. Shortly after birth, mothers can reliably distinguish their offspring through either visual, olfactory, auditory, or tactile cues (see Porter, 1991, for review). In one study, for example, 9 of 10 mothers correctly identified their newborn's odour after only 10–60 minutes postnatal contact with the infant (Kaitz, Good, Rokem & Eidelman, 1988). Although the data is more limited, fathers also seem to have the ability to identify their offspring soon after birth. Fathers with an average of less than 7 hours of postnatal contact, were able to recognize their offspring, blindfolded, by touch of the infant's hand alone (Kaitz et al., 1994). Conversely, infants very quickly develop kin preferences. Two week old breast feeding infants seem to be capable of recognizing their mother by olfactory cues alone (see Porter, 1991, for review).

Familial mentality

Before turning to psychopathology, one additional concept needs to be introduced. 'Mentality' is a term which refers to 'the notion of various internal competencies being co-assembled to create certain types of self–other roles' (Gilbert, 1998: 364; Gilbert, Chapter 6, this volume). I use the term 'familial mentality' to refer to a co-assembly of adaptive kin-directed behaviours which integrate the self-kin role. Some individuals are far more adept at familial relationships than others. Those who are adept have secure, mutually fulfilling, familial bonds which contribute to their well-being. Familial mentality refers to this type of social competency.

At birth, many adaptations exist only as propensities, and require specific kinds of external stimulation to develop properly. The visual system is a good example. Without normal visual input in early life, neural networks serving vision do not develop properly and vision is consequently impaired (Wiesel & Hubel, 1963). Similarly, I will argue that familial mentality exists as a propensity, at birth, and requires specific environmental input to develop. Responsivity is, in essence, optimal altruism. As such, it is the first reliable social signal of kinship and therefore an ideal stimulus to cultivate familial mentality.

Attachment researchers, notably Mary Ainsworth (1967), observed that 'secure' attachment in infants tends to develop when parents are responsive to the infant's needs (see also Isabella, 1993; Isabella & Belsky, 1991; Smith & Pederson 1988). More recent research suggests that parents, who were securely attached in their own childhood (as judged by the Adult Attachment Inventory; AAI) are likely to be responsive to, and have securely attached offspring (as measured by the Ainsworth Strange Situation). Conversely, mothers who were insecurely attached in their childhood (as judged by the AAI) were found to be less responsive to, and more likely to have insecurely attached infants (infants rated either insecure avoidant or insecure resistant as measured by the Ainsworth Strange Situation) (Steele, Steele & Fonagy, 1996; see van IJzendoorn, 1995, for a meta-analysis of similar studies). These data suggest an intergenerational pattern: responsivity begets responsivity in the next generation and an early lack of responsivity tends to beget unresponsive parents in the next generation. (See Belsky, Steinberg & Draper, 1991 for an evolutionary hypothesis regarding this pattern.)

Responsivity initiates the earliest familial dialogue. Learning the nuances of familial dialogue is a complex developmental task which provides the individual with the skills to maintain stable social bonds throughout life, both within the family and within the culture of birth. (See Johnson, 1993, for an extensive description of Japanese socialization.) A responsive milieu constitutes an environment where the subtleties of kinship can be best learned.

In sum, I am proposing that a responsive childhood milieu optimally stimulates familial mentality. Later in life, such individuals have highly stable boundaries between familial and sexual forms of relatedness and are therefore extremely unlikely to be incestuous (Erickson, 1989, 1993; Wolf, 1993, 1995). This boundary functions at an unconscious level. There is no need to think, 'This is my child, I should not behave in a sexualized way'. Appropriate behaviour occurs fluidly and without conscious thought. By contrast, in a neglectful childhood milieu familial mentality is less well developed. The subjective sense of kinship is diminished. The unconscious boundary between familial and sexual relatedness is less stable and incestuous behaviour is far more likely (see Alexander, 1992; Haynes-Seman & Krugman, 1989; Sroufe et al., 1985).

The notion that a positively reinforcing early experience – a responsive milieu – establishes incest avoidance departs dramatically from earlier hypotheses. Oedipal psychology assumes that all social bonds are ultimately sexual. This assumption forced Freud to explain how sexual behaviours are directed away from kin.

Childhood castration fears were invoked. Other authors followed a similar paradigm, arguing that punishment in the childhood home (Demerest, 1977), or frustrating childhood sexual play (Fox, 1962, 1980), were the developmental antecedents of incest avoidance (for a discussion of problems with these hypotheses see Erickson, 1983,1989).

Later psychoanalytic writers, contrary to traditional theory, argued or inferred that a nonsexual form of affiliation emerges between kin under normal developmental conditions (e.g., Bacal & Newman, 1990; DeVos, 1975; Doi, 1989; Ferenczi, 1949; Johnson, 1993; Kohut, 1984; Suttie, 1935). Yet, these authors lacked an explanation of how nonsexual bonds could exist. We now know that nonsexual, or familial bonds, can exist because evolutionary pressures shaping kin-directed behaviours (altruism, attachment, incest avoidance) are significantly different from those shaping sexual behaviour.

Psychopathologies of kinship

The are two basic ways that psychopathologies of kinship arise: familial bonds may be misdirected and/or familial mentality may have not been adequately developed. In either case, behaviours such as neglect or incest are more likely to occur, which may reflect psychopathology in the perpetrator and lead to psychopathology in the victim.

Misdirected familial bonds and psychopathology

If early proximity is necessary to establish a familial bond and hence, incest avoidance, then a lack of proximity should create a condition in which incest is particularly likely. Clinical research, although limited in scope, is clearly supportive. The only occasions in which incest seems clearly motivated by mutual sexual passion occur when kin are separated early on and are later reunited (Greenberg & Littlewood, 1995; Weinberg, 1955). Weinberg (1955) writes, 'Six pairs of siblings were separated in infancy. . . . Though intellectually aware of an incest taboo, each did not feel an aversion to the other as a sex partner' (p. 78; see also Greenberg & Littlewood, 1995).

In poems, novels, and plays in which incest is a theme, a frequent storyline is of separation in early childhood with a later incestuous reunion (Cory & Masters, 1963; Rank, 1992). The myth of Oedipus is by far the best-known example. Oedipus is separated from his mother, Jocasta, at birth and much later reunites incestuously with her. Mary Shelly's *Frankenstein* portrays the reverse circumstance in which early proximity precluded later sexuality between Victor and his betrothed (foster sister) Elizabeth (Price, 1995).

Little is known of the long-term effects of incestuous relationships following early separation. In some cases it does not seem to create psychological difficulties. (For example, see the discussion of Patty and Alan Muth in *Esquire*, July 1998.) In others the effect is devastating (see the memoir of Kathryn Harrison entitled,

The Kiss, 1997). Individuals may view themselves as 'freaks' of nature (Harrison, 1997). They may experience powerful sexual feelings for their refound kin, recognize such feelings as highly aberrant, and yet consciously desire a familial relationship. If this rare case is encountered in therapy, an explanation of the profound importance of early proximity for establishing familial boundaries may help such individuals understand their unusual struggle and view themselves in a more accepting light.

Clinically, the most pervasive cause of psychopathology, resulting from 'misdirected' familial bonds probably occurs in families with stepparents. Stepparents are not biological kin; however, society rightly expects them to assume a parental role together with the behavioural boundaries appropriate to that role. Because stepparents are not likely to be present during the critical period they are less likely to develop a familial bond with stepchildren and are probably more likely to violate boundaries. Consistent with this, a study of stepparents revealed that only 53 per cent of stepfathers and 25 per cent of stepmothers claimed to have 'parental feelings' for their stepchildren (Duberman, 1975, as cited in Daly & Wilson, 1981). Families with a stepparent appear to be predisposed to abuse and neglect offspring (Daly & Wilson, 1981) and sexual abuse is known to be much more likely to occur if a stepfather is present in the home (Parker & Parker, 1986; Russell, 1984).

In a family therapy setting acknowledging that a step family does not have nature on its side may be helpful. The therapist's goal is then to help the family develop a sense of psychological kinship (see Bailey, Chapter 3, this volume) and to set appropriate parent–child boundaries. Research shows that stepfathers who are extensively involved in the early care of stepdaughters are less likely to be sexually abusive (Williams & Finkelhor, 1995). This finding suggests that simply having step families make a conscious effort to behave like a family, may, to some extent, evoke appropriate familial affiliation.

Familial mentality and psychopathology

A responsive developmental milieu seems to provide the foundation of robust familial mentality. With this foundation the psychological boundaries of kinship are stable. To my knowledge, no data exist on the incidence of incest in families in which parents were judged to be highly responsive. Clinical experience would suggest that it is very low.

In contrast, a profile of families in which incest has occurred is characterized by emotional deprivation and rejection during the childhood of all involved. In the case of father–daughter incest, the father typically comes from a background of emotional deprivation, having experienced maternal rejection, and abandonment by his father. The daughter is typically starved for affection and the mother usually has also had an emotionally deprived childhood (Herman, 1981; Justice & Justice, 1979). A similar pattern is evident in mother–son incest in which the mother was usually deprived of a nurturant relationship as a child (Justice & Justice, 1979;

Weinberg, 1955). A son who attempts an incestuous relationship with his mother may do so because he has been severely rejected by her and perceives incest as a way to force her to be close to him (Weinberg, 1955). Although the data concerning sibling incest is rather limited, a similar pattern seems to exist (Mrazek, 1981). Thus it seems that an extreme lack of early responsivity characterizes the childhood of both perpetrators and victims of incest. (See also Alexander, 1992; Haynes-Seman & Krugman, 1989; Sroufe *et al.*, 1985.)

The familial bond hypothesis: A summary

First, Hamilton's (1964) inclusive fitness hypothesis predicted that kinship would be a fundamental organizing principle in nature. This prediction has been robustly supported. Altruistic and attachment behaviours are overwhelmingly kin-directed behaviours. The discovery of incest avoidance adaptations in nature, and in humans, provides further evidence of the evolutionary salience of kinship.

Second, kin-recognition is crucial to establish adaptive social behaviour. Association, during critical periods, establishes kin-recognition in many species, including humans.

Third, the critical period for incest avoidance in humans has been shown to be approximately the first 2½ years of life (Wolf, 1995). A key assumption of the familial bond hypothesis is that this critical period functions, more broadly, as a developmental boundary of kinship. Bonds formed during this critical period are typified by specific behaviours, (attachment and altruistic behaviours and incest avoidance) and by a subjective sense of kinship – regardless of actual genetic relatedness (e.g., simpua couples and kibbutz peers).

Fourth, the complex social interactions which occur within a familial bond are assumed to be integrated by a single mental network called familial mentality. To develop robustly, familial mentality is dependent on an adequately responsive childhood milieu. In an unresponsive childhood milieu the subjective sense of kinship is diminished. The unconscious boundaries which normally develop between familial and sexual forms of affiliation are unstable and consequently, incest, neglect, and other forms of abuse are more likely. Even if familial mentality is well developed in a parent, association with offspring during the critical period seems to be crucial for developing a familial bond.

Finally, an enduring sense of kinship, and incest avoidance, are not established by repression of sexual impulses. They are, rather, established by the development of a familial bond, an evolutionarily distinct form of affiliation, which precludes sexuality. Incest avoidance may be maintained by repression under conditions of impaired familial bonding. It is in this relatively uncommon circumstance that Oedipal conflicts may arise.

Kinship and psychotherapy

What is curative in long-term psychotherapy is still unclear. The therapeutic alliance is surely central (e.g., see Bailey, Chapter 3, this volume; see Gilbert, Chapter 6, this volume; Glantz & Pierce, 1989; Holmes, 1993; Kreigman, Chapter 4, this volume). The element most crucial to alliance formation is probably empathy. The responsivity of a parent which elicits secure attachment, and the empathy of psychotherapists in successful therapy are probably closely related. Such an environment creates an 'as if' circumstance which allows the individual the opportunity to experience a kin-like relationship and occasionally 'psychological kinship' in the therapeutic setting (Bailey, 1988; Bailey, Chapter 3, this volume; Bailey & Nava, 1989; Bailey, Wood & Nava, 1992; Bailey & Wood, 1998).

This chapter does not add substantively to what the other authors have said about the therapeutic relationship. What it does offer therapists is a novel construct for conceptualizing a patient's history. To illustrate, I will use a vignette from Sigmund Freud's self-analysis.

Sigmund Freud: A case of a misdirected kinship and early loss?

As is widely known, Freud never entered therapy. He did, however, engage in a 'self-analysis' which began in the mid-summer of 1897. Little of Freud's correspondence has survived but we do have a remarkable window into his self-analysis through letters written to his friend and colleague, Wilhelm Fleiss (Freud, 1985). Particularly important for this analysis is that Freud, to some unknown extent, was raised by a nanny. Her name was Monika Zajic and she was present during Freud's earliest childhood. Little else is known about his nanny, aside from Freud's comments in his correspondence to Fleiss.

In a letter dated 3 October 1897, it is apparent that Freud is reaching a crossroads in his self-analysis. Freud writes (1985: 268):

> For the last four days my self analysis, which I consider indispensable for the clarification of the whole problem, has continued in dreams and has presented me with the most valuable elucidations and clues.

Freud then comments, seemingly dismissively, about his father:

> I can only indicate that the old man plays no active part in my case . . .

Continuing, his tone changes distinctly as he recalls his nanny (1985: 268):

> In my case the 'prime originator' [emphasis Freud's] was an ugly, elderly, but clever woman, who told me a great deal about God Almighty and hell and who instilled in me a high opinion of my own capacities . . .

Freud again changes course and comments about his mother:

> later (between two and two and a half years) [parenthesis Freud's] my libido towards *matrem* [emphasis Freud's] was awakened, namely, on the

occasion of a journey with her from Leipzig to Vienna, during which we must have spent the night together and there must have been an opportunity of seeing her *nudam* [emphasis Freud's].

In the same letter Freud again comments, glowingly, about his nanny (1985: 269):

I have not yet grasped anything at all of the scenes themselves which lie at the bottom of the story. If they come to light and I succeed in resolving my own hysteria, then I shall be grateful to the memory of the old woman who provided me, at such an early age with the means for living and going on living.

In his next letter, dated 15 October 1897, we learn that Freud has since asked his mother about this nanny and has found that she had been fired and jailed for stealing from the family. Freud then writes (1985: 271):

Thereupon a scene occurred to me which in the course of twenty-five years has occasionally emerged from conscious memory without my understanding it. . . . I was crying in despair. My brother Philip unlocked a wardrobe for me, and when I did not find my mother inside I cried even more until slender and beautiful she came in through the door. What can this mean? . . . I suddenly understand it. When I missed my mother, I was afraid she had vanished from me, just as the old woman had a short time before.

Later in the same letter Freud begins to perceive what will become his Oedipus hypothesis, he writes (1985: 272):

A single idea of general value dawned on me. I have found in my case too, being in love with my mother and jealous of my father, and I now consider it a universal event in childhood, . . . If this is so we can grasp the gripping power of Oedipus Rex, . . .

It was at this time, during the summer and autumn of 1897, that Freud gave up the seduction hypothesis and began to formulate the Oedipal hypothesis (Sulloway, 1979).

According to traditional views, Freud's self-analysis led directly to his notions on infantile sexuality and Oedipal conflicts (cf. Sulloway, 1979). The interpretation which he makes of his own early experience fits, at least in his mind, within the Oedipal model. He may have directed his attention to sexualized feelings for his mother (the trip to Vienna), and his dismissive feelings towards his father, in interpreting his internal conflicts *vis-a-vis* the myth of Oedipus.

Looking at the same material from an evolutionary perspective, our attention may be drawn along a different path. Recalling the power of early association to influence the relationship of simpua couples and kibbutz peers, one wonders about Freud's relationship with his nanny. The nanny was, by Freud's own recollection, present during the critical phase for familial bonding. Moreover, she appears to have been a highly responsive figure in the young child's life. Freud describes her as his 'prime originator'. He states that she, 'Instilled in me a high opinion in my own capacities'. Freud is 'grateful' to this woman who gave him at an early age, 'the means for living and going on living'. Notably, Freud, now in his early forties, had had no contact with his nanny for nearly four decades.

Perhaps Freud's nanny was the most responsive individual in his early childhood. She may then have been young Freud's most secure attachment. In this regard, Freud, like Oedipus, may have been raised, during his earliest years, by someone other than his mother. Freud does long for his mother when he realizes his nanny is gone, 'I cried until slender and beautiful she came through the door'. Yet, in these letters he never describes his mother in the immediate, glowing terms reserved for his nanny. From this perspective we can understand why the young Freud was so deeply troubled at his nanny's sudden disappearance, and why a recollection of her loss had persisted well into adulthood.

There are, however, hints of a darker side to the nanny relationship. In a postscript dated 4 October 1897, he comments (presumably) about his nanny (1985: 269):

> Today's dream . . . produced the following . . . she was my teacher in sexual matters and complained I was clumsy and unable to do anything . . . .she washed me in reddish water in which she had previously washed herself (the interpretation is not difficult; I find nothing like this in the chain of my memories; so I regard it as a genuine discovery.)[parenthesis Freud's] . . . she made me steal zehners . . . to give to her.

Freud suggests that his nanny sexualized their relationship when he states, 'she was my teacher is sexual matters'. What did he mean by this? Was she sexually abusive? Or was she merely an earthy individual who perhaps without embarrassment explained sexual anatomy and what the dogs were doing in the park? We will never know. However, if she did transgress boundaries, Freud was sexually abused. Early sexual abuse may be a precursor of precocious sexuality in children (Haynes-Seman & Krugman, 1989) possibly explaining Freud's particular emphasis on infantile sexuality. Further, the pathogenic effects of sexual abuse are well documented (Chu & Dill, 1990; Courtois, 1979; Gelinas, 1983; Herman, 1981; Kluft, 1985; Meiselman, 1978; Morrison, 1989; Putnam, 1989; Schetky, 1990; Shearer et al., 1990; Stone, 1990; Summit & Kryso, 1978). In sum, if he was sexually abused by someone whose relationship was held dear, Freud's perception of familial relationships could have been significantly distorted.

Conclusion

In recent decades it has become abundantly clear that kinship is a basic organizing principle in nature. Critical periods provide the developmental underpinning of kinship in many species, including humans. The critical period for kinship, or familial bonding, in our species is approximately the first 2½ years of life. Bonds formed during this period are typified by specific behaviours including incest avoidance, and attachment and altruistic behaviours. Psychopathologies of kinship can emerge if kin are (1) separated during the critical period, or (2) if the early milieu is markedly unresponsive and therefore inhibits the development of a familial mentality.

Despite its fundamental importance, kinship has continued to play a peripheral role in psychological constructs often used to guide the therapeutic process, e.g., self-psychology, object relations, and classic Freudian/Oedipal psychology. Understanding the evolved and largely unconscious underpinnings of kinship draws a therapist's attention to important aspects of a patient's life history that otherwise may be overlooked. While incest avoidance is an evolved adaptation, like many adaptations it operates optimally in certain environments but can be weakened or become maladaptive in others. The concept of a kin recognition mentality, that is sensitive to proximity and attachment security during critical periods, offers a very different view on incestuous desires and behaviours to that proposed by Freud. It thus suggests very different mechanisms for the violations of incestuous boundaries and the serious pathologies that can arise in its wake.

References

Adams, M.S. & Neel, J.V. (1967) 'Children of incest', *Pediatrics* 40: 55–62.

Agren, A. (1984) 'Incest avoidance and bonding between siblings in gerbils', *Behavioral Ecology and Sociobiology* 14: 161–9.

Ainsworth, M.D.S. (1967) *Infancy in Uganda: Infant Care and the Growth of Love*, Baltimore: Johns Hopkins University Press.

Alexander, P.C. (1992) 'Application of attachment theory to the study of sexual abuse', *Journal of Consulting and Clinical Psychology* 60: 185–95.

Amos, B., Schlotterer, C. & Tautz, D. (1993) 'Social structure of pilot whales revealed by analytical DNA profiling', *Science* 260: 670–2.

Arnold, G., Quinett, B., Cornuet, J., Masson, C., Schepper, B., Estoup, A. & Gasqui, P. (1996) 'Kin recognition in honeybees', *Nature* 379: 498.

Axelrod, R. & Hamilton, W.D. (1981) 'The evolution of cooperation', *Science* 211: 1390–6.

Bacal, H.A. & Newman, K.M. (1990) *Theories of Object Relations: Bridges to Self Psychology*, New York: Columbia University Press.

Bailey, K.G. (1988) 'Psychological kinship: Implications for the helping professions', *Psychotherapy* 25: 132–41.

Bailey, K.G. & Nava, G. (1989) 'Psychological kinship, love, and liking: Preliminary validity data', *Journal of Clinical Psychology* 45: 587–94.

Bailey, K.G. & Wood, H.E. (1998) 'Evolutionary kinship therapy: Basic principles and treatment implications', *British Journal of Medical Psychology* 71: 509–23.

Bailey, K.G., Wood, H.E. & Nava, G. (1992) 'What do clients want? Role of psychological kinship in professional helping', *Journal of Psychotherapy Integration* 2: 125–47.

Bateson, P. (1979) 'How do sensitive periods arise and what are they for?', *Animal Behavior* 27: 470–86.

Bateson, P. (1983) 'Optimal outbreeding', in P. Bateson (ed.), *Mate Choice*, London: Cambridge.

Belsky, J., Steinberg, L. & Draper, P. (1991) 'Childhood experience, interpersonal development, and reproductive strategy: An evolutionary theory of socialization', *Child Development* 62: 647–70.

Bettleheim, B. (1969) *The Children of the Dream*, New York: Macmillan.

Bevc, I. & Silverman, I. (1993) 'Early proximity and intimacy between siblings and incestuous behavior: A test of the Westermarck theory', *Ethology and Sociobiology* 14: 171–81.

Bischof, N. (1975) 'Comparative ethology of incest avoidance', in R. Fox (ed.), *Biosocial Anthropology*, New York: Wiley.

Bowlby, J. (1969) *Attachment and Loss, Volume 1: Attachment*, New York: Basic Books.

Brenner, C. (1955) *An Elementary Textbook of Psychoanalysis*, New York: Anchor Books.

Burda, H. (1995) 'Individual recognition and incest avoidance in eusocial common mole-rats rather than reproductive suppression by parents', *Experientia* 51: 411–13.

Carter, C.O. (1967) 'Risk to offspring of incest', *Lancet* 1: 436.

Chu, J.A. & Dill, D.L. (1990) 'Dissociative symptoms in relation to childhood physical and sexual abuse', *American Journal of Psychiatry* 147: 887–92

Cory, D.W. & Masters, R.E.L. (1963) *Violation of Taboo: Incest of the Great Literature of Past and Present*, New York: Julian Press.

Courtois, C.A. (1979) 'The incest experience and its aftermath', *Victimology* 4: 337–47.

Daly, M. & Wilson, M.I. (1981) 'Abuse and neglect of children in the evolutionary perspective', in R.D. Alexander & D.W. Tinkle (eds), *Natural Selection and Social Behavior.*,New York: Chiron Press.

Demarest, W.J. (1977) 'Incest avoidance among human and nonhuman primates', in S. Chevalier-Skolnikoff & E.F. Poirer (eds), *Primate Social Behavior*, New York: Garland Press.

DeVos, G.A. (1975) 'Affective dissonance and primary socialization: Implications for a theory of incest avoidance', *Ethos* 3: 165–82.

Doi, T. (1989) 'The concept of amae and its psychoanalytic implications', *International Review of Psychoanalysis* 16: 349–54.

Enmoto, T. (1978) 'On social preference in sexual behavior of Japanese monkeys (Macaca fuscata)', *Journal of Human Evolution* 7: 283–93.

Erickson, M.T. (1983) *An Analysis of the Biological Hypothesis of Incest Avoidance and Presentation of an Alternate Neo-Westermarckian Model.* Unpublished Thesis, Graduate Division, University of California, Berkeley.

Erickson, M.T. (1989) 'Incest avoidance and familial bonding', *Journal of Anthropological Research* 45: 267–91.

Erickson, M.T. (1993) 'Rethinking Oedipus: An evolutionary perspective of incest avoidance', *American Journal of Psychiatry* 150: 411–16.

Erickson, M.T. (1999) 'Incest avoidance: Clinical implications of the evolutionary perspective', in J. McKenna, E.O. Smith & W. Trevathan (eds), *Evolutionary Medicine*, New York: Oxford University Press.

Evans, S. (1986) 'The pair bond of the common marmoset', in D.M. Taub & F.A. King (eds.), *Current Perspectives in Primate Social Dynamics*, New York: Van Nostrand Reinhold.

Ferenczi, S. (1949) 'Confusion of tongues between the adult and the child', *International Journal of Psychoanalysis* 30: 225–30.

Fox, J.R. (1962) 'Sibling incest', *British Journal of Sociology* 13: 128–50.

Fox, J.R. (1980) *The Red Lamp of Incest*, New York: Dutton.

Freud, S. (1953/1913) *Totem and Taboo. In Complete Psychological Works* (Standard ed.), (Vol. 13), London: Hogarth Press.

Freud, S. (1985) *The Complete Letters of Sigmund Freud to Wilhelm Fliess 1887–1904*. J.M. Masson (ed. & trans.), Cambridge, MA: Belknap Press.

Gavish, L., Hofmann, J.E. & Getz, L.L. (1984) 'Sibling recognition in the prairie vole, *Microtus Ochrogaster, Animal Behavior* 23: 362–6.

Gelinas, D.J. (1983) 'The persistent negative effects of incest', *Psychiatry* 46: 312–32.

Gilbert, P. (1998) 'Evolutionary psychopathology: Why isn't the mind designed better than it is?', *British Journal of Medical Psychology* 71: 353–73.

Glantz, K. & Pearce, J.K. (1989) *Exiles from Eden*, New York: Norton.

Goodall, J. (1986) *The Chimpanzees of Gombe*, Cambridge, MA: Belknap Press (Harvard University Press).

Greenberg, J.R. & Mitchell, S.A. (1983) *Object Relations in Psychoanalytic Theory*, Cambridge, MA: Harvard Press.

Greenberg, M., & Littlewood, R. (1995) 'Post-adoption incest and phenotypic matching: Experience, personal meanings and biosocial implications', *British Journal of Medical Psychology* 68: 29–44.

Hamilton, W.D. (1964) 'The genetical evolution of social behavior, I and II', *Journal of Theoretical Biology* 7: 1–52.

Hanby, J.P. & Brown, C.E. (1974) 'The development of sociosexual behavior in Japanese macaques', *Behavior*, 49: 152–96.

Harrison, K. (1997) *The Kiss*, New York: Random House.

Haynes-Seman, C. & Krugman, R.D. (1989) 'Sexualized attention: Normal interaction or precursor to sexual abuse?', *American Journal of Orthopsychiatry* 59: 238–45.

Herman, J.L. (1981) *Father-Daughter Incest*, Cambridge, MA: Harvard University Press.

Holmes, J. (1993) 'Attachment theory: A biological basis for psychotherapy?', *British Journal of Psychiatry* 163: 430–8.

Holmes, W.G. & Sherman, P.W. (1982) 'Kin recognition in animals', *American Scientist* 71: 46–55.

Hoogland, J.L. (1982) 'Prairie dogs avoid extreme inbreeding', *Science* 215: 1639–41.

Isabella, R.A. (1993) 'Origins of attachment: Maternal interactive behavior across the first year', *Child Development* 64: 605–21.

Isabella, R.A. & Belsky, J. (1991) 'Interactional synchrony and the origins of infant-mother attachment: A replication study', *Child Development* 62: 373–84.

Johnson, F.A. (1993) *Dependency and Japanese socialization: Psychoanalytic and Anthropological Investigations into Amae*, New York: New York University Press.

Justice, B. & Justice, R. (1979) *The Broken Taboo*, New York: Human Sciences Press.

Kaitz, M., Good, A., Rokem, A.M. & Eidelman, A.I. (1988) 'Mothers' recognition of their newborn by olfactory cues', *Developmental Psychology* 20: 582–91.

Kaitz, M., Shuri, S., Danziger, S., Hershko, Z. & Eidelman, A.I. (1994) 'Fathers can also recognize their newborns by touch (brief report)', *Infant Behavior and Development* 17: 205–7.

Keller, L. & Passera, L. (1993) 'Incest avoidance, fluctuating asymmetry, and the consequences of inbreeding in *Iridomyrmex humilis*, an ant with multiple queen colonies', *Behavioral Ecology and Sociobiology* 33: 191–9.

Kluft, R.P. (ed.) (1985) *Childhood Antecedents of Multiple Personality*, Washington, DC: American Psychiatric Press.

Koenig, W.D. & Pitelka, F.A. (1979) 'Relatedness and inbreeding avoidance: Counterploys in the communally nesting acorn woodpecker', *Science* 206: 1103–5.

Kohut, H. (1984) 'How does analysis cure?', in A. Goldberg & P. Stepansky (eds), *Contributions to the Psychology of the Self*, Chicago: University of Chicago Press.

Levi-Strauss, C. (1969) *The Elementary Structures of Kinship*, Boston: Beacon Press.

Lorenz, K.Z. (1937) 'The companion in the bird's world', *Auk* 54: 245–73.

McCabe, J. (1983) 'FBD marriage: Further support for the Westermarck hypothesis of the incest taboo?', *American Anthropologist* 85: 50–69.

Meiselman, K.C. (1978) *Incest: A Psychological Study of Causes and Effects*, San Francisco: Jossey-Bass.

Morrison, J. (1989) 'Childhood sexual histories of women with somatization disorder', *American Journal of Psychiatry* 146: 239–41.

Mrazek, P.K. (1981) 'The nature of incest: A review of contributing factors', in P.B. Mrazek & C.H. Kempe (eds), *Sexually Abused Children and their Families*, Elmsford, NY: Pergamon Press.

Murray, R.D. & Smith, E.O. (1983) 'The role of dominance and intrafamilial bonding in the avoidance of close inbreeding', *Journal of Human Evolution* 12: 481–6.

Oliver, J.E. (1993) Intergenerational transmission of child abuse: Rates, research, and clinical implications. *American Journal of Psychiatry* 150: 1315–24.

Packer, C. (1979) 'Inter-troop transfer and inbreeding avoidance in Papio anubis', *Animal Behavior* 27: 1–36.

Parker, H. & Parker, S. (1986) 'Father–daughter sexual abuse: An emerging perspective', *American Journal of Orthopsychiatry* 56: 531–49.

Paul, A. & Kuester, J. (1985) 'Intergroup transfer and incest avoidance in semi-free ranging Barbary macaques (Macaca sylvanus) at Salem (FRG)', *American Journal of Primatology* 8: 317–22.

Pereira, M.E. & Weiss, M.L. (1991) 'Female mate choice, male migration, and the threat of infanticide in ringtailed lemurs', *Behavioral Ecology and Sociobiology* 28: 141–52.

Pfennig, D.W. & Sherman, P.W. (1995) 'Kin recognition', *Scientific American* June: 98–103.

Piper, W.H. & Slater, G. (1993) 'Polyandry and incest avoidance in the cooperative stripe-backed wren of Venezuela', *Behavior* 124 (3–4): 227–47.

Porter, R.H. (1991) 'Mutual mother–infant recognition in humans', in P.G. Hepper (ed.), *Kin Recognition*, Cambridge: Cambridge University Press

Price, J.S. (1995) 'The Westermarck trap: A possible factor in the creation of Frankenstein', *Ethology and Sociobiology* 16: 349–53.

Pusey, A.E. (1980) 'Inbreeding avoidance in chimpanzees', *Animal Behavior* 28: 543–52.

Putnam, F.W. (1989) *The Diagnosis and Treatment of Multiple Personality Disorder*, New York: Guilford Press.

Rabin, I.A. (1965) *Growing up on a Kibbutz*, New York: Springer.

Ralls, K. & Ballou, J. (1982a) 'Effects of inbreeding on juvenile mortality in some small mammal species', *Laboratory Animals* 16: 159–66.

Ralls, K. & Ballou, J. (1982b) 'Effects of inbreeding on infant mortality in captive primates', *International Journal of Primatology* 4: 491–505.

Rank, O. (1992) *The Incest Theme in Literature and Legend*, (G.C. Richter, trans.), Baltimore: Johns Hopkins University Press (Original work published 1912).

Russell, D.E.H. (1984) 'The prevalence and seriousness of incestuous abuse: Stepfathers vs. biological fathers', *Child Abuse and Neglect* 8: 15–22.

Rutter, M. (1995) 'Clinical implications of attachment concepts: Retrospect and prospect', *Journal of Child Psychology and Psychiatry* 36: 549–71.

Sade, D.S. (1968) 'Inhibition of son–mother mating among free ranging rhesus monkeys', *Science and Psychoanalysis* 12: 18–38.

Schetky, D.H. (1990) 'A review of the literature on the long-term effects of childhood sexual abuse', in R.P. Kluft (ed.), *Incest-Related Syndromes of Adult Psychopathology*, Washington, DC: American Psychiatric Press.

Scott, L.M. (1984) 'Reproductive behavior of adolescent female baboons in Kenya', in M.F. Small (ed.), *Female Primates: Studies by Women Primatologists*, New York: Alan R. Liss.

Seemanova, E. (1971) 'A study of children of incestuous matings', *Human Heredity* 21: 108–28.

Shearer, S.L., Peters, C.P., Quaytman, M.S. & Ogden, R.L. (1990) 'Frequency and correlates of childhood sexual and physical abuse histories in adult female borderline patients', *American Journal of Psychiatry* 147: 214–16.

Shepher, J. (1971) 'Mate selection among second generation kibbutz adolescents and adults: Incest avoidance and negative imprinting', *Archives of Sexual Behavior* 1: 293–307.

Sherman, P.W. (1977) 'Nepotism and the evolution of alarm calls', *Science* 197: 1246–53.

Sherman, P.W., Jarvis, J. & Braude, S.H. (1992) 'Naked mole rats', *Scientific American*, August: 72–78.

Smith, P.B. & Pederson, D.R. (1988) 'Maternal sensitivity and patterns of infant–mother attachment', *Child Development* 59: 1097–101.

Smuts, B.B. (1985) *Sex and Friendship in Baboons*, New York: Aldine-de-Gruyter.

Spiro, M.E. (1965) *Children of the Kibbutz*, New York: Schocken Books.

Sroufe, L.A., Jacobvitz, D., Mangelsdorf, S., DeAngelo, E. & Ward, M.J. (1985) 'Generational boundary dissolution between mothers and their preschool children: A relationship systems approach', *Child Development* 56: 317–25.

Steele, H., Steele, M. & Fonagy, P. (1996) 'Association among attachment classifications of mothers, fathers, and their infants', *Child Development* 67: 541–55.

Stone, A.A. (1997) 'Where will psychoanalysis survive?', *Harvard Magazine*, January: 35–39.

Stone, M.H. (1990) 'Incest in the borderline patient', in R.P. Kluft (ed.), *Incest-Related Syndromes of Adult Psychopathology*, Washington, DC: American Psychiatric Press.

Sulloway, F.J. (1979) *Freud, Biologist of the Mind*, New York: Basic Books.

Summit, R. & Kryso, J. (1978) 'Sexual abuse of children: A clinical spectrum', *American Journal of Orthopsychiatry* 48: 237–51.

Suttie, I.D. (1935) *The Origins of Love and Hate*, London: Kegan Paul.

Talmon, S. (1964) 'Mate selection in collective settlements', *American Sociological Review* 29: 491–508.

Tokuda, K. (1961) 'A study of sexual behavior in the Japanese monkey troop', *Primates* 3: 1–40.

Tutin, C. (1979) 'Mating patterns and reproductive strategies in a community of wild chimpanzees', *Behavioral Ecology and Sociobiology* 6: 29–38.

van den Berghe, P.L. (1980) 'Incest and exogamy: A sociobiological reconsideration', *Ethology and Sociobiology* 1: 151–62.

van IJzendoorn, M.H. (1995) 'Adult attachment representations, parental responsiveness, and infant attachment: A meta-analysis on the predictive validity of the adult attachment interview', *Psychological Bulletin* 117: 387–403.

Vogel, C. (1985) 'Helping, cooperation and altruism in primate societies', in B. Holldobler & M. Lindauer (eds), *Experimental Behavioral Ecology and Sociobiology*, New York: Sinauer.

Weinberg, S.K. (1955) *Incest Behavior*, Secaucus, NJ: Citadel.

Westermarck, E.A. (1922/1889) *The History of Human Marriage*, Vol. 2, New York: Allerton Press.

White, L.A. (1948) 'The definition and prohibition of incest', *American Anthropologist* 50: 416–35.

Wiesel, T.N. & Hubel, D.H. (1963) 'Single-cell responses in the striate cortex of kittens deprived of vision in one eye', *Journal of Physiology* 165: 1003–17.

Williams, G.C. & Nesse, R.M. (1991) 'The dawn of Darwinian medicine', *Quarterly Review of Biology* 66: 1–22.

Williams, L.M. & Finklehor, D. (1995) 'Paternal caregiving and incest: Test of a biosocial model', *American Journal of Orthopsychiatry* 65: 101–13.

Wilson, E.O. (1998) *Consilience: The Unity of Knowledge*, New York: Alfred A. Knopf.

Wolf, A.P. (1970) 'Childhood association and sexual attraction: A further test of the Westermarck hypothesis', *American Anthropologist* 72: 503–15.

Wolf, A.P. (1993) 'Westermarck redivivus', *Annual Review of Anthropology* 22: 157–75.

Wolf, A.P. (1995) *Sexual Attraction and Childhood Association: A Chinese Brief for Edward Westermarck*, Stanford: Stanford University Press.

Wolf, A.P. (1998) 'Childhood association, sexual attraction, and the sexes: Or was Dr. Ellis right?', Unpublished talk, Conference on Edward Westermarck, Turku, Finland, November 1998.

Woolfenden, G.E. & Fitzpatrick, J.W. (1978) 'The inheritance of territory in group-breeding birds', *Bioscience* 28: 104–108.

Yamazaki, G.K., Beauchamp, G.K., Kupriewski, D., Bard, J., Thomas, L. & Boyce, E.A. (1988) 'Familial imprinting determines H-2 selective mating preferences', *Science* 240: 1331–2.

11

DISORGANIZED ATTACHMENT, MODELS OF BORDERLINE STATES AND EVOLUTIONARY PSYCHOTHERAPY

Giovanni Liotti

The evolution of parental investment, such that the parent provides sources of protection and care to offspring, and offspring are motivated to stay close rather than disperse after birth or avoid parents, is fundamental to all vertebrate species (MacLean, 1985; Trivers, 1985). The bond that develops between parent and offspring has been referred to as attachment (Bowlby, 1969/1982) and attachment relationships are now often used to describe many types of relationship (bond) where an individual is motivated to stay close to another and seek care. Bowlby (1969/1982) outlined, from an evolutionary perspective, why mammalian infants (especially primates) are born with the innate dispositions to search for closeness to conspecifics when distressed or frightened. He also specified that the inborn, evolved mechanisms of attachment strongly contribute, 'from the cradle to the grave' (Bowlby, 1979: 129), to the organization of behaviour, the regulation of emotional experience, social cognition and self-definition. Attachment, in Bowlby's theory, appears as a major organizing principle that may explain important aspects of human interpersonal relations in general, and of the therapeutic relationship in particular (Bowlby, 1979, 1988). Thus, Bowlby was one of the first psychotherapists to root human experiences in the inborn mechanisms of mind, as they are conceived by evolutionary biology and ethology.

In this chapter I outline how the innate motivational system underpinning attachment behaviour anticipates specific types of interaction and the developmental problems that arise when these are not forthcoming, e.g., the parent is as much a threat or thwarting object as a helpful resource to the child. The chapter pursues five goals:

1   To outline current thinking on how the innate attachment strategies can take on different forms according to the history of attachment interactions between infants and caregivers (phylogeny and ontogeny, in the perspective of attachment theory, are reciprocally interacting processes).

2   To focus on the disorganization of attachment. The different forms of attachment behaviour to be first identified by developmental psychologists showed up as organized patterns. Recently, however, the possibility that early attachment behaviour becomes disorganized deservedly received much attention in attachment research.
3   To argue that attachment disorganization is a risk factor in the development of various disturbances implying splitting and dissociation, or expressing themselves in intense and unstable styles of interpersonal relationships – first and perhaps foremost among these disturbances being the borderline personality disorder (BPD).
4   To hint at the possibility that two rival models of borderline pathology – Kernberg's (1975, 1984) psychoanalytic and Linehan's (1993) cognitive–behavioural models are both understandable from the theoretical perspective of attachment disorganization.
5   To describe how to work with the attachment needs of the borderline patient within the therapeutic relationship.

Organization and disorganization of attachment

Research on early attachment shows that, during the second year of life, most infants are able to organize their attachment behaviour according to three patterns (Ainsworth, Blehar, Waters & Wall, 1978; Main, 1995). Pattern A of attachment behaviour is called *avoidant* because the infant actively avoids asking for the caregiver's attention and also avoids proximity to the caregiver, both at the moment of a brief separation and at the moment of reunion after such a separation. Pattern B is called *secure* because the infant, who protests at separation, is readily comforted by the caregiver's attention immediately after reunion. Finally, pattern C is called *resistant* or *ambivalent* because the infant, who (like the B infant) protests at separation, continues to express distress as the caregiver is offering the required attention during the episode of reunion.

Infants organize their attachment behaviour according to the caregivers' style of response to the babies' inborn requests for proximity, protection and comfort (Bowlby, 1969/1982, 1988; for recent discussions of empirical support to this assertion, see Belsky, Rosenberg & Crnic, 1995; Pederson, Gleason, Moran & Bento, 1998; van IJzendoorn, 1995). The avoidant pattern of attachment usually appears in infant–caregiver dyads where the caregiver dismisses the infant's wishes for protective attention and comfort (e.g., the caregiver regards the infant's requests of attachment as a nuisance, and believes that to comply with them amounts to spoiling the baby). Infants whose caregivers are dismissing of attachment organize their behaviour accordingly: they take pains to avoid bothering their caregivers with the requests for proximity and comfort they have learned to expect will be rejected. The secure pattern is typical of the dyads where the caregiver has a positive attitude toward the infant's need for closeness and comfort. The caregivers of securely attached babies are relatively prompt and dependable in responding to the infants' attachment signals. The resistant pattern is characteristically related to the caregiver's inconsistent responses to the infant's requests for attachment, and to the caregiver's interfering attitude with respect to the child's autonomous exploration of the environment.

In the hitherto studied parent–child samples at low risk for psychological disturbances, most infants proved able to *organize* attachment behaviour according to one of the patterns outlined above (secure, avoidant and resistant). Even in these low-risk samples, however, a substantial minority of infants – about 20 per cent according to recent estimates (Carlson, Cicchetti, Barnett & Braunwald, 1989; Main & Morgan, 1996) – are unable to give organization and orientation to attachment behaviour (Main, 1995; Main & Solomon, 1990; Solomon & George, 1999). It is noteworthy that in samples at high risk for emotional disorders (e.g., mother–child dyads where the mother suffers from depression, mother–child dyads living in chaotic or maltreating families, or mother–child dyads characterized by prenatal alcohol abuse) disorganization of infant attachment is the rule: up to about 80 per cent of the children in these samples proved unable to organize attachment behaviour along any identifiable pattern (Carlson *et al.*, 1989; Lyons-Ruth, Repacholi, McLeod & Silva, 1991; O'Connor, Sigman & Brill, 1987; Radke-Yarrow, McCann, De Mulder & Belmont, 1995).

Phenotypic aspects of attachment disorganization

In the Strange Situation (the experimental procedure for the assessment of attachment behaviour during the first 2 years of life: Ainsworth *et al.*, 1978), disorganized attachment shows up as incompatible responses emitted simultaneously or in quick sequence, or else as lack of orientation during attachment interactions (Main & Solomon, 1990). For instance, attachment behaviour is labelled disorganized when the infant calls loudly for the parent during the phase of separation (approach behaviour similar to that emitted in the secure and the resistant patterns), but then, two to three minutes later, actively avoids contact with the parent at reunion (avoidance behaviour akin to that shown in the avoidant pattern). Children who, at reunion, approach the caregiver with head or gaze averted, or who cling to the caregiver while arching the body away (two examples of simultaneous display of contradictory patterns), are also considered disorganized in their attachment behaviour.

Extreme examples of contradictory behaviour patterns, that illustrate the interest of disorganized attachment (henceforward mentioned by the initials, DA, for the sake of brevity) for developmental psychopathology, have been described by Main and Solomon (1990: 142–143). For instance, a little girl, about 12 months old, approaches her father, on all fours, after a brief separation; she then stops, suddenly and out of the blue ceasing to smile; her face assumes an uncanny, blank expression while, in an obviously angry gesture, she hits the floor with her hand (redirected aggression?); finally, she resumes the smile and proceeds again towards her father. Another 1-year-old girl is looking at her mother; her gaze is blank, then the expression on her face splits in two; on one half of the face it is possible to detect a smile, on the other there is rage or disgust (the baby's corpus callosum has not yet matured, which allows for two different centres, one in each brain hemisphere, to control her emotional-motor behaviour). Disorganization of attachment may be also manifested in lack of orientation, in frightened expression or in freezing behaviour, as in the case of a toddler who, while he approaches his mother after the first brief separation of the Strange Situation, suddenly stops any movement, hands in air, gazing blankly into the void for thirty interminable seconds.

Disorganization of attachment has been empirically linked to unresolved memories of losses, abuses and other traumas in the caregiver (Main & Hesse, 1990). If DA characterizes the interaction between a child and a caregiver in the Strange Situation, then it is highly probable that the caregiver will rehearse, in the course of a properly devised semi-structured interview (Adult Attachment Interview, AAI: George, Kaplan & Main, 1985), memories of loss of an attachment figure or of traumas suffered at the hand of their attachment figures (emotional, sexual or other physical abuses). These memories, moreover, are narrated in such a way (lapses, serious space–time confusions regarding when and where the events happened, other cognitive distortions) as to suggest that they have not been elaborated and resolved. Caregivers of children who are organized (secure, resistant or avoidant) in their attachment seldom report unresolved traumatic memories in their response to the AAI. The link between DA in the child and unresolved traumatic memories in the caregiver is a statistically robust finding, that has been replicated repeatedly (Ainsworth & Eichberg, 1991; Benoit & Parker, 1994; Lyons-Ruth & Block, 1996; Ward & Carlson, 1995).

How attachment processes become disorganized: The evolutionary perspective

Evolutionary psychology offers important insights into the mechanisms whereby attachment behaviour can become disorganized. This is linked to the simultaneous and conflicting activation of both the defence and the safety system in the infant, as the consequence of both reassuring and threatening social signals sent by a caregiver in response to the infants' requests for attachment. This is especially noted when the infant interacts with a caregiver suffering from unresolved traumatic memories.

The defence and the safety systems

From an evolutionary perspective threat signals, whether they come from other sources or from a caregiver, activate defensive responses in the infant. Defensive responses have been classified by Marks (1987) and others (Gilbert, 1993), into a number of basic behavioural strategies that may be elicited by perceived danger in most vertebrate species: flight, freezing, defensive aggression and submissive behaviour. The similarities between specific strategies in different species strongly support the idea that these defensive responses have been favoured by natural selection and therefore are innately available in the brain of vertebrates. Taken together, the inborn algorithms for the processing of information related to defensive responses, and the neural structures upon which these algorithms operate, constitute the defence system (Gilbert, 1989, 1993; LeDoux, 1996). By contrast, all sensory information indicating absence of danger or protection from danger is related by Gilbert (1989, 1993) to the operations of a safety/safeness system.

In vertebrate species endowed with a well-developed limbic cortex (mammals in general and primates in particular), another inborn strategy adds to the defence system as a possible response to danger: the active search for the protective proximity of a conspecific. This strategy (attachment behaviour) is regulated by an inborn behavioural control system, called 'attachment system' by Bowlby (1969/1982), and considered by Gilbert (1989) a part of the safety system. Finally, the evolution of the neocortex endows human beings with a further strategy in the face of danger, based on the symbolic rehearsal of information related to previously-met dangerous situations. When the context of human behaviour and experience becomes similar to past contexts of hurt or threat, not only feelings but also thoughts related to danger and defence automatically surface in the stream of consciousness. These thoughts may help in devising better strategies for coping with actual or immediately forthcoming danger, but they may also be utterly inappropriate to the present situation, as exemplified by the ruminations accompanying post-traumatic phobias (LeDoux, 1996).

Disorganized attachment: conflict between the defence and the safety system

The coexistence in humans of different inborn organizing response systems for avoiding dangers and approaching rewarding stimuli allows, in certain circumstances, for a peculiarly paradoxical relationship that gives way to disorganized attachment. Basically, a parent who can be both a source of comfort but also a source of threat can activate both systems simultaneously. Such a circumstance is further complicated by the fact that the two more recently evolved strategies for coping with danger – the symbolic, intrapsychic one and the interpersonal one linked to the evolution of the attachment system – may seriously conflict with the evolutionarily older defensive strategies (freezing, flight, defensive fight and submission). Gilbert (1989) expresses this idea in terms of a conflict between the defence system and the safety system. Infants are highly attentive to the non-verbal signals of parents including proximity, holding, stroking and facial expressions (Schore, 1994). Not only is the infant's psychobiological state regulated by such interactions (Hofer, 1984) but infants use signals of the facial expression of parents to work out if something is a threat or not. It follows then that parents whose facial expressions and other verbal and non-verbal behaviours are ambivalent, or who signal mixtures of positive and negative emotions will create confusion in the infant. Empirical research suggests that one group of parents where such contradictory types of signalling takes place are in those suffering from unresolved traumatic memories (Main & Hesse, 1990; Main & Morgan, 1996).

To suffer from unresolved traumatic memories means that fragments of past painful events emerge unpredictably in the stream of consciousness, and that these fragments cannot be integrated in any organized process of thought (Horowitz, 1986; Main & Morgan, 1996). From the point of view of evolutionary psychology, such a compulsive surfacing of traumatic memories is the outcome of the inborn tendency to rehearse dangerous events in the face of new situations that may involve similar dangers (in this context, also the concept of phylogenetic regression – as formulated by Bailey, 1987 – may be relevant). Parents who were abused children, or who suffered the loss of an attachment figure or of another child, may tend (at some level of mental processes) to remember these events while taking care of their infants. Just as they did not receive adequate care, so they may fear this being repeated. This is present in the infant–parent interaction by signals that the parent is anxious, distressed, fearful, avoidant, uncertain or confused. When people experience an intrusion of unresolved traumatic memories in their stream of consciousness, they will unwittingly, and often unconsciously, express fear.

Main and Hesse (1990) originally formulated the hypothesis that infants whose caregivers are suffering from unresolved traumatic memories will quite often witness, in the caregiver's face, an expression of fear (together with expressions of frustration, hurt and anger). Among the emotional signals related to the automatic surfacing of unresolved traumatic memories, fear is particularly important in the context of DA. To the infant, the expression of fear in an adult's face is in itself frightening, i.e., it is interpreted as a signal of danger and it activates the defence system (Fields & Fox, 1985; Main & Hesse, 1990). The activation of the defence system by the same source of signals that modulate attachment creates the paradoxical situation underlying DA. In children of parents suffering from unresolved traumatic memories, the inborn strategies regulated by the defence system – flight, freezing, defensive aggression or submission – conflict with the approach, explorative or calming strategies regulated by the safety system (attachment behaviour).

It is important to emphasise that – with the notable exception of violent, abusive parental behaviour that directly frightens children while they are asking for protective proximity – no other pattern of caregiving can bring over such a conflicting activation of the safety and the defence system. Indifferent, dismissing or even openly rejecting parental behaviour discourages the infant's overtures aimed at proximity-seeking, but does not frighten the infant and therefore does not summon other defensive strategies together with attachment. Therefore, children of parents who are dismissing of attachment will be able to organize coherently their attachment behaviour (they will come to use avoidance of the attachment figure as an organized strategy whenever the motivational system controlling attachment is activated: avoidant pattern of attachment). Parental behaviour, corresponding to the resistant pattern of attachment, that unpredictably oscillates between acceptance and refusal of the infant's attachment overtures may be disappointing or distressing but not frightening to the child. It may yield an abnormally intense activation of the attachment system, not the simultaneous, conflicting activation of attachment and defensive strategies that is necessary to seriously hamper the organization of attachment behaviour.

In the face of the simultaneous activation of safety and defensive strategies – both elicited by the same social releasers (the caregiver's non-verbal behaviour) – attachment behaviour cannot be organized because the conflict is intrinsically irresolvable (George, 1996; Main & Hesse, 1990). The caregiver, who is the source of the infant's safety, appears *at the same time* to be a source of danger. The infant's inborn defence system, in such circumstances, is activated and directed toward the caregiver. Infants tend to attack defensively the frightened/frightening caregivers, or to withdraw (through flight or freezing) from them. Withdrawing from the caregiver, however, means loneliness, and any threat of loneliness forces infants to approach the caregivers because of the inborn structure of the attachment system (Bowlby, 1969/1982, 1988). Caught in this unsolvable dilemma, infants display a disorganized admixture of approach and avoidance behaviour toward the caregiver, or else freeze or display defensive aggressiveness in the middle of a friendly approach (see the description of disorganized attachment in the preceding paragraph).

The link between unresolved trauma, frightened *but not otherwise maltreating* parental behaviour, and disorganized infant attachment helps in the understanding also of those instances of DA in which the caregiver abuses the infant or in other ways acts so as to directly induce fear in the infant: in these cases, even more obviously than in the case of frightened but not maltreating parental behaviour, the simultaneous activation of attachment strategies and of more archaic evolved responses to danger, both directed toward the caregiver, is the hypothesized mechanism of disorganization.

Disorganized attachment and psychopathology

DA is an interesting theme of inquiry for developmental psychopathology (Carlson & Sroufe, 1995; George, 1996; Main, 1995). The mere fact that it is by far the more frequent (up to 80 per cent) type of attachment behaviour in families at high risk of emotional disorders, while it is observed only in about 20 per cent of children in low-risk samples, would already suffice to justify this interest. Moreover, DA: (1) provides us with an interesting model of dissociative processes (Carlson, 1997; Lichtenberg, Lachmann & Fosshage, 1992; Liotti, 1992, 1999a,b; Main & Morgan, 1996); (2) suggests useful interpretations of the dynamics underlying ruptures of the therapeutic alliance (and other difficulties in the therapeutic relationship) during the treatment of severe dissociative and personality disorders (Liotti, 1993, 1995; Liotti & Intreccialagli, 1998); (3) is a putative risk factor for any emotional disorder implying experiences of uncontrollable anxiety (Hesse & Main, 1999). In order to understand the psychopathological implications of DA, it is mandatory to reflect on the representations of self and others that accompany early experiences of attachment.

Attachment theory holds that children construct structures of implicit memory concerning the self and the attachment figure (internal working models, IWMs) on the basis of their actual experience with the attachment figure (Amini *et al.*, 1996; Bowlby, 1969/1982, 1988; Bretherton, 1990). The IWMs soon assume the control of the inborn system regulating attachment behaviour, and are reflected in the behavioural patterns observed in the Strange Situation. There are important differences between the IWM of DA and the IWMs of the three organized patterns of attachment. The IWM regulating the infant's attachment behaviour in the secure pattern, as inferred by the type of relationship between the infant and the caregiver, is unitary and coherent. It portrays the caregiver as trustworthy, and the self as the bearer of meaningful emotions and meaningful wishes for closeness and protection when in danger. In the other two organized patterns of attachment, the avoidant and the resistant, the IWM portrays a far less favourable representation of the self and the caregiver. The caregiver is likely represented as unavailable in the avoidant and as unpredictable or controlling in the resistant pattern (theoretical reflections and reviews of empirical findings on the representations of self and the attachment figure are offered in Bretherton, 1990, Carlson & Sroufe, 1995, and George, 1996). However unfavourable the representations of self and caregiver in the avoidant and resistant patterns may sometimes be, they still are such as not to exceed the infant mind's capacity of synthesizing relatively coherent and unitary meaning structures. By contrast, the information available to infants disorganized in their attachment behaviour is such as to disrupt the construction of a unitary IWM of self and the attachment figure: the IWM of DA is multiple, fragmented and incoherent (Main, 1991). It conveys representations of the self and of the attachment figure so contradictory or incompatible that they cannot be reciprocally integrated: they tend to remain dissociated at least in the first steps of personality development, and may stay so even in adult life (Carlson,1997; Liotti, 1992, 1995, 1999a,b).

Rescuer, persecutor and victim: Split representations in DA

The IWM of DA induces an oscillation of the representational processes, regarding both the self and the attachment figure, between the three dramatic stereotypes of the Victim, the Rescuer and the Persecutor (Liotti, 1999a, b). The attachment figure may be represented negatively, as the cause of the ever-growing fear experienced by the self (self as Victim of a Persecutor), but also positively, as a Rescuer (a parent frightened by unresolved traumatic memories may be willing to offer comfort to the child, and may be unaware of the facial expression and of its effect on the infant; the child may feel such comforting availability together with the fear). Together with these two opposed representations of the attachment figure (Persecutor and Rescuer) meeting a vulnerable and helpless (Victim) self, the IWM of DA conveys also a negative representation of a powerful, evil self meeting a fragile or even devitalized attachment figure (Persecutor self, held responsible for the fear expressed by the attachment figure). Moreover, there is the possibility, for the child, to represent both the self and the attachment figure as the helpless victims of a mysterious, invisible source of danger. And finally, since the frightened attachment figure may be comforted by the tender feelings evoked by contact with the infant, the implicit memories of DA may also convey the possibility of construing the self as the powerful Rescuer of a fragile attachment figure (the little child perceives the self as able to comfort a frightened adult). Descriptions of the shifts of a patient's self-representations between the poles of the Victim, the Persecutor and even the Rescuer (while the therapist is represented, in sometimes very quick succession, as Rescuer, Persecutor and Victim) may be easily found in the literature on the treatment of borderline and dissociative patients (Davies & Frawley, 1994; Liotti, 1995). It is possible that similar experiences of multiple, incompatible, dissociated, dramatic representations of self and caregiver (Persecutor–Victim, Victim–Persecutor, Victim–Victim, Rescuer–Victim, Victim–Rescuer) lie at the heart of DA.

Metacognitive deficits and DA

Research on attachment yields evidence that the development of the integrative functions of consciousness during childhood and adolescence is hindered if the attachment relationship to the caregivers remains disorganized. The integrative functions of consciousness are based on the capacity of momentarily suspending decision and action, so as to compare with each other different representations of self, of other people's states of mind, and of reality. The development of this capacity manifests itself, during childhood and adolescence, with the growing abilities: (1) to distinguish between appearance and reality (Flavell, Flavell & Green, 1983; Wimmer & Penner, 1983); (2) to construct a theory of mind (Baron-Cohen, 1995); (3) to reflect on mental states (Fonagy *et al.*, 1995); (4) to monitor thoughts, feelings and language (metacognitive monitoring: Flavell, 1979; Main, 1991); (5) to perform formal operations of thought (Flavell, 1963), and (6) to pay attention to external stimuli without being unwittingly absorbed in daydreams.

The development of all these abilities is hindered by insecure attachment in general, and by the persistence of that pattern of relationship whose early prototype is manifested by infant DA in particular. Pre-school children who had been infants disorganized in their attachment behaviour rank very low, particularly if compared with formerly securely attached children, in the false-belief tests used for the assessment of the child's theory of mind (Fonagy, Redfern & Charman, 1997; Meins, 1997). In a longitudinal study, children whose attachment behaviour in infancy had been disorganized, were judged by their teachers as significantly more confused and 'absent minded' than their peers with a different attachment history (Carlson, 1997). Children 5–8 years old, judged disorganized in their response to the Children Attachment Interview (Green, Stanley, Smith & Goldwyn, 1999), show marked impairment of metacognitive and mentalizing capacities in comparison to securely attached peers. Adolescents who had been fearful/disorganized children showed marked difficulties in tests of formal reasoning, when compared with peers who had different attachment experiences (Jacobsen, Edelstein & Hofmann, 1994).

240

Metacognitive and mentalizing (i.e., theory of mind) deficits during development bring over concurrent difficulties in understanding, naming, discriminating and therefore controlling mental states in general and emotions in particular (Fonagy *et al.*, 1995; Maffei, 1998). Therefore, children with metacognitive deficits should have difficulties in controlling emotions and impulses. In accordance with this hypothesis, a number of studies provide evidence that disorganized infants tend to grow into children with difficulties in the control of anxiety (Hesse & Main, 1999) and aggression (Lyons-Ruth, 1996; Van IJzendoorn, 1997).

Finally, a metacognitive deficit implies a poor capacity to reflect on one's own mental representations. This capacity yields the possibility of integrating contra-dictory features (thesis and antithesis) in cohesive wholes (syntheses). It is therefore not surprising that children who have been infants disorganized in their attachments show negative and disorganized self-representations more often than controls (Cassidy, 1988; Hesse & Main, 1999; Main, 1995; Solomon, George & DeJong, 1995).

All these findings suggest that the effects of early DA may extend into childhood and adolescence and may become a risk factor for psychopathological develop-ments. As to the nature of these developments, the dissociative disorders and the borderline personality disorder (BPD) seem likely candidates. Theoretical-clinical considerations (Lichtenberg, Lachmann & Fosshage, 1992; Liotti, 1992, 1995, 1999a,b; Main, & Morgan, 1996) and the results of a few empirical studies (Anderson & Alexander, 1996; Carlson, 1997; Coe, Daleenberg, Aransky & Reto, 1995; Liotti, Intreccialagli & Cecere, 1991) suggest that DA not only illustrates and contains, as in a nutshell, the dynamics of the dissociative processes, but may also be an actual risk factor in the development of the dissociative disorders.[1]

Disorganized attachment and borderline pathology

The hypothesis that DA may be a risk factor for BPD (Cotugno,1997; Liotti, 1999a,b), has not yet been explored with comparable depth as in the case of the dissociative disorders.[2] There are, however, good reasons for advancing this hypothesis. First, the Dissociative Identity Disorder (DID, formerly called multiple personality disorder: American Psychiatric Association, 1994) and the borderline states have been considered by many as overlapping disorders or as parts of the same psychopathological continuum (Benner & Josceline, 1984; Buck, 1983; Horevitz & Braun, 1984; Marmer & Fink, 1994; Ross, 1989). Both the DID and the BPD have been regarded as chronic subtypes of the post-traumatic stress disorder, and both are diagnosed predominantly in females (Gunderson & Sabo, 1993a; Spiegel, 1984). Frankly dissociative episodes are one of the key diagnostic features of the BPD (American Psychiatric Association, 1994; Perry & Herman, 1993). The differential diagnosis between the DID and the BPD may be difficult or impossible if the clinician does not contact the patient's alter personalities (Fink & Galinkoff, 1990). Comorbidity, according to DSM-III and DSM-IV criteria, between DID and BPD is extremely frequent (Fyer, France & Sullivan, 1988). Semantically and conceptually, it is not easy to distinguish splitting, the alleged basic defence mechanism in the borderline states, from dissociation.[3] If the dissociative and the borderline disorders are somehow linked, then it is not unlikely that an early risk factor for the first category, such as DA, may be such also for the second.

Another reason for paying heed to DA when reflecting on the origins of borderline states is that its possible role in such psychopathological developments seems compatible with the basic assumptions of two major theories of borderline pathology, Kernberg's (1975, 1984) psychoanalytic theory and Linehan's (1993) cognitive–behavioural theory.

The central theme of Kernberg's model of borderline states is the idea that many of the patient's disturbances are linked to the existence of split representations of positive and negative features of self and others. These representations are held to be present since infancy, and to remain in a split condition throughout personality development. Kernberg's thesis is readily matched with the idea that DA is linked to multiple and incompatible representations of self and the attachment figure. An important difference between Kernberg's idea of splitting and the description of a multiple IWM (Liotti, 1995, 1999a,b; Main, 1991) is that the development of a multiple IWM does not necessarily imply defensive processes (but is not absolutely incompatible with them: Fonagy, Moran, Steele & Steele, 1992). Moreover, the status of the non-integrated representations in DA may be more similar to dissociation (i.e., multiple and incompatible) than to splitting (i.e., dual and contradictory: see Young, 1988, for differences between dissociation and splitting within the psychoanalytic theory of defence mechanisms; see also Ross, 1989: 151 for a rebuttal of such differences). These differences notwithstanding, the basic idea of incompatible and disassociated representations of self and others at the beginning of personality development is alike in Kernberg's model and in the DA model of borderline development.[4]

The DA model also acknowledges the importance of the dysfunction of the system regulating the emotions, which is emphasized in the cognitive–behavioural theory of BPD advanced by Linehan (1993). The developmental defect in the integrative functions of consciousness (theory of mind, metacognitive monitoring, reflective-self capacity, formal or operational thinking) observed in relation to insecure attachment in general and DA in particular (see the preceding paragraph), may be linked to the deficit in the 'system' regulating the emotions (the nuclear disturbance of BPD according to Linehan). Linehan describes the functions of this system as the capacity to reflect on the emotions as discrete mental states, to name them properly, and to acknowledge their origin, function and value both in the inner and in the interpersonal life. Linehan's system of emotional regulation, therefore, is linked to the development of metacognitive monitoring and of an adequate theory of one's own and of others' minds (cf. Maffei, 1998). Metacognitive deficits have been assessed in samples of BPD patients (Barone, 1998; Fonagy et al., 1995).

The DA model of borderline states not only acknowledges the importance both of the split self-representations and of the poor metacognitive capacity of emotional regulation: it also explains how the affective instability, the dramatically mutable relational style, the self-damaging behaviour and the identity disturbance are related to the frantic efforts of avoiding real or imagined abandonment. All these features of the borderline states are explained by the DA model as the consequence of the *recurrent activation of the attachment motivational system*. When active, the attachment system of these patients causes fear of abandonment and frantic efforts to avoid it, while the multiple, shifting representations of the IWM are responsible for the uncertain sense of self, the dramatically changing attitudes toward significant others, and the self-damaging behaviour (Self as Persecutor, deserving punishment). Paranoid ideation (Self as Victim, Others as Persecutors) – that is as transient as the representations of self and others portrayed by the attachment IWM are mutable – may also be related to the episodic activation of the attachment system within unfavourable interpersonal relationships. The dissociative experiences may also be explained as the outcome of the activation of the attachment system in interpersonal contexts that are particularly confusing: these experiences would then reflect the disordered state of a consciousness that is forced to deal with multiple and incompatible *simultaneous* self-representations.

The emphasis on the activation of the attachment system as a mediator of the borderline symptoms and disturbances has important consequences on the therapeutic strategy, and particularly on the understanding of the therapeutic relationship.

Disorganized attachment in the psychotherapy of borderline states

The clinician who pays heed to DA while treating a borderline patient may become aware that the more dramatic shifts in the patient's representations of self and/or the therapist are contingent upon the activation, within the therapeutic relationship, of the patient's attachment system. In order to deal properly with such an awareness, the therapist should think of interpersonal exchanges and interpersonal motivation in evolutionary terms – which makes the psychotherapy of borderline patients according to the DA model a particularly interesting example of evolutionary psychotherapy.

A reminder: attachment and the modular model of social motivation

In the evolutionary perspective, human interpersonal behaviour is regulated by a number of motivational systems, linked each to a distinct brain module (in Edelman's terminology, to a distinct, ethologically defined 'value' of the old mammalian brain: see Migone & Liotti, 1998). The development of each motivational system during the personal learning history is based on a well-defined set of inborn dispositions. These systems evolved in mammals to pursue independent even if interrelated biosocial goals such as attachment, mating, ranking and co-operation (Bowlby, 1969/1982, 1988; DeWaal, 1996; Gilbert, 1989, Chapter 6, this volume, LeDoux, 1996; Liotti, 1994). In the therapeutic relationship, as in every human relationship of sufficient duration and meaningfulness, various types of interaction succeed and alternate, each regulated by one or the other of the basic interpersonal motivational systems: attachment, competitive, seductive and co-operative inter-actions. The important theme to be emphasized here is that every motivational system, when it becomes active at any given time in the therapeutic relationship, potentially affords to the patient's and the therapist's subjective experience two types of information: emotional information linked to the inborn operations of that system, and cognitive information linked to memories of previous activation of that system (cf. LeDoux, 1996, for a discussion of the representation of these functional systems in the brain). In the case of the attachment system, its activation within the therapeutic relationship will bring forth, together with pleasant or unpleasant specific emotions, coherent and unitary representations of the self and of the therapist if the patient's attachment behaviour has been organized – or incoherent, dramatic, multiple and dissociated representations if it has been mostly disorganized during personality development. If the attachment system is disorganized, its activation during the therapeutic dialogue could also induce dissociative experiences within the session (Liotti, 1993, 1995; Liotti & Intreccialagli, 1998).

The therapeutic relationship in the evolutionary perspective

The evolutionary psychotherapist will monitor the motivational ground of every therapeutic interaction according to the evolutionary theory of human motivation summarized earlier. In agreement with cognitive psychotherapists, evolutionary psychotherapists may strive to shape the therapeutic relationship, since the very first session, according to the ideal of collaborative empiricism (Beck & Emery, 1985). This is performed through the active search of an explicit agreement on goals and rules of the therapeutic work (a particularly convincing example of how this mutual agreement is constructed at the beginning of the treatment of borderline patients may be found in Linehan, 1993). If the joint formulation of a shared goal for the treatment has been successful, the inborn motivational system mediating co-operative behaviour is likely to become active both in the therapist and in the patient at the beginning of the treatment. Patients, however, do suffer. Since the beginning of psychotherapy, they are gradually disclosing their troubles to benev-olent persons (the therapists) that they come to perceive as emotionally available and as 'stronger and/or wiser' than themselves (Bowlby, 1979: 129). Disclosing one's suffering to an available person who is perceived as stronger and wiser than the self is the typical situation in which, 'from the cradle to the grave' (Bowlby, 1979: 129), the inborn attachment system is activated. Therefore, in the course of psychotherapy, the co-operative system will give way to the attachment system. The activation of the attachment system within the therapeutic relationship may be detected in a variety of ways: through an analysis of the patient's and the therapist's emotional reactions (see the concept of the therapist's emotions as 'markers' of particular interpersonal cycles and schemata: Safran & Segal, 1990), or through the patient's representations of self and the therapist as they may appear during the therapeutic dialogue (e.g., the patient idealizes the therapist) or in a dream.

In most borderline patients, the activation of the attachment system is accompanied, since early childhood, by unpleasant states of mind related to the dramatic and multiple IWM of DA (disorientation, altered states of consciousness, a loop of increasing fear whether one approaches or avoids the attachment figure, dramatic shifts between the representation of self and the attachment figure as a Rescuer, a Persecutor and a Victim). It is therefore likely that these patients have learned to inhibit, as far as possible, the activation of the attachment system in order to avoid the unpleasant experiences that accompany it. One way to inhibit the activation of the attachment system is to shift to another inborn motivational system, whose operations manifest themselves with emotions and behaviour alike to those of attachment. For instance, anger may appear as an operation of the care-seeking attachment system whose goal is to ask energetically for the attachment figure's attention (e.g., the secure child protests during the separation from the mother in Ainsworth's Strange Situation: Ainsworth et al., 1978). This kind of anger is to elicit 'something' from the other. Anger can also be used to give a signal of 'stay away', that is to stop the other from intruding or doing something – e.g., getting too close. Hence, anger may also appear as an operation of the competitive system (e.g., threat display aimed at defining the social rank, exerting control over the other – making the other submit – and defending boundaries; Gilbert, 1989, 1992). It is therefore possible that, in their relationships, borderline patients quickly switch from attachment anger into competitive (defensive) anger, thereby facilitating the activation of the agonistic rather than the care-giving system in the other person. In this way, an interpersonal cycle is facilitated that cuts off the activation of attachment in the borderline patients and of care giving in their partners, thereby protecting the patients from dissociative and other unpleasant experiences linked to their attachment system. Hence, the patient may not so much fear the therapist as fear the inner experiences the therapist will trigger as they become attached. To feel deeply ashamed of, or frightened by, one's own attachment feelings/ needs is a case in point. And people often defend themselves from 'shame' of their feelings by withdrawing or becoming competitive and aggressive (Gilbert, personal communication). Of course, such a 'protection' is earned at a cost: the patient will appear to suffer from the affective instability and the inappropriate, intense anger that are listed among the diagnostic criteria for BPD (American Psychiatric Association, 1994).

Another way of inhibiting the activation of the attachment system implies a shift of the meaning attributed to the wish for bodily contact with another human being. Since both the attachment system (whose goal is *protective* proximity and comforting hug) and the sexual system imply a wish for physical closeness, borderline patients may misinterpret as sexual, both in themselves and in other people, wishes that are instead related to attachment needs. It is because of the confusion between sexual and attachment wishes that borderline patients may appear improperly seductive within the therapeutic relationship, and may get trapped into promiscuous or dangerous sexual affairs within other social relationships.[5]

A clinical example

A clinical case illustrates how the evolutionary psychotherapist dealing with a borderline patient may monitor the activation of the patient's attachment system, and deal with its various manifestations.

Mario, a borderline patient in his thirties, began his psychotherapy with a fairly co-operative attitude. A few weeks later, after having described his painful emotions in a stormy love relationship (to which the therapist listened with empathy), Mario became competitive and challenging towards the therapist. The therapist thought that this shift in Mario's attitude could be a way of inhibiting the attachment system, by activating the ranking system in its stead. Thereupon, he provided calm and understanding responses to the patient's challenges. As a consequence, Mario gradually assumed a more positive stance during the therapeutic dialogues. About 5 months from the beginning of the treatment, there were clear signs that the patient's attachment system had been activated. Mario now seemed to look at his therapist as at a powerful and benevolent rescuer rather than at a rival in a power struggle. Two sessions after the one in which the therapist had noticed that Mario now looked upon him as an idealized attachment figure, Mario reported a dream. In the dream, Mario's best friend had been killed and changed into a zombie. The friend in the dream was a psychologist. In the uncanny, frightening atmosphere of the dream it was unclear whether or not Mario killed his friend before he had been transformed in a zombie. The zombie tried to embrace Mario, and it was also unclear whether the intention of such approach was to express friendly feelings or rather to strangle him.

The characters in this dream recall the multiple, dissociated representations in the IWM of DA: the attachment figure (the friend, the therapist, as once one or both Mario's parents) is devitalized (a zombie) while the self, appearing as a persecutor, is held responsible for this loss of vitality; *at the same time*, the self is construed as the helpless victim of an evil attachment figure (the zombie strangling an innocent Mario); and also, the self is seen as the object of the positive attention of a benevolent, forgiving attachment figure (the friend expressing affection). Soon after having reported this dream, Mario's attitudes towards the therapist and the treatment became very complex. Mario shifted quickly between opposite representations of self and the therapist, reminding the dramatic characters of Persecutor, Rescuer and Victim (multiple transferences).

Oscillation of attitudes toward self and the therapist are common in the therapeutic relationship with borderline patients as they are in these patients' other relations: in a short span of time, even within a single session, borderline patients may dramatically ask for help, look distant and indifferent, state their wish to quit therapy because of the fear of being damaged, express the fear of being dangerous to beloved persons, and make the therapist feel important and loved but also threatened or oppressed. If the multiple transferences are linked to the activity of the patients' attachment system, then the therapist would better monitor carefully the intensity and duration of the operations of this system within the therapeutic relationship. Linehan's treatment manual (Linehan, 1993), suggests an interesting way of preventing the problems[6] created by a too intense activation of the attachment system in the psychotherapy of borderline states.

Why two settings are better than one in the psychotherapy of borderline patients

Linehan suggests engaging the patient in a mutually agreed upon therapeutic contract from the very beginning of the therapeutic dialogues (the co-operative system is thereby powerfully activated both in the patient and in the therapist). With respect to therapeutic relationships in which the therapist acts as a benevolent caregiver (the motivational register in the beginning therapeutic relationship being attachment–caregiving) or as a prosocial dominant (the motivational register being provided by the ranking system), Linehan's therapeutic manoeuvre makes it relatively easier, when the patient's attachment system becomes active, to try immediately to retrieve the original co-operative order. Furthermore, Linehan's model makes use, since the beginning of treatment, of two independent even if correlated therapeutic settings (individual and group). Provided that there is theoretical and technical agreement between the individual and the group therapists, the co-ordination of two simultaneous therapeutic settings is demonstrably superior to any of the single settings in reducing both drop-outs and self-destructive behaviour (Linehan, 1993).

The positive effect of two simultaneous settings in the treatment of borderline states may be explained on the basis of attachment dynamics. The simultaneous existence of another caregiving relationship (with the group therapist) protects the relationship with the individual therapist from the consequences of an intense activation of the patient's attachment system. If the activation of the patient's attachment system within an individual psychotherapy brings over an increased propensity to painful dissociative experiences, and to dramatic shifts in the way of construing self and therapist, both patient and therapist are likely to find the therapeutic relationship too difficult to be either tolerated (on the patient's side) or dealt with successfully (on the therapist's side). What happens in these circumstances, according to attachment theory, is a repetition of the situation leading to DA: to relinquish a relationship that alone appears capable of affording comfort from unbearable emotional pain is frightening, but to approach the attachment figure is equally frightening. *Each pole of this dilemma increases the intensity of the painful emotions implied by the other.* One of the likely consequences of this state of affairs is the patient's dropping out from treatment; another is a therapeutic stalemate (both are unfortunately common occurrences in the treatment of borderline patients: Gunderson & Sabo, 1993b). If, however, a second therapist is engaged in the therapeutic programme (e.g., the group therapist in Linehan's model), the patient may feel that there is another source of help available, and this perception may reduce the emotional strain on the first therapeutic relationship (e.g., with the individual psychotherapist).

If one reason for the usefulness of two simultaneous settings in the treatment of borderline patients is the distribution of the patients' attachment needs on more than a single therapist, then such usefulness should appear also with combined interventions other than individual and group. Combined individual psychotherapy and family therapy, or even individual psychotherapy and pharmacological therapy (if the drugs are prescribed by a psychiatrist who is well grounded in psychological treatments), could protect the individual psychotherapy from drop-outs as well as individual and group interventions do.

Mario's therapist had been aware, since the beginning of the treatment, of the risks inherent in the activation of his patient's attachment system. He had thereupon planned Mario's treatment in close co-operation with a psychiatrist who was also an expert psychotherapist, well aware of the DA model of borderline states. The psychiatrist (P) was supposed to help Mario with periodic prescriptions of antidepressants during the whole unfolding of the psychotherapeutic process. When multiple transferences and the consequent sharp increase in emotional suffering came to characterize Mario's relationship with the therapist (T), P came to the aid: instead of merely increasing the dosage of antidepressants, P (who had been informed by T of the stalemate in the therapeutic relationship) examined how Mario was perceiving the difficulty in his psychotherapy. While overwhelming emotions of DA hampered his responses to such an inquiry when T attempted it, Mario was able to discuss the problem with P (who had not yet been invested in the role of attachment figure). Mario was painfully trying to synthesize in a single meaning structure two sets of emotional-interpersonal information: (1) his rage at noticing his suffering was increasing and T was unable to soothe it (Self as Victim); and (2) his guilt for devaluing and aggressing such a nice person as T had proven to be (Self as Persecutor). The synthesis he was constructing portrayed both himself and T as the helpless victims, in his words, of a 'hideous, invincible illness' (perceiving both the self and the therapist as the helpless 'victims' of some unconquerable evil, within the meaning domain of DA, is, according to this model, the most likely antecedent of premature interruptions of therapy by borderline patients). To this construction, P opposed a clearly stated, firmly held belief that: (1) he (P) was able to help Mario, both with drugs and with dialogue; (2) also T was able to help Mario, and was available to discuss with him the future prospects of their treatment if Mario allowed him to do so. This intervention greatly relieved Mario from his suffering, and prompted his decision to resume the dialogue with T he had planned to quit. Within the following dialogues between Mario and his psychotherapist, T made good use of the exchange between P and Mario, as both his colleague and his patient had reported it to him. This exchange was repeatedly examined according to the analysis of 'model scenes' proposed by Lichtenberg, Lachmann and Fosshage (1992, 1996). The exchange between P and Mario (what Mario thought and felt during his dialogue with P, and in how many ways these thoughts and feelings were different from those he had had during the more dramatic sessions with T) became the model scene of a proper attachment interaction, to be gradually contrasted with the dramatic, unstable interactions that had come to characterize the attachment-caregiving interactions between Mario and T. In this way, a therapeutic goal not dissimilar from Kernberg's concept of integration was gradually pursued.

Concluding remarks

The clinical vignette exemplifies how an evolutionary approach to psychotherapy helps in the understanding of the interpersonal dynamics responsible for a major problem in the treatment of borderline patients – namely, the high risk of drop-out – and in devising a solution to this problem by exploiting the opportunities offered by two therapists working in close co-operation. In order to use these opportunities fully, it is useful for the two therapists to understand the evolved rules that govern human interpersonal behaviour (e.g., the increased intensity of activation of the attachment system when only one attachment figure is available). Such an understanding may greatly facilitate the integration of ideas coming from psychoanalytic and cognitive–behavioural models of borderline states: a major reward of approaching psychotherapy from an evolutionary perspective.

One of the main goals of this chapter is to hint at the integrative power of an evolutionary approach to psychotherapy in reducing the fragmentation and dispersion of valuable clinical insights, that are often considered incompatible only because they stem from different traditions, epistemologies or meta-theories. Evolutionary psychology provides the psychotherapist with a way of thinking about human behaviour, motivation, and cognitive-emotional processes that is free from the constraints of the classical approaches to psychotherapy (e.g., from the psychoanalytic emphasis on conflict between drives, from the behaviourist's emphasis on learning and observable behaviour, and from the assertion of a primacy of cognitions over emotional-motivational processes that characterizes cognitive therapy). Yet, evolutionary psychology is wide enough in scope as to take into consideration all the major themes of the classical approaches to psychotherapy: motivational and interpersonal dynamics, developmental processes, interdependence of emotions and cognitions, and relationships between conscious and non-conscious aspects of mental life. Thus, from the point of view of evolutionary psychology, different therapeutic techniques and clinical insights, that had their origin from approaches focused on one or the other of these themes, often do not appear incompatible.

Disorganized attachment and borderline pathology provide just one illustration of how the integrative power of an evolutionary approach may be reflected in the practice of psychotherapy, combining the insights of both psychoanalytic and cognitive–behavioural models. By reading the other chapters of this book, and the wide literature quoted in the references, it becomes clear that other examples of this integrative power are accumulating quickly, so that evolutionary psychotherapy already appears as a strong ecumenical approach to the practice of psychotherapy, yet an approach that remains solidly grounded in contemporary biological science.

References

Ainsworth, M.D.S., Blehar, M.C., Waters, E. & Wall, S. (1978) *Patterns of Attachment*, Hillsdale, NJ: Lawrence Erlbaum Inc.

Ainsworth, M.D.S. & Eichberg, C. (1991) 'Effects on infant–mother attachment of mother's unresolved loss of an attachment figure, or other traumatic experiences', in C.M. Parkes, J. Stevenson-Hinde & P. Marris (eds), *Attachment Across the Life Cycle*, (pp.160–183), London: Routledge.

American Psychiatric Association (1994) *Diagnostic and Statistical Manual of Mental Disorders*, (4th ed) *DSM-IV*, Washington, DC: American Psychiatric Association.

Amini, F., Lewis, T., Lannon, R., Louie, A., Baumbacher, G., McGuinnes, T. & Zirker, E. (1996) 'Affect, attachment, memory: Contributions toward psychobiologic integration', *Psychiatry* 59: 213–39.

Anderson, C.L. & Alexander, P.C. (1996) 'The relationship between attachment and dissociation in adult survivors of incest', *Psychiatry* 59: 240–54.

Bailey, K.G. (1987) *Human Paleopsychology: Implications for Aggression and Pathological Processes*, Hillsdale, NJ: Lawrence Erlbaum Associates Inc.

Baron-Cohen, S. (1995) *Mindblindness: An Essay on Autism and the Theory of Mind*, Cambridge, MA: MIT Press.

Barone, L. (1998) *Attaccamento e Metacognizione nei Disturbi di Personalità*, Articolo presentato al IX Congresso della Società Italiana di Terapia Cognitiva (SITCC), Torino, 13–15 November 1998 [*Attachment and Metacognition in Personality Disorders*. Paper presented at the IX Conference of the Italian Association for Cognitive Therapy].

Beck, A.T. & Emery, G. (1985) *Anxiety Disorders and Phobias: A Cognitive Perspective*, New York: Basic Books.

Belsky, J. Rosenberg, K. & Crnic, K. (1995) 'The origins of attachment security: Classical and contextual determinants', in S. Goldberg, R. Muir & J. Kerr (eds), *Attachment Theory: Social, Developmental and Clinical Perspectives*, (pp. 153–84), Hillsdale, NJ: Analytic Press.

Benner, D.G. & Joscelyne, B. (1984) 'Multiple personality as a borderline disorder', *Journal of Nervous and Mental Disease* 172: 98–104.

Benoit, D. & Parker, K.C. (1994) 'Stability and transmission of attachment across three generations', *Child Development* 65: 1444–56.

Bowlby, J. (1969/1982) *Attachment and Loss. Vol.1*, (2nd edition), London: Hogarth Press.

Bowlby, J. (1979) *The Making and Breaking of Affectional Bonds*, London: Tavistock.

Bowlby, J. (1988) *A Secure Base*, London: Routledge.

Bretherton, I. (1990) 'Open communication and internal working models: Their role in attachment relationships', in R. Thompson (ed.), *Socioemotional Development*, (pp. 57–113), Lincoln: University of Nebraska Press.

Buck, O.D. (1983) 'Multiple personality as a borderline state', *Journal of Nervous and Mental Disease* 17: 162–65.

Carlson, E.A. (1997, April) 'A prospective longitudinal study of consequences of attachment disorganization/disorientation', *Paper presented at the 62nd Meeting of the Society for Research in Child Development*, Minneapolis, MN.

Carlson, E.A. & Sroufe, L.A. (1995) 'Contribution of attachment theory to developmental psychopathology', in D. Cicchetti & D. Cohen (eds), *Developmental Psychopathology: Theory and Methods* (vol.1), (pp. 581–617), New York: Wiley.

Carlson, E.A., Cicchetti, D., Barnett, D. & Braunwald, K. (1989) 'Disorganized/disoriented attachment relationships in maltreated infants', *Developmental Psychology* 25: 525–31.

Cassidy, J. (1988) 'Child-mother attachment and the self in six-year-olds', *Child Development* 59: 121–34.

Coe, M.T., Daleenberg, C.J., Aransky, K.M. & Reto, C.S. (1995) 'Adult attachment style, reported childhood violence history and types of dissociative experiences', *Dissociation* 8: 142–54.

Cotugno, A. (1997) 'Psicoterapia cognitiva e stati borderline', *Psicobiettivo* 17: 17–34.

Davies, J.M. & Frawley, M.G. (1994) *Treating the Adult Survivor of Childhood Sexual Abuse: A Psychoanalytic Perspective*, New York: Basic Books.

DeWaal, F. (1996) *Goodnatured: The Origins of Right and Wrong in Humans and Other Animals*, Cambridge, MA: Harvard University Press.

Fields, T.M. & Fox, N.A. (1985) *Social Perception in Infants*, Norwood, NJ: Ahler.

Fink, D. & Galinkoff, M. (1990) 'Multiple personality disorder, borderline personality disorder and schizophrenia: A comparative study of clinical features', *Dissociation* 3: 127–34.

Flavell, J.H. (1963) *The Developmental Psychology of Jean Piaget*, New York: Van Nostrand.

Flavell, J.H. (1979) 'Metacognition and cognitive monitoring: A new area of cognitive-developmental inquiry', *American Psychologist* 34: 906–11.

Flavell, J.H., Flavell, E.R. & Green, F.L. (1983) 'Development of the appearance-reality distinction', *Cognitive Psychology* 15: 95–120.

Fonagy, P., Moran, G., Steele, M. & Steele, H. (1992) 'L'integrazione della teoria psicoanalitica e del lavoro sull'attaccamento: La prospettiva intergenerazionale', in M. Ammaniti & D. Stern (eds), *Attaccamento e Psicoanalisi*, (pp. 61–85), Roma: Laterza.

Fonagy, P., Redfern, S. & Charman, A. (1997) 'The relationship between belief–desire reasoning and a projective measure of attachment security', *British Journal of Developmental Psychopathology* 15: 51–63.

Fonagy, P., Steele, M., Steele, H., Leigh, T., Kennedy R., Mattoon, G. & Target, M. (1995) 'Attachment, the reflective self, and borderline states', in S. Goldberg, R. Muir & J. Kerr (eds), *Attachment Theory: Social, Developmental and Clinical Perspectives*, (pp. 233–78), Hillsdale, NJ: Analytic Press.

Fyer, M.R., France, A.J. & Sullivan, T. (1988) 'Comorbidity of borderline personality disorder', *Archives of General Psychiatry* 45: 348–52.

George, C. (1996) 'A representational perspective of child abuse and prevention: Internal working models of attachment and caregiving', *Child Abuse and Neglect* 20: 411–24.

George, C., Kaplan, N. & Main, M. (1985) *The Adult Attachment Interview*, Unpublished manuscript, available at the University of California, Berkeley. (To appear in: *Assessing Attachment through Discourse, Behaviour and Drawing*, M. Main (ed.), Cambridge: Cambridge University Press).

Gilbert, P. (1989) *Human Nature and Suffering*, Hove, UK: Lawrence Erlbaum Associates Ltd.

Gilbert, P. (1992) *Depression: The Evolution of Powerlessness*, Hove, UK: Psychology Press.

Gilbert, P. (1993) 'Defence and safety: Their function in social behaviour and psychopathology', *British Journal of Clinical Psychology* 32: 131–53.

Green, J. Stanley, C., Smith, V. & Goldwyn, R. (1999) *The identification of repesentations of attachment in 5–8 years old children: Validation of a Child Attachment Interview.* Paper presented at the European Science Foundation Workshop, 'Attachment Disorganisation and Psychopathology in Development', 9 September, Leiden, The Netherlands.

Gunderson, J.C. & Sabo, A. (1993a) 'The phenomenological and conceptual interface between borderline personality disorder and post-traumatic stress disorder', *American Journal of Psychiatry* 150: 19–27.

Gunderson, J.C. & Sabo, A. (1993b) 'The treatment of borderline personality disorder: A critical review', in J. Paris (ed.), *Borderline Personality Disorder: Etiology and Treatment*, (pp. 399–419), Washington, DC: American Psychiatric Press.

Hesse, E. & Main, M. (1999) 'Second-generation effects of trauma in non-maltreating parents: Previously unexamined risk factor for anxiety', *Psychoanalytic Inquiry*, 19: 481–540.

Hofer, M.A. (1984) 'Relationships as regulators: A psychobiologic perspective on bereavement', *Psychosomatic Medicine* 46: 183–97

Horevitz, R.P. & Braun, B.G. (1984) 'Are multiple personalities borderline?', *Psychiatric Clinics of North America* 7: 69–87.

Horowitz, M.J. (1986) *Stress Response Syndromes*, (2nd ed.), New York: Aronson.

Jacobsen, T., Edelstein, W. & Hofmann, V. (1994) 'A longitudinal study of the relation between representation of attachment in childhood and cognitive functioning in childhood and adolescence', *Developmental Psychology* 30: 112–24.

Kernberg, O.F. (1975) *Borderline Conditions and Pathological Narcissism*, New York: Jason Aronson.

Kernberg, O.F. (1984) *Severe Personality Disorders: Psychotherapeutic Strategies*, New Haven, CT: Yale University Press.

LeDoux, J. (1996) *The Emotional Brain*, New York: Simon & Schuster.

Lichtenberg, J.D., Lachmann, F. & Fosshage, D. (1992) *Self and Motivational Systems: Toward a Theory of Technique*, Hillsdale, NJ: Analytic Press.

Lichtenberg, J.D., Lachmann, F. & Fosshage, D. (1996) *The Clinical Exchange*, Hillsdale, NJ: Analytic Press.

Linehan, M.M. (1993) *Cognitive–Behavioral Treatment for Borderline Personality Disorder*, New York: Guilford Press.

Liotti, G. (1992) 'Disorganized/disoriented attachment in the etiology of the dissociative disorders', *Dissociation* 5: 196–204.

Liotti, G. (1993) 'Disorganized attachment and dissociative experiences: An illustration of the developmental-ethological approach to cognitive therapy', in K.T. Kuehlvein & H. Rosen (eds), *Cognitive Therapies in Action*, (pp. 213–39), San Francisco: Jossey-Bass.

Liotti, G. (1994) *La Dimensione Interpersonale della Coscienza* [*The Interpersonal Dimension of Consciousness*]. Roma: NIS.

Liotti, G. (1995) 'Disorganized/disoriented attachment in the psychotherapy of the dissociative disorders', in S. Goldberg, R. Muir & J. Kerr (eds), *Attachment Theory: Social, Developmental and Clinical Perspectives*, (pp. 343–63), Hillsdale, NJ: Analytic Press.

Liotti, G. (1999a) 'Disorganization of attachment as a model for understanding dissociative psychopathology', in J. Solomon & C. George (eds), *Attachment Disorganization*, (pp. 291–317), New York: Guilford Press.

Liotti, G. (1999b) 'Understanding the dissociative processes: The contribution of attachment theory', *Psychoanalytic Inquiry*, 19: 757–83.

Liotti, G. & Intreccialagli, B. (1998) 'Metacognition and motivational systems in psychotherapy: A cognitive-evolutionary approach to the treatment of difficult patients', in C. Perris & P. McGorry (eds), *Cognitive Psychotherapy of Psychotic and Personality Disorders*, (pp.333–349), Chichester: Wiley.

Liotti, G., Intreccialagli, B. & Cecere, F. (1991) 'Esperienza di lutto nella madre e predisposizione ai disturbi dissociativi della prole: Uno studio caso-controllo', *Rivista di Psichiatria* 26: 283–91.

Lyons-Ruth, K. (1996) 'Attachment relationships among children with aggressive behavior problems: The role of disorganized early attachment patterns', *Journal of Consulting and Clinical Psychology* 64: 64–73.

Lyons-Ruth, K. & Block, D. (1996) 'The disturbed caregiving system: Relations among childhood trauma, maternal caregiving and infant attachment', *Infant Mental Health Journal* 17: 257–75.

Lyons-Ruth, K., Repacholi, B., McLeod, S. & Silva, E. (1991) 'Disorganized attachment behavior in infancy: Short-term stability, maternal and infant correlates and risk-related subtypes', *Development and Psychopathology* 3: 377–96.

MacLean, P. (1985) 'Brain evolution relating to family, play and the separation call', *Archives of General Psychiatry* 42: 405–17.

Maffei, C. (1998) *Disturbo Borderline di Personalità, Metacognizione ed Autoregolazione*, Articolo presentato al IX Congresso della Società Italiana di Terapia Cognitiva (SITCC), Torino, 13–15 November 1998 [*Borderline Personality Disorder, Metacognition and Emotional Self-Regulation*. Paper read at the IX Conference of the Italian Association for Cognitive Therapy].

Main, M. (1991) 'Metacognitive knowledge, metacognitive monitoring, and singular (coherent) versus multiple (incoherent) models of attachment', in C.M. Parkes, J. Stevenson-Hinde & P. Marris (eds), *Attachment Across the Life Cycle*, (pp. 127–59), London: Routledge.

Main, M. (1995) 'Recent studies in attachment: Overview, with selected implications for clinical work', in S. Goldberg, R. Muir & J. Kerr (eds), *Attachment Theory: Social, Developmental and Clinical Perspectives*, (pp. 407–74), Hillsdale, NJ: Analytic Press.

Main, M. & Hesse, E. (1990) 'Parents' unresolved traumatic experiences are related to infant disorganized attachment status: Is frightened and/or frightening parental behavior the linking mechanism?', in M.T. Greenberg, D. Cicchetti & E.M. Cummings (eds), *Attachment in the Preschool Years*, (pp. 161–82), Chicago: Chicago University Press.

Main, M. & Morgan, H. (1996) 'Disorganization and disorientation in infant Strange Situation behavior: Phenotypic resemblance to dissociative states?', in L. Michelson & W. Ray (eds), *Handbook of Dissociation*, (pp.107–37), New York: Plenum Press.

Main, M. & Solomon, J. (1990) 'Procedures for identifying infants as disorganized/disoriented during the Ainsworth Strange Situation', in M.T. Greenberg, D. Cicchetti & E.M. Cummings (eds), *Attachment in the Preschool Years*, (pp. 121–60), Chicago: Chicago University Press.

Marks, I. (1987) *Fears, Phobias and Rituals: Panic, Anxiety and their Disorders*, Oxford: Oxford University Press.

Marmer, S.S. & Fink, D. (1994) 'Rethinking the comparison of borderline personality disorder and multiple personality disorder', *Psychiatric Clinics of North America* 17: 743–71.

Meins, E. (1997) *Security of Attachment and the Social Development of Cognition*, Hove, UK: Psychology Press.

Migone, P. & Liotti, G. (1998) 'Psychoanalysis and cognitive-evolutionary psychology: An attempt at integration', *International Journal of Psychoanalysis* 79: 1071–95.

O'Connor, M.J., Sigman, M. & Brill, N. (1987) 'Disorganization of attachment in relation to maternal alcohol consumption', *Journal of Consulting and Clinical Psychology* 55: 831–6.

Ogden, T.H. (1982) *Projective Identification and Psychotherapeutic Technique*, New York: Jason Aronson.

Pederson, D., Gleason, K., Moran, G. & Bento, S. (1998) 'Maternal attachment representations, maternal sensitivity, and the infant–mother attachment relationship', *Developmental Psychology* 34: 925–33.

Perry, J.C. & Herman, J.L. (1993) 'Traumas and defences in the etiology of the borderline personality disorder', in J. Paris (ed.), *Borderline Personality Disorder: Etiology and Treatment*, (pp.129–46), Washington, DC: American Psychiatric Press.

Radke-Yarrow, M., McCann, K., De Mulder, E. & Belmont, B. (1995) 'Attachment in the context of high-risk conditions', *Development and Psychopathology* 7: 247–65.

Ross, C. (1989) *Multiple Personality Disorder*, New York: Wiley.

Safran, J.D. & Segal, Z.V. (1990) *Interpersona Process in Cognitive Therapy*, New York: Basic Books.

Schore, A.N. (1994) *Affect Regulation and the Origin of the Self: The Neurobiology of Emotional Development*, Hillsdale, NJ: Lawrence Erlbaum Associates Inc.

Solomon, J. & George, C. (eds) (1999) *Attachment Disorganization*, New York: Guilford Press.

Solomon, J., George, C. & DeJong, A. (1995) 'Children classified as controlling at age six: Evidence of disorganized representational strategies and aggression at home and at school', *Development and Psychopathology* 7: 447–63.

Spiegel, D. (1984) 'Multiple personality as a posttraumatic stress disorder', *Psychiatric Clinics of North America* 7: 101–10.

Trivers, R. (1985) *Social Evolution*, Melano Park, CA: Benjamin/Cummings.

Van IJzendoorn, M.H. (1995) 'Adult attachment representations, parental responsiveness and infant attachment: A meta-analysis on the predictive validity of the Adult Attachment Interview', *Psychological Bulletin* 117: 382–403.

Van IJzendoorn, M.H. (1997) 'Attachment, emergent morality and aggression: Towards a developmental socio-emotional model of antisocial behaviour', *International Journal of Behavioral Development* 21: 703–27.

Ward, M.J. & Carlson, E.A. (1995) 'The predictive validity of the adult attachment interview for adolescent mothers', *Child Development* 66: 69–79.

Wimmer, H. & Penner, J. (1983) 'Beliefs about beliefs: Representations and constraining function of wrong beliefs in young children's understanding of deception', *Cognition* 13: 103–28.

Young, W. (1988) 'Psychodynamics and dissociation: All that switches is not split', *Dissociation* 1: 33–8.

Notes

1   This assertion by no means implies that infants whose attachment behaviour is disorganized are inescapably destined to develop psychiatric disturbances as they grow up. A risk factor in the development of psychological disturbances is not a linear cause of them. Children or adolescents, whose attachment has been disorganized in infancy, may gradually become capable of organizing their attachment behaviour and the corresponding representations, either as a function of their parents' gradual elaboration of traumatic memories, or as a function of other, more positive attachment relationships. Even if the attachment relationship with a caregiver suffering from unresolved traumas persists unmodified throughout childhood and adolescence, other risk factors should usually add up to disorganized attachment if a serious psychiatric disorder (e.g., a dissociative identity disorder or a borderline personality disorder) is to be developed. Risk factors that very likely add up to disorganized attachment in the genesis of most dissociative and borderline disorders are unfavourable temperamental traits (e.g., emotional vulnerability according to Linehan, 1993) and traumatic experiences (incest and other types of abuses within the family: Gunderson & Sabo, 1993a; Perry & Herman, 1993; Spiegel, 1984).

2   The preliminary results of a wide survey of clinical populations, conducted by an Italian Group for the Study of Attachment and Dissociation (under the leadership of Paolo Pasquini, an epidemiologist of the *Istituto Superiore di Sanità*, Italy's National Health Institute) show that patients suffering from personality disorders of the impulsive spectrum, had the early experience of being cared for by a recently bereaved mother more often than other psychiatric patients. The difference is statistically significant (Pasquini, personal communication). A *recently* bereaved mother is very likely suffering from an unresolved mourning process, and her children are therefore more likely than other infants to develop a disorganized attachment (Main & Hesse, 1990; Main & Morgan, 1996).

3   See, on this topic, Young (1988) and Ross' comments to Young's paper (Ross, 1989: 151).

4   Another key theme in Kernberg's theory of borderline pathology is the idea of projective identification. Projective identification combines: (1) projective processes (e.g., on the part of a caregiver, or of an adult patient in psychotherapy), and (2) identification with the projected unconscious mental state (e.g., on the part of an infant, or of the psychotherapist), with (3) a powerful interpersonal pressure on which it is impossible to reflect (Ogden, 1982). Such a scheme fits well the type of relationship between a disorganized child and a frightened/frightening parent during most of their attachment interactions. Parents 'project' into children the fear that a dangerous situation could be repeated because they cannot deal consciously with their unresolved traumatic memories. Children identify with the central emotional theme of the parents' memories, because in their brain the tendency to react with fear to an adult's expressed fear is wired in. The attachment relationship provides the context for the required 'powerful interpersonal pressure', in that the emotions expressed within such a relationship by each party are powerful sign-stimuli, or social releasers, for both parties. Other human relationships in which the inborn systems of attachment and caregiving could be easily activated become the forum for a repetition of this scheme through the mediation of the IWM (Liotti, 1995; Liotti & Intreccialagli, 1998).

5   The improper activation of the agonistic and of the sexual system in the place of the attachment system may be a feature of other personality disorders in the impulsive cluster, such as the antisocial and the histrionic.

6   These problems are manifold. Because of multiple transferences, patients and therapists share the very unpleasant and disheartening experience of disorientation and disorganization within the therapeutic relationship; patients have renewed

contradictory and painful emotions of attachment, that they are unable to modulate; multiple, contradictory and dramatic self-representations pose serious obstacles to the already poor metacognitive capacity, which hinders the understanding of transference interpretations; there is enhanced risk of aggressive or self-aggressive acting out, or else of dropping out of treatment.

12

THE SYNDROME OF REJECTION SENSITIVITY

An evolutionary perspective

Leon Sloman

This chapter focuses on the evolutionary role of attachment strategies and their pivotal role in rejection sensitivity. The chapter also notes how sensitivity to rejection can affect people's concerns about social rank and their tendency to engage in submissive and subordinate behaviours when socially threatened. After describing how rejection sensitivity can be understood in terms of the close relationship between attachment theory and social rank theory, I will explore how an evolutionary model of rejection sensitivity can be used to integrate other explanations based on psychodynamics, family interactions, neurotransmitter changes and genetic factors. Clinical examples demonstrating the central importance of rejection sensitivity to emotional disorders are given and discussed within an evolutionary framework.

Rejection sensitivity

From an evolutionary point of view rejections can be serious. In many species, infants rejected by their mothers not only lose their protection and access to food but also lose an important source of psychobiological regulation (Hofer, 1984). And in later life, many animals who live in groups, rejection due to abnormal behaviours or appearance can result in ostracism and even attacks. For example, when polio swept through the Gombe valley, crippling a number of chimpanzees under study (Goodall, 1990), those deformed were often ignored by the others and eventually died. To a social species such as humans, acceptance and help from others is essential for survival and reproduction (Bowlby, 1969; Gilbert, 1989). Not surprisingly, then, humans have a built-in sensitivity to cues signalling abandonment and rejection, and a menu of response for reducing its probability, e.g., distress calling, minimizing its impact, and reduced activity in the case of despair (Bowlby, 1973).

The concept of rejection sensitivity refers to heightened concerns with rejection and is associated with an exquisitely sensitive fear of real or imagined slights. Feeling rejected means one feels rebuffed, dismissed, spurned, or that one is the object of disapproval. Some individuals are so perceptive that they are able to recognize very subtle cues of rejection. Other individuals can perceive rejection where no rejection exists and greatly magnify the importance of minor rejections. As with all innate potentials there is individual variation in the ease, degree, regularity and chronicity of their arousability.

Donald Klein (1971) introduced the concept of hysteroid dysphoria, characterized by heightened pain in response to loss. He highlighted the physiological under-pinnings by showing that, after being given monoamine oxidase inhibitors (antidepressants), the subjects no longer became dysphoric on loss of admiration, or in response to the kind of rejections that would previously have elicited the dysphoric reaction. Klein subsequently renamed the syndrome 'rejection-sensitive dysphoria'. He saw the pattern of response to loss as a critical factor in shaping personality, self-image, habitual behaviour and symptom complexes. Peter Kramer (1993) subsequently broadened the concept of rejection sensitivity to include those who seek attention through seductive behaviour, who feed applause addiction by competitive behaviour and those who react to negative feedback by social avoidance and diminished self-worth. Kramer provided anecdotal accounts of the efficacy of a new class of antidepressants, namely, selective serotonin re-uptake inhibitors (SSRIs) in treating rejection sensitivity, but also acknowledged the role that psychotherapy can play in some of these patients.

Rejection sensitivity, fear of disapproval, being marginalized, ignored, loss of emotional support and abandonment have been linked to a variety of emotional disorders for many years reaching back to the pioneering work of Bowlby (1969) and Harlow (e.g. see Harlow & Mears, 1979). For example, Beck (1983) delineated a type of vulnerability to depression called sociotropy which is marked by fears of disapproval and separation from loved ones. Blatt *et al.* (1982) and Zuroff and Mongrain (1987) used the term anaclitic when describing a similar vulnerability to excessive dependency, fear of interpersonal loss and rejection. Within our current nosology, rejection sensitivity is particularly associated with borderline personality disorder and atypical depression (DSM-IV, American Psychiatric Association, 1994).

Downey and Feldman (1996) found that people who were high in rejection sensitivity felt rejected following experimentally manipulated ambiguous rejection feedback from a new acquaintance. When exposed to the same feedback, people who were not rejection sensitive did not feel rejected. The researchers also found, using another group, that people who enter relationships disposed to anxiously expect rejection, more readily perceived rejection in their romantic partner's insensitive behaviour. Rejection-sensitive people exaggerated their partner's dissatisfaction and lack of commitment to the relationship. Rejection-sensitive men were jealous and suspicious and sought to control their partner's contact with others. Rejection-sensitive women tended to blame their partners unjustly and were hostile and unsupportive towards them, which paradoxically would increase the chances of rejection.

Downey, Freitas, Michaelis and Khori (1998) tested the hypothesis of a self-fulfilling prophecy whereby those with rejection sensitivity behaved in ways that elicited rejection from their dating partners. Results showed that high rejection-sensitive people's relationships tended to break up more frequently than those of low rejection-sensitive people. Further, high rejection-sensitive women behaved more negatively than low rejection-sensitive women during conflictual discussions. This helps explain why high rejection-sensitive women's partners were more rejecting than low rejection-sensitive women's partners following naturally occurring relationship conflicts. These findings lead to the paradoxical conclusion that women, who are more sensitive to rejection, are due to their behaviour more likely to provoke rejection by their dating partners.

The Involuntary Defeat Strategy (IDS)

Rejection is not the only threat that group living animals have to confront. Another is day-to-day conflicts over resources (such as food, nesting sites, and mates). In these contexts, animals need to avoid getting into costly fights and be prepared rapidly to submit in situations of attack from conspecifics. In extreme cases, social defeats and states of inhibition induced by losing conflicts have also been linked to depression. Price (1967: 244) was one of the first to suggest that 'states of depression, anxiety and irritability are the emotional concomitants of behaviour patterns which are necessary for the maintenance of dominance hierarchies in social groups. A dominance hierarchy is necessary in a social group if aggressive animals are to live together without fighting each other'. Price claimed that states of depression, anxiety and irritability 'arose during the course of our evolution as adaptive mechanisms – mechanisms which, in all probability, are no longer of any advantage in modern social conditions'.

The key idea of Price's theory is that mechanisms that underpin human depression evolved from the strategic importance of having de-escalating or losing strategies. These strategies have an important signal function to self and others. To self, it reduces social confidence and inhibits challenging or acquisitive behaviour, and to others it sends signals that lead potential attackers to de-escalate their attacks (Gilbert & Allan, 1998).

Price (1969) subsequently labelled the reaction to agonistic defeat 'the yielding subroutine of ritual agonistic behaviour' and Price and Sloman (1987) distinguished between voluntary yielding, which refers to conscious rational submission that is a function of the forebrain, and the yielding subroutine – a more primitive mechanism for yielding that may be automatically triggered when losing an agonistic encounter. These evolved defensive mechanisms are also present in other vertebrates. They proposed that the 'hardware' for this primitive mechanism is situated in the reptilian brain. This conclusion was derived from the work of MacLean (1985) who noted changes in the physical state of reptiles associated with

259

changes in the status hierarchy. For example, reptiles that had lost rank lost their bright colours and died shortly thereafter. According to Levitan, Hasey and Sloman (2000), the IDS can be thought of as a preprogrammed neural circuit linking the limbic system, prefrontal cortex and striatum, which mediate, respectively, the emotional, cognitive and behavioural components of the IDS. Levitan, Hasey and Sloman (2000) discuss how abnormal serotonergic activity may contribute to a persistent IDS and depression, and this condition may be compounded by the depressed state via lowered social rank. Price *et al.* (1994) in their presentation of the social competition model of depression call the yielding subroutine the 'Involuntary Subordinate Strategy' and currently Sloman (in press) has in the interest of clarity renamed it the 'Involuntary Defeat Strategy' (IDS). Gilbert has labelled this model 'social ranking theory' (Gilbert, 1992; Gilbert & Allan, 1994).

Success in the struggle for status or power is associated with feelings of pride and euphoria (Weisfeld & Wendorf, 2000), which encourages more vigorous competition. Mazur and Booth (1998) explain this biologically, when they propose that high or rising testosterone, by encouraging dominant behaviour, induces men to compete for high status. The experience of winning or successfully defending high rank boosts testosterone, which in turn encourages more dominant behaviour. This reciprocal model implies feedback between testosterone and dominance, each reinforcing the other. This represents a positive feedback cycle whereby success leads to more success. This is the converse of the IDS which is part of a cycle in which failure triggers discouragement (the IDS) which can lead to more failure.

The IDS in action

The IDS is a core concept of social rank theory. Individuals, who are engaged in competitive struggles, react differently according to whether their fortunes are waxing or waning. For example, when I make a poor shot in tennis, I feel bad, but when I am hitting the ball well and winning against a skilled opponent, I feel good. During the average game, my feelings oscillate between the two, but, if I am making many mistakes and losing, I may become so discouraged and frustrated that my game deteriorates further. This illustrates how, after frequent triggering, the IDS becomes more persistent. An alternative possibility, after my IDS has been triggered a number of times, is my acceptance that my opponent is a better player which allows me to enjoy the opportunity of improving my game. In this case, my acceptance of subordinate status leads to a switching off of my IDS which, in turn, allows me to enjoy the rest of the game.

The individual's first reaction, when the tide turns against him or her, may be increased aggressiveness that is associated with a greater determination to win (Klinger, 1977). However, as the inevitability of defeat looms larger, aggressiveness may be replaced by feelings of discouragement, hopelessness and inadequacy. In many instances this pattern could be attributable to the IDS. The IDS has the function of triggering flight, or submission and, if the initial resentment was not too strong, psychological acceptance of the loss follows. The IDS may manifest as discouragement and helplessness, which serves to terminate the competitive encounter. Acceptance of loss, or successful escape, or the decision to retaliate and fight on, all lead to the IDS being terminated and this frees the individual to move on to other, perhaps more productive, activities.

The term 'involuntary' indicates the IDS is automatically triggered and, therefore, not under conscious control, although it may be modified by cognitive factors that lead an individual to accept 'defeat' without it being seen as a serious loss of status or indicating a major personal inadequacy. The term 'defeat' indicates that the IDS is normally triggered by loss or failure, and the term 'strategy' indicates that it is a genetically based pattern of response. The IDS assists the individual to adopt subordinate status. One intriguing aspect of Price's formulation was his demonstration that negative feelings could have the important adaptive function of regulating conflict and reducing the risk of unnecessary injury or death.

Price saw depression as one component of the IDS and shame is another (Gilbert & McGuire, 1998). Human groups rank members by attractiveness and the presence of supportive relationships. As Gilbert and McGuire (1998) note, shame 'is an involuntary response to an awareness that one's attractiveness is under threat. In such contexts of demotion in the eyes of others, all the inclusive fitness benefits of having high(ish) ranking friends and lovers and having access to resources can be damaged too'. Gilbert and McGuire say that shame alerts people to the fact that certain social signals they send will elicit a negative response from others so that sending these inappropriate signals is likely to lead to loss of status. The shame effect can be seen as 'an involuntary submissive response, typically triggered by social threat, the function of which is to de-escalate conflict' (Gilbert & McGuire, 1998). This suggests that shame may be a conspicuous feature of the IDS triggered by failure in competition to be more attractive and have affiliative relationships and is less evident in the IDS triggered by failure in agonic competition. Thus the nature of the IDS varies depending on the situation.

An effective IDS is flexible in that it is appropriately triggered and readily terminated. An ineffective IDS may be automatically and, perhaps prematurely, triggered in any potentially competitive encounter, even with a weaker opponent. When the IDS is ineffective, the conflict is generally not resolved so that the IDS is not deactivated and remains overly persistent. This may result in the individual feeling at a disadvantage – even when there is no need. He may then overcompensate by an involvement in unproductive power struggles or become overly submissive. If the IDS is ineffective in terminating the conflict and becomes overly persistent, it may manifest as psychopathology. The main differences between effective and ineffective functioning of the IDS are listed in Table 12.1. Although Allan and Gilbert (1997) claim that theorizing on the nature, functions, biologies and psychopathologies has raced ahead of measurement, their own preliminary findings suggest that submissive behaviours and passive/withdrawal are associated with depression and other psychopathologies.

Table 12.1 Difference between effective and ineffective functioning of the IDS

Effective functioning

Flexible. Generally of short duration. Appropriately triggered (i.e., defeat is inevitable or very likely)

Associated with
1   secure attachment
2   good social skills
3   high self-esteem
4   ability to respond to new challenges

Ineffective functioning

Rigid (often persistent). Prematurely triggered or delayed (may be triggered when the opponent is weaker or not triggered when the opponent is clearly more powerful)

Associated with
1   insecure attachment
2   low self-esteem
3   unproductive power struggles often characterized by put-downs
4   rejection sensitivity
5   strong feelings of frustration, hostility and depression

Competing to be valued and wanted

Humans compete in many different domains, and rarely these days (outside of prison and street gangs) on the basis of physical strength and aggressiveness. These competitions take many forms. For example, we compete sexually, to be selected for a job, to get onto a sports team, and even to be valued as a friend. We seek to be held in high regard rather than low regard – to be seen as worthy, able and attractive rather than as unworthy, unable and unattractive. What one competes for affects the strength of reactions to defeat. This leads to the question of why some people cannot tolerate being judged less adequate than others in some domain. Envy, rage and depression are often related to the perception that one is judged inferior to others. Our anger is a protest against negative judgements from others, while our depression triggers painful resignation.

If the maintenance of a high social attractiveness is considered a main priority, any fall in social attractiveness is perceived as a loss of status. When the individual feels rejected, this is likely to be experienced as a loss of status. This might partly account for why there is an inextricable link in people with rejection sensitivity between attachment disruptions and loss of social status. For them, being unlovable is equivalent to being of low rank in the social ranking system based on attractiveness (see also Hilburn-Cobb, in press; Gilbert & McGuire, 1998).

Other competitions revolve around goals, aims, wants and desires within relationships. You want to have a quiet weekend, but your family wants to take a trip. You want sex, but your partner does not, or you want to play football, but your partner wants you to help paint the house. These competitions relate to getting your way, or giving in, or compromising over everyday issues.

Competitions and conflicts of interest are everyday occurrences and we need to learn to be able to live comfortably with others more talented than ourselves and to be able to both compromise and be assertive. Some are able to navigate these domains without feeling overwhelmed by depression, anxiety or anger. Others, however, are prone to more serious feelings of defeat, frustration and anger – that is, they are prone to frequent and excessive triggering of the IDS. Some of the reasons for this variation of response are considered later in this chapter under the heading of biological and experiential factors.

Different practitioners approach the patient suffering from depression from radically different perspectives. Some focus on the biochemical and neurotransmitter changes and how these can be normalized by the use of psychopharmacological agents. Those with a psychological perspective view the low self-esteem as a product of earlier unresolved conflicts, traumas and frustrations and seek to resolve conflicts, or modify negative basic assumptions by changing cognitions. Therapists, trained in family therapy, focus on the communicative function of the patient's feelings of helplessness, hopelessness and low self-esteem. They endeavour to improve communication between family members, to promote secure attachments between family members and to establish a more functional family hierarchy.

The evolutionary approach adds a useful new dimension to the clinical inquiry by examining how the changes associated with depressive mood might be derived from earlier evolved mechanisms (i.e., submissive behaviour) that at one time helped raise inclusive fitness or at least had minimized deleterious effects on it. This is a major advance, because it shows how the processes highlighted by the biological, psychological and communicative approaches act in unison to serve a common function. From an evolutionary perspective, low self-esteem, feelings of helplessness and hopelessness, psychomotor retardation, neurotransmitter changes and submissive demeanour are all possible manifestations of the IDS.

Relation between social competition and attachment theories

I suggest that both the defensive behaviours that mediate submissiveness in situations of conflict, and attachment strategies, which mediate seeking and avoiding loss of interpersonal bonds, play a pivotal role in rejection sensitivity. Whereas attachment theory covers strategies that maintain proximity between individuals, social rank theory deals mainly with the regulation of conflict. However, since most everyday risks to disruption of interpersonal ties are the result of conflict, I shall argue that the fear of rejection also activates defensive responses related to conflicts – that is involuntary defeat strategies and submissive behaviour.

Attachment theory and social hierarchy theory both have their roots in ethology. Superficially the models appear separate and distinct, but closer examination reveals a reciprocal relationship between a secure attachment and effective dominance–submission mechanisms (Hilburn-Cobb, 1998). In fact, the functioning of the social ranking and attachment systems seem so interconnected that they could be said to generally function synchronously.

The clue from attachment theory suggests that the inner models of the self and relationships, built up in childhood, enable us to accept that some people are superior to us in various domains and help us to handle everyday conflicts of interest. Those with poor attachment relationships have two problems. First, they require constant signals that they are desired, wanted and attractive, and fear being seen as unattractive and not able to call on others for support. Second, they see attachment as something that must be earned – in competition; a need to prove their worth. They may feel that there are others who might be viewed as more attractive and to whom potential lovers/helpers might defect. Their inner models of attachment are organized around dimensions of power, control and competitiveness. For example, anxious attachment is associated with unfavourable social comparisons and excessive concern with approval (Gilbert, Allan & Trent, 1995). Those who are anxiously attached start off with the feeling that their attractive/desirability rating in the market-place is low. Narcissists on the other hand will make bids to improve their social attractiveness rating, by grandiose appeals and display, and to constantly inflate their perceived rank (in terms of attractiveness or sense of entitlement) in the eyes of others. The narcissists' rage is related to their attempts to coerce others who do not comply with their demands or accept their inflated self-representations.

Securely attached people are likely to have an effectively functioning IDS (Sloman, 2000). As a result they are better able to establish meaningful relationships and deal with conflict and, therefore, are better equipped to enter the world of competition without needing to set their sights too low because of feelings of inadequacy, or to try to compensate by setting goals that are unrealistically high.

The IDS is associated with feelings of helplessness and inadequacy and this is generally accompanied by feeling unloved and unlovable. One reason is that the individual's own competitiveness and the rage and frustration associated with losing and not having his or her needs met will likely be subjectively perceived as negative qualities by self and others. Losing is also interpreted by the loser as evidence of his or her own inadequacy. In addition the IDS reinforces negative feelings about the self as well as the belief that others have negative thoughts about him or her – characteristic features of the depressed individual. All these feelings could contribute to the individual concluding that others do not like him or her and that he or she is unlovable. In general rising rank will increase the individual's social attractiveness, while falling rank, which is generally associated with a triggering of the IDS, has the reverse effect (Weisfeld & Wendorf, 2000). Those with rejection sensitivity already feel unlovable and the frequent triggering of their IDSs would tend to make them feel even more unlovable.

The ambivalent type of insecure attachment is associated with a constant need for reassurance that one is loved so that a failure to receive the reassurance one seeks triggers feelings of rejection. For these reasons, those with an ambivalent insecure attachment are particularly prone to develop rejection sensitivity. The initial feeling is often one of rage or anger, but this cannot be expressed, because of the fear that direct expression would only intensify the initial rejection (Hilburn-Cobb, 1998). The other person's power to reject leads to the perception that the other person is more powerful than oneself so that one's anger leads one into a struggle one will inevitably lose, which therefore leads to a triggering of the IDS.

When the individual, who is securely attached, loses a competitive encounter, he or she is more likely to obtain emotional support and more able to make productive use of such support. This lowers levels of arousal and facilitates de-escalation, which leads to rapid acceptance of loss and submission (Hilburn-Cobb, 1994). The securely attached individual is, therefore, less likely to experience rejection sensitivity. According to this integrated model, any progress that the client makes in terms of achieving a more secure attachment will, in turn, promote a more effective functioning of both dominant and subordinate mechanisms. Furthermore, progress in learning to avoid premature or inappropriate triggering of subordinate mechanisms (i.e., constructive self-assertion) enables the client to develop more affiliative relationships with others.

When the IDS has been triggered in a competitive encounter with someone towards whom one is insecurely attached, the nature of the relationship will often make it harder for the person to accept defeat so that the IDS becomes overly persistent. This often manifests as oversubmissiveness which has been shown by Allan and Gilbert (1997) to be associated with increased vulnerability to various forms of psychopathology. It may also contribute to unproductive power struggles that can also lead to psychopathology (Sloman, 1981).

Troy and Sroufe (1987) have shown that an insecure attachment is likely to lead to either victim or victimizing behaviour and that securely attached children were not likely to become either victims or bullies. This supports the proposition that there is a close relationship between form of attachment and effectiveness of dominant subordinate mechanisms.

When an activation of the attachment system fails to down-regulate negative affect, the subordinate system may be activated and may manifest as a dramatic display of helplessness and hopelessness designed to enlist support by playing on the other person's sympathies. The IDS is an integral part of this helpless response so that, if this becomes a habitual way of relating for that individual, his or her IDS will be easily triggered. This may then manifest as rejection sensitivity. Such individuals tend to be easily aroused to anger or resentment and an activation of the IDS fails to terminate the conflict leaving the individual with the feeling that he or she is engaged in a futile struggle. These individuals exhibit a persistent IDS which may manifest as chronic low self-esteem. Their sensitivity to criticism and rejection makes them prone to react with anger to real or imagined slights. This anger can then trigger an escalation of the IDS which creates a self-perpetuating vicious cycle that manifests as depression or other psychopathological conditions. Ehlers, Maercker, and Boos (2000: 51) showed that 'consistent with previous data on sexual and physical assault' the 'experience of "mental defeat" during political imprisonment clearly distinguished between survivors with and without post-traumatic stress disorder and correlated with PTSD severity'. Their description of 'mental defeat' corresponds closely to our concept of the IDS. These findings suggest that excessive stimulation of the IDS is likely to impair the functioning of the attachment system in the down-regulation of negative affect.

The role of biological factors

Biological factors play an important role in contributing to rejection sensitivity. Kagan and Snidman (1991) have shown that some infants are born with raised reactivity of their stress-hormone systems and are more sensitive than others to separation from their mothers.These infants exhibit a greater variability of their heart rates in stress situations. Behavioural inhibition is a behavioural syndrome, identifiable at an early age, characterized by shyness, avoidance, uneasiness, fear of unfamiliar situations, people, objects and events (Garcia-Coll, Kagan & Reznick, 1984). Available data indicate that it is not immutable but is governed to some extent by environmental factors (Turner, Beidel & Wolff, 1996).Current data also suggest that there is a limited relationship between behavioural inhibition and maladaptive social anxiety. Those infants who have a highly reactive stress hormone system or a high degree of behavioural inhibition are probably more vulnerable to the stressors that lead to rejection sensitivity.

The role of experiential factors

Downey, Khouri and Feldman (1997) found that childhood exposure to family violence and rejection was associated with a heightened sensitivity to rejection. Downey and Feldman (1996: 1328) have drawn on interpersonal theories of personality and in particular attachment theory 'to propose that early rejection experiences leave a psychological legacy that emerges in the disposition to be sensitive to rejection by significant others'.

I have already discussed how an insecure attachment can contribute to rejection sensitivity. Sometimes parents interact with their child as if they are in a competitive struggle. Parents, who feel very insecure in their parenting role, may misinterpret their child's behaviour as disrespect or a put-down and may try to assert control by coercion, intimidation and threat. They operate on the premise that, if they can instill fear and submission in their child, the child will be better behaved. One of the techniques they may use is shaming by calling the child 'stupid' or 'bad'. This locates the child as very low status in terms of his competency or attractiveness. In this case, the child's subordinate strategies are triggered in the context of an insecure parent–child relationship. The same will hold true for physical or sexual abuse within the context of the parent–child relationship. All forms of abuse are, by definition, forms of power distinctions where the abused is forced into a subordinate – controlled – position by the abuser. The case of Hillary, later, illustrates how this scenario can be replayed in the therapeutic relationship. As the relationship between the patient and therapist is strengthened, the IDS is activated and this may lead to a flight from therapy. In other words, as the patient comes closer to the therapist – who is seen as dominant, more powerful, the defensive behaviour of 'flight from a potentially abusing dominant' is triggered. Thus a variety of experiences can lead to premature triggering of the IDS and to rejection sensitivity. With regards to precipitating factors, the dysphoria in rejection sensitivity may be elicited by real or imagined put-downs or loss of affection.

Excessive shaming can be both a predisposing and precipitating factor. Shame often involves a rumination on the negative aspects of the self. It acts as an alerting mechanism to those aspects of the self that should stay hidden from others and those aspects of the self that one would like to get rid of (Gilbert, 1997: 121). The central function of shame is to alert the self to actual or possible losses of social attractiveness and prime submissive strategies which include desires to escape, hide, conceal or signal to others that one is submitting and not fighting back. Excessive shaming can contribute to submissiveness (constant triggering of the IDS) and to delinquent behaviour and may lead to rejection sensitivity.

Rejection sensitivity can be maladaptive in a number of ways. It can lead to pointless bickering, to power struggles, to social isolation, or to depression. However, although the premature triggering of the IDS is maladaptive now, it may have once been adaptive. For example, it may be adaptive for a small child with a very punitive or authoritarian parent to avoid the risks of confrontation by submitting quickly. However, the pattern that was once adaptive is no longer adaptive in adulthood. Moving from ontogenetic to phylogenetic adaptation (because most of man's evolution occurred in the hunter–gatherer phase) it may well be that the IDS played a more crucial role in prehistoric times than today. Because a lot of competition has become ritualized, as in sporting events, the IDS may be less important than it once was.

The child who has constantly had to submit in the face of overpowering threats from a parent is unable to develop the skill of knowing when to submit and when to be assertive, which is crucial to becoming a successful negotiator in conflicts with parents and others. It is also relevant to the development of skill in emotional regulation in conflict situations. The insecurely attached child is likely to think only in terms of winning or losing and constantly feels the threat of aggression, withdrawal of love or even abandonment. By contrast, secure families reconcile quickly and easily (Sloman, 1981).

Psychotherapeutic implications

One can draw a parallel between the IDS and anxiety in that both can be adaptive, but can in excess become maladaptive. Therefore, one aim may be to reduce the client's anxiety and another may be to teach the client how to avoid triggering the IDS or learn how to switch it off.

The focus here will be on rejection sensitivity, but the principles have a broader application. If the therapist has concluded that the IDS plays an important role in case formulation, one can highlight the biological nature of the IDS, its evolutionary function and its phenomenology. The therapist can illustrate the adaptive function of feelings of helplessness in bringing the individual's own aggressiveness under control and communicating 'no threat' to the adversary. Attributing the client's sensitivity to rejection or depression to a biological adaptive strategy helps to normalize the symptoms.

Another strategy is to incorporate one's understanding of the adaptive function of the behaviour by the use of 'positive reframing' (Minuchin & Fishman, 1981). That is, one attributes a positive function to negative symptoms. For example, I inform a family member that self-sacrifice is their way of avoiding hurting or getting angry with another family member. Individuals will often respond that they do not want to be self-sacrificing, which gives me the chance to say, if they want to change their way of responding, this is something we can work on. One of my aims is to demonstrate how the IDS is being triggered in situations where clients might well be able to stand their ground. One may then help clients recognize that their IDS is being triggered by out-of-date assumptions. At times, one may assist clients to withdraw from an arena where there is little prospect of success by enabling them to recognize that their goals are unrealistic, or they need to move on.

When the individual's IDS has been prematurely triggered on a regular basis for many years, progress in psychotherapy is likely to be slow. The effectiveness of antidepressants in both depressive illness and rejection sensitivity might be attributable to their inhibitory effect on the IDS (Levitan, Hasey & Sloman, 2000). Pharmacotherapy and psychotherapy could both be directed towards avoiding a triggering of the IDS so that each could have a facilitating effect on the other.

Premature triggering of the IDS does not always lead to rejection sensitivity; it may also manifest as submissive personality or as dysthymic disorder. One determining factor is that those with rejection sensitivity feel that they have been unjustly treated and then react with anger. Those with dysthymic disorder or submissive personality feel that they do not deserve any better treatment than what they already receive. However, there is often an overlap between these syndromes.

It can be difficult, at times, to differentiate between 'true self-assertion' and those who overcompensate for their IDS by trying to prove that they are not inferior or inadequate. In this case the therapist needs to assist clients to distinguish between 'true' and 'false' self-assertion by enabling those with the false impression that they are asserting themselves to recognize that they are overcompensating. A key aspect of false self-assertion is the sense of revenge and injustice and personal slight, 'how could they do that to me?' and this leads to a desire for revenge, possibly accompanied by an attitude of contempt which is expressed verbally or nonverbally. In true self-assertion, one wants to get one's own way without seeing the other as being unfair, and there is an attitude of respect towards the other.

In order to clarify this distinction, I sometimes tell my clients the story of the film called *Mr Baseball*. The story deals with an American major league baseball player, who in the twilight of his career is traded to a Japanese baseball team which required a move to Japan. The team assigns an attractive young Japanese woman to him as translator/cultural facilitator. Reflecting on how many aging athletes must feel in the twilight of their career, he confesses, 'Don't miss, don't miss, my whole life I'm trying to hit the ball, but now I'm saying, don't miss'. The one-time fast learner and confident achiever was now racked with self-doubt. After he indulges in this, for him, rare moment of self-revelation, the Japanese translator responds sympathetically and supportively, 'You will hit the ball, accept: I will hit, I will hit, I will hit'.

The Case of Sam

This vignette was given to me by Sam, a 53-year-old single male who was suffering from rejection sensitivity and dysthymic disorder. He had been a good baseball player as a youth and was now twice divorced. He was working on how to avoid triggering his own IDS. He said that this film struck a resonant chord in him. Prior to seeing the film, he had developed a good deal of insight into the relation between his depression and subordinate strategies, but concluded, 'in therapy if the learning cannot be applied for the sake of creating positive changes in your life, you run the risk of becoming the most insightful depressive in the universe'. He desperately wanted to 'hit the ball', 'to live life and my biggest challenge would be finding the way to actualize this wish'. When I had spoken about self-assertion geared to avoid triggering the IDS, he had understood what was meant intellectually but, when he saw the movie, these concepts really resonated. This vignette illustrates how a dramatic presentation can complement the effect of an intellectual explanation. It also highlights how focusing on winning can be a means of avoiding triggering the IDS. However, recognizing that one's chance of success is slim enables one to avoid competitive encounters, where defeat is almost inevitable. Thus, it is important objectively to evaluate the likelihood of success, before confronting an adversary.

After relating this story, I sometimes ask my clients what they would be able to say to themselves equivalent to, 'I am going to hit the ball'. This is sometimes quite productive. A wife, who was in couples therapy, had been summoned to an interview and was expecting to be hauled over the coals by a boss who was rude and disrespectful of employees. We discussed what would be the most helpful thing to say to herself on the way to the interview. After some discussion, she decided it would be helpful to say, 'the following people are rooting for me' (the list included both her husband and the therapist). Keeping her supporters in mind enabled her to deal more effectively with her adversary. This indicates how the knowledge that one has support behind one is reassuring when engaging in an adversarial encounter. For this reason, the presence of secure attachments helps avoid premature triggering of the IDS.

In order to make the concept of the IDS more meaningful, I often refer to it as the 'shivering response', a term coined by John Price who noted that both the IDS and the 'shivering response' are automatically triggered and both have an adaptive function. One can avoid shivering by dressing warmly, or turning up the central heating. One can learn how to avoid triggering the IDS, but it can be a slow process.

In order to help clients learn to avoid the premature triggering of the IDS, I often relate the story of Mr Baseball and go on to discuss what one could say to oneself to help 'hit the ball' – to avoid triggering the IDS. In couples sessions, the partner can contribute suggestions.

The Case of Rosemary

Rosemary was a highly intelligent and attractive woman in her mid twenties with a history of sexual abuse as a child. She suffered from periodic bouts of depression. Being the youngest of five siblings, she played the child role in the family. She said, 'My mother criticizes me for not taking any responsibility. She makes me feel like a little kid. I feel, if I do what she tells me, I have lost the battle. Whenever she says something, I feel so small because I feel that she has more power than I. I would like to be grown up enough not to be easily threatened by my mother.' She later said, 'I don't want to discuss my anger with my mother, because if I tell her how I feel, she cries and says "Why are you being so nasty to me?" She makes me feel terrible.' Rosemary often stayed away from school, which prevented her from getting through high school. However, she had developed a great talent for coming up with plausible excuses for not showing up.

Although she was inclined to relate in a child role to others, she also felt uncomfortable due to giving others power over her. Relating to men was particularly threatening, because it reminded her of how she had been abused sexually and being seductive towards men was her way of coping with this anxiety. Rosemary's use of 'coy' behaviour and difficulty in asserting herself probably made it more difficult to protect herself from sexual abuse. This in turn compounded her problems in self-assertion. In physiological terms, her IDS had been kindled at an early age, and any new encounter with an authority figure would trigger her IDS which reinforced her feeling of incompetence. Because she felt sufficiently secure with her fiancé, she would try to alleviate this discomfort by provoking fights which led to an escalating cycle of rage and frustration accompanied by an overly persistent IDS. This would frequently culminate in depression.

Because Rosemary was insecurely attached, she was unable to self-soothe via her attachment system so she turned to the subordinate strategy for self-regulation by using it to elicit support from others. However, because the subordination strategy evoked shame (Hilburn-Cobb *et al.*, submitted, Weisfeld & Wendorf, 2000) Rosemary felt uncomfortable about turning to others for support, which made it hard for this form of self-regulation to succeed. This would also account for her initial resistance to therapy. This was an unconscious process rather than a conscious manipulative act. Children, who are insecurely attached, may use 'coy' behaviour to disarm parental anger and turn it into nurturance (Crittenden, 1997: 56). Crittenden says that coy behaviour is morphologically very similar to flirtatious behaviour and may make the child more susceptible to being sexually abused. This coy behaviour has its roots in both submission (as it is a form of subordination) and dominance (as it is a form of control). The child continues to display angry threats until the parent responds. If the parent's response is appeasing, the display of anger usually escalates. If the parents' response is angry, the child switches to coy behaviour. The parent then melts and the child is likely to act weak and incompetent until the parent becomes exasperated at which point the child switches to anger. The parent placates the child who then demands more. When initially seen, Rosemary displayed this coy behaviour and expressed anger by coming late or failing to show for appointments, but this coy behaviour gradually lessened as her attendance improved.

In therapy, Rosemary's insight and ability to grasp new concepts were very appealing, but her therapist found her constant lateness and frequent missed appointments frustrating. She informed the therapist that she had to hide her insecurities from him because, if she showed her weakness, he would be more powerful than her, and would become arrogant like her stepfather who had sexually abused her. When she suggested that the therapist must be angry because of her slow progress, he responded by suggesting that perhaps she was feeling frustrated with him for the slow progress she had made. She agreed and as she developed sufficient trust in the therapist she became better able to challenge and express frustration with him. The task of helping her to learn how to avoid 'shivering' (i.e., avoid triggering the IDS) played a key role in therapy. The therapist gave her the therapeutic assignment of thinking about what she could say to herself that would enable her to avoid shivering. Not long after, she related how she had been dreading calling up an employer to explain why she had been absent from work, but then began to say to herself, 'I am as powerful as she is' and after saying this a few times, she was able to call this person and offer an explanation. One might say that she had developed a successful way of switching off her IDS.

One hurdle in therapy was her use of the subordinate mechanism to solicit support. Once able to acknowledge the inappropriateness of this manner of approach, she began to explore a more adult way of relating to others. This entailed becoming more open and direct and also more assertive. At the same time she became less coy and flirtatious and more able to take responsibility and be more trusting of the therapist. When last seen, her depression had cleared and she said she no longer saw the therapist as a more powerful figure whose chair loomed over her's – she saw her chair as being just as high as the therapist's.

The Case of Hillary

At times, one may find oneself in a competitive struggle with a patient so that it becomes difficult to say anything without feeding into the struggle. For example, Hillary, a 40-year-old women, said, 'I am in a middle of a fight with you, but I really don't know what the fight is about – about me or about you. You are trying to convince me that my voice/opinion matters, but I believe that you don't really mean this – your behaviour shows, the structure that you are part of shows that you are the authority so I can't allow you to win. I will tie my mind and integrity in knots trying to defeat you and what I experience is incredible frustration.' This client had written me a note saying that she had very warm feelings towards me that she had never verbalized. It appeared that fighting with me was a defence against allowing herself to express her wish for closeness. Because of previous experiences of abuse by men, it was very difficult for her to trust any man. Her relationships with women were by contrast fairly stable.

In terms of the IDS, it appeared that her previous experiences had left her with a fear of intimacy and her adversarial relationship with men was a form of self-protection. However, when she challenged a man, she felt at a disadvantage so that her IDS was quickly triggered. This left her feeling even more inadequate and her usual response was to break off the relationship, as a result of her IDS triggering avoidant flight behaviour. In the therapeutic relationship, she defended against the shame associated with the IDS by challenging the therapist. The task of the therapist was to win her trust before her avoidant flight behaviour was triggered.

Conclusion

The evolutionary approach enables us to formulate both healthy functioning and certain types of psychopathology in terms of the effective functioning of biological strategies. Ineffective functioning is exemplified by insecure attachment and an overly persistent IDS and when one of these strategies is ineffective it tends to render the other strategy ineffective as well.

More work needs to be done to define the IDS more precisely and new techniques of intervention are required to facilitate more flexible and efficient functioning of the IDS which would enable clients to avoid confrontations or submit quickly when it became apparent that there was no hope of victory. Alternatively, the ability to fight or disagree, without triggering the IDS, enables one to enjoy certain confrontations so that they do not become negative experiences. It is normal to enjoy winning games and sporting encounters and normal to feel bad about losing. However, the tendency to over-react to winning or losing may reflect a poor 'sense of self' (Kohut & Wolfe, 1978). The more angry the individual, the more likely he is to see the interaction as adversarial. If he sees the interaction as adversarial, his IDS may, because of previous experience, be quickly triggered and, the more angry he is, the more powerful the IDS required. As described above, the IDS and anger can reinforce each other and this can culminate in depressive illness. We must find the best ways to resolve this negative cycle and avoid a premature triggering of the IDS. This would be relevant in the treatment of rejection sensitivity.

Finally, we need to recognize that a variety of treatment modalities such as psychotherapy, pharmacotherapy and perhaps physical education may all in different ways end up having a similar effect. For example, all may contribute to enabling the individual to become more self-assertive. Because evolutionary psychotherapy is a new field, there is still a need to develop more of a consensus about the evolutionary model and intervention techniques. This book should go some way towards the development of this badly needed consensus. A belief in evolutionary principles does not preclude the use of other models such as psycho-analysis or cognitive therapy model (Gilbert, Chapter 6, and Kriegman, Chapter 4, this volume). However, the evolutionary model can enrich other models (Swallow, 2000). The social competition model provides a useful paradigm for enabling clients to become more self-assertive.

References

Allan, S. & Gilbert, P. (1997) 'Submissive behaviour and psychopathology', *British Journal of Clinical Psychology* 36: 467–88.

American Psychiatric Association (1994) *Diagnostic and Statistical Manual of Mental Disorders*; DSM IV, Washington, DC: American Psychiatric Association.

Beck, A.T. (1983) 'Cognitive therapy of depression; new perspectives', in P.J. Clayton & J.E. Barrett (eds), *Treatment of Depression: Old Controversies and New Approaches*, (pp. 263–90), New York: Raven Press.

Blatt, S.J., Quinlan, D.M., Chevron, E.S., McDonald, C. & Zuroff, D. (1982) 'Dependency and self criticism: psychological dimensions of depression', *Journal of Consulting and Clinical Psychology* 50: 113–24.

Bowlby, J. (1969) *Attachment: Attachment and Loss*, (Vol. 1), London: Hogarth Press.

Bowlby, J. (1973) *Separation, Anxiety and Anger: Attachment and Loss*, (Vol. 2), London: Hogarth Press.

Crittenden, P.M. (1997) 'Patterns of attachment and sexual behavior; risk of dysfunction versus opportunity for creative integration', in L. Atkinson & K.J. Zucker (eds), *Attachment and Psychopathology*, New York: Guilford Press.

Downey, G. & Feldman, S.I., (1996). 'Implications of rejection sensitivity for intimate relationships', *Journal of Personality and Social Psychology* 70: 1327–43

Downey, G,. Freitas, A.L., Michaelis, B. & Khori, H. (1998) 'The self fulfilling prophecy in close relationships: rejection sensitivity and rejection by romantic partners', *Journal of Personality and Social Psychology* 75: 545–60.

Downey, G., Khouri, H. & Feldman, S. (1997) 'Early interpersonal trauma and adult adjustment: The mediational role of rejection sensitivity', in D. Cicchetti & S. Toth (eds), *Rochester Symposium on Developmental Psychopathology: Vol. VIII. The Effects of Trauma on the Developmental Process*, (pp. 85–114), Rochester, NY: University of Rochester Press.

Ehlers, A., Maercker, A. & Boos, A. (2000) 'Posttraumatic stress disorder following political imprisonment: The role of mental defeat, alienation, and perceived permanent change', *Journal of Abnormal Psychology* 109: 45–55.

Garcia-Coll, C., Kagan, J. & Reznick, J.S., (1984) 'Behavioral inhibition in young children', *Child Development* 55: 1005–19.

Gilbert, P. (1989) *Human Nature and Suffering*, Hove, UK: Lawrence Erlbaum Associates Ltd.

Gilbert, P. (1992) *The Evolution of Powerlessness*, Hove, UK: Psychology Press.

Gilbert, P. (1997) 'The evolution of social attractiveness and its role in shame, humiliation, guilt and therapy', *British Journal of Medical Psychology* 70: 113–47.

Gilbert, P. & Allan, S. (1994) 'Assertiveness, submissive behaviour and social comparison', *British Journal of Clinical Psychology* 33: 295–306.

Gilbert, P. & Allan, S. (1998). 'The role of defeat and entrapment (arrested flight) in depression: an exploration of an evolutionary view', *Psychological Medicine* 28: 1–14.

Gilbert, P. & McGuire, M.T. (1998) 'Shame, status and social roles: psychobiology and evolution', in P. Gilbert & B. Andrews (eds), *Shame; Interpersonal Behavior, Psychopathology and Culture*, (pp. 99–124), New York: Oxford University Press.

Gilbert, P., Allan, S. & Trent, D. (1995) 'Involuntary subordination or dependency as key dimensions in depressive vulnerability', *Journal of Clinical Psychology* 51: 740–52.

Goodall, J. (1990) *Through a Window. Thirty Years with the Chimpanzees of Gombe*, Harmondsworth: Penguin.

Harlow, H.F. & Mears, C. (1979) *The Human Model; Primate Perspectives*, New York: Winston.

Hilburn-Cobb, C. (1994) Hierarchical challenge, involuntary subordinate strategy and adolescent attachment to parents: A hypothetical model of adolescent depression. *Paper presented at the International Society of Human Ethology*, 4 August 1994, Toronto.

Hilburn-Cobb, C. (1998) 'Adaptation and survival through a hierarchy of behavioral systems: Attachment, subordination, dominance, defeat and psychopathology', Unpublished manuscript.

Hilburn-Cobb, C. (in press) 'Adolescent psychopathology in terms of multiple behavioural systems. The role of attachment and controlling strategies and frankly disorganized behaviour', in L. Atkinson (ed.), *Clinical Applications of Attachment Theory*, New York: Guilford Press.

Hofer, M.A. (1984) 'Relationships as regulators: a psychobiological perspective on bereavement', *Psychosomatic Medicine* 46: 183–97.

Kagan, J. & Snidman, N. (1991) 'Infant predictors of inhibited and uninhibited profiles', *Psychological Science* 2: 40–4.

Klein, D.F. (1971) 'Approaches to measuring the efficacy of drug treatment of personality disorders: analysis and program, in *Principles and Problems in Establishing the Efficacy of Psychotropic Agents*, US Department of HEW, Public Health Service No 2138 Washington, D.C.

Klinger, E. (1977) *Meaning and Void*, Minneapolis: University of Minnesota Press.

Kohut, H. & Wolfe, E. (1978) 'The disorders of the self and their treatment: An outline', *International Journal of Psycho Analysis* 59: 413–25.

Kramer, P.D. (1993) *Listening to Prozac*, New York: Viking, Penguin Books.

Levitan, R., Hasey, G. & Sloman, L. (2000) 'Major depression and the involuntary defeat strategy: Biological correlates', in L. Sloman & P. Gilbert (eds), *Subordination and Defeat: Towards a New Evolutionary Model of Mood Disorders*, Hillsdale, NJ: Lawrence Erlbaum Associates Inc.

MacLean, P. (1985) 'Brain evolution relating to family, play, and the separation call', *Archives of General Psychiatry* 42: 405–417.

Mazur, A. & Booth, A. (1998) 'Testosterone and dominance in men', *Behavioral and Brain Sciences* 21: 353–97.

Minuchin, S. & Fishman, H.C. (1981) *Family Therapy Techniques*, (pp. 73–7), Cambridge, MA: Harvard University Press.

Price, J.S. (1967) 'Hypothesis: the dominance hierarchy and the evolution of mental illness', *Lancet* 11: 243–6.

Price, J.S. (1969) 'The ritualization of agonistic behavior as a determinant of variation along the neuroticism stability dimension of personality', *Proceedings of the Royal Society of Medicine*. 62: 1107–10.

Price, J.S. & Sloman, L. (1987) 'Depression as yielding behavior: An animal model based on Schjelderup-Ebbe's pecking order', *Ethology and Sociobiology* 8(suppl): 85–98.

Price, J.S., Sloman, L., Gardner, R., Gilbert, P. & Rohde, P. (1994) 'The social competition hypothesis of depression', *British Journal of Psychiatry* 164: 309–15.

Sloman, L. (1981) 'Intrafamilial struggles for power: An ethological perspective', *International Journal of Family Therapy* 2: 13–33.

Sloman, L. (2000) 'The involuntary defeat strategy', in L. Sloman & P. Gilbert (eds), *Subordination and Defeat: Towards a New Model of Mood Disorders and Evolution*, Hillsdale, NJ: Lawrence Erlbaum Associates Inc.

Swallow, S. (2000) 'Social comparisons, subordination and depression: evidence for a rank-mediated IDS', in L. Sloman & P. Gilbert (eds), *Subordination and Defeat: Towards a New Evolutionary Model of Mood Disorders*, Hillsdale, NJ: Lawrence Erlbaum Associates Inc.

Troy, M. & Sroufe, L.A. (1987) 'Victimization among preschoolers. Role of attachment relationship history', *Journal of American Academy of Child and Adolescent Psychiatry* 26: 166–72.

Turner, S.M., Beidel, D.C. & Wolff, P.L. (1996) 'Is behavioural inhibition related to the anxiety disorders?' *Child Psychology Review* 16: 157–72.

Weisfeld, G. & Wendorf, C.A. (2000) 'The involuntary defeat strategy and discrete emotions theory', in L. Sloman & P. Gilbert (eds), *Subordination and Defeat: Towards a New Evolutionary Model of Mood Disorders*, Hillsdale, NJ: Lawrence Erlbaum Associates Inc.

Zuroff, D.C. & Mongrain, M. (1987) 'Dependency and self criticism: Vulnerability factors for depressive states', *Journal of Abnormal Psychology* 96: 14–22.

13

PATHOGENIC BELIEFS AND GUILT IN HUMAN EVOLUTION

Implications for psychotherapy

Lynn E. O'Connor

Introduction

This chapter discusses the therapy process as one in which people, motivated by a drive for wellness and life satisfaction, work with the therapist to change their pathogenic beliefs and overcome their problems. Many pathogenic beliefs are related to an exaggerated sense of responsibility for others, and people with psychological problems are often suffering from a conflict between self-interest and a concern for others, resulting in maladaptive interpersonal guilt.

The capacity to form beliefs and to engage in problem solving and planning are evolved psychological mechanisms in *Homo sapiens*. In addition, our species, adapted to larger group living and stable group composition, has a highly developed capacity for altruism, empathy, sympathy and guilt, along with a levelling mechanism, all of which contributed to sharing and other successful social adaptations in the Environment of Evolutionary Adaptedness (EEA). However, in post-EEA culture, behaviour associated with these adaptive psychological mechanisms may sometimes be 'mismatched' with contemporary conditions, and contribute to disturbances in the guilt system and the development of pathogenic beliefs and dysfunctional behaviour.

To date, much psychoanalytic theory has assumed the unconscious mind to be rooted in disorganized, aggressive, antisocial and individualistic motivations, and has failed to recognize that self-interest can also be advanced by seeing others prosper, and that there may also be powerful unconscious prosocial motivations. This chapter suggests that the evolved social mentalities for altruistic and caring behaviour have been fundamental to human evolution, and can operate at both conscious and unconscious levels to produce serious internal conflicts, inhibitions, and psychological problems that bring people to therapy.

It is proposed that patients begin psychotherapy with an unconscious plan to change their maladapative beliefs and overcome problems, particularly those connected to guilt, shame and inhibitions. They do this through a process of testing their pathogenic beliefs with the therapist. Several assumptions, common in clinical practice, are questioned: the belief in resistance, the belief in neutrality, and the focus on process and transference interpretations. It is suggested that successful therapy is an intimate, kin-like social activity regulated by normal rules for helpful human interactions, and that optimal therapeutic technique is highly case-specific.

The evolution of pathogenic beliefs and guilt

Adaptation

An evolutionary perspective on psychological problems and their treatment centres on the fundamental principle of adaptation; through time, evolution has shaped life at every level of organization to be adapted to the environment in which it evolved. Understanding psychopathology and treatment in terms of ultimate adaptations in evolutionary history, on the one hand, and local adaptations or adjustment to the current environment on the other, forms the foundation of evolutionary psychotherapy.

Ultimate adaptations have been selected by an evolutionary process, while local adaptations have not themselves evolved, as there has not been time for evolution to shape them. However, local adaptations make use of mechanisms evolved as ultimate adaptations. For example, a child's inclination to imitate the behaviour and cultural style of his or her family is an ultimate adaptation, permitting the child to fit into his or her family and to carry on the culture. However, the actual behaviours that the child adopts are local adaptations. Psychological mechanisms, embedded in the structure of the mind, are ultimate adaptations. Shaped by selection and serving the 'ultimate' purpose of survival and reproduction, they provide a link between evolution and behaviour (Cosmides & Tooby, 1992a, b). Psychological problems may be particularly well understood and treated from the perspective of both local and ultimate adaptations (Glantz & Pearce, 1989; Gilbert, 1989, 1992, 1995; McGuire & Troisi, 1998; Sampson, 1992, 1997; Slavin & Kriegman, 1992; Stevens & Price, 1996; Weiss, Sampson & The Mount Zion Psychotherapy Research Group, 1986; Weiss, 1993).

Common psychological mechanisms in *Homo sapiens*, such as the proneness to comply with others, the ability to learn through imitation, and the capacity to feel guilt, shame, and other self-conscious emotions, are ultimate adaptations that serve to ensure survival at various levels of organization. Local adaptations, however, may or may not serve the ultimate purpose of survival and reproduction. While in most cases local adaptations contribute to survival, in some instances they result in maladaptive behaviours and lead to psychopathology.

Psychological mechanisms

The mind as posited by Freud and his followers was ruled by disorganized, antisocial and maladaptive unconscious processes (Freud, 1895/1950; Freud,

1900/1950; Isaacs, 1983; Klein, 1927/1975; Kernberg, 1967). In contrast, modern cognitive and evolutionary science is demonstrating that the human mind – including the unconscious – is an organized set of evolved mechanisms that makes local adaptation possible (Bowers, Regehr, Baltharzard & Parker, 1990; Cosmides & Tooby, 1992a; Dorfman, Shames & Kihlstrom, 1996; Kihlstrom, 1987; Lewicki, Hill & Czyzewska, 1992).

Human cognitive and emotional capacities are psychological adaptations shaped by evolution for the pursuit of basic biological goals such as survival, reproduction, kin investment, and reciprocation (Buss, 1999; Cosmides & Tooby, 1992a, b; Gilbert, 1989, 1997; McGuire & Troisi, 1998; Nesse, 1990, 1994) in the Environment of Evolutionary Adaptedness (EEA) (Bowlby, 1982/1969; Glantz & Pearce, 1989). These mechanisms or 'social mentalities' (Gilbert, Chapter 6, this volume) provide the means by which people are able, through behaviour, to adapt to their environments, and to function successfully in work, social relationships and procreation. The structure of the human mind, its ability to solve problems, to form beliefs and expectations based on prior experience, to assess for danger and safety, to make plans and carry out actions, to communicate with other people, and to engage in social relations, involves mechanisms that are used in local adaptation. The capacity to experience and express emotions that serve as a call for attention and action is another psychological adaptation (LeDoux, 1996; Nesse, 1990; Nesse & Williams, 1994; Tooby & Cosmides, 1990; Gilbert, 1989, 1997).

People are highly motivated to adapt to their environments, and when psychological problems interfere with functioning, people want to resolve them and recover. Thus people begin psychotherapy determined to overcome their problems. In a cognitive psychodynamic theory developed by Weiss (1986, 1993) and often referred to as Control Mastery theory, it is posited that patients, motivated by a biological drive for wellness and life satisfaction, work with the therapist to modify the conscious and unconscious distortions and problem-causing beliefs that may underlie their inhibitions, symptoms and maladaptive behaviours.

The capacity to form beliefs

The ability to form beliefs based on experience begins in early childhood (Baron-Cohen, 1995; Gelman, 1990; Leslie, 1988, 1994; Leslie & Thaiss, 1992; Premack & Premack, 1994; Stern, 1985). Small children, like scientists, have been shown to generate theories about the world and test hypotheses derived from them (Kagan, 1984; Repacholi & Gopnik, 1997; Gopnik & Meltzoff, 1997). Expectations and beliefs are formed even before children are able to communicate verbally (Lewis, Alessandri & Sullivan, 1990).

Throughout life people form new beliefs and expectations, based on new experiences, while often holding on to those formed earlier. In most circumstances, beliefs mediate locally adaptive behaviour and the capacity to form theories and beliefs is evolutionarily adaptive. However, when a child grows up in a dysfunctional family or a disturbed broader socioeconomic environment, beliefs which may have been locally adaptive in the context where they were formed become pathogenic and may lead to maladapative behaviours and psychopathology (see Liotti, Chapter 11, this volume).

Pathogenic beliefs

Children are particularly vulnerable to the development of pathogenic beliefs because they lack prior life experience by which to judge what is going on in their families and what happens in their interactions with others. Children are likely to believe that what happens in their families is what is supposed to happen; it is all that they know. They are likely to consider even severely disturbed parental behaviour acceptable, or something for which they themselves are responsible (Bowlby, 1982/1969). For young children, parents are the ultimate authorities, representing truth and morality (Weiss, 1993). Children work to adjust to the family environment, to maintain their connections to their parents and siblings, and to make a contribution to the family. The beliefs that children develop are part of their efforts at local adaptation.

Social behaviour in many primate species is primarily learned by imitation (Bernhard, 1988; Boesch, 1996; Whiten, 1998), and human children often directly imitate their parents and other caretakers, with little capacity for judgement about the effectiveness or functionality of the behaviours imitated. In their attempt to make sense of the world, to establish decision rules governing behaviour, children develop beliefs and systems of beliefs that rationalize parental behaviours. Additionally, children are often confused by psychological causality and tend to have an exaggerated sense of responsibility for their loved ones, the result of adaptive mechanisms aimed at maintaining relationships and supporting the family (Bowlby, 1982/1969; Modell, 1965, 1971; Weiss, 1986; Zahn-Waxler & Kochanska, 1990; Zahn-Waxler & Radke-Yarrow, 1983).

For example, when a girl grows up in a family with a frightening alcoholic father, she may develop the belief that men are supposed to be frightening. When she later begins the process of mate selection, she may maladaptively choose a mate who resembles her father, following her mother's decision in mate selection. Or a girl who grows up with a depressed mother may develop the belief that women are supposed to be depressive, and in adulthood she may demonstrate maladaptive symptoms like her mother, based on imitation, identification and loyalty to the family.

The girl with a depressed mother may also believe that she is responsible for her mother's chronic unhappiness and is obligated to try to make her mother happy. Research has demonstrated that children often attempt to engage or even cheer up depressed mothers (Cohn, Campbell, Matias, & Hopkins, 1990; Mulherin, 1998; Radke-Yarrow *et al.*, 1994; Tronick, Als & Brazelton, 1977; Weiss, 1993). When a child fails in this endeavour she may develop the belief that she is a failure and this belief may inhibit her from the successful pursuit of normal goals. Pathogenic beliefs are grim and constricting, predicting danger for the person holding them, and danger for their loved ones.

Pathogenic beliefs about harming others

Particularly common pathogenic beliefs are those predicting that a person's pursuit of normal goals will cause others to suffer. Based on the psychological mechanisms of altruism, empathy, sympathy and guilt and related to caretaking behaviour (Batson, Fultz & Schoenrade, 1987; Gilbert, 1989; Scott, 1958), people are often excessively worried that pursuing their own interests will cause harm to others.

For example, a person who grows up with an unhappy and unsuccessful father may develop the pathogenic belief that his or her success will accentuate the father's feelings of inadequacy. Or a person who grows up with a mother whose life is focused entirely on her children – even past their adolescence – may develop the pathogenic belief that to leave home and be independent will leave the mother without purpose. Or an academically gifted child with a learning disabled sibling may develop the belief that if she fulfils her academic potential, she will make her sibling suffer by comparison. She may even develop the belief that her natural talents are in fact the cause of her sibling's dysfunction, whether or not she is successful. These types of pathogenic beliefs give rise to a pervasive, ruminating and maladaptive sense of interpersonal guilt related to fears of harming others, and result in symptoms, inhibitions and dysfunction (Bush, 1989; Ferguson, Stegge, Miller & Olsen, 1999; Ferguson & Stegge, 1998; Ferguson & Eyre, 1998; Ferguson, 1996; Harder, Cutler & Rockert, 1992; O'Connor, Berry, Weiss, Bush & Sampson, 1997a; O'Connor, Berry & Weiss, 1999; O'Connor, Berry, Weiss & Sevier, 1997b; O'Connor, Berry, Weiss & Gilbert, 1998; Weiss, 1983, 1986, 1993).

The evolution of altruism and guilt

Altruism, a subject of discussion in both psychological and biological theory, has been attributed to a number of motivations and ultimate purposes. Inclusive fitness theory (Hamilton 1963, 1964) explains acts of altruism that are aimed at helping individuals who are genetically related, and that lead to the maximum reproduction of the gene (Dawkins, 1976) even at the expense of the altruistic individual. Reciprocal altruism (Axelrod & Hamilton, 1981; Trivers, 1971, 1985) provides an explanation for altruistic acts performed for non-kin, with the expectation of reciprocation. In both inclusive fitness and reciprocal altruism, the underlying motivation may be described as egoistic. Recently, several evolutionary biologists and psychologists have described altruistic behaviour as best explained by multiple levels of selection – including selection at the level of the individual, the genetically related family, and the group (Buss, 1999; O'Connor et al., 1997b; Sober & Wilson, 1998; Wilson, 1977, 1989; Wilson & Sober, 1994). In group selection, altruistic behaviour increases fitness at the level of the group, in between-group competition. Sober and Wilson (1998) have hypothesized that group selection is a factor in altruistic acts aimed at the good of the group.

While altruism, empathy, sympathy and guilt may contribute to holding people, groups and families together, to reconciliations in situations of conflict, in some cases they may be associated with the kinds of pathogenic beliefs and self-sacrificing behaviours associated with psychopathology and maladaptive interpersonal guilt.

The capacity to feel guilt is an evolved psychological mechanism, an adaptation to group living, serving the purpose of maintaining social ties and holding people together (Baumeister, Stillwell & Heatherton, 1994; Gilbert, 1989, 1997; Tangney, Wagner & Gramzow, 1992; Tangney & Fischer, 1995). Connected to caregiving behaviour and a sense of responsibility for others, guilt is based on the capacity for empathy and sympathy, the ability to feel another's distress (Batson, Fultz & Schoenrade, 1987; Caporael, Dawes, Orbell & van de Kragt, 1989; Hay, Nash & Pedersen, 1981; Plutchik, 1987; Sagi & Hoffman, 1976; Simner, 1971). Guilt takes this capacity a step further; not only are people able to feel another's discomfort, they also take responsibility for it and try to relieve it (Chapman, Zahn-Waxler, Cooperman & Iannotti, 1987; Eisenberg *et al.*, 1989; Olthof, Ferguson & Luiten, 1989; Zahn-Waxler & Kochanska, 1990; Zahn-Waxler & Radke-Yarrow, 1983; Zahn-Waxler, Radke-Yarrow & King, 1979; Zahn-Waxler, Radke-Yarrow, Wagner & Chapman, 1992). Guilt links empathy to altruistic behaviour (Eisenberg-Berg & Neal, 1979; Hoffman, 1975, 1976, 1978, 1982; Thompson & Hoffman, 1980;).

The evolution of guilt in humans provided a mechanism by which both genetically related and non-related people in a social group could successfully stay connected to one another. This may have occurred when environmental conditions made larger and more stable group formation a more adaptive strategy than the smaller and more unstable group composition noted in many higher primates (Maryanski, 1996). Under conditions in which stable group composition, larger group size, and the presence of the pair-bond are particularly adaptive forms of social organization, guilt provides a psychological mechanism that mitigates the effects of within-group competition. A person who feels harmed by another is often more willing to forgive the harm-doer, and to maintain the connection, upon perceiving that the person who harmed them feels guilty (Worthington *et al.*, 1999). Guilt is an unpleasant emotion, and when people feel guilty they are inclined to make restitution and increase the probability of conflict resolution (Adams, 1965; Baumeister, Stillwell & Heatherton, 1994; Walster & Berscheid, 1973).

Thus guilt is ordinarily highly adaptive, and in recent years the adaptive form of guilt has been studied empirically (Gilbert, 1997; Tangney, Wagner & Gramzow, 1992; Tangney & Fischer, 1995). The maladaptive functions of guilt have also been described by clinicians (Modell, 1965, 1971; Neiderland, 1961, 1981; Weiss, 1983, 1986, 1993) and studied empirically, demonstrating a significant correlation with depression and other psychological symptoms (Ferguson *et al.*, 1999; Ferguson & Stegge, 1998; Ferguson & Eyre, 1998; Ferguson, 1996; Harder, Cutler & Rockert, 1992; O'Connor *et al.*, 1997a, b; O'Connor, Berry & Weiss, 1999; O'Connor *et al.*, 1998; Zahn-Waxler, Cummings, Iannotti & Radke-Yarrow, 1984; Zahn-Waxler, Kochanska, Krupnick & McKnew, 1990).

281

Survivor guilt

Informed by a clinical perspective, Weiss (1983, 1986, 1993), Bush (1989) and O'Connor *et al.* (1997a) have focused on the proneness to survivor or outdoing guilt. People tend to feel survivor guilt when they survive the death of a loved one, or when they believe they are better off than others. This kind of guilt has been referred to as inequity guilt by Baumeister and Leary (1995), outperformance distress by Exline and Lobel (1999), and as survivor guilt in more clinically-focused literature (Bush, 1989; Friedman, 1985; Modell, 1965, 1971; Neiderland, 1961, 1981; O'Connor *et al.*, 1997a, b, 1998, 1999; Weiss 1983, 1986, 1993)

Survivor guilt serves as a levelling mechanism, promoting group cohesion and inhibiting within-group competition and may be associated with the levelling impulse in hunter–gatherer groups (Boehm 1993, 1997). People feel survivor guilt when hearing about a friend's misfortune, for example when someone they know loses a job, is diagnosed with an illness, or is otherwise suffering. We even feel survivor guilt towards strangers, for example when seeing homeless beggars, or hearing about an airplane crash, a major fire, or an epidemic of illness. The most literal kind of survivor guilt is that which people tend to feel after the death of a loved one.

The experience of survivor guilt is often unconscious – that is people are not quite aware of it, although they may notice feelings of discomfort and anxiety. For example, when a friend announces that she has been diagnosed with a serious illness, many people initially feel a moment of relief that they have not been so inflicted, followed by feelings of guilt for their 'selfishness'. This may then be followed by anxiety and thoughts of punishment, 'that's going to happen to me too'. The last step in this sequence serves to make things equal, to momentarily put the witness in the same position as the victim, thereby reducing survivor guilt. There is evidence that sibling rivalry may sometimes be a manifestation of unconscious survivor guilt and an attempt to make things equal between siblings (Webster, 1998). For example, it is common to have a child express jealousy towards a disabled sibling, ostensibly because of the extra parental care the disabled child receives. This expression of jealousy may constitute a way to build up the disabled sibling, in order to reduce the guilt that the more fortunate sibling feels.

The capacity to feel survivor guilt is linked to people's ability to make social comparisons and to evaluate equity in social exchange, employing the specific algorithms that evolved to assess social exchange and detect cheating (Cosmides & Tooby, 1992b). Survivor guilt, a reversal and/or inhibition of competition, is dependent on people being able to assess their status in relation to others, and to evaluate whether their situation is equitable when compared to that of others. People are thus alert to their own penchant for cheating; that is in order for a person to feel survivor guilt, the algorithm related to cheater detection must be turned inward. If people feel they have obtained more than others, they tend to feel guilty. This is especially true within the close social group or family (Boszormenyi-Nagy & Spark, 1973; Modell, 1965, 1971), and extends to the larger social environment.

The evolution of survivor guilt

The capacity to experience survivor guilt was an adaptation to life in the Environment of Evolutionary Adaptedness (EEA). From paleoanthropology and the study of contemporary hunter and gatherer society, it has been suggested that EEA societies were based on a foraging, immediate return economy, in conditions of high variability of essential nutrient sources, leading to a highly co-operative and egalitarian social environment and culture (Boehm, 1993; 1997; Cosmides & Tooby, 1992b; Itani, 1988; Power, 1988; Service, 1966; Turnbull, 1968; Woodburn, 1982).

Survivor guilt is a proximate motive for sharing, and adults sharing food with infants, children and young mothers is a necessary phenomenon in human child rearing. Juvenile chimpanzees, in contrast to humans, are able to provision for themselves through foraging immediately after weaning. Human children, however, are unable to provide all of their own food until late adolescence (Charnov, 1993; O'Connell, Hawkes & Blurton-Jones, 1999). Beginning with *Homo ergaster*, there were dietary changes including the use of tubers, which required cooking. These changes were associated with delayed maturity, and depended on adults being willing to share food with children, adolescents, and even grown women with infants (O'Connell *et al.*, 1999; Wood & Brooks, 1999; Wood & Collard, 1999; Wrangham, Jones, Laden, Pilbeam & Conklin-Brittain, 1999). Grandmothers' sharing food with grandchildren and even with women of childbearing years contributes to fitness (Hawkes, O'Connell, Blurton-Jones, Alverez & Charnov, 1998). Guilt at inequality creates an internal discomfort in the absence of sharing, and promotes provisioning to offspring into adulthood.

As part of their evolution as a social organism, people exhibit a highly tuned drive to help others, to equity and fairness (Baumeister, Stillwell & Heatherton, 1994; Baumeister & Leary, 1995; Caporael 1997; Caporael & Brewer, 1995; Cosmides & Tooby, 1992b; Gilbert, 1989; Sober & Wilson 1998; Tooby & Cosmides, 1990, 1996), along with a drive to uniqueness and individual achievement (McClelland, 1985) or what has been noted as the 'appetite for individuality' (Tooby & Cosmides, 1996, p. 133). D.S. Wilson (personal communication, 1996) has noted that in many hunter–gatherer groups individuals who strive to dominate others are held in check by other members of the group, creating an enforced egalitarianism 'in which it is considered immoral for one person to have more status or resources than others'. Wilson suggests that this social force was common in small-scale human societies for a long enough period to have evolutionary consequences, noting that to be better off than others in the group was a precarious situation in the ancestral social environment, making survivor guilt an adaptive psychological mechanism.

In highly egalitarian cultures, sharing on the part of the whole group appears to be extensive. While sharing, and particularly food sharing, may serve the social purpose of promoting social cohesion (Kent, 1993), it appears from ethnographic and primate studies, to develop most dramatically in environments in which

283

the food source is highly variable, such that the widespread sharing of food was a highly adaptive strategy (Cosmides & Tooby, 1992b) for dealing with times of scarcity. Proneness to survivor guilt may have contributed to this adaptation. Furthermore, antecedents to survivor guilt may be seen in higher primates who regularly share food with one another. It has anecdotally been reported that chimpanzees and bonobos respond to begging behaviour first by exhibiting discomfort, and then in some cases by sharing (de Waal, 1996; de Waal & Lanting, 1997). Begging, seen between infants and parents in many species, may have extended through selection into a behaviour between non-related adult higher primates, in conjunction with the proneness to feel uncomfortable when faced with another's discomfort.

Survivor guilt and psychopathology

While the need to maintain attachments and social cohesion in the group upholds the drive to care for others and the maintenance of equality, the need to be successful in work and reproduction supports self-interest and the drive to uniqueness and individual achievement (Tooby & Cosmides, 1996). Both the drive to care for others and to maintain equality, and the drive to care for the self and to seek personal achievement, appear to exist in all cultures and people. The relative importance of each is highly culture-specific, and even within a unified culture, there exists variation among individuals. Furthermore, while both drives may have functioned well together in the social environment of the EEA, in post-EEA cultures – and particularly in industrial and post-industrial culture – they may come into conflict within an individual, and indeed within a changing culture (Asano, 1998). Many common pathogenic beliefs in contemporary culture are related to this conflict. These centre around the belief that a person's individual success or happiness will cause others to suffer. This common contemporary conflict between self-interest and concern for others may represent a nature–culture mismatch problem (Bailey & Wood, 1998; Bailey, Chapter 3, this volume; Buss 1999; Cosmides and Tooby, 1992; Glantz & Pearce, 1989). This conflict is often unconscious, and may become a central focus in an evolutionary psychotherapy.

In the clinical literature, survivor guilt was mentioned in passing by Freud, in the wake of his father's death (1897/1960), and was then brought into focus by Neiderland (1961, 1981), who described the suffering of people who survived Second World War prison camps, having witnessed the brutal murder of their families at the hands of Nazi Germany. Modell (1965, 1971) expanded the concept of survivor guilt to the guilt people feel when they believe they are better off than other members of their families, and linked it to the development of psychopathology as well as to evolutionary theory. Weiss (1983, 1986, 1993) noted that survivor guilt was likely to result in psychological problems when it was linked to irrational pathogenic beliefs that led to the suppression of normal developmental strivings. Recent empirical research demonstrated a significant correlation between survivor guilt and psychological symptoms, submissive behaviour and depression (O'Connor et al., 1997a,b, 1998; O'Connor, Berry & Weiss, 1999).

In summary, it is hypothesized that the proneness to survivor guilt was developed by selection pressure related to group living. Although highly adaptive in the EEA, in the post-industrial era it appears to have become increasingly associated with pathogenic beliefs, psychological problems and resulting dysfunction. In the contemporary environment, many people stop themselves from the normal pursuit of success and achievement as the result of an often unconscious concern that their success will harm others. The resulting psychological symptoms and suffering are what bring many people to therapy.

Implications for evolutionary psychotherapy

The patient's plan for therapy

When people begin therapy, it is with the purpose of overcoming their problems and impediments to local adaptation. Motivated by the drive to pursue normal life goals, patients set out to work with the therapist to modify the pathogenic beliefs that contribute to their problems, and to change their dysfunctional behaviours. Organized by an adaptive unconscious mind – shaped by evolution to evaluate the environment for danger and safety and to solve the particular problems they face (Miller, Galanter & Pribram, 1960; Bowlby, 1982/1969; Sampson, 1990a, b; Weiss, 1986, 1993) – people begin therapy with a plan to work on their specific pathogenic beliefs and problematic behaviours (Fretter, 1995; Rosbrow, 1993; Silberschatz, Curtis & Nathans, 1989; Silberschatz & Curtis, 1993; Weiss & Sampson, 1986; Weiss, 1993, 1998). As noted by Tooby and Cosmides (1990: 406), 'human beings have cognitive mechanisms whose function is planning, . . . and these mechanisms are adaptations to the problem of decision making . . . the capacity to plan is an evolved adaptation'. This capacity to plan mediates goal-directed human activities, including psychotherapy.

The patient's plan for treatment – which may be unconscious – usually includes disclosing and mastering adverse prior experiences that led to their maladaptive beliefs, having new experiences both in and out of therapy that will help change these beliefs, overcoming their pathogenic inhibitions, and pursuing goals which have been out of reach. The pathogenic beliefs that patients commonly work on concern negative views of the self and exaggerated worries about harming others. The conflict between concern for status and ranking and worry about others often underlies many pathogenic beliefs, and developing strategies to more effectively deal with this is often a part of the patient's unconscious plan.

The hypothesis that patients have a plan for therapy and are the primary agents of change calls into question several common assumptions about the therapeutic process. In our approach, patients and therapists are not assumed to be at cross purposes or adversarial. Patients have agency in the conduct of the therapy, and their in-therapy behaviour is not ruled by resistance, nor is it motivated by the tendency to homeostasis in the case of family-based therapy. Although many practitioners find it hard to accept the hypothesis of the patient's plan for positive change in therapy, they do not find it difficult to imagine that patients plan their resistance to therapy, a widely held assumption in traditional psychodynamic psychotherapy (Weiss, 1998).

The therapist's task

Assuming a patient's planfulness and motivation for health, the therapist forms hypotheses about the patient's case-specific plan for treatment, attempts to understand the patient's pathogenic beliefs and the conditions under which they developed, attempts to reframe problems in an evolutionary perspective, and helps patients learn to negotiate the conflict between self-interest and concern about others. Through these efforts, the therapist helps the patient to modify his or her pathogenic beliefs.

The evolutionary psychotherapist is always asking basic questions:

- 'What was the adaptive purpose of this belief or behaviour when it developed?'
- 'What were the particular conditions that contributed to this problem, and what in the environment was the patient responding to?'
- 'Who in the social group was the patient trying to help, protect or comply with?'
- 'Who might the patient have been imitating when he or she developed this problem?'
- 'How might we reframe this problem in an evolutionary and ethological perspective?'
- 'What normal biological motivational systems have been inhibited by this problem?'

In reaction to current moods and experiences that the patient brings to the therapist, the therapist is also asking:

- 'How does this problem relate to the patient's concern about status and ranking?'
- 'How does this problem relate to the patient's worry about others?'

Informed by these questions, patients' life histories, pathogenic beliefs and problems are put in an evolutionary perspective and normalized in terms of clarifying the local adaptation for which they developed, and the ultimate psychological mechanisms to which they are connected.

Concern for others as well as self-interest and concerns about status, are linked to primary biological motives; however, concern about others is often less conscious than is concern about the self. For example, patients often come into therapy well aware of their antisocial feelings and personal ambitions, their jealousy, anger and competitiveness, but they may be less aware of their worry about others. As children many patients were chastised by parents for 'selfishness' and this often becomes an underlying and pathogenic component to patients' self-definition. In therapy, the conflict between ranking and care-giving may be made explicit, and experiences and behaviours may be interpreted and reframed in prosocial terms. Even apparently harmful behaviours may be understood and interpreted, not as a function of unconscious greed, competitiveness, jealousy, lust or destructiveness, but as the patient's effort to adapt to a dysfunctional family system or to a disturbing current environment, and in many cases, as the result of the patient's unconscious imitations of disturbed parents. In contrast to therapy which emphasizes antisocial impulses, therapy conducted from this perspective focuses on people's prosocial care-giving motives.

For example, Susan is a 40-year-old woman suffering from proneness to depression and self-hate. In therapy, Susan revealed that she believed herself to be a cruel person. To illustrate, she disclosed that as a child she was sometimes cruel to her younger brother. She locked him out of the house and pretended that she wasn't there, leaving him outside and frightened. From this experience, Susan inferred that she was an evil person, harmful to others and deserving of punishment. The therapist questioned the adaptive purpose of this behaviour, and wondered whom Susan was trying to help, comply with, or imitate. She asked Susan, 'Had this ever happened to you?' and it emerged that she had been imitating her mother who had locked Susan and her siblings out of the house, pretending she wasn't there. Susan's imitation of her mother was driven, not by hostility or competition, but by identification, attachment, and unconscious loyalty to her mother. As the therapist pointed this out, Susan felt relief and one of her pathogenic beliefs was modified.

Testing in therapy

In therapy, patients carefully and deliberately – although often outside of awareness – test their pathogenic beliefs, in order to change them (Rangell, 1969; Weiss, 1986, 1993). That is, patients initiate highly directed concrete actions designed to elicit a response from the therapist, with implications for the irrational beliefs that lead to guilt, shame, fear and inhibitions. The patient who believes that she is supposed to be a failure because her parents told her she was a failure, or that she is supposed to be depressed because her mother was depressed, or that she is supposed to fail in her job because to be successful would make her unsuccessful brother feel like a failure, will test these beliefs with the therapist. She hopes that by passing her tests, the therapist will provide evidence that her beliefs are not true, and thereby help to disconfirm them. For example, the patient who believes her success will harm others, may test the therapist by describing a success, to see if it will be perceived as harmful.

The process of testing the therapist proceeds according to the patient's assessment of danger and safety (Sampson, 1990a,b; Weiss & Sampson, 1986; Weiss, 1993). When the patient feels a sense of safety – established by tests early in treatment – when she has hopes that the therapist will disconfirm her pathogenic beliefs, she tells the therapist her secrets, reveals usually hidden experiences and feelings, tests her pathogenic beliefs and makes progress. When the patient feels endangered, she expects the therapist to confirm her pathogenic beliefs, she withdraws, does little self-disclosure, and fails to make progress. And most of this goes on outside of conscious awareness. This process cuts across many therapies – psychodynamic, humanistic, interpersonal, family and cognitive–behavioural therapy.

While patients have a broad overarching plan for therapy, they also consciously and unconsciously plan the specific tests that occur within the therapy. Sometimes the patient's planning of a test becomes explicit, as the following example illustrates.

The case of Denise

Denise, a public interest attorney, came into treatment for a mild proneness to depression and anxiety. A brilliant and beautiful woman, she graduated from a prestigious law school and at the time she began therapy, she was highly successful in her work. However, she was holding herself back in taking leadership at the firm.

As a child, Denise had been in a caretaker role in the family, tending to her erratic, self-centred and successful professional mother. From this experience she developed the pathogenic belief that she was not to be a 'star' or a leader, that she was always to be sensitive and caregiving to authorities, and that she was to view herself as slightly flawed and inadequate. In adolescence, her mother frequently criticized her for not paying close attention to her appearance and fashion, for not 'taking care of herself'. In compliance, she saw herself as a person who couldn't take care of herself, and her success as an academic and professional woman had not altered that opinion. In one session, she said to her therapist, 'I don't eat right, I never cook, I don't dress right, I can't take care of myself'. The therapist responded with reassurance. 'You do take care of yourself, you're spending your time focused on your career, that's what you should be doing.' Denise continued, 'I'm not eating enough vegetables, I'm not taking care of myself'. The therapist again responded with reassurance. Seeming dissatisfied, Denise continued, 'Well I don't look right, I'm not well put together'. Again the therapist responded with reassurance, 'You always look well put together, you always look great in my opinion'. At this point, abruptly, Denise relaxed, and a shy smile came across her face. She said, 'I just thought of something, you know this is so embarrassing, I just remembered this thing. You know how you think about what you're going to wear to work the next day – draw a mental image of what you'll wear, what it will look like? Well I always do that. And I just realized on the days that I'm coming to see you, I deliberately dress down, more casually, to show you what a mess I am.' The therapist again reassured Denise about her appearance, and Denise then disclosed painful details of how her mother had made her feel badly about her appearance and her lack of interest in fashion and the impact that had on her sense of self-esteem. This exemplifies the testing process, and the planfulness and specificity of the patient's tests, and was particularly compelling in that Denise was able to articulate and remember the partly unconscious process of planning her test of the therapist.

In some tests, patients do something to the therapist that they believe they did to their parents that caused their parents or siblings to put them down, chastise them or otherwise traumatize them. In other tests, patients turn 'passive into active', that is they actively imitate the traumatizing behaviours carried out by their parents or siblings, that they found so disturbing in childhood and that they had to endure passively (Foreman, 1996; Weiss, 1993).

When patients felt unprotected as children, they may offer the therapist tests that call for a protective reaction, which would demonstrate that they deserve protection. For example, patients who suffer from the belief that they do not deserve protection, may test the therapist by threatening to carry out a dangerous action, hoping that the therapist will respond protectively. When patients felt rejected by parents, they may offer the therapist tests that give the therapist the opportunity to reject them, hoping that instead the therapist will be accepting. For example, they may act difficult or rejecting of the therapist, and when the therapist reacts with reassurance and acceptance, the pathogenic belief that the patients deserve rejection is modified.

Patients who felt omnipotently responsible for parents or siblings may test this belief by trying to make the therapist feel omnipotently responsible towards them. For example, they may blame the therapist for being inadequate, and tell the therapist that therapy isn't helping them enough, in order to test their belief that they did not do enough for their families, and to obtain from the therapist a model of how to respond when someone is overly demanding. Likewise, when patients felt put down by a parent, or of low status in the family, they may test this belief by giving the therapist the opportunity to put them down or treat them as low ranking. When patients believed that their successes threatened the hierarchy in the family, they may test the belief by bragging about their achievements, to see if the therapist will feel threatened or disapproving.

Therapists know when patients are testing by their own reactions; when the therapist feels pulled to provide reassurance or advice, to provide protection, to do more for the patient, or to be accepting or rejecting, that indicates a patient's testing. When the therapist feels an aversive emotion, like shame, guilt, fear, or confusion, it is often because patients are turning passive into active; that is, they are imitating the traumatizing parental or sibling behaviours that in childhood made them feel shame, guilt, fear or confusion. The following case of Maureen demonstrates the specificity and purposefulness of a patient's testing, and its relationship to a patient's pathogenic beliefs.

The case of Maureen

Maureen was a highly intellectual woman, who, after a number of years of treatment, finished a PhD in history from a major university. When she began therapy she was working as a secretary, having dropped out of graduate school some years before. She initially presented as full of shame and self-hate. The therapist hypothesized that Maureen was holding herself back out of survivor guilt towards her parents, and her inhibitions had the purpose of keeping her from being more successful than her parents, who were from working class backgrounds.

In the course of treatment, as Maureen began to feel better and to consider returning to graduate school, she started to test the therapist by listing all of her accomplishments, in an almost exaggerated manner. The therapist, believing that Maureen was testing her belief that being successful would be harmful, encouraged her and praised her achievements. Maureen visibly relaxed, and went on to tell a story from her childhood. She described coming home after school, excited to tell her mother about something she had excelled at, as she had been doing with the therapist. She vividly portrayed her pride at her accomplishment. Her mother responded with anger, telling Maureen, 'Stop bragging, keep your success in school quiet, you will give your brother an inferiority complex'. Maureen remembered feeling guilt and shame, certain that she had harmed her younger brother who had learning and behaviour problems. In the wake of this and other similar experiences, she developed the pathogenic belief that if she did well in school it would harm her brother and subsequently she became increasingly inhibited about taking herself and her intellectual ambitions and talents seriously.

In therapy Maureen tested this belief, repeating the experience with her therapist, in the hopes of modifying the pathogenic belief. When the therapist was encouraging Maureen felt reassured, the belief was modified, and she was able to remember and describe this and other experiences, to which the belief had been an adaptation.

When the therapist makes an intervention that the patient finds helpful – and especially when the therapist does or says something that specifically counters the particular pathogenic belief on which the patient is working, or directly passes a test that the patient is conducting – the patient often relaxes, demonstrates considerable relief and feels better. Often, as in the case of Maureen, the patient responds by describing new memories, feelings or experiences (Fretter, 1984; Fretter, Bucci, Broitman & Silberschatz, 1994; Silberschatz, Fretter & Curtis, 1986).

The immediate effects of therapeutic interventions

The patient–therapist relationship, like other close relationships, involves the regulation and deregulation of the patient's neurochemical and psychological well-being (Troisi & McGuire, Chapter 2, this volume; McGuire & Troisi, 1987, 1998). The therapy relationship is an intimate individual or group social activity, regulated by the normal rules for helpful human interactions. Patients develop their problems in the context of close attachments, and it is in new close attachments that they are best able to recover. The therapist is in a kin-like relationship with the patient (Bailey, 1988; Bailey & Nava, 1989; Bailey, Wood & Nava, 1992; Nava & Bailey, 1991; Bailey & Wood, 1998; Bailey, Chapter 3, this volume) and becomes a part of the patient's social network, support clique, or reference group (Dunbar & Spoors, 1994). As in other social relations, when the therapist is rejecting, critical, or treats the patient as lower ranking, the patient is likely to become neurochemically deregulated, and to feel shame, guilt or depression. And when the therapist is accepting, respectful, and provides helpful interventions, she is likely to help regulate the patient, causing direct and immediate positive changes on the physiological and neurochemical as well as cognitive and affective levels of organization (see also Troisi & McGuire, Chapter 2, this volume). Some evidence for this was gathered in a 16-session case conducted by Ablon, as part of a psychotherapy research project carried out by Pole (Pole, Ablon & O'Connor, 1997). The patient and therapist were monitored throughout, for physiological reactivity including heart rate, skin conductivity and movement, in order to study the patient's reactions to the therapist's interventions. This research demonstrated that when the therapist made a helpful interpretation, the patient relaxed as shown by decreased heart rate and skin conductivity, and disclosed new material.

The case of Maria

Maria was a 30-year-old woman, married with two children. She came into treatment complaining of depression, having dropped her own career aspirations in order to take care of her children and to support her graduate student husband in his professional development. Four months before beginning treatment her mother had died after a long and painful illness, an event Maria rarely mentioned in the early phase of the therapy. Maria's mother had, like Maria, sacrificed pursuing her own interests for the sake of staying at home and taking care of her children and husband. The therapist hypothesized that Maria had the pathogenic belief that she was supposed to be like her mother and to sacrifice her own interests for those of her family, in order to avoid feeling survivor guilt for being better off than her mother and to avoid sex-role guilt for doing something not traditionally 'feminine'. He also hypothesized that the patient felt worried about her husband, and feared that if she continued to pursue her own career interests, her husband would feel threatened. Finally, he hypothesized that the patient was suffering from immediate survivor guilt in the wake of her mother's death.

In session 13, Maria was describing her feelings of jealousy towards her husband, and putting herself down for what she related as her competitiveness. She said that whenever she got interested in an activity – and gave the example of roller blading – if her husband also got interested, she would become competitive, convinced that she wouldn't be as good as he was, and quit entirely. The therapist responded, saying, 'I think maybe you were really afraid you would be better at roller blading than your husband, and if that happened, you feared you would be threatening his sense of manhood'. Maria replied quietly, 'No . . . no . . . ' and grew very still and thoughtful. And within a few minutes she said, 'You know I just thought of something very silly . . . ' and went on to describe a scene with her mother when her mother was dying. She was sitting with her mother in the hospital, her mother was emaciated and she was thinking, '"I wish I was skinny like my mother, I wish I was dying, to be with my mother'. She then spoke for the first time of her grief at her mother's death.

Later in the same session, Maria admitted to her intense worry about her husband, and to her concern that she was better off than he was. She described his proneness to procrastination and sloppy study habits, and confessed that she knew that before she had dropped out of her own graduate programme, she had been a much more conscientious and organized student than her husband. After this session Maria's depression lifted, as demonstrated by the Beck Depression Inventory as well as by clinical impression. Furthermore, from the physiological data it was found that Maria's heart rate had dropped significantly immediately after the therapist's interpretation, even while she was saying 'No . . . no . . . ', denying its accuracy. This indicated that the therapist's understanding of Maria's unconscious guilt and worry about her husband – which had been covered up by what she thought were feelings of 'jealousy' – provided her with immediate relief and increased feelings of safety, and allowed new painful material to emerge and be worked through in the therapy. After this session Maria become less depressed and was able to go out and get a part-time job, in line with the career she had been pursuing. This case, and the research conducted, demonstrates not only the importance of unconscious guilt and worry about others in relation to people's problems, but the direct effect of therapist–patient interactions on the physiological, cognitive and effective level of organization.

Technique and case-specificity: Neutrality, advice, reassurance, self-disclosure

Many standard assumptions of therapeutic technique are called into question for the psychotherapist working from an evolutionary perspective. Not constrained by the implications of the inherently disorganized and antisocial unconscious underlying many psychoanalytically-informed therapies, the therapist is free to utilize a variety of techniques, to select therapeutic strategies and attitudes specifically tailored to particular patients with their unique history and set of problems. Thus the techniques of treatment are highly case-specific and sometimes may contradict commonly accepted traditions of therapy. For example, across many schools of treatment it is assumed that the therapist should maintain an attitude of inquiry and neutrality, and practise what is referred to as 'abstinence', that is, the avoidance of relaxed two-way social interactions including self-disclosure. It is believed that the therapist needs to attempt to be a 'blank screen' on which the patient may place her projections, in order to analyse them. It is assumed that unconscious material will emerge and become manageable when the therapist avoids 'gratifying' the patient, through abstinence or neutrality. While it is also understood that the stance of abstinence will raise a patient's anxiety, it is believed that this is a positive event, and that increased anxiety results in the emergence of unconscious material. This has been countered by empirical research demonstrating that a decrease in anxiety may be associated with the emergence of new, previously unconscious, information (Gassner, Sampson, Brumer & Weiss, 1986; Pole, Ablon & O'Connor, 1997). In fact, when patients feel safe – that is when they feel less, not more, anxious – they reveal to the therapists their experiences and feelings, and when they feel endangered they withdraw.

From an evolutionary perspective with the assumption of an adaptive and organizing unconscious, particularly one with a specific mechanism for the detection of cheating, the possibility that a social and highly intelligent animal might consistently conceal important social information – that is be truly abstinent – seems highly unlikely. Patients are able to piece together important information about their therapists, despite therapists' efforts to be non-revealing. And the wisdom of avoidance of self-disclosure and ordinary two-way human interactions may be questioned in light of regulation–deregulation theory (Troisi & McGuire, Chapter 2, this volume). Many if not most patients respond to abstinent behaviour on the part of the therapist, or any other intimate kin-like relationship, by experiencing a sense of rejection, or at best, confusion. And for many, this is hardly a situation of optimal safety, conducive to intimate disclosures (Bailey & Wood, 1998).

While a non-abstinent approach in which the therapist utilizes self-disclosure, or gives advice or reassurance, may be extremely helpful for many patients, it may be problematic for others. In order for some patients to feel comfortable they need the therapist to be in the role of an expert who is also a friend, who regularly engages in relaxed and friendly conversations, while other patients feel more comfortable with the therapist taking a distant professional approach. The methods by which the therapist helps to establish a therapeutic alliance varies tremendously from case to case, although many patients appear to benefit most from therapies conducive to establishing the therapeutic relationship as kin-like (Bailey, 1988; Bailey & Nava, 1989; Bailey, Wood & Nava, 1992; Nava & Bailey, 1991; Bailey & Wood, in press; Bailey, Chapter 3, this volume). Because pathogenic beliefs ordinarily develop in kin relationships, kin-like relationships are more likely to facilitate a corrective emotional experience.

For example, a patient who grew up in a very distant family in which she was unable to feel close or important to her parents, began to feel safe with her therapist only after he had shared with her that he was in mourning for his mother who had died recently. However, another patient who grew up taking responsibility for her siblings, withdrew when the therapist used self-disclosure in an effort to use himself as a model related to a particular problem. His self-disclosure made her worry that she would have to care for him as she had had to care for her parents and siblings.

The case of Anna exemplifies a case in which a neutral approach might be counter-productive. Anna grew up in an alcoholic family system, with a mother who, severely impaired by alcohol use, was unavailable emotionally and unable to fulfil normal protective functions. Her father was usually at work, or when home was preoccupied with his work or with his wife's drinking. As a result, Anna was neglected and grew up feeling rejected, unlovable, and unprotected. She believed that she deserved neither help nor protection, and as a result was dysfunctional both in terms of protecting herself and establishing herself in a successful career or intimate relationship. In therapy she tested the therapist by threatening to do something self-destructive, and by asking advice about career decisions. The therapist hypothesized that in order to help Anna modify her pathogenic beliefs, she needed to be overtly protective, and to be willing to provide the kinds of advice that children usually get from functional parents.

When Anna posited various possibilities related to career development, her therapist responded by engaging in active conversation, thinking over possibilities out loud, and giving advice and suggestions. Anna responded by making progress. And when Anna tested the therapist by hinting that she was going to take some potentially dangerous action, the therapist responded by telling her, 'Don't do that', maintaining that Anna deserved protection. Anna responded positively, becoming less guarded in therapy and more self-protective in her life. In this case an attitude of inquiry and neutrality would have been perceived as rejection and would have been counter-productive.

In contrast, Mark was a 32-year-old man who grew up with an intrusive, overly directive and advice-giving mother. In childhood he developed the belief that he was inadequate to make his own decisions and plans, and to do so would displease his mother and deprive her of a sense of competence and purpose. In treatment, he tested this belief by claiming that he couldn't make a simple decision or plan, and requesting advice. At first, the therapist took these requests at face value, and tried to offer helpful suggestions, after which Mark withdrew and appeared dissatisfied. By carefully noting Mark's reaction, the therapist realized her error and began to better understand the test Mark was conducting. She began to assume a more neutral approach to the treatment, responding to requests with questions, avoiding any specific direction or advice. Mark responded by relaxing and making progress, appearing more self-confident and able to make decisions. In this case, neutrality was most helpful to the patient.

The effectiveness of other commonly accepted therapeutic methods is also highly case-specific. For example, in psychodynamic treatment, it is often considered particularly helpful for the therapist to make transference interpretations, that is to bring the patient's attention to his or her relationship with the therapist, to explain current events and feelings in terms of the therapeutic relationship, and to then trace these feelings back to the family of origin. While this strategy may in some cases be helpful, particularly when the patient him or herself brings up the therapeutic relationship, empirical research has suggested that transference interpretations may often be counter-productive and lead to poor therapy outcome (Piper, Azim, Joyce & McCallum, 1991; Fretter et al., 1994; Haglend et al., 1993). A focus on 'in the room' interactions in many cases may result in the patient feeling uncomfortable, self-conscious and exposed, and may suggest to the patient that the therapist is feeling the need for attention. Not infrequently, patients respond to transference comments by withdrawing or attempting to placate the therapist.

Optimally, the therapist working from an evolutionary perspective has a wide range of behaviours available, and matches therapeutic technique to the case-specific needs of the patient. Techniques that provide conditions of safety for one patient may constitute danger for another. The need for case-specificity applies to the frame of the therapy – the rules and parameters of the therapy relationship; the frame may need to differ according to the patient's unique history and problems. A patient who was frequently neglected as a child may need to have frequent phone contact with the therapist between sessions, before settling in with a sense of safety. The patient who was given little or no autonomy as a child may need evidence that the therapist is willing to let the patient set the terms of the therapy, to change or cancel appointments, before the patient feels comfortable and respected, and is able to make progress.

Conclusion

In summary, this perspective on evolutionary psychotherapy suggests that selection pressures have resulted in our species having particular characteristics, including an adaptive, organized and organizing unconscious mind, capable of complex planning and assessing for danger and safety, and containing highly developed cognitive and emotional mechanisms that support group living. The human mind, adapted to complex and interdependent social life, is specifically designed to develop beliefs, from infancy on, that determine the decisions and plans that rule social behaviour. When maladjusted family structure and disturbed parental personalities lead to pathogenic beliefs that counter normal developmental goals, a person is likely to develop psychological problems that cause suffering, and this suffering leads a person to therapy. Pathogenic beliefs are most often related to a person's relational world, and involve concerns about connections to others. They are particularly likely to involve profound loyalty to the family, concerns about harming loved ones, and the resulting self-conscious and relational emotions such as interpersonal guilt and shame. People with pathogenic beliefs are highly motivated to master their problems. Patients begin therapy with an unconscious plan to change these beliefs and pursue the goals for which the human mind is designed. They work to change their pathogenic beliefs by testing them with the therapist. When the therapist is able to help patients alter these beliefs, to reduce guilt and shame and overcome their inhibitions, patients make progress and, in many cases, resolve their problems.

References

Adams, S. (1965) 'Inequity in social exchange', in L. Berkowitz (ed.), *Advances in Experimental Social Psychology*, (Vol. 2), (pp. 267–99), New York: Academic Press.

Asano, E. (1998) *A Comparison of Japanese Americans and European Americans: Cultural Values, Ethnic Identity, Guilt, and Shame*. Unpublished Dissertation, The Wright Institute, Berkeley, CA.

Axelrod, R. & Hamilton, W.D. (1981) 'The evolution of cooperation', *Science* 211: 1390–6.

Bailey, K.G. (1988) 'Psychological kinship: Implications for the helping professions', *Psychotherapy* 25: 132–141.

Bailey, K.G. & Nava, G. (1989) 'Psychological kinship, love and liking: Preliminary validity data', *Journal of Clinical Psychology* 45: 587–94.

Bailey, K.G. & Wood, H.E. (1998) 'Evolutionary kinship therapy: Basic principles and treatment implications', *British Journal of Medical Psychology* 71, 4: 509–23.

Bailey, K.G., Wood, H.E. & Nava, G.R. (1992) 'What do clients want? Role of psychological kinship in professional helping', *Journal of Psychotherapy Integration* 2: 125–41.

Baron-Cohen, S. (1995) *Mindblindness: An Essay on Autism and Theory of Mind*, Cambridge, MA: MIT Press.

Batson, C.D., Fultz, J. & Schoenrade, P.A. (1987) 'Adults' emotional reaction to the distress of others', in N. Eisenberg & J. Strayer (eds), *Empathy and its Development*, (pp. 163–81), Cambridge: Cambridge University Press.

Baumeister, R.F. & Leary, M.R. (1995) 'The need to belong: Desire for interpersonal attachments as a fundamental human motivation', *Psychological Bulletin* 117: 497–529.

Baumeister, R.F., Stillwell, A.M. & Heatherton, T.F. (1994) 'Guilt: An interpersonal approach', *Psychological Bulletin* 115: 243–67.

Bernhard, J.G. (1988) *Primates in the Classroom*, Boston: University of Massachusetts Press.

Boehm, C. (1993) 'Egalitarian behavior and reverse dominance hierarchy', *Current Anthropology* 34: 227–54.

Boehm, C. (1997) 'Impact of the human egalitarian syndrome on Darwinian selection mechanics', *The American Naturalist* 150: S100–21.

Boesch, C. (1996) 'The emergence of cultures among wild chimpanzees', in W.G. Runciman, J. Maynard Smith & R.I.M. Dunbar (eds), *Evolution of Social Behaviour Patterns in Primates and Man*, (pp. 251–68), Oxford: Oxford University Press.

Boszormenyi-Nagy, I. & Spark, G.M. (1973) *Invisible Loyalties: Reciprocity in Intergenerational Family Therapy*, New York: Harper and Row.

Bowers, K., Regehr, G., Balthazard, C. & Parker, K. (1990) 'Intuition in the context of discovery', *Cognitive Psychology* 22: 72–110.

Bowlby, J. (1982/1969) *Attachment*, (2nd edition), (Vol. I), New York: Basic Books.

Bush, M. (1989) 'The role of unconscious guilt in psychopathology and psychotherapy', *Bulletin of the Menninger Clinic* 52: 97–103.

Buss, D.M. (1999) *Evolutionary Psychology: The New Science of the Mind*, Needham Heights, MA: Allyn & Bacon.

Caporael, L.R. (1997), 'The evolution of truly social cognitition: The core configurations model', *Personality and Social Psychology Review* 1: 276–98.

Caporael, L.R. & Brewer, M. B. (1995) 'Hierarchical evolutionary theory: There *is* an alternative and it's not creationism', *Psychological Inquiry* 6: 31–4.

Caporael, L.R., Dawes, R.M., Orbell, J.M. & van de Kragt, A.J.C. (1989) 'Selfishness examined: Cooperation in the absence of egoistic incentives', *Behavioral and Brain Sciences* 124: 683–99.

Chapman, M., Zahn-Waxler, C., Cooperman, G. & Iannotti, R. (1987) 'Empathy and responsibility in the motivation of children's helping', *Developmental Psychology* 23: 140–5.

Cohn, J.F., Campbell, S.B., Matias, R. & Hopkins, J. (1990) 'Face-to-face interactions of postpartum depressed and nondepressed mother-infant pairs at 2 months', *Developmental Psychology* 26: 15–23.

Cosmides, L. & Tooby, J. (1992a) 'From evolution to adaptations to behavior: Toward an integrated evolutionary psychology', in R. Wong (ed.), *Biological Perspectives in Motivated and Cognitive Activities*, Norwood: Ablex.

Cosmides, L. & Tooby, J. (1992b) 'Cognitive adaptations for social exchange', in J.H. Barkow, L. Cosmides & J. Tooby (eds), *The Adapted Mind: Evolutionary Psychology and the Generation of Culture*, (pp. 163–228), New York: Oxford University Press.

Dawkins, R. (1976) *The Selfish Gene*, Oxford: Oxford University Press.

de Waal, F. & Lanting, F. (1997) *Bonobo: The Forgotten Ape*, Berkeley: University of California Press.

de Waal, F. (1996) *Good Natured*, Cambridge, MA: Harvard University Press.

Dorfman, J., Shames V. & Kihlstrom J.F. (1996) 'Intuition, incubation, and insight: implicit cognition in problem solving', in J. Underwood (ed.), *Implicit Cognition*, New York: Oxford University Press.

Dunbar, R.I.M. & Spoors, M. (1994) 'Social networks, support cliques, and kinship', *Human Nature* 6: 273–90.

Eisenberg, N., Fabes, R.A., Miller, P.A., Fultz, J., Shell, R., Mathy, R.M. & Reno, R.R. (1989) 'Relation of sympathy and personal distress to prosocial behavior: A multimethod study', *Journal of Personality and Social Psychology* 57: 55–66.

Eisenberg-Berg, N. & Neal, C. (1979) 'Children's moral reasoning about their own spontaneous prosocial behavior', *Developmental Psychology* 15: 228–9.

Exline, J.J. & Lobel, M. (1999) 'The perils of outperformance: Sensitivity about being the target of a threatening upward comparison', *Psychological Bulletin*, 125: 307–37.

Ferguson, T.J. (1996, August). *Is Guilt Adaptive? Functions in Interpersonal Relationships and Mental Health*, Symposium conducted at the annual meeting of the American Psychological Association, Toronto, Canada.

Ferguson, T.J. & Eyre, H.L. (1998, August) 'The interpersonal (mal)functions of guilt', in T. J. Ferguson (Chair), *Guilt and Shame as Interpersonal Communications and Regulators*. Symposium presented at the annual meeting of the American Psychological Association, San Francisco, California.

Ferguson, T.J. & Stegge, H. (1998) 'The measurement of guilt in children: A rose by any other name still has thorns', in J. Bybee (ed.), *Guilt in Children*, (pp. 19–74), New York: Academic Press.

Ferguson, T.J., Stegge, H., Miller, E.R. & Olsen, M.E. (1999) 'Guilt, shame, and symptoms in children', *Developmental Psychology*, 35: 347–57.

Foreman, S. (1996) 'The significance of turning passive into active in control mastery theory', *Journal of Psychotherapy Practice and Research* 5: 106–21.

Fretter, P.B. (1984) 'The immediate effects of transference interpretations on patient's progress in brief, psychodynamic psychotherapy', Doctoral dissertation. University of San Francisco, 1984, *Dissertation Abstracts International* 46 (6). (University Microfilm No. 85–12, 112.)

Fretter, P.B. (1995) 'A control-mastery case formulation of a successful treatment for major depression', *In Session: Psychotherapy in Practice* 1 (2): 3–17.

Fretter, P., Bucci, W., Broitman, J. & Silbershatz G. (1994) 'How the patient's plan relates to the concept of transference', *Psychotherapy-Research* 4: 58–72.

Freud, S. (1895/1950) *Project for a Scientific Psychology, The Standard Edition of the Complete Psychological Works of Sigmund Freud*, (Vol. 1), (pp. 283–399), London: The Hogarth Press.

Freud, S. (1897/1960). As cited in Jones, E. (1960). *The Letters of Sigmund Freud*, New York: Basic Books.

Freud, S. (1900/1950). *The Interpretation of Dreams*, New York: The Modern Library

Friedman, M. (1985) 'Toward a reconceptualization of guilt', *Contemporary Psychoanalysis* 21: 501–47.

Gassner, S., Sampson, H., Brumer, S. & Weiss, J. (1986) 'The emergence of warded off contents', in J. Weiss, H. Sampson & The Mount Zion Psychotherapy Research Group (eds), *The Psychoanalytic Process: Theory, Clinical Observations and Empirical Research*, (pp. 171–86), New York: Guilford.

Gelman, R. (1990) 'First priorities organize attention to and learning about relevant data: Number and the animate–inanimate distinction as examples', *Cognitive Science* 14: 79–106.

Gilbert, P. (1989) *Human Nature and Suffering*, Hove, UK: Lawrence Erlbaum Associates Ltd.

Gilbert, P. (1992). *Depression: The Evolution of Powerlessness*, Hove, UK: Psychology Press.

Gilbert, P. (1995) 'Biopsychosocial approaches and evolutionary theory as aids to integration in clinical psychology and psychotherapy', *Clinical Psychology and Psychotherapy* 2: 135–56.

Gilbert, P. (1997) 'The evolution of social attractiveness and its role in shame, humiliation, guilt and therapy', *British Journal of Medical Psychology* 70: 113–47.

Gilbert, P. & Andrews, B. (1998) *Shame: Interpersonal Behavior, Psychopathology and Culture*, New York, Oxford: Oxford University Press.

Glantz, K. & Pearce, J. (1989) *Exiles from Eden: Psychotherapy from an Evolutionary Perspective*, New York: Norton.

Gopnik, A. & Meltzoff, A.N. (1997) *Words, Thoughts and Theories*, Cambridge, MA: The MIT Press.

Haglend, P., Heyerdahl, O., Amlo, S., Engelstad, V., Fossum, A., Sarbye, A. & Sarlie, T. (1993) 'Interpretations of patient therapist relationship in brief dynamic psychotherapy', *Journal of Psychotherapy Practice and Research* 2: 296–306.

Hamilton, W.D. (1963) 'The evolution of altruistic behavior', *American Naturalist* 97: 354–6.

Hamilton, W.D. (1964) 'The evolution of social behavior', *Journal of Theoretical Biology* 7: 1–52.

Harder, D.W., Cutler, L. & Rockert, L. (1992) 'Assessment of shame and guilt and their relationships to psychopathology', *Journal of Personality Assessment* 59: 584–604.

Hawkes, K., O'Connell, J.F., Blurton-Jones, N.G., Alverez, H. & Charnov, E.L. (1998) 'Grandmothering, menopause, and the evolution of human life histories', *Proceedings of the National Academy of Sciences*, 95: 1336–39.

Hay, D.F., Nash, A. & Pedersen, J. (1981) 'Responses of six-month olds to the distress of their peers', *Child Development* 52: 1071–5.

Hoffman, M.L. (1975) 'Developmental synthesis of affect and cognition and its implications for altruistic motivation', *Developmental Psychology* 11: 607–22.

Hoffman, M.L. (1976) 'Empathy, role taking, guilt, and development of altruistic motives', in T. Lickona (ed.), *Moral Development and behavior: Theory, Research and Social Issues*, (pp. 124–43), New York: Holt, Rinehart and Winston.

Hoffman, M.L. (1978) 'Psychological and biological perspectives on altruism', *International Journal of Behavioral Development* 1: 323–39.

Hoffman, M.L. (1982) 'Development of prosocial motivation: Empathy and guilt', in

N. Eisenberg (ed.), *The Development of Prosocial Behavior*, (pp. 281–313), San Francisco: Academic Press.

Isaacs, S. (1983) 'The nature and function of phantasy', in M. Klein, P. Heimann, S. Isaacs & J. Riviere (eds), *Developments in Psycho-Analysis*, New York: De Capo Press.

Itani, J. (1988) 'The origin of human equality', in M.R.A. Chance (ed.), *Social Fabrics of the Mind*, Hove, UK: Lawrence Erlbaum Associates Ltd.

Kagan, J. (1984) *The Nature of the Child*, New York: Basic Books.

Kent, S. (1993) 'Sharing in an egalitarian Kalahari community', *Man* 28: 479–514.

Kernberg, O. (1967) *Object Relations Theory and Clinical Psychoanalysis*, New York: Jason Aronson.

Kihlstrom, J. (1987) 'The cognitive unconscious', *Science* 237: 1445–52.

Klein, M., (1927/1975) *Love, Guilt and Reparation*, New York: Free Press.

LeDoux, J. (1996) *The Emotional Brain: The Mysterious Underpinnings of Emotional Life*, New York: Simon and Schuster.

Leslie, A. (1988) 'Some implications of pretense for the development of theories of the mind', in J.W. Astington, P.L. Harris & D.R. Olson (eds), *Developing Theories of the Mind*, (pp. 19–46), New York: Cambridge University Press

Leslie, A. (1994) 'Core architecture and domain specificity', in L.A. Hirshfeld, & S.A. Gelman (eds), *Mapping the Mind: Domain Specificity in Cognition and Culture*, (pp. 119–148), New York: Cambridge University Press.

Leslie, A. & Thaiss, L. (1992) 'Domain specificity in conceptual development: Neuropsychological evidence from autism', *Cognition* 43: 225–51.

Lewicki, P., Hill, T. & Czyzewska, M. (1992) 'Nonconscious acquisition of information', *American Psychologist* 47: 796–801.

Lewis, M., Alessandri, S.M. & Sullivan, M.W. (1990) 'Violation of expectancy, loss of control, and anger expressions in young infants', *Developmental Psychology* 26: 745–51.

Maryanski, A. (1996) 'African ape social networks: A blueprint for reconstructing early hominid social structure', in J. Steele & S. Shennan (eds), *The Archaeology of Human Ancestry: Power, Sex and Tradition*, London and New York: Routledge.

McClelland, D.C. (1985) *Human Motivation*, Dallas, TX: Scott, Foresman & Co.

McGrew, W.C. & Feistner, A.T., (1992) 'Two nonhuman primate models for the evolution of food sharing: Chimpanzees and Callitrichids', in J.H. Barkow, L. Cosmides & J. Tooby (eds), *The Adapted Mind: Evolutionary Psychology and the Generation of Culture*, (pp. 229–48), New York: Oxford University Press.

McGuire, M.T. & Troisi, A. (1987) 'Physiological regulation-deregulation and psychiatric disorders', *Ethology and Sociobiology* 8: 9S—25S.

McGuire, M. & Troisi, A. (1998) *Darwinian Psychiatry*, New York: Oxford University Press.

Miller, G.A., Galanter, E. & Pribram, K.H. (1960) *Plans and the Structure of Behavior*, New York: Holt, Rinehart, & Winston.

Modell, A.H. (1965) 'On having the right to a life: An aspect of the superego's development', *International Journal of Psycho-Analysis* 46: 323–31.

Modell, A.H. (1971) 'The origin of certain forms of pre-oedipal guilt and the implications for a psychoanalytic theory of affects', *International Journal of Psychoanalysis* 52: 337–46.

Mulherin, K. (1998) *Interpersonal Guilt in Children and Adolescents*, Unpublished Doctoral Dissertation, The Wright Institute, Berkeley CA.

Nava, G.R. & Bailey, K.G. (1991) 'Measuring psychological kinship: Scale refinement and validation', *Psychological Reports* 68: 215–27.

Neiderland, W.G. (1961) 'The problem of the survivor', *Journal of Hillside Hospital* 10: 233–47.

Neiderland, W.G. (1981) 'The survivor syndrome: Further observations and dimensions', *Journal of American Psychoanalytic Association* 29: 413–25.

Nesse, R.M. (1990) 'Evolutionary explanations of emotions', *Human Nature* 1: 261–89

Nesse, R.M. (1994) 'An evolutionary perspective on substance abuse', *Ethology and Sociobiology* 15: 339–48.

Nesse, R.M. & Williams, G.C. (1994) *Why we Get Sick: The New Science of Darwinian Medicine*, New York: Random House.

O'Connell, J.F., Hawkes, K. & Blurton-Jones, N.G. (1999) 'Grandmothering and the evolution of homo erectus', *Journal of Human Evolution*, 36: 461–85.

O'Connor, L.E., Berry, J.W., Weiss, J. (1999) 'Interpersonal guilt, shame and psychological problems', *Journal of Social and Clinical Psychology*, 18: 181–203.

O'Connor, L.E., Berry, J.W., Weiss, J., Bush, M. & Sampson, H. (1997a) 'Interpersonal guilt: development of a new measure', *Journal of Clinical Psychology* 53: 73–89

O'Connor, L.E., Berry, J.W., Weiss, J. & Gilbert, P. (1998, July) *Guilt, Fear, Empathy and Depression in College Students and Clinically Depressed Patients*, Poster presented at the meetings of the Human Behavior and Evolution Society, Davis, CA.

O'Connor, L.E., Berry, J.W., Weiss, J. & Sevier, M. (1997b, April) *Guilt-Based and Fear-Based Submissive Behavior: An Evolutionary Perspective*, Poster presented at the Western Psychological Association Meetings, Seattle, Washington.

Olthof, T., Ferguson, T.J. & Luiten, A. (1989) 'Personal responsibility antecedents of anger and blame reactions to children', *Child Development* 60: 1328–36.

Piper, W.E., Azim, H.F.A., Joyce, A.S. & McCallum, M. (1991) 'Transference interpretations, therapeutic alliance and outcome in short term individual psychotherapy', *Archives of General Psychiatry* 48: 946–53.

Plutchik, R. (1987) 'Evolutionary bases of empathy', in N. Eisenberg & J. Strayer (eds), *Empathy and its Development*, (pp. 38–46), New York: Cambridge University Press.

Pole, N., Ablon, J.S. & O'Connor, L. (1997) 'Theory-driven single case research: Integrating clinical theory with emotion research', Panel presented at the North American Society for Psychotherapy Research Conference, Tucson, AZ.

Power, M.D. (1988) 'The cohesive foragers: Human and chimpanzee', in M.R.A. Chance (ed), *Social Fabrics of the Mind*, (pp. 75–104), Hove, UK: Lawrence Erlbaum Associates Ltd.

Premack, D. & Premack, A. (1994) 'Origins of human social competence', in M. Gazaniga (ed.), *The Cognitive Neurosciences*, Cambridge, MA: MIT Press.

Radke-Yarrow, M., Zahn-Waxler, C., Richardson, D.T., Susman, A. & Martinez, P. (1994) 'Caring behavior in children of clinically depressed and well mothers', *Child Development* 65: 1405–14.

Rangell, L. (1969) 'Choice, conflict and the decision making function of the ego: A psychoanalytic contribution to decision theory', *International Journal of Psychoanalysis* 50: 599–602.

Repacholi, B.M. & Gopnik, A. (1997) 'Early reasoning about desires: Evidence from 14-and 18-month olds', *Child Development* 33: 12–21.

Rosbrow, T. (1993) 'Significance of the unconscious plan for psychoanalytic theory', *Psychoanalytic Psychology* 10: 515–52.

Sagi, A. & Hoffman, M.L. (1976) 'Empathic distress in the newborn', *Developmental Psychology* 12: 175–76.

Sampson, H. (1990a) 'The problem of adaptation to reality in psychoanalytic theory', *Contemporary Psychoanalysis* 26: 677–91.

Sampson, H. (1990b) 'How the patient's sense of danger and safety influence the analytic process', *Psychoanalytic Psychology*, 7: 115–24.

Sampson, H. (1992) 'The role of "real" experience in psychopathology and treatment', *Psychoanalytic Dialogues* 2: 509–28.

Sampson, H. (1997) 'Review of M.O. Slavin & Daniel Kriegman, *The adaptive design of the human psyche: Psychoanalysis, evolutionary biology, and the therapeutic process*, *Psychoanalytic Psychology* 14: 135–9.

Scott, J.P. (1958) *Animal Behavior*, Chicago: University of Chicago Press.

Service, E.R. (1966) *The Hunters*, Foundations of Modern Anthropology Series. New Jersey: Prentice Hall.

Silberschatz, G. & Curtis, J. (1993) 'Measuring the therapist's impact on the patient's therapeutic progress', *Journal of Consulting and Clinical Psychology* 61: 403–11.

Silberschatz, G., Curtis, J. & Nathans, S. (1989) 'Using the patient's plan to assess progress in psychotherapy', *Psychotherapy* 26: 40–6.

Silberschatz, G., Fretter, P. & Curtis, J. (1986) 'How do interpretations influence the process of psychotherapy?', *Journal of Consulting and Clinical Psychology* 54: 646–52.

Simner, M.L. (1971) 'Newborn's response to the cry of another infant', *Developmental Psychology* 5: 136–50.

Slavin, M.O. & Kriegman, D. (1992) *The Adaptive Design of the Human Psyche: Psychoanalysis, Evolutionary Biology, and the Therapeutic Process*, New York: Guilford.

Sober, E. & Wilson, D.S. (1998) *Unto Others: The Evolution and Psychology of Unselfish Behavior*, Cambridge: Harvard University Press.

Stern, D.N. (1985) *The Interpersonal World of the Infant: A View from Psychoanalysis and Developmental Psychology*, New York: Basic Books.

Stevens, A. & Price, J. (1996) *Evolutionary Psychiatry: A New Beginning*, London: Routledge.

Tangney, J.P., Wagner, P. & Gramzow, R. (1992) 'Proneness to shame, proneness to guilt, and psychopathology', *Journal of Abnormal Psychology* 101: 469–78.

Tangney J.P. & Fischer, K.W. (1995) *Self-Conscious Emotions: The Psychology of Shame, Guilt, Embarrassment, and Pride*, New York: Guilford Press.

Thompson, R.A. & Hoffman, M. L. (1980) 'Empathy and the development of guilt in children', *Developmental Psychology* 16: 155–6.

Tooby, J. & Cosmides, L. (1990) 'The past explains the present: Emotional adaptations and the structure of ancestral environments', *Ethology and Sociobiology* 11: 375–424.

Tooby, J. & Cosmides, L. (1996) 'Friendship and the banker's paradox: Other pathways to the evolution of adaptations for altruism', *Proceedings of the British Academy* 88: 119–143.

Trivers, R.L. (1971) 'The evolution of reciprocal altruism', *Quarterly Review of Biology* 46: 35–57.

Trivers, R.L. (1985) *Social Evolution*, California: Benjamin/Cummings.

Tronick, E.D., Als, H. & Brazelton, T.B. (1977) 'Mutuality in mother–infant interaction', *Journal of Communication* 27: 74–9.

Turnbull, C. (1968) Hunting and gathering. Part III. Contemporary societies. *International Encyclopedia of the Social Sciences.*

Walster, E. & Berscheid, E. (1973) 'New directions in equity research', *Journal of Personality and Social Psychology* 25: 151–76.

Webster, R. (1998) *Sibling Rivalry and Interpersonal Guilt*, Unpublished Doctoral Dissertation, The Wright Institute, Berkeley, CA.

Weiss, J. (1983) 'Notes on unconscious guilt, pathogenic beliefs, and the treatment process', *Bulletin #6*. The San Francisco Psychotherapy Research Group (formerly the Mount Zion Psychotherapy Research Group), Department of Psychiatry, Mount Zion Hospital and Medical Center.

Weiss, J. (1986) 'Unconscious guilt', in J. Weiss & H. Sampson (eds), *The Psychoanalytic Process: Theory, Clinical Observation and Empirical Research*, New York: Guilford Press.

Weiss, J. (1993) *How Psychotherapy Works: Process and Technique*, New York: Guilford Press.

Weiss, J. (1998) 'Patient's unconscious plans for solving their problems', *Psychoanalytic Dialogues* 8: 411–53.

Weiss, J., Sampson, H. & The Mount Zion Psychotherapy Research Group (1986) *The Psychoanalytic Process: Theory, Clinical Observation and Empirical Research*, New York: Guilford Press.

Whiten, A. (1998) 'Imitation of the sequential structure of actions by chimpanzees (Pan troglodytes)', *Comparative Psychology* 112: 270–81.

Wilson, D.S. (1977) 'Structured demes and the evolution of group-advantageous traits', *The American Naturalist* 111: 157–85.

Wilson, D.S. (1989) 'Levels of selection: An alternative to individualism in biology and the human sciences', *Social Networks* 11: 257–72

Wilson, D.S. & Sober, E. (1994) 'Reintroducing group selection to the human behavioral sciences', *Behavioral and Brain Sciences* 17: 585–654.

Wood, B. & Brooks, A. (1999) 'We are what we ate', *Nature*, 400 (6741): 219–20.

Wood, B. & Collard, M. (1999) 'Grades among the African early hominids', in T. Bromage & F. Schrenck (eds), *African Biogeography, Climate Change and Early Hominid Evolution*, New York: Oxford University Press.

Woodburn, J. (1982) 'Egalitarian societies', *Man* 17: 431–51.

Worthington, E.L., Jr., Berry, J.W., Parrott, L., III, O'Connor, L.E., Gramling, S. & Nicholson, R. (1999) *Studies in Trait Unforgivingness and States of Unforgiveness.* Paper presented at the annual convention of the American Psychological Association, Boston.

Wrangham, R.W., Jones, J.H., Laden, G., Pilbeam, D. & Conklin-Brittain, N.L. (1999) 'The raw and the stolen: Cooking and ecology of human origins', *Current Anthropology*, 40: 567–94.

Zahn-Waxler, C., Cummings, E.M., Iannotti, R.M. & Radke-Yarrow, M. (1984) 'Young offspring of depressed parents: A population at risk for affective problems', in D. Cicchetti & K. Schneider-Rosen (eds), *Childhood Depression*, (Vol. 26), San Francisco: Jossey-Bass.

Zahn-Waxler, C. & Kochanska, G. (1990) 'The origins of guilt', in R.A. Thompson (ed.), *Socioemotional Development: Nebraska Symposium on Motivation, 1988*, (Vol. 36), (pp. 183–259), Lincoln, Nebraska: University of Nebraska Press.

Zahn-Waxler, C., Kochanska, G., Krupnick, J. & McKnew, D. (1990) 'Patterns of guilt in children of depressed and well mothers', *Developmental Psychology* 26: 51–9.

Zahn-Waxler, C. & Radke-Yarrow, M. (1983) 'Early altruism and guilt', *Academic Psychology Bulletin* 5: 247–59.

Zahn-Waxler, C., Radke-Yarrow, M. & King, R A. (1979) 'Child rearing and children's prosocial initiations toward victims of distress', *Child Development* 50: 319–30.

Zahn-Waxler, C., Radke-Yarrow, M., Wagner, E. & Chapman, M. (1992) 'Development of concern for others', *Developmental Psychology* 28: 126–36.

Acknowledgements

I would like to thank Jack Berry, Joseph Weiss, David Stiver, Peter Dybwad, Kathy Mulherin, Bill Meehan, Denise Scatena, Virginia Morgan, Eunice Yi and my students at the Wright Institute for our on-going discussions in the development of this chapter, as well as for their helpful suggestions about this manuscript. I would also like to thank Paul Gilbert for his collaboration in our empirical studies of guilt and depression and for his helpful suggestions about this chapter. Finally, I wish to thank Kent Bailey for his thoughtful suggestions and editing.

14

THE PSYCHOTHERAPY OF SHAME-RELATED PATHOLOGY FROM AN EVOLUTIONARY PERSPECTIVE

David W. Harder and Deborah F. Greenwald

Past anthropological and psychological theorists (Benedict, 1946/1974; Erikson, 1950, 1968; Piers & Singer, 1953) have regarded shame as a relatively primitive emotion that is largely supplanted by guilt in more advanced societies. More recently, some prominent empirical research (summarized by Tangney, 1995) has taken a similar viewpoint, contending that shame is an almost uniformly harmful emotion correlated with anger, self-absorption and numerous varieties of psychopathology.

However, in a previous paper we (Greenwald & Harder, 1998) argued that such a position is inconsistent with evolutionary theory, which presumes that all basic human emotions are useful for adaptation (Ekman, 1994; Ekman & Davidson, 1994; Frijda, 1994), that is, for physical survival and for reproduction. Any universal affect (Ekman & Friesen, 1984) is very likely to serve such functions after withstanding millennia of natural and cultural selective pressures (de Waal, 1996; Wright, 1994). We presented the principal idea that, under most circumstances, shame in a mild and transitory form is a helpful signal of social norm violations that can occur in a variety of behavioural domains important for inclusive fitness (i.e., the ability to transfer one's genes directly or indirectly into the next generation; Hamilton, 1964, 1972; Wenegrat, 1990). Although individuals do not, in their own minds, behave so as to enhance fitness directly, the pursuit of their own personal goals, money, influence, sexual gratification and the care of children, tends to facilitate the passage of their genes to descendants (Gilbert, Bailey & McGuire, Chapter 1, this volume). In evolutionary terms support from one's social group is helpful in this regard. Thus, knowledge that a moral or social norm has been violated can lead the individual to correct his or her behaviour for acceptance by the social group and for future fitness. Schneider (1977), Goldberg (1991), and Scheff (1995) have similarly suggested that shame can normally be a guide rather than a burden, although they do not link the idea to genetic advantage. The subjective sense of psychological well-being maintained by the avoidance of, or removal of, acute shame emotion thus mediates socially approved (Broucek, 1991) and genetically advantageous behaviour.

It has been noted frequently (e.g., Lewis, 1971; Scheff, 1995) that shame is an affect of relationship. Some theorists (Goldberg, 1991; Lewis, 1971; Tomkins, 1963) have even implied that it is the master emotion of social connectedness and conduct. Developmentally, shame is originally triggered by the reaction of others, most importantly the parents, whose responses attain premier salience. Gradually, the child is socialized by internalizing societal norms, mediated by the family's approval and disapproval patterns, and by a continued vulnerability to similar shame cues from other members of society outside the family circle. Hence, shame feelings can be initiated by actual criticism from others or by an imagined negative reaction from an audience (Lewis, 1971). In all such experiences the sense of at least one other's presence underlines the relationship-based nature of shame emotion and the potential control of one's behaviour that is ceded to observers. Shameless individuals can be socially rejected (Guisinger & Blatt, 1994; Scheff, 1988, 1995), because they do not allow others to exert sufficient control over their behaviour, whereas prominently shame-prone persons may give away too much control. In broad terms the former group might be considered undersocialized and the latter, oversocialized. In clinical terms the former would include narcissistic, antisocial, addictive substance abusers, and several other types of personality disorders while the latter would most typically include depressives and other overly inhibited neurotic conditions (DSM-IV; American Psychiatric Association, 1994).

Relationship, actual or implied, and the possibility of control by others are two sides of the same coin. Erikson (1950, 1968) makes this point in naming autonomy versus shame and doubt the focal conflict of the second phase of personality development in his theory and by emphasizing the importance of that stage for the eventual acquisition of socially reasonable self-regulation. His work also implies that personal problems issuing from this stage can manifest themselves in later life either as excessive shame or as a defensive refusal to experience shame consciously, which results in an apparently shameless person who wishes to avoid the influence of others upon him or her. An optimal level of readiness to experience shame, then, is the aim of socialization, where regulation of one's behaviour is socially acceptable to some minimal degree while, simultaneously, self-assertiveness is not entirely crushed. It follows that outside of this optimal range shame at levels that are too high or too low will constitute problems in behavioural adaptation.

Previously we (Greenwald & Harder, 1998) discussed four shame domains that contribute to the ultimate degree of inclusive fitness achieved: conformity, prosocial reciprocity, competition/status, and sexual behaviour. The first two areas are particularly instrumental in the maintenance of one's participation in a coherent, co-operative and supportive social group (Axelrod, 1984; Axelrod & Hamilton, 1981; Cosmides & Tooby, 1992; Dawkins, 1989; Scheff, 1988; Sherif et al., 1988; Sherif & Sherif, 1964; Tajfel, 1978, 1982). Minimal levels of conformity to social expectations identify one as a member of the in-group, known from experimental research to receive preferential treatment in comparison to outsiders (Crocker, Thompson, McGraw & Ingerman, 1987; Krebs & Denton, 1997; Tajfel, 1982; Tajfel & Turner, 1986; Wilder & Allen, 1978). Prosocial activities, such as help given to associates, or the reciprocal exchange of gifts, can support the social bonds necessary for increased fitness (English, 1994; Fiske, 1992). If, on the other hand, one is excluded from the group because of violations of conformity or prosocial norms, there is the potential for serious loss of inclusive fitness, both in terms of reduced access to reproductive partners and access to communal resources in raising offspring. Although the individual is only aware of the feeling of discomfort attendant upon exclusion from the group, and not the effect on his or her inclusive fitness, the discomfort shapes the willingness to modify behaviour so as to maintain positive contact with the group and thus avoid the ultimate lowering of inclusive fitness. The undersocialized clients referred to above manifest their most obvious psychopathology in these two domains.

The third and fourth domains are more directly central to the individual's efforts to obtain mates and to acquire the resources necessary to raise offspring successfully, processes that involve much competition among same-sex individuals within the encompassing social collective. In this connection Gilbert (1997) has indicated that both the intimidation of potential competitors – which we (Greenwald & Harder, 1998) relate to status/competition strivings – and the ability to attract mates – which we relate to one's status and one's sexual attractiveness and aggressiveness – are crucial to the success of one's reproductive efforts. Oversocialized clients often exhibit their major difficulties in these two domains.

It should also be noted that efforts in one shame domain may have implications for one's position in the other domains as well, as when prominent prosocial activities raise an individual's place in the competitive social hierarchy (Hill, 1984), making him or her also more attractive as a mate. However, at the same time, it appears likely that a responsiveness to shame and shame signals in the first two domains may be inversely correlated with sensitivity in the last two domains. Nevertheless, we assume a significant degree of independence among these domains, so that strong reactivity in one realm does not invariably predict one's reactivity in the others. Thus, whenever we speak of high or low sensitivity to shame, it is important to consider in what domains the individual is likely to feel shame emotion or manifest concerns about the possibility of experiencing such feelings.

According to this evolutionary psychological perspective, the capacity to regulate oneself in response to external shame cues in all four domains is vital to the maintenance of connections with the social group and the realization of individual opportunities for successful reproduction. Difficulties in functioning emerge when a person is either under- or over-responsive to such cues, so that behaviour is maladaptively regulated. Such eventualities can lead either to social rejection or exclusion or to disadvantages in the competitive areas of status-seeking and the securing of willing reproductive partners. Inclusive fitness, then, is substantially linked with the capacity to attune one's internal signal shame to an optimum level in response to social expectations and inner dictates. Such an accomplishment facilitates behaviour that is both minimally acceptable to the group and also supportive of the individual's strivings.

It should be noted that sensitivity to shame does not require the actual presence of an audience. It can be a response either to external shaming cues from others or to internally-generated negative feelings (or cognitive expectations) about the self in the contemplation of possible behaviours. We use the term *signal shame* here to refer to mild feelings or cognitions of anticipatory shame that do not cause significant distress but can serve as a warning guide to behaviour. These signals presage the dysphoric acute shame that would occur if a 'shameful' behaviour were performed. Wide cultural variation in the norms that trigger such shame can be observed (de Rivera, 1989; Kitayama, Markus & Matsumoto, 1995; Scherer & Wallbott, 1994; Wallbott & Scherer, 1995), so that the specific behavioural corrections required to avoid more acute shame affect vary accordingly. At the same time, all societies make use of this human capacity to enforce appropriate conduct. It should be noted that although most norms of this sort tend to support the conforming and prosocial behaviours and the curbs on excessive competitiveness and sexuality that contribute to social cohesion, cultures do also include norms that bolster the appropriate levels of competitiveness and sexuality necessary for the successful reproduction of most of their members.

The particular role position an individual occupies within the social surroundings may also play an important part in determining the extent of shame-responsiveness in any of the four particular domains. For example, a religious official may have very different occupational and societal role constraints upon acceptable behaviour than a prominent sports figure. Conformity and prosocial expectations would ordinarily be quite strong for the first of these roles, while they would be much reduced for the second, and the reverse would be true for competition and sexuality. Similarly, pre-existing social status can also help determine the amount and type of comportment demanded by others. In the conformity area, for example, very high and very low status persons show less need to follow group dictates (Dittes & Kelley, 1956), particularly if their loyalty to the group has already been demonstrated by previous indications of conformity (Hollander, 1958, 1960). Very high status individuals will face more pressure to engage in prosocial gift-giving, whether in the form of charity or public works, than the very low. Competition for heightened or maintained status may be less of a concern for those already low in the social scale, because efforts to rise may well face overwhelming obstacles. There is, of course, also much individual variation in the readiness to experience signal shame, presumably because of inborn predispositions as well as the formative developmental influences of experience. Some, for example, will feel better with a relatively strong bond to others, while others, narcissistic individuals, say, may see themselves as superior to others and, consequently, not subject to the same constraints. Thus, sensitivity to signal shame will be a complex product of culture, the immediate surrounding social group, social role demands, and individual personality.

Towards a psychotherapeutic approach to signal shame problems

Most clinical writings (e.g., Lewis, 1971; Levin, 1967, 1971; Mayman, 1974) and empirical studies (Harder, 1995; Tangney, 1995, Tangney, Burggraff & Wagner, 1995) have emphasized the problems that involve an excess of manifest, experienced shame. These individuals tend to attack themselves, withdraw from others, or avoid social contact to protect themselves from additional acute shame dysphoria (Nathanson, 1994a). In our categorization of domains, such individuals would be seen as excessively responsive to shame signals regarding violations of conforming and prosocial norms, the group cohesion shame domains. Such oversocialized people would be relatively constricted and worried about doing something wrong or foolish, so that they typically find it hard to be spontaneous. In this chapter we also want to focus new attention upon the signal shame defects of the undersocialized: those who have problems inherent in having too little responsiveness to conformity and prosocial shame signals and those, often the same individuals, who have problems with behavioural regulation of their own competitive and sexual strivings. In these cases the potential guiding function of shame is seriously compromised and social norms can be dangerously disregarded, with consequences for inclusive fitness just as negative as those that can be produced by too much sensitivity to such norms. These narcissistic and other undersocialized cases often exhibit excessive responsiveness to the possible shame that they imagine would occur if they were not compulsively competitive or sexual. Thus, in this chapter we highlight defects in sensitivity to signal shame that appear in apparently 'shameless' persons as well as those that occur in the characteristically shame prone.

The shame domains and therapeutic strategies: Case illustrations

To begin our presentation of therapeutic strategies, in this section case material will be presented in two of the domains discussed earlier, conformity and status/competition, to illustrate how we recommend approaching the various kinds of signal shame problems.

Conformity and Prosocial Domains

As indicated previously, the extremes of responsiveness to signal shame – either excessive or insufficient – can create difficulties in any of the four behavioural domains – conformity, prosocial behaviour, status/competition, and sexuality. In the area of conformity too little shame sensitivity can bring about ostracism or rejection (Scheff, 1988). Whether from defensiveness or mere obliviousness, the insistent assertion of one's own wishes without regard to custom can make others uncomfortable, rejecting, and hostile (Asch, 1952; Schachter, 1951). Unstigmatized acceptance by the group is essential to the welfare of most human beings (Baumeister & Leary, 1995; Goffman, 1963; Hogg & Abrams, 1988), so that the risk is serious. Even when private preferences diverge significantly from custom, most individuals are highly aware that they need to create an impression (Leary & Kowalski, 1990) of minimally acceptable conventionality. But those with insufficient concerns about signals regarding conformity shame can forge blindly ahead without conscious awareness that they are in violation of that necessity.

Similarly, those whose sense of shame does not impel participation in prosocial activities, such as reciprocity in gift-giving or helping a neighbour, that promote the support of others in times of need (Fiske, 1992; Greenwald & Harder, 1998), may run the risk of being isolated from the group. Both of these shame domains, the boundaries of which are defined by the expectations and shaming responses of one's particular culture and social position, can guide one to a minimally acceptable level of conformity and prosocial involvements only if the external cues and internal shame signals are perceived accurately and heeded.

Those who are, in contrast, excessively responsive to signal shame in the areas of conformity and prosocial behaviour, the shame-prone individuals of most empirical research (Gilbert, Allan, Ball & Bradshaw, 1996; Harder, 1995,1996; Harder, Cutler & Rockart, 1992; Harder & Lewis, 1987; Harder & Zalma, 1990; Tangney, Burggraf & Wagner, 1995), will put others' expectations and needs above their own, leading to diminished personal freedom, constrained expressiveness, and, ultimately, lowered fitness (Greenwald & Harder, 1998). Excessive worries in these domains can produce extremely painful affect and low self-regard, which can independently reduce fitness. Here, too, accurate perception of shaming cues and internal shame signals is important for optimum functioning, although, in these cases, this goal would entail a reduction of shame responsivity rather than a heightening.

We hypothesize that those very aware of signal shame in the domains of conformity and prosocial behaviour are likely to be those who have the most to gain (or perceive that they do) from keeping a close tie to the group, while the reverse is true for those who are more aware of status/competition and sexual shame. This perception of the relationship to the group may be based on a number of factors. For example, an individual may be relatively fearful and feel safer, psychologically and physically, with a strong bond to others, viewing them as a source of protection. Conversely, narcissistic individuals may see themselves as vastly superior to others, not subject to the same constraints, while antisocial personalities may largely lack the capacity to feel connected to others.

The importance of belonging may also vary with social class. Those in both the highest and lowest social classes possibly obtain less benefit from the group, the former because they have sufficient resources themselves, and the latter because their low status does not entitle them to many benefits, even when they are loyal members. As a result, members of each of these classes are likely to show less concern with conformity and prosocial shame. They do not gain much by putting group concerns ahead of their own personal wishes and may not improve their inclusive fitness substantially by doing so. For those in the middle classes, as for the fearful individuals, group membership is very important, as their connection to others, and their moderate status, allows them access to the resources of the group as a whole, which increases their fitness.

Case illustrations

This case illustrates some of the difficulties of too little responsivity to signal shame in the area of conformity, although, as is characteristic with real-life psychopathology, issues in other shame domains appeared during the treatment as well. Mr S. was the adult son of immigrant parents, who were very ambitious for him but also had contempt for many aspects of American culture, which they disparaged. S. was an extremely hard-working man, relatively impervious to peer pressure and, generally, very uncomfortable with any pressure on him exerted by others. He developed a successful career as a legal consultant but had difficulty maintaining relationships with co-workers. An essential aspect of S.'s working style was to research his topic thoroughly and pay little attention to prevailing opinion, which often enabled him to provide unusual and very useful advice. This same strategy in interpersonal areas led him to ignore others' wishes, expectations, and opinions. At times, he appeared to be completely oblivious to what was expected, as when he delivered a professional presentation in a very soiled and wrinkled suit. He felt angry at comments made about his appearance and hurt by social rejection, yet he was also scornful of the importance of such trivia. He was repeatedly exposed to the 'shameful' results of not conforming to these social expectations and would suffer, not shame, but hurt and ostracism, with consequent irritated puzzlement. Although he was quite capable of feeling shame about other, status-related issues at his work, S. ignored shaming cues about conformity-related situations, often, it seemed, because he felt compelled to maintain his autonomy and not be influenced by others. He thought that others generally gave him poor advice that would lead him in a direction profitable to them but harmful to himself. This strategy served him well in his professional, but not in his personal, life.

Three general approaches were used in treating Mr S. The first was to focus on the personal cost he paid in ignoring the cues that he received. The second was to challenge his perception that responding to such shaming cues was an intolerable submission of his will to others (which made any conformity for him a struggle around status/competition as well). The third was to urge S. to try out new behavioural patterns consistent with a heightened sense of others' shame cues and a revised view of his usual way of dealing with them. Because his chief complaint was the unsatisfying nature of his interpersonal relationships, therapy began by linking his experience of interpersonal rejection to his disregard for social expectations. S. had been so dismissive of such 'arbitrary' conventions that he did not consider how others would feel when he blatantly flouted them. It helped to point out that he did not have to subscribe to the prevailing rules in order to follow them, just as in another country, he could behave according to local social norms while maintaining his own (cultural) values. In addition, the therapist suggested that by behaving more appropriately S. could enhance his respect and status among his colleagues, rather than losing status, as he feared. Although at first S. was quite resistant to these intervention strategies, insisting on the foolishness of the social rules in question, he gradually came to accept that, nonetheless, there was a serious price to be paid for their violation. Gradually, he came to think that he would not be untrue to himself if he were to abide by these rules for his own benefit. While he did not become socially adept, his interactions with others improved considerably. His capacity to respond, at least on a cognitive level, to signal shame in the domain of conformity had obviously increased.

Ms R., who was excessively reluctant to disregard convention, is an example of a contrasting clinical situation. She was so preoccupied with intense self-consciousness and a sense of shame about how she appeared that she could hardly bear to let others watch her walk across a room, assuming that they would be snickering at her. Although the therapy of this case was in some ways very different from that of Mr S., the principles of focus upon what the client loses by a continuation of the current behavioural style and therapist challenges to the client's current belief system were common to both cases. Ms R. was helped to realize that she was sacrificing major personal satisfactions and freedoms because of her intense worries about violating social norms. It was useful for her to examine the many activities that she could not engage in and choices she would never make, for fear of being shamed. She was urged to question whether she would regard similar behaviour on the part of others as equally shameful, which she could readily agree was not the case. Challenges were made to her beliefs that she would always stand out negatively no matter how innocuously she behaved, along with therapist recommendations that she experiment with small exposures of herself in feared situations to observe whether or not the expected shaming from others actually occurred. After a time of such experimentation she came to realize that others were not as negative about her and that she did not stand out in such a shameful way as she had previously supposed. She was also able to recall early shaming experiences with her father, almost abusive in nature, that had set the tone for her developing self-evaluation. Gradually, Ms R. became more attractive in appearance and manner, less depressed, more interpersonally responsive, and much happier.

Status/competition

As with the conformity and prosocial areas, in the domains of status/competition and sexuality, either excessive or insufficient responsiveness to signal shame will cause difficulties. If, for example, responsiveness to the possibilities of shame (loss of status) is excessive, the individual will perceive his or her own personal goals, such as winning or attaining a superior position, as more important than the maintenance of group connections. This person will experience signal shame when he or she is tempted to back down from a competitive challenge, regarding such behaviour as spineless or cowardly. This drivingly competitive approach is likely to alienate others, fraying the connection to a supportive social network. Such a person may view the group largely in terms of a hierarchy, with the value of membership primarily in having high status, not in interconnectedness. There is little attempt to bond or share with others, but rather only to surpass them. Attempts by others to elicit conformity are perceived as strategies to control and enforce submission; accedence to this pressure would be seen as shameful.

Because the desire to defeat others is so prominent, this individual ignores indications that the socially acceptable limits of competitiveness have been reached and thus runs the risk of causing humiliation rage in others when he or she 'wins', yet suffers a continuous threat of internal shame (and rage) if the other 'wins' (Gilbert, 1997; Lewis, 1971, 1987). Such preoccupations can cause much interpersonal damage even in intimate relationships. An individual who is highly responsive in this way to signals of possible shameful status loss can ultimately run further serious risks of loss of position, or even of life. Those who must accept every challenge, and who see challenges to their status everywhere, will often enter into risky interpersonal confrontations and/or physically dangerous situations in order to avoid the shame they perceive in any act of backing down. They will accept every battle, even when they are at a disadvantage and will give ultimatums that may put them at risk of great loss of status and/or personal safety.

Some individuals feel excessive competitiveness in numerous areas of comparison with others; some feel it only in one or two. For example, some might be indifferent to such general social status considerations as overall income or education, but feel intensely upset by personal, face-to-face 'slights' that might, in actuality, be only minor, unintended annoyances, or even nonexistent snubs. Under this kind of pre-eminent competitiveness, whatever its particular situational triggers, needs for gratifying relatedness, ultimately necessary for inclusive fitness, can be forever frustrated.

Case illustrations

Mr J. was an example of this kind of person. He grew up in a family of very competitive, confident, and assertive physicians. He was always expected to hold his own in the many competitive discussions and sporting activities engaged in by his kin. As a young adult he gained admission to medical school but found it much too regimented for his sense of personal autonomy and honour. He promptly withdrew, combatively asserting to all of his disappointed family members that medical school was excessively hierarchical and that he would make a considerable name for himself in another field. He did, indeed, perform extremely well in his new profession with a hard-driving sense of purpose that did not allow for co-operation with colleagues, except when they could serve his own aims. He became known as a brilliant but argumentative, uncooperative, competitive individual who would only contribute to the greater good of his employer when it did not distract him from the advancement of his own reputation. He took up various sports with focused intensity, always ready to engage others in a test of his own skills versus theirs. Even when he was clearly at a disadvantage or in physical danger, he could not back down, once rising to a joking dare from an acquaintance to ski down an extremely steep slope when he had only taken up the sport a short time before. When he was faced with a sporting challenge in another state while his wife was seriously ill, Mr J. refused to remain by her bedside, because, above all, he felt that he had to uphold his position as a competitor who would not give in. Not surprisingly, he had stormy relationships with family and colleagues and was often mentally and physically exhausted from constantly maintaining the overdriven competition strivings.

In therapy J. was directed to notice clearly the costs of his usual behaviour. At first, the loss of gratifying relationships and the hostility of colleagues were seen more as others' problems than anything he, himself, contributed to, but over time he did come to realize more fully the payment that his behaviour exacted. A moderately serious skiing injury also helped to bring home to him the potential risks he was exposing himself to by never allowing himself to avoid a competitive struggle or confrontation. In addition, challenges were made to his way of seeing almost every interaction as a competitive provocation. Although he found it difficult to believe in the beginning that others were not as competitive as he and that many interactions could be seen in other terms, he gradually came to accept some of the therapist's alternative interpretations of social contacts. Eventually, it also became possible to point out that his excessive need to assert his higher status versus others actually often lost him status in others' eyes, because his aggressive efforts of this sort often looked absurd to observers. Thus, always having to win actually exposed him to losing. Mr J. was also urged to realize that his fear of losing status from not behaving in a constantly competitive manner actually led him to be 'controlled' by others. Real control of others would first entail his controlling his own behaviour to promote his own best self-interest. For example, if a ski slope was too steep for him, it made no sense to allow someone else's dare to 'control' his behaviour and perhaps lead him to another injury. If he still experienced some residual shame at avoiding such a challenge, the therapist suggested that perhaps J. could tolerate that, given his knowledge that this decision was in his own best interests. Therefore, once again, the principles of alerting the client to the costs of his or her habitual behaviour and posing cognitive challenges to the accuracy of the existing belief system engendered gradual change.

On the other side of the status/competition coin, too little responsiveness to signal shame in this domain can produce an excessively compliant person, who passes up opportunities for individual advancement and, hence, opportunities for reproductive success as well (Greenwald & Harder, 1998). He or she attempts to reduce conflict with others by avoiding competition and/or by resorting rapidly to submissive displays (de Waal, 1996; Keltner & Harker, 1998; Wright, 1994), but by doing so, will sacrifice personal goals. Because this individual makes a virtue out of his or her docility, he or she is rarely involved in potentially beneficial competitive behaviour. A 'nice guy' of this sort may, indeed, finish last.

Mr L., for example, always stressed co-operation with others, and avoided voicing disagreements and being assertive, particularly in situations where a clear

313

competitive atmosphere was present. He had difficulty understanding why he never received promotions at his insurance adjustment job despite a six-year record of conscientious performance warmly appreciated by his supervisors. He was also puzzled by the characteristic lack of interest shown by women he tried to date. In treatment Mr L. only gradually realized that his extremely pleasant, non-competitive persona was actually leading to considerable losses in terms of promotions, respect from colleagues and friends, and responsiveness from women. Simultaneously, the therapist challenged L.'s assumption that he avoided social disapproval and shaming ridicule by his low-risk behaviour. In fact, others ridiculed L. for being excessively yielding and submissive. As L. was urged to press more for his own interests, and this became a treatment focus, his feelings of resentment over others' control of him (which he was allowing) came to the fore. The force of this anger became a strong motivation to support his increasing competitiveness.

The sexual domain

In the sexual realm, too, insufficient or excessive responsivity to signal shame can create serious difficulties. Immoderately low levels of sexual shame are associated with a lack of sexual restraint, which can improve reproductive success in the short run. However, if this behaviour is negatively sanctioned in the cultural environment, it is likely to reduce the individual's attractiveness to mates who have the strongest chance for long-term reproductive success. In the long run his or her violations of sexual propriety can reduce social status, access to resources and partners, and the parental involvement in childcare necessary to enhance inclusive fitness (Greenwald & Harder, 1998).

In contrast, the person with excessive shame sensitivity in the sexual area can be overly inhibited. Shame, as a check upon rampant sexuality, has long been associated (e.g., Freud, 1905/1953, 1909/1963; Fenichel, 1945) with bodily and psychological exposure of sexual feelings, attractions, and preferences, and with inhibiting anxiety that makes many shy away from potentially sexual relationships (e.g., Lewis, 1987). The person who readily expects shaming around such feelings, from without or within, can become overly restrained, to the detriment of reproductive success. Such an individual, who may actively avoid efforts to be sexually active, can, in reality, become the butt of jokes and ridicule about sexual inadequacy or a pathetic lack of life experience, which further inhibits the initiation of appropriate sexual behaviours. In one sense, such a pattern could be seen as a special type of conformity shame, because it involves concerns about the violation of group norms. As with other types of conforming behaviour guided by shame, the individual gives up his or her own (sexual) goals in order to reduce potential conflicts with group standards, and thereby impairs his or her chances against sexual competitors.

For all four domains described above, it should be noted that the sensitivity to shame for some clients may be unconscious and denied, particularly in cases of narcissistic and other personality disorders (Kaufman, 1989, 1996; Kernberg, 1970; Kohut, 1971; Morrison, 1989; Wurmser, 1987). In these cases, despite a surface lack of concern with a particular domain of shame, the individual may in fact be struggling with these issues in a way that will have a strong, yet not easily predictable, impact on therapy. Therapist awareness of this possibility can inform effective discussion of all the domains that are importantly involved in the client's shame problems.

Recommendations for psychotherapy

A large volume of clinical writings over the past quarter century suggests that shame is a critical aspect of a broad range of presenting problems that covers nearly every possible diagnosable disorder and many subclinical instances of distress as well. The most comprehensive of such writers is Kaufman (1989, 1996), whose catalogue of shame-based disorders spans the entire realm of psychopathology. A sampling of other theorists, practitioners, and researchers who focus more on specific types of pathology also provides a feel for the extent of influences that shame experience, or desperate attempts to avoid it, have been granted: alcoholism and drug abuse (Cook, 1993; Evans, 1987; Gomberg, 1987; O'Connor, Berry, Inaba & Weiss, 1994); antisocial personality, delinquency, and criminal violence (Cassorla, 1986; Gilligan, 1996; Katz, 1988; Wright, 1987); anxiety disorders (Glickauf-Hughes & Wells, 1995; Harder, 1995; Harder & Lewis, 1987; Lewis, 1971; Mayman, 1974); borderline personality (Fischer, 1985, Lansky, 1987b; Nathanson, 1994b); depression (Harder, 1995; Hoblitzelle, 1987; Lewis, 1971, 1986; Wright, O'Leary & Balkin, 1989; Tangney, Burggraf & Wagner, 1995); domestic violence and marital dysfunction (Lansky, 1987a; Petrik, Gildersleeve-High, McEllistrem & Subotnik, 1994; Retzinger, 1991; Scheff, 1987; Wallace & Nosko, 1993); eating disorders (Floyd & Floyd, 1985; Frederickson & Roberts, 1997; Sanftner, Barlow, Marschall & Tangney, 1995); narcissistic personality (Kernberg, 1970; Kohut, 1971; Lewis, 1987; Morrison, 1989); paranoia (Blos & Shane, 1981; Colby, 1976; Lewis, 1971); post-traumatic stress disorders (Cook, 1993; Lansky, 1994; Stone, 1992); sexual and physical abuse (Cook, 1993; James, 1992; Migdow, 1994); sexual disorders (Frederickson & Roberts, 1997; Katz, 1988; Stoller, 1987); and suicide (Harper & Hoopes, 1990; Shreve & Kunkel, 1989; Yufit, 1991). Shame has been cited as a critical aspect of all of these conditions, making it highly likely that painful shame experiences will be involved in the treatment of all types of emotional or behavioural disturbance.

Obviously, any recommendations for shame-focused clinical work with such a wide range of pathology must allow for the heterogeneity of such a catalogue of problems. In addition, we are suggesting here that clinicians can helpfully conceptualize pathologies in terms of defects in optimal signal shame capacity within the four domains described earlier. Traditionally, many of the presenting problems listed above might have been seen simply as involving too much apparent shame (e.g., depression, eating disorders) or too little (e.g., narcissistic and antisocial personalities). We believe that our classification of problems by domain and typical level of signal shame provides a more differentiated picture of the changes needed.

315

Specialized clinical techniques undoubtedly will ultimately prove useful for the various disorders enumerated in diagnostic manuals such as the DSM-IV (American Psychiatric Association, 1994) as well as for the eight types of shame domain problems we have outlined (four domains, excessive or insufficient use of signal shame in each). Nevertheless, we believe that some general notions of treatment for the clinical management of shame-related issues are worth consideration. We recommend five guidelines for the therapist.

1) *The evolutionary necessity of shame experiences can be helpfully communicated to the client, indicating their general adaptive purpose and the importance of developing an optimum level of signal shame*, along with acknowledgement that unfortunate circumstances in the client's personal life have led to the current maladaptive state. Such a strategy would tend to legitimate the client's own shame experiences or worries about being shamed by others, to avoid the client possibly feeling blamed (and shamed) for being in his or her difficulties, and to support the subjective sense of righteous outrage (Lewis, 1987) that often issues from acute shame feelings or the threat that others (including the therapist) will induce such feelings. This approach would reduce the anxiety around shame threats and make acute shame emotion more tolerable. We do not recommend here an intellectual discussion of the role of shame in adaptation and genetic fitness, but rather comments from the therapist that indicate where, in the particulars of the patient's life, the adaptive potential of the client's shame capacities may be utilized for personal advantage. Client awareness that more accurate readings of others' shame cues and moderate responses to them can prove quite adaptively beneficial can thus be heightened. Because most clients will misread their internal shame signals either to an exaggerated or a harmfully minimized degree, the therapist's task is, in one sense, educational.

This educational component of the intervention must be mixed with a good measure of personal empathy, in order to modulate client tendencies towards disruptive, overemotional reactions, including shame about having shame (Levin, 1967; Lewis, 1971), which can lead, in some cases, to a complete abandonment of treatment. Even the most empathic therapists find it difficult to avoid entirely the inadvertent shaming of a client who is sensitive to any hints that their shame experiences are defects about which to feel more ashamed. For these cases, particularly those who show strong defensive denial of shame, this proposed evolutionary perspective would normally be introduced very cautiously and slowly, because of extreme vulnerability. It is often these very clients who most need awareness about the usefulness of shame signals, so that they can become sensitive to their own slight anticipatory twinges of shame and more successfully curb their heedless behaviour. Osherson and Krugerman (1990) suggest that such a therapeutic dilemma may well be a more prevalent problem with males, because of possible status loss associated with a help-seeking role and the heightened status/competition concerns of many men. It could be expected to be present for those of both genders who are especially sensitive to status shame and who may experience therapeutic interventions as assaults on their self-respect, causing them to lose face. Thus, while the therapist must educate the client to greater responsiveness in the domains of conformity and prosocial behaviour, he or she might also need to educate the client to less responsiveness in another realm, status/competition.

Whenever treatment disruption threatens, the therapist may need to re-emphasize the evolutionary usefulness, even the necessity, of experiencing shame feelings now and then and to reiterate their potential usefulness in guiding future, more reasonable and adaptive behaviours, that can lead to a more gratifying life. This must be done in a gentle, empathically attuned manner (Stolorow & Lachmann, 1980), but carefully, so that it does not take on the appearance of condescension. Accurate empathy also must be maintained for the humiliated fury that acute shame experiences are likely to produce, even if the shame itself is not consciously felt and is thus 'bypassed' (Lewis, 1971). Both clinical and empirical evidence (Livingston & Farber, 1996; Morrison, 1989) suggest that the therapist's maintenance of a helpful, empathic stance with all aspects of shame manifestations is a difficult, yet essential, thing to do.

2) An additional evolutionary aspect of our approach is *the conceptualization of the client's problems within our four-domain scheme of major human activities.* We suggest that therapist attention be directed to the specific shame domain, or domains, in which the client's major troubles with shame signals occur. If, for example, such analysis suggested the presence of pronounced, but not excessive, status/competition shame issues and simultaneous insufficient responsiveness in the prosocial domain, active therapist promotion of minimally adaptive prosocial reciprocity might be required, while leaving the client with an unchallenged, appropriate level of status/competition preoccupation. Therapist judgements about which domains show excessive or insufficient shame signal responsiveness should also be leavened by awareness of the life situation faced by a client. For example, someone from an inner-city environment, where survival requires a strong sensitivity to any possible slights regarding status (honour) and a readiness to assert one's position, even with violence (Cohen, Vandello & Rantilla, 1998), may lead a counsellor to see appropriate status/competition responsiveness in a level that would appear excessive in other life surroundings.

3) As to general *treatment tactics*, we recommend the three that were outlined above in our case illustrations of shame problems:

- *The costs to the client of the current inflexible behavioural pattern should be stressed.* This will be necessary to increase client motivation for change, but – as indicated in this section of the chapter – should be performed with care and empathic concern, to avoid the problem of inadvertent shaming of the client.
- *The therapist should challenge the belief system* that supports the pre-existing behavioural pattern.

- *The therapist can urge experimentation* with new behaviours to assess the consequences for the client. New appraisals can demonstrate the irrationality of the client's beginning belief system and demonstrate the utility of mild signal shame.

With regard to all three of the foregoing, it will usually be necessary, especially at the inception of treatment, to indicate that the client's style is not one fixed for all time, although many clients may initially believe that it is and will maintain vigorously that they are powerless to alter it, partly to make a (defensive) virtue of the status quo. Others will assert that they would not want to alter it for fear of 'losing' or of being controlled by others. Obviously, the costs will differ greatly depending on which shame domains are involved, the specific social and cultural circumstances present, and whether the pathology is more the undersocialized or oversocialized variety.

The clinical literature (Kernberg, 1970; Kohut, 1971; Morrison, 1989; Kaufman, 1989) suggests that with undersocialized clients, who will often show defensive denial regarding their shame signals, actively refuse to yield to others, and/or pre-emptively attack others for their shortcomings (Nathanson, 1994a), the therapist must perform a particularly difficult balancing task. At one and the same time patients should be pressed to heed others' shame cues and their own internal shame signals, but do so without also causing intense shame (and shame-rage; Lewis, 1987). The therapist can stress repeatedly what the client stands to gain from change despite the difficulties and pain that arise, to support continued motivation, but this literature indicates that sailing is not usually smooth. Part of the therapist's task in the experimentation phase of this kind of case is to promote new, socially approved control mechanisms in the various behavioural domains. However, care must be exercised constantly, so that the therapist's urgings do not continuously trigger patient shame and resistance, either simply by concentration upon the client's shortcomings or by the therapist being perceived as condescending and/or controlling.

4) Whenever the pain of acute shame is experienced during treatment or the threat of shame becomes the focus, *the therapist can point out the adaptive advantages of the client's own characteristic way of dealing with shame threats, even while he or she also continues to highlight its clear negative consequences.* For example, the avoidance of social contacts to protect against the possibility of others' criticisms can be given credit for its protective function, even while the untoward effects of such avoidance can also be mentioned. Open acknowledgement of the adaptive elements of the pre-existing coping style should reduce tendencies to be shamed by one's troubles under the gaze of the therapist. Probably, at the beginning of treatment the incidents focused on will not be explicitly labelled as involving shame, which itself could induce a painful and infuriating shame experience. But as therapy progresses and the therapist is viewed as a more trustworthy figure and less as a potential shamer, such overt labelling could become more customary without presenting the same danger of treatment disruption.

5) As indicated several times in the previous four principles, *empathic acceptance of the client's experience should comprise the background tone of all therapist efforts, primarily to avoid the problem of inadvertently shaming the client.* We do not believe that such acceptance is sufficient unto itself for optimal change, as maintained by Rogers (1976) and some of the self-psychologists (Kohut, 1971; Stolorow & Lachmann, 1980), but we do believe that the atmosphere of safety (Horney, 1950, 1953; Kaufman, 1989) and a sense that one's affective experience is partly legitimate, even when it also seems inappropriate (Lewis, 1987), are necessary conditions for the adaptive integration of powerful emotional experiences (Socarides & Stolorow, 1986) such as shame. Some basic level of self-acceptance (Rogers, 1976) and self-forgiveness for intensely shameful aspects of the self (Halling, 1994) are probably preconditions for the consistent, adaptive reading of others' shame cues and the adaptive activation of one's own signal shame.

Kaufman (1989: 164–168) argues that the therapist being a real person, rather than adopting a more distant, blank-screen stance, is a crucial addition to empathy for the client's feelings, especially for clients of the undersocialized variety. The aim is to have the client see the therapist as a person who will occasionally be willing to discuss matters of common interest and reveal aspects of the unique individual in the therapist's chair. By this route Kaufman (1989) expects the client to develop trust in the therapist, such that shameful formative experiences can become conscious and eventually divulged without the occurrence of further debilitating shame. Such a trusting therapeutic relationship is analogous to the bond between a child and a supportive parent, wherein potentially shameful exposures of the self will not be magnified by criticism but soothed, instead, by empathic understanding. The centrality of such trust to effective therapy is certainly suggested by research (Ainsworth, Blehar, Waters & Wall, 1978) on the crucial importance of secure, nurturing childhood attachments for healthy personality development and on the implications of secure attachment for psychological health in adults (Henderson, 1977; Jones, 1983; Shaver & Hazan, 1994). Without the client having a securely positive sense of attachment to the therapist the danger of shame-rage remains high whenever the patient's misreading of others' signals is identified by the therapist and examined in the open.

Self-psychologists (Kohut, 1971; Stolorow & Lachmann, 1980) agree that trust is an essential element of effective treatment, particularly when self (shame) vulnerability is marked, but they would typically argue that consistent empathy with the client's distorted views of the world should not generally be accompanied by disclosures of the therapist's reality. Such reality can destroy the patient's necessary fantasy about the therapist's attitudes towards the patient. Furthermore, the therapist's injection of real feelings into the treatment process always runs the risk of countertransference involvement. In the case of the shame-endangered patient such therapist reactions tend to involve subtle shaming and blaming (Wurmser, 1987), just the tack that can trigger shame-rage or, via defensive resistance, imprison the patient even more rigidly within his current pathological condition. A somewhat atypical self-psychologist, Morrison (1994), does advocate

319

some self-disclosure, going so far as to reveal his own shame feelings occasionally to patients. Empathy and trust are also his aims, which he feels require the therapist to relinquish the silent confessor role in favour of his real, sometimes shameful, reality. This is done to reduce the shame inherent in the frequent personal disclosures of one party to another who remains largely silent, and who can thus appear, at least in fantasy, as a critical, haughty, condescending person.

We view the positions of Kaufman (1989) and Morrison (1994) as potentially appropriate responses to the empathic needs of some clients, but whatever else along these lines that a therapist introduces, the basic principle is still the maintenance of an attitude of empathic acceptance as the patient's shame-related experiences are gradually exposed.

Once the client's awareness of shame signals and mastery of shame threats has progressed, an ideal treatment regimen might also include a period of group psychotherapy. A group format can be particularly helpful with all the issues that relate to shame in psychopathology, because it constitutes a social 'laboratory' where one's readings of and responses to the shame signals of others can be observed in a broader context than that afforded by individual treatment. Other group members can become ancillary therapists in the provision of feedback about the patient's understanding of social signals and the provision of the supportive environment required for the safe absorption of such feedback. In his classic study of curative factors in group treatment Yalom (1970: 70–71) reported the ten statements that patients felt were most representative of what helped them in therapy. Five of them carried implications for potential shame experience and the usefulness of group feedback for correcting socially inappropriate (shameful) behaviour. The statements were: 'discovering and accepting previously . . . unacceptable parts of myself', 'other members honestly telling me what they think of me', 'the group teaching me about the type of impression I make on others', 'learning how I come across to others', 'seeing that others could reveal embarrassing things . . . and benefit from it helped me do the same'. These patients also listed feeling more trustful of groups and other people as a curative influence, suggesting that the information received about themselves was delivered in just the kind of safe atmosphere we believe to be so crucial to the management of shame in individual treatment. Lear (1990) and Nicholas (1993) detail some of the scapegoating and condemnatory dangers of feedback delivered in an unsafe group environment, particularly to socially repugnant or morally deficient clients, who, we maintain, would run the highest risk of shaming from others. Both of these authors indicate that a properly maintained group atmosphere can circumvent the potential dangers and engender the positive outcomes afforded by most groups.

Group therapy approaches that are conducted under emotionally supportive conditions have also been noted to reduce the shame experienced by trauma victims (Turner, 1993) and also by 'acter-outers' who have come to feel shame over their transgressions, even if only after the fact (Buchele, 1994). Group therapy, then, provides an excellent medium to convey the importance of one's appearance to others and the necessary corrections for minimal social acceptability. Once a minimal level of safety is attained in the group a client with too little conscious shame can be supportively confronted with his or her norm violations, perhaps to a greater degree than is possible by a single therapist.

Summary and theoretical affiliations of the recommended therapeutic approach

Collectively, the foregoing five core therapeutic guidelines can be regarded as underlining the necessity of managing the client's affect, so that therapy does not become disruptively disturbing, in concert with attempts to correct erroneous cognitions about his or her adaptive prospects whenever shame signals are experienced. In pursuit of positive client motivation and efforts towards change, it is important to help the client make accurate assessments of the shame messages sent by others, and of the threats of possible acute shame feelings, so that new, more effective behaviour patterns can be evolved. Always, the ultimate aim of therapy would be the same: to improve the client's awareness of the adaptability offered by using his or her own mild shame feelings or the cognitive anticipation of shame emotion as signals that can effectively guide behaviour. If such proto-shame experiences come to be regarded more as information to be used for personal benefit than as dangerous eventualities that must be denied, ignored, or capitulated to, the patient will be well advanced towards a healthier life.

Many elements of our recommended approach – the focus upon the evolutionarily adaptive purposes of shame, the emphasis upon alteration of maladaptive beliefs, the building of accurate assessment skills regarding external shaming cues and internal shame threats, and the examination of cognitive expectancies about possible positive changes – make this primarily a cognitive–behavioural treatment (Mahoney & Arnkoff, 1978). Within this orientation we expect that more beneficial results will be achieved with a gentle, empirically collaborative style (Beck, 1976; Hollon & Beck, 1994) than with a confrontative, less empathetic one (Ellis, 1986), which could leave a sensitive patient extremely anxious and vulnerable, or, alternatively, furious and poised to quit treatment.

However, our insistence upon the importance of empathic attunement to the client's potentially painful shame experiences and subsequent shame-rage introduce elements of Rogerian therapy (Rogers, 1976) and self-psychology (Kohut, 1971; Morrison, 1989; Stolorow & Lachmann, 1980). In addition, recognition that apparently excessive or insufficient conscious shame may differ from more unconscious, opposite feelings and attitudes also makes this approach somewhat psychodynamic in nature. In particular, cognizance of the extreme unconscious sensitivity of clients to humiliation and shame-rage (Lewis, 1971, 1987), which can be easily and unwittingly triggered, also gives this perspective a psychodynamic stamp. Further, awareness that countertransferential factors within the therapist are crucial elements to monitor for a successful treatment of shame problems (Retzinger, 1998; Kaufman, 1989) also makes this a partially psychodynamic approach. The recently popular idea of internal schemas, whether primarily seen as cognitive (Young, 1990;

Young & Klosko, 1993) or as affective (Kaufman, 1989, 1996) in nature, may ultimately provide a means by which theoretical integration of the combined cognitive and dynamic approach that we recommend here might be favourably accomplished.

Overall, we believe that the integration of evolutionary and other points of view using the guidelines provided previously would ultimately enable the client to pay more accurate and appropriate attention to shame signals, to face more easily the shame of exposing shame experiences in treatment (Harder, 1990; Levin, 1967; Lewis, 1971, 1987), to better tolerate the extreme pain associated with shame emotions, to stave off the therapy-crippling effects of suppressed or unconscious shame-rage (Lewis, 1971, 1987), and to avoid some of the preoccupation with oneself that can block constructive action after a shame experience (Tangney, 1995).

Summary

The major points we make in this chapter are that while, traditionally, shame theorists and researchers have focused on the negative effects of excessive shame experience,

1) insufficient responsiveness to shame presents just as much a shame-related problem as excessive shame and creates as many difficulties for the client, and
2) the concept of shame can be profitably broadened to include not only concerns about violating social norms of conformity and prosocial behaviour but also personal goals in the status/competition and sexuality domains.

This viewpoint allows psychological thinking to be more consistent with an evolutionary perspective, in which shame is viewed as a useful, in fact, a necessary, emotion that can guide adaptive behaviour. The 'problem' of shame is not that it exists, but that it can be felt either too keenly or too lightly. The therapist's goal, then, is to optimize the level of shame responsiveness, so that clients can best regulate their functioning.

References

Ainsworth, M.D.S., Blehar, M., Waters, E. & Wall, S. (1978) *Patterns of Attachment*, Hillsdale, NJ: Lawrence Erlbaum Associates Inc.

American Psychiatric Association (1994) *Diagnostic and Statistical Manual of Mental Disorders-fourth edition (DSM-IV)*. Washington, DC: APA.

Asch, S.E. (1952) *Social Psychology*, New York: Prentice-Hall.

Axelrod, R. (1984) *The Evolution of Cooperation*, New York: Basic Books

Axelrod, R. & Hamilton, W.D. (1981) 'The evolution of cooperation', *Science* 211: 1390–6.

Baumeister, R.F. & Leary, M.R. (1995). 'The need to belong: Desire for interpersonal attachments as a fundamental human motivation', *Psychological Bulletin* 117: 497–529.

Beck, A.T. (1976) *Cognitive Therapy and the Emotional Disorders*, New York: International Universities Press.

Benedict, R. (1946/1974) *The Chrysanthemum and the Sword*, Boston: Houghton-Mifflin.

Blos, P. & Shane, M. (1981) 'Psychoanalytic perspectives on the "more disturbed" adolescent', *Journal of the American Psychoanalytic Association* 29: 161–75.

Broucek, F.J. (1991) *Shame and the Self*, New York: Guilford Press.

Buchele, B.J. (1994) 'Innovative uses of psychodynamic group psychotherapy', *Bulletin of the Menninger Clinic* 58: 215–23.

Cassorla, A.A. (1986) 'A preliminary investigation of the experience of shame in psychiatrically hospitalized, conduct disordered adolescents', *Dissertation Abstracts International* 47: 1715B. (University Microfilms No. DA 8614664).

Cohen, D., Vandello, J. & Rantilla, A.K. (1998) 'The sacred and the social: Cultures of honor and violence', in P. Gilbert & B. Andrews (eds), *Shame: Interpersonal Behavior, Psychopathology, and Culture*, (pp. 261–282), New York: Oxford University Press.

Colby, K.M. (1976) 'Clinical implications of a simulation model of paranoid processes', *Archives of General Psychiatry* 33: 854–7.

Cook, D.R. (1993) *The Internalized Shame Scale Manual*, Menomonie, WI: Channel Press. (Available from the author at Rt. 7, Box 270A, Menomonie, WI 54751).

Cosmides, L. & Tooby, J. (1992) 'Cognitive adaptations for social exchange', in J.H. Barkow, L. Cosmides & J. Tooby (eds), *The Adapted Mind: Evolutionary Psychology and the Generation of Culture*, (pp. 163–228), New York: Oxford University Press.

Crocker, J., Thompson, L.L., McGraw, K.M. & Ingerman, C. (1987) 'Downward comparison, prejudice, and evaluation of others: Effects of self-esteem and threat', *Journal of Personality and Social Psychology* 52: 907–16.

Dawkins, R. (1989) *The Selfish Gene*, (3rd edition), Oxford: Oxford University Press.

de Rivera, J. (1989) 'Comparing experiences across cultures: Shame and guilt in Americans and Japanese', *Hiroshima Forum for Psychology* 14: 113–20.

de Waal, F.M.B. (1996) *Good Natured: The Origins of Right and Wrong in Humans and Other Animals*, Cambridge, MA: Harvard University Press.

Dittes, J.E. & Kelley, H.H. (1956) 'Effects of different conditions of acceptance upon conformity to group norms', *Journal of Abnormal and Social Psychology* 53: 100–7.

Ekman, P. (1994) 'All emotions are basic', in P. Ekman & R.J. Davidson (eds), *The Nature of Emotion*, (pp. 15–19), New York: Oxford University Press.

Ekman, P. & Davidson, R.J. (1994) 'Afterword: What is the function of emotions?', in P. Ekman & R.J. Davidson (eds), *The Nature of Emotion*, (pp. 137–9). New York: Oxford University Press.

Ekman, P. & Friesen, W.V. (1984) *Unmasking the Face*, (2nd edition), Palo Alto, CA: Consulting Psychologists Press.

Ellis, A. (1986) 'Rational-emotive therapy', in I.L. Kutash & A. Wolf (eds), *Psychotherapist's Casebook: Theory and Technique in the Practice of Modern Therapies*, (pp. 277–87), San Francisco: Jossey-Bass

English, F. (1994) 'Shame and social control revisited', *Transactional Analysis Journal* 24: 109–20.

Erikson, E.H. (1950) *Childhood and Society*, New York: Norton.

Erikson, E.H. (1968) *Identity, Youth, and Crisis*, New York: Norton.

Evans, S. (1987) 'Shame, boundaries and dissociation in chemically dependent, abusive and incestuous families', *Alcoholism Treatment Quarterly* 4: 25–38.

Fenichel, O. (1945) *The Psychoanalytic Theory of Neurosis*, New York: International Universities Press.

Fischer, S.F. (1985) 'Identity of two: The phenomenology of shame in borderline development and treatment', *Psychotherapy* 22: 101–9.

Fiske, A.P. (1992) 'The four elementary forms of sociality: Framework for a unified theory of social relations', *Psychological Review* 99: 689–723.

Floyd, D.S. & Floyd, W.A. (1985) 'Bulimia: The secretive cycle of shame/superiority', *Journal of Human Behavior and Learning* 2: 6–12.

Frederickson, B.L. & Roberts, T.A. (1997) 'Objectification theory: Toward understanding women's lived experiences and mental health risks', *Psychology of Women Quarterly* 21: 173–206.

Freud, S. (1905/1953) 'Three essays on the theory of sexuality', in J. Strachey (ed., & trans.), *The Standard Edition of the Complete Psychological Works of Sigmund Freud*, (Vol. 7), (pp. 125–243), London: Hogarth Press.

Freud, S. (1909/1963) 'Analysis of a phobia in a five-year-old boy', in P. Rieff (ed.), *Freud, the Sexual Enlightenment of Children*, New York: Collier.

Frijda, N.H. (1994) 'Emotions are functional, most of the time', in P. Ekman & R.J. Davidson (eds), *The Nature of Emotion*, (pp. 112–22), New York: Oxford University Press

Gilbert, P. (1997) 'The evolution of social attractiveness and its role in shame, humiliation, guilt and therapy', *British Journal of Medical Psychology* 70: 114–43.

Gilbert, P., Allan, S., Ball, L. & Bradshaw, Z. (1996) 'Overconfidence and personal evaluations of social rank', *British Journal of Medical Psychology* 69: 59–68.

Gilligan, J. (1996) 'Exploring shame in special settings: A psychotherapeutic study', in C. Cordess & M. Cox (eds), *Forensic Psychotherapy: Crime, Psychodynamics and the Offender Patient, Vol. 2: Mainly Practice*, (pp. 475–89), London: Jessica Kingsley Publishers.

Glickauf-Hughes, C. & Wells, M. (1995) 'Narcissistic characters with obsessive features: Diagnostic and treatment considerations', *American Journal of Psychoanalysis* 55: 129–43.

Goffman, E. (1963) *Stigma: Notes on the Management of Spoiled Identity*, Englewood Cliffs, NJ: Prentice-Hall.

Goldberg, C. (1991) *Understanding Shame*, Northvale, NJ: Jason Aronson.

Gomberg, E.L. (1987) 'Shame and guilt issues among women alcoholics', *Alcoholism Treatment Quarterly* 4: 139–55.

Gomberg, E.L. (1987) 'Shame and guilt issues among women alcoholics', *Alcoholism Treatment Quarterly*, 4: 139–55.

Greenwald, D.F. & Harder, D.W. (1998) 'Domains of shame: Evolutionary, cultural, and psychotherapeutic aspects', in P. Gilbert & B. Andrews (eds), *Shame: Interpersonal Behavior, Psychopathology, and Culture*, (pp. 225–45), New York: Oxford University Press.

Guisinger, S. & Blatt, S.J. (1994) 'Individuality and relatedness: Evolution of a fundamental dialectic', *American Psychologist* 49: 104–11.

Halling, S. (1994) 'Shame and forgiveness', *Humanistic Psychologist* 22: 74–87.

Hamilton, W.D. (1964) 'The genetical evolution of social behavior. I. and II', *Journal of Theoretical Biology* 7: 1–52.

Hamilton, W.D. (1972) 'Altruism and related phenomena, mainly in the social insects', *Annual Review of Ecological Systems* 3: 193–232.

Harder, D.W. (1990) Comment on Wright *et al.*, 'Shame, guilt, narcissism, and depression: Correlates and sex differences', *Psychoanalytic Psychology* 7: 285–9.

Harder, D.W. (1995) 'Shame and guilt assessment, and relationships of shame- and guilt-proneness to psychopathology', in J.P. Tangney & K.W. Fischer (eds), *Self-Conscious Emotions: The Psychology of Shame, Guilt, Embarrassment and Pride*, (pp. 368–92), New York: Guilford Press.

Harder, D.W. (1996, August) 'Guilt and symptoms of psychopathology: Chronic versus moral standards guilt', in J.A. Bybee & J. Tangney (co-chairs), *Is Guilt Adaptive? Functions in Interpersonal Relationships and Mental Health*, Symposium conducted at the 104th annual convention of the American Psychological Association, Toronto, Canada.

Harder, D.W. & Lewis, S.J. (1987) 'The assessment of shame and guilt', in J.N. Butcher & C.D. Spielberger (eds), *Advances in Personality Assessment*, (Vol. 6), (pp. 89–114), Hillsdale, NJ: Lawrence Erlbaum Associates Inc.

Harder, D.W. & Zalma, A. (1990) 'Two promising shame and guilt scales: A construct validity comparison', *Journal of Personality Assessment* 55: 729–45.

Harder, D.W., Cutler, L. & Rockart, L. (1992) 'Assessment of shame and guilt and their relationships to psychopathology', *Journal of Personality Assessment* 59: 584–604.

Harper, J.M. & Hoopes, M.H. (1990) *Uncovering Shame*, New York: Norton.

Henderson, S. (1977) 'The social network, support and neurosis: The function of attachment in adult life', *British Journal of Psychiatry* 131: 185–91.

Hill, J. (1984) 'Human altruism and sociocultural fitness', *Journal of Social and Biological Structures* 7: 17–35.

Hoblitzelle, W. (1987) 'Differentiating and measuring shame and guilt: The relation between shame and depression', in H.B. Lewis (ed.), *The Role of Shame in Symptom Formation*, (pp. 207–35), Hillsdale, NJ: Lawrence Erlbaum.

Hogg, M.A. & Abrams, D. (1988) *Social Identifications*. London and New York: Routledge.

Hollander, E.P. (1958) 'Conformity, status, and idiosyncrasy credit', *Psychological Review* 65: 117–27.

Hollander, E.P. (1960) 'Competence and conformity in the acceptance of influence', *Journal of Abnormal and Social Psychology* 61: 361–5.

Hollon, S.D. & Beck, A.T. (1994) 'Cognitive and cognitive-behavioral therapies', in S. Garfield & E. Bergin (eds), *Handbook of Psychotherapy and Behavior Change*, (4th edition), New York: Wiley.

Horney, K. (1950) *Neurosis and Human Growth*, New York: Norton.

Horney, K. (1953) 'Constructive forces in the therapeutic process', *American Journal of Psychoanalysis* 13: 4–19.

James, S.R. (1992) 'Treatment of the shame involved in the experience of incest', in J.S. Rutan (ed.), *Psychotherapy for the 1990s*, (pp. 273–85), New York: Guilford Press.

Jones, B.A. (1983) 'Healing factors of psychiatry in light of attachment theory', *American Journal of Psychotherapy* 37: 235–44.

Katz, D.S. (1988) 'An analysis of defense mechanisms, moral reasoning, and shame-guilt proneness in pedophiles, rapists, and nonoffenders', *Dissertation Abstracts International* 49: 544B–5B. (University Microfilms No. DA 8801218).

Kaufman, G. (1989) *The Psychology of Shame: Theory and Treatment of Shame-Based Syndromes*, New York: Springer.

Kaufman, G. (1996) *The Psychology of Shame: Theory and Treatment of Shame-Based Syndromes*, (2nd edition), New York: Springer.

325

Keltner, D. & Harker, L. (1998) 'The forms and functions of the nonverbal signal of shame', in P. Gilbert & B. Andrews (eds), *Shame: Interpersonal Behavior, Psychopathology, and Culture*, (pp. 78–98), New York: Oxford University Press.

Kernberg, O.F. (1970) 'Factors in the psychoanalytic treatment of narcissistic personalities', *Journal of the American Psychoanalytic Association* 18: 51–85.

Kitayama, S., Markus, H.R. & Matsumoto, H. (1995) 'Culture, self, and emotion: A cultural perspective on "self-conscious" emotions', in J.P. Tangney & K.W. Fischer (eds), *Self-Conscious Emotions: The Psychology of Shame, Guilt, Embarrassment and Pride*, (pp. 439–64), New York: Guilford Press.

Kohut, H. (1971) *The Analysis of the Self*, New York: International Universities Press.

Krebs, D.L. & Denton, K. (1997) 'Social illusions and self-deception: The evolution of biases in person perception', in J.A. Simpson & D.T. Kenrick (eds), *Evolutionary Social Psychology*, (pp. 21–48), Mahwah, NJ: Lawrence Erlbaum Associates Inc.

Lansky, M.R. (1987a) 'Shame and domestic violence', in D.L. Nathanson (ed.), *The Many Faces of Shame*, (pp. 335–62), New York: Guilford Press.

Lansky, M.R. (1987b) 'Shame in the family relationships of borderline patients', in J.S. Grotstein, M.F. Solomon & J.A. Lang (eds), *The Borderline Patient*, (pp. 187–99), Hillsdale, NJ: Analytic Press.

Lansky, M.R. (1994) 'Nightmares of a hospitalized rape victim', *Bulletin of the Menninger Clinic* 59: 4–14.

Lear, T.E. (1990) 'Shameful encounters, alienation, and healing restitution in the group', *Group-Analysis* 23: 155–61.

Leary, M.R. & Kowalski, R.M. (1990) 'Impression management: A literature review and two-component model', *Psychological Bulletin* 107: 34–47.

Levin, S. (1967) 'Some metapsychological considerations on the differentiation between shame and guilt', *International Journal of Psycho-Analysis* 48: 267–76.

Levin, S. (1971) 'The psychoanalysis of shame', *International Journal of Psycho-Analysis* 52: 355–62.

Lewis, H.B. (1971) *Shame and Guilt in Neurosis*, New York: International Universities Press.

Lewis, H.B. (1986) 'The role of shame in depression', in M. Rutter, C.E. Izard, & P.B. Read (eds.), *Depression in Young People: Developmental and Clinical Perspectives*, (pp. 325–39), New York: Guilford Press.

Lewis, H.B. (1987) 'Shame and the narcissistic personality', in D.L. Nathanson (ed.), *The Many Faces of Shame*, (pp. 93–132), New York and London: Guilford Press.

Livingston, R.H. & Farber, B.A. (1996) 'Beginning therapists' responses to client shame', *Psychotherapy* 33: 601–10.

Mahoney, M.J. & Arnkoff, D.B. (1978) 'Cognitive and self-control therapies', in S.L. Garfield & E.A. Bergin (eds), *Handbook of Psychotherapy and Behavior change*, (2nd edition), New York: Wiley.

Mayman, M. (1974, August) *The shame experience, the shame dynamic, and shame personalities in psychotherapy*. Paper presented at the annual convention of the American Psychological Association, New Orleans. (Available from the Psychological Clinic, 1027 E. Huron St., Ann Arbor, MI 48109).

Migdow, J. (1994) 'Silencing the child', *Transactional Analysis Journal* 24: 178–84.

Mineka, S. & Kelly, K.A. (1989) 'The relationship between anxiety, lack of control and loss of control', in A. Steptoe & A. Appels (eds), *Stress, Personal Control, and Worker Health*, New York: Wiley.

Morrison, A.P. (1989) *Shame: The Underside of Narcissism*, Hillsdale, NJ: Analytic Press.

Morrison, A.P. (1994) 'The breadth and boundaries of a self-psychological immersion in shame', *Psychoanalytic Dialogues* 4: 19–35.

Nathanson, D.L. (1994a) *Shame and Pride: Affect, Sex and the Birth of the Self*, New York: Norton.

Nathanson, D.L. (1994b) 'Shame, compassion, and the "borderline" personality', *Psychiatric Clinics of North America* 17: 785–810.

Nicholas, M.W. (1993) 'How to deal with moral issues in group therapy without being judgmental', *International Journal of Group Psychotherapy* 43: 205–21.

O'Connor, L.E., Berry, J.W., Inaba, J. & Weiss, J. (1994) 'Shame, guilt, and depression in men and women in recovery from addiction', *Journal of Substance Abuse Treatment* 11: 503–10.

Osherman, S. & Krugerman, S. (1990) 'Men, shame, and psychotherapy', *Psychotherapy* 27: 327–39.

Petrik, N.D., Gildersleeve-High, L., McEllistrem, J.E. & Subotnik, L.S. (1994) 'The reduction of male abusiveness as a result of treatment: Reality or myth?', *Journal of Family Violence* 9: 307–16.

Piers, G. & Singer, M.B. (1953) *Shame and Guilt: A Psychoanalytic and Cultural Study*, New York: Norton.

Retzinger, S.M. (1991) *Violent Emotions: Shame and Rage in Marital Quarrels*, Newbury Park, CA: Sage.

Retzinger, S.M. (1998) 'Shame in the therapeutic relationship', in P. Gilbert & B. Andrews (eds), *Shame: Interpersonal Behavior, Psychopathology, and Culture*, (pp. 206–22), New York: Oxford University Press.

Rogers, C.R. (1976) 'Non-directive counseling: Client-centered therapy', in W.S. Sahakian (ed.), *Psychotherapy and Counseling: Techniques in Intervention*, (pp. 382–422), Chicago: Rand-McNally.

Sanftner, J.L., Barlow, D.H. & Marschall, D.E., Tangney, J.P. (1995) 'The relation of shame and guilt to eating disorder symptomatology', *Journal of Social and Clinical Psychology* 14: 315–24.

Schachter, S. (1951) 'Deviation, rejection, and communication', *Journal of Abnormal and Social Psychology* 46: 190–207.

Scheff, T.J. (1987) 'The shame-rage spiral: A case study of an interminable quarrel', in H.B. Lewis (ed.), *The Role of Shame in Symptom Formation*, (pp. 109–49), Hillsdale, NJ: Lawrence Erlbaum.

Scheff, T.J. (1988) 'Shame and conformity: The deference-emotion system', *American Review of Sociology* 53: 395–406.

Scheff, T.J. (1995) 'Shame and related emotions: An overview', *American Behavioral Scientist* 38: 1053–9.

Scheff, T.J. & Retzinger, S.M. (1991) *Emotions and Violence: Shame and Rage in Destructive Conflicts*, Lexington, MA: Lexington Books.

Scherer, K.R. & Wallbott, H.G. (1994) 'Evidence for the universality and cultural variation of differential emotion response patterning', *Journal of Personality and Social Psychology* 66: 310–28.

Schneider, C. (1977) *Shame, Exposure, and Privacy*, Boston: Beacon.

Shaver, P.R. & Hazan, C. (1994) 'Attachment', in A.L. Weber & J.H. Harvey (eds), *Close Relationships*, (pp. 110–30), Boston: Allyn & Bacon.

Sherif, M. & Sherif, C.W. (1964) *Reference Groups: Exploration into Conformity and Deviation of Adolescents*, New York: Harper & Row.

Sherif, M., Harvey, O.J., White, B.J., Hood, W.R. & Sherif, C.W. (1988) *Intergroup Conflict and Cooperation: The Robber's Cave Experiment*, Middletown, CT: Wesleyan University Press.

Shreve, B.W. & Kunkel, M.A. (1989, August) *The role of shame in adolescent suicide: A self-psychological perspective*. Paper presented at the annual meeting of the American Psychological Association, New Orleans.

Socarides, D.D. & Stolorow, R.D. (1986) 'Self psychology and psychoanalytic phenomenology', in I.L. Kutash & A. Wolf (eds), *Psychotherapist's Casebook: Theory and Technique in the Practice of Modern Therapies*, (pp. 43–54), San Francisco: Jossey-Bass.

Stoller, R. (1987) "Pornography: Daydreams to Cure Humiliation", in D.L. Nathanson (ed.), *The Many Faces of Shame*, (pp. 292–307), New York: Guilford Press.

Stolorow, R. & Lachmann, F. (1980) *Psychoanalysis of Developmental Arrests*, New York: International Universities Press.

Stone, M.H. (1992) 'Incest, Freud's seduction theory, and borderline personality', *Journal of the American Academy of Psychoanalysis* 20: 167–81.

Tajfel, H. (1978) *Differentiation Between Social Groups: Studies in the Psychology of Inter-Group Relations*, San Diego, CA: Academic Press.

Tajfel, H. (ed.) (1982) *Social Identity and Intergroup Relations*, London: Cambridge University Press.

Tajfel, H. & Turner, J.C. (1986) 'The social identity theory of intergroup behavior', in S. Worchel & W.G. Austin (eds), *The Psychology of Intergroup Relations*, (2nd edition, pp. 7–24) Chicago: Nelson Hall.

Talbot, N.L. (1996) 'Women sexually abused as children: The centrality of shame issues and treatment implications', *Psychotherapy* 33: 11–18.

Tangney, J.P. (1995) 'Recent advances in the empirical study of shame and guilt', *American Behavioral Scientist* 38: 1132–45.

Tangney, J.P., Burggraf, S.A. & Wagner, P.E. (1995) 'Shame-proneness, guilt-proneness, and psychological symptoms', in J.P. Tangney & K.W. Fischer (eds), *Self-Conscious Emotions: The Psychology of Shame, Guilt, Embarrassment and Pride*, (pp. 343–67), New York: Guilford Press

Tomkins, S.S. (1963) *Affect/Imagery/Consciousness*, (Vol. 2), New York: Springer.

Tomkins, S.S. (1987) 'Shame', in D.L. Nathanson (ed.), *The Many Faces of Shame*, (pp. 133–61), New York and London: Guilford Press.

Turner, S. (1993) 'Talking about sexual abuse: The value of short-term groups for women survivors', *Journal of Group Psychotherapy, Psychodrama, and Sociometry* 46: 110–21.

Wallace, R. & Nosko, A. (1993) 'Working with shame in the group treatment of male batterers', *International Journal of Group Psychotherapy* 43: 45–61.

Wallbott, H.G. & Scherer, K.R. (1995) 'Cultural determinants in experiencing shame and guilt', in J.P. Tangney & K.W. Fischer (eds), *Self-conscious Emotions: The Psychology of Shame, Guilt, Embarrassment and Pride*, (pp. 465–87), New York: Guilford Press.

Wenegrat, B. (1990) *Sociobiological Psychiatry*, Lexington, MA: Lexington Books/Heath.

Wilder, D.A. & Allen, V.L. (1978) 'Group membership and preference for information about others', *Personality and Social Psychology Bulletin* 4: 106–10.

Wright, F. (1987) 'Men, shame, and antisocial behavior: A psychodynamic perspective', *Group*, 11: 238–46.

Wright, F., O'Leary, J.O. & Balkin, J. (1989) 'Shame, guilt, narcissism, and depression: Correlates and sex differences', *Psychoanalytic Psychology* 7: 285–9.

Wright, R. (1994) *The Moral Animal: Evolutionary Psychology and Everyday Life*, New York: Pantheon.

Wurmser, L. (1987) 'Shame: The veiled companion of narcissism', in D.L. Nathanson (ed.), *The Many Faces of Shame*, (pp. 64–92), New York and London: Guilford Press.

Yalom, I.D. (1970) *The Theory and Practice of Group Psychotherapy*, New York: Basic Books.

Young, J.E. (1990) *Cognitive Therapy for Personality Disorders: A Schema-Focused Approach*, Sarasota, FL: Professional Resource Exchange.

Young, J. & Klosko, J. (1993) *Reinventing Your Life*, New York: St. Martin's Press.

Yufit, R.I. (1991) 'American Association of Suicidology Presidential Address: Suicide assessment in the 1990s', *Suicide and Life Threatening Behavior* 21: 152–63.

Section IV

OVERVIEW AND CONCLUDING COMMENTS

15

EVOLUTIONARY PSYCHOTHERAPY:

Where from here?

Kent G. Bailey and Paul Gilbert

This book has explored how our understanding of evolution can inform psychotherapy. Both client and therapist each share the same ancestral heritage that goes back into the distant reaches of mammalian, primate, hominid and human evolution. Consequently, each shares the same fundamental desires, needs, goals, and defensive strategies (e.g., flight, fight, submit, proximity seek, deceive and so forth). Although variations in culture, class, socioeconomic status, race, gender, and nationality draw attention to individual differences, there remains the opportunity for clients and therapists – and any two human beings – to readily empathize with the other and reach a deep common ground. Indeed, our species 'family' has come a long, difficult way together since the common ancestor to humanity walked the savannas of Africa some six to seven million years ago.

The evolutionary approach helps to answer three fundamental questions about humanity that go to the heart of professional helping and clinical practice: First, what and who are we as human beings – that is, what is human nature or species 'normality'?; second, how and why do humans develop and/or behave in less than optimal ways – that is, what can evolution tell us about the causes of suffering and psychopathology?; and, third, what can professional helpers and psychotherapists do to ameliorate or even 'cure' the suffering of heart and mind? All the chapters in this book address each of these questions, although individual authors differ in their weighting of the questions and their particular theoretical and clinical emphases.

This book casts the net widely in bringing evolutionary concepts to bear on traditional clinical practice and psychotherapy. Some of these concepts include functional analysis and regulation/dysregulation of internal processes (Troisi & McGuire, Chapter 2), proximate versus ultimate causes of behaviour (Kriegman, Chapter 4; O,Connor, Chapter 13), social strategies and mentalities (Gilbert, Chapter 6), archetypes (Stevens, Chapter 5) attachment and mal-attachment (Erickson, Chapter 10; Liotti, Chapter 11; Sloman, Chapter 12), kinship, kin selection, and inclusive fitness (Bailey, Chapter 3; Erickson, Chapter 10; Gilbert, Bailey & McGuire, Chapter 1; Kriegman, Chapter 4), theory of mind and deception (Allen & Gilbert, Chapter 7), altruism and reciprocity (Bailey, Chapter 3; Gilbert, Bailey & McGuire, Chapter 1), activation/deactivation of psychological mechanisms (Troisi & McGuire, Chapter 2), aggression, ranking behaviour, and formation of alliances (Gilbert; Chapter 6; Gilbert, Bailey & McGuire, Chapter 1; Liotti, Chapter 11; Sloman, Chapter 12), sexual reproductive strategies and sexual jealousy (Glantz & Moehl, Chapter 8), gender in psychotherapy (Rasgon, McGuire & Troisi, Chapter 9), shame (Harder & Greenwald, Chapter, 14), guilt (O'Connor, Chapter 13) and incest avoidance (Erickson, Chapter 10).

These concepts help to flesh out a meaningful view of human nature (question 1) and also help to cement links between human nature and the domain of psychopathology (question 2). Many authors also discuss evolution-based concepts that address – directly or indirectly – questions 2 (psychopathology) and 3 (clinical applications in the helping context). The therapeutic implications include those of the value of evolution-informed case formulation (Troisi & McGuire, Chapter 2); self and sub-selves relations and internal conflict (Gilbert Chapter 6; Stevens, Chapter 5), internal working models of self and relationships (Liotti, Chapter 11; Sloman, Chapter 12); the nature of pathogenic beliefs (Allen & Gilbert, Chapter 7; O'Connor, Chapter 13), role of client "testing" in therapy (O,Connor; Chapter 13), kin-like relations and psychological kinship in therapy (Bailey, Chapter 3), transference/countertransference (Kriegman, Chapter 4), therapist and client gender (Rasgon, McGuire & Troisi, Chapter 9), failure to achieve biological goals (Troisi & McGuire, Chapter 2), key issues in couples therapy (Glantz & Moehl, Chapter 8), shame (Harder & Greenwald, Chapter 14) and guilt (O'Connor, Chapter 13).

What emerges is a picture of the evolved human brain as a repository of ancient mechanisms and mentalities that proximally impel us to survive and do those things that have in the past, ultimately, led to individual reproduction and/or reproduction of closely related kin (i.e., inclusive fitness). All human beings are so impelled, and in that fact lies the seeds of evolutionary psychology, evolutionary psychopathology, and evolutionary psychotherapy.

Some overarching trends

Normal functions and their disruption or malfunction

Virtually all models of psychological dysfunction and disorder are implicitly based on the fundamental premise that abnormality is a variation and/or departure from some pre-existing normality (Wakefield, 1999). Although culture may at times define which strategies are deemed abnormal (e.g., high aggressiveness may be regarded as justified in one culture but as deviant in another), malfunction or dysfunction of psychological processes typically reflect 'normality abnormally expressed' (Bailey, 1991). Similarly, in physical medicine disease exists 'when some of the structures and functions of the body deviate from the norm to the point where the ability to maintain homeostasis is destroyed or threatened or where the individual can no longer meet environmental challenges' (Abrams, 1986: 4). In medicine, normality of the body's structures, functions, and structure–function relationships are often assumed at the outset and focus is primarily on diagnosing and treating the deviation. For the physician, normality and health are basically one and the same thing (see Offer & Sabshin, 1966, 1984, 1991). For example, when the pathologist examines a sample of cells microscopically from a patient's breast, the focus is entirely on identifying the presence or absence of deviant cells not normal ones. But this logic, commonly carried over into the psychiatric view of mental illness, readily breaks down when the diagnostician and therapist move into the domains of emotion, behaviour, and thought, for no consensual agreement has been reached on baseline normality. Consequently, either the normality problem is ignored entirely by psychoanalysts, behaviourists, cognitivists, and others, or reasoning risks falling into circular attempts at definition such as Rosenhahn and Seligman's (1995: 16): *Normality is simply the absence of abnormality* (emphasis in original). Clearly, in the absence of some reasonable consensus on what constitutes pre-existing normality, the fields of both psychopathology and psychotherapy resemble large, fine homes erected on shifting sands rather than a firm foundation.

There are various reasons why our understanding of normality can become confused. First, because as various chapter authors point out, an apparent dysfunction may in fact be a 'normal' adaptation to a specific environment. For example, if someone is severely traumatized in early life (e.g., via abuse) it may be a part of normal defensive organization to become highly threat sensitive, distrustful, anxious, aggressive, or depressed. Although this may compromise his or her ability to pursue biosocial goals (Troisi & McGuire, Chapter 2) and is not conducive to happiness, we may be observing basically 'normal' adaptations to abnormal or traumatizing environments (see Nesse & Williams, 1995, for further discussion of such issues in medicine).

Second, while there are specific evolved strategies subserving normal adaptations (e.g., for mate selection, attachment), there is both genetic variation in these strategies and cultural variation in how they are expressed. For example, there is wide variation in the genetic underpinnings of personality and susceptibility to pathology. In bipolar affective illness, evidence suggests that genes for excessive mood variation may have been positively selected and offer advantages provided their rates do not exceed certain frequencies in populations (Wilson, 1998). Similar arguments apply to disorders like psychopathy, anxiety, depression, and even schizophrenia (Stevens & Price, 2000). So there is little doubt that some people are genetically disposed to various 'psychopathologies'. Thus we should be careful not to mix our levels between sociobiological concerns about what factors influence gene frequencies in specific populations, and what is essentially 'normal' psychology in terms of species-wide needs that must be met to enable people to secure goals, and form health promoting, psychobiological regulating relationships with themselves and others. There is clear evidence now that certain types of relationship are associated with good health outcomes, whereas others compromise the stress hormones and immune systems (Gilbert, Bailey & McGuire, Chapter 1).

This raises complex issues of what is adaptive in modern environments (see Troisi & McGuire, Chapter 2, this volume; and McGuire & Troisi, 1998). No evolutionist argues that disorders such as panic disorder, paranoia or severe depression are healthy in modern environments, because more often than not they interfere with biosocial goals. The question is a different one: what normal functions, that previously had adaptive significance, are involved in a particular psychopathology? And in exactly what ways (Wakefield, 1999)? For example, in panic it may be the threat detection and flight systems that are maladaptively triggered (e.g., by certain types of thinking – as in the cognitive model). Nesse and Williams (1995) have given a good airing to these issues for physical medicine. But in the field of psychopathology we are a long way from understanding, much less agreeing on, what the normal mechanisms are that may be functioning maladaptively in particular disorders. For example, is depression a disorder of attachment, social rank systems, or a more general thwarting of biosocial goals? Are there different types of depression that reflect dysfunction in different systems? Only a scientific, data-driven approach can answer these questions but until recently there have been no theories to encourage such research.

Fourth, because the mind is modular-like (with a variety of different and at times competing strategies) in its operation, dysfunction can arise either because one or more modules are dysfunctional or absent and/or the *interactions* between modules produce maladaptive feedback and spin out of control (Gilbert, 1995). For example, people with autism seem to have dysfunctions in basic modules for processing social information (Baron-Cohen, 1997). Many depressed people do not. Their social processing biases are often mood dependent and they may run into problems when (for example) the normal capacities for introspection and rumination set up negative feedback loops (Gilbert, Chapter 6); i.e., modules come to interact dysfunctionally with each other.

Fifth, Harder and Greenwald (Chapter 14) offer another angle with their view that some functions and modules (e.g., for shame) can be over-developed or under-developed. And this view fits well with others who see some psychopathologies as arising out of skewed development with the under- or over-development of certain strategies (e.g., Beck *et al.*, 1990). Horowitz *et al.* (1988) developed a questionnaire (Inventory of Interpersonal Problems; IIP) which focused specifically on inter-personal problematic behaviours of 'too much or too little'. This scale explores things people find hard to do (e.g., trust others) and things people overdo (e.g., open up to people too much). In a factor analytic study of the IIP, Barkham, Hardy and Startup (1994) found that interpersonal problems (of doing things too much or too little) factored out into similar constructs as suggested by Gilbert (1989); that is, problems revolved around care eliciting, helping others, sharing, and asserting oneself.

The idea that different strategies can be under- or over-developed also helps us conceptualize the adaptive–maladaptive issue in new ways. For example, sensitivity to rejection is adaptive but can become maladaptive (Sloman, Chapter 12), normal attachment mechanisms can become dysfunctional (Liotti, Chapter 11) and similar reasoning is suggested for guilt (O'Conner, Chapter 13), shame (Harder & Greenwald, Chapter 14), deception mechanisms (Allen & Gilbert, Chapter 7), and the internal rehearsal of self–other role enactments (Gilbert, Chapter 6). These fine-grain analyses of adaptive mechanisms (and their dysfunctions) will add substantially to our understanding of various disorders and offer the beginnings of new ways to classify disorders and their therapy.

Commonalties

Whether it is in dysfunctional 'modules', dysfunctional interactions between 'modules' or under- or over-development, the evolution-based chapters in this volume provide the researcher, diagnostician and therapist with an implicit menu of species norms, that are contextually and developmentally sensitive, as baselines for estimating pathological deviations. For example, when we explored the social strategies of caring (giving and receiving), mate selection, ranking behaviour, and formation of alliances in the introductory chapter, or when Troisi and McGuire discuss suboptimal outputs, functional incapacities, or system dysregulation, it is implicitly against the baseline of species typicality, or, more loosely, 'normality'. Fundamentally, this is another way at looking at question 1, human nature. Whereas other social sciences lack a baseline or species norm, evolutionary psychology and psychopathology – and now psychotherapy – start from the foundation of a universal human nature (Buss, 1990; Gilbert, 1989; Tooby & Cosmides, 1990), grounded in the evolutionary sciences of this century (classic Darwinian theory, neo-Darwinian theory, ethology, sociobiology, biocultural anthropology, evolutionary anthropology, paleopsychology, evolutionary paleontology, and so forth).

These separate evolutionary strands all converge on two ruling principles. First, there is a univeral human nature that arose, over eons of time, through natural and sexual selection of gene-traits (Gilbert, Bailey & McGuire, Chapter 1) that helped our prehuman, hominid, and human ancestors to first survive and then reproduce individually and inclusively. Second, in modern contexts, some environments are now toxic and deeply thwarting and damaging of our nature (see Bailey, Chapter 3 on mismatch theory). Just as easy access to high fat foods, sugar and salt foods, cigarettes and alcohol, and low requirements for exercise damage our physical health, so do deviations from early attachment 'norms' (namely, intimate relations between infant and caregiver(s) during first years of life) and deviations from ancestral patterns of family intimacy (namely, kin relations) and group cohesion (namely, band and tribal patterns) damage our mental health.

Clearly, mental health flourishes in some environments and not in others and the reason for this resides as much in the thwarting of natural needs (especially social ones) as in any genetic vulnerability. Once the fields of psychopathology and psychotherapy ground themselves in this logic, then psychopathologists naturally turn their attention to unhealthy deviations from the species norm in their assessments and diagnoses, and psychotherapists naturally turn theirs to ways of reducing or normalizing these deviations (e.g., helping the client effectively to pursue biosocial goals or establish healthier and more species-normal kinship and social support systems).

The social brain and natural sociality

The brain regulates life itself through metabolic and other vital functions, and it also regulates the mind's panoply of functions – consciousness, emotion, behaviour and thought. As such, the brain codes, stores, and de-codes vast amounts of information ranging from the simplest spinal reflex, to relatively fixed action patterns (e.g., the orgasmic response or the pupillary reflex), to mixtures of ancient and simple patterns with newer, learned material (e.g., patterns of sexual foreplay and intercourse in various cultures), to predominantly learned patterns (e.g., preferences in politics, entertainment, fashion and the like), and, finally, to the realm of 'pure thought' that transcends the instincts (see Bailey, 1987). Paul MacLean's (1990) triune brain model stipulates that this hierarchical complexity can be simplified once the brain is decomposed into the three domains of (i) reptilian automaticity, (ii) paleomammalian emotionality and motivational impulsions, and (iii) neocortical thought, reasoning, self-control, and future orientation. Much of human nature is encoded into the first two phylogenetically older levels of the brain, but the human species has also been a 'thinker' since the early stages of evolution from the common ancestor, and early hominids evolved in an environment that was distinctly cognitive as compared to that of other animals. Indeed, *the core of our zoological distinctiveness is our entry into this cognitive niche* (Tooby & DeVore, 1987: 209, emphasis in original; see also Allen & Gilbert, Chapter 7).

The brain appears infinite in its capabilities, but what does it really do most of the time? More than anything else, the human brain is a social brain that houses the psychological mechanisms and social mentalities (Gilbert; Chapter 6 Liotti, Chapter 11; Sloman, Chapter 12; Troisi & McGuire, Chapter 2) that subserve the day-to-day social behaviour of human beings. Kriegman (Chapter 4) states the familiar evolutionary view, *The human brain evolved as a powerful social "computer" that evolved to deal with the incredible complexity of kin and reciprocal relatedness and conflict in . . . a web of social connections* (emphasis in original). From the earliest attachment of infant to mother, to later child–parent relations, parent-to-parent relations, and numerous other configurations, human beings reveal themselves to be highly social creatures who love, nurture, share, and sometimes hate and kill with an alacrity not seen anywhere else in nature.

Biosocial goal-seeking and failure to achieve goals

As a highly social organism, human beings are naturally designed to meet a wide range of biological and biosocial goals and failure to meet these goals is associated with feelings of frustation, helplessness, depression, and many other forms of psychopathology. Troisi and McGuire (Chapter 2) say that, 'Human beings, like all other organisms, have been designed by natural selection to strive for the achievement of specific goals and or experiences . . . These are the goals that concern humans and that are responsible for most of human behaviour.' In general, biosocial goals include, but are not limited to, satisfactory outcomes in the areas of food acquisition and nutrition, finding shelter, mating, mate protection and retention, parenting, alliance building, status acquisition, managing agonistic conflicts, being a valued in-group member in kinship and inclusive fitness contexts, managing fairness and reciprocity in relationships, and experiencing meaning in one's life (Gilbert, 1989, 1997). When human beings enjoy success in meeting their natural biosocial goals (Gilbert, 1989, 1992; Nesse, 1990) or in any way 'succeed' as a member of their species (Bailey, 1987; Herrnstein, 1977), they tend to be emotionally satisfied, happy, and fulfilled, and perhaps more optimistic about life in general. In contrast, any real or perceived failure in the species mission is likely to be accompanied by displeasure, frustration, tension, depression, and, in the extreme, serious forms of physical and psychological pathology.

Two cautions to working with a species wide nature

We offer two cautions to working with species wide biosocial goals. First there is a cultural and moral dimension to helping people achieve biosocial goals. There are some goals that may have adaptive value but therapists will try to inhibit them on moral grounds. For example, vengeful killing (outside of war) is not encouraged. Nor is (say) a male's sexual desires for under-age girls. And no reputable therapist would attempt to help a married man or woman become successful at attracting and (deceiving) men or women so she or he could have multiple affairs – even if each has understandable (evolved) desires to do so. So understanding species norms does not mean evolutionary therapists stand outside of the cultural values and morality of their society.

Second, evolutionary psychotherapy is based on the evolutionary fact that there will be individual differences within populations. So that when we speak of species norms this is a very high level view. In other words, to articulate species norms is *not to try to impose specific values*. For example, the social interest and orientation of the schizoid or introvert personality will be very different to that of the extravert. And of course people will come to therapy with very different culturally acquired beliefs and experiences. Like other psychotherapies, evolutionary psychotherapy is respectful of these individual variations and the particular needs, aspirations and capabilities of each client. One person may seek to find ways of eliciting more supportive relationships, whereas another may seek ways to have more personal control and autonomy from others. While one person may seek ways to control his or her anger another may seek ways to cope with grief. Given a secure enough base from which to explore, people will often come up with their own novel ways of coping and changing.

Methods of repairing and restoring disrupted biosocial functions

This discussion implies that a major function of evolutionary psychotherapy is to reduce harmful dysfunctions (Wakefield, 1999) and to aid clients in defining and optimizing *their* goal-seeking and goal-realization. Troisi and McGuire (Chapter 2) are clear on this: the primary aim of evolutionary psychotherapy 'is improving the patient's chances of achieving short-term biological goals'. *However, this aim is achieved in various ways depending on what the client brings to therapy.* For the seriously ill person (e.g., the schizophrenic or manic-depressive), psychotropic medication in conjunction with psychotherapy may be required to elicit even rudimentary goal-seeking (see Troisi & McGuire, Chapter 2) and the impoverished or undereducated client may require financial help, advice, and other forms of support at the outset. Moreover, people with disorganized attachment backgrounds and otherwise problematic social histories (e.g., borderline and other seriously disturbed individuals – see Kriegman, Chapter 4; Liotti, Chapter 11), are likely to need great support and 'kinship' (Bailey, Chapter 3) from the therapist before they are emotionally strong enough to pursue their biosocial goals in health promoting ways. Ultimately, however, evolutionary psychotherapists seek to help the person become a well-functioning member of species *Homo sapiens* whose biosocial goals, as reflected in personal aspirations and needs, are reasonably sought and met. And it does not matter what kind of illness a person suffers (e.g., schizophrenia, depression or alcohol dependence) or how severe it is, as members of the human race they all require some control over their goals and access to health promoting resources (e.g., helpful, supportive and non-abusing relationships).

Cognitive restructuring and repair of the mind

As mentioned earlier, human beings lived and evolved in a cognitively demanding social niche for a long time, and the capacity for thought, reflection, and self-reflection is one of our most distinctive species traits. Each individual lives in a public world of perception and behaviour on the one hand, but also traverses in his or her own private, internal world of perceptions, images, and thoughts about the self, others, and material objects. Cognitive therapists are aware of the power of these internal functions, and many argue that distorted cognitions lie at the base of much human misery and pathology (Beck, 1987). The evolutionary cognitive therapist adds a major element to traditional approaches; that is, the internal cognitive world of the client reflects not only his or her own ontogenetically constructed mind with its panoply of selves and subselves (Gilbert, Chapter 6), modular processes, psychological mechanisms, social mentalities, and the like, but these also contain ancient 'wisdom' of ancestral minds that came before as well (Stevens, Chapter 5). This does not imply innate ideas *per se*, but rather innate competencies (strategies and algorithms) and design mechanisms of the brain that bias motivations, emotions, and thinking in directions that favour survival proximally and inclusive fitness ultimately (Gilbert, Bailey & McGuire, Chapter 1). As contributors to this volume have stated time and again, human beings do not just feel, want, and think about anything and everything, they focus on basically similar themes, goals, and preoccupations as have all of the humans that came before them (see Bailey, 1987).

Finally, the evolutionary therapist is very cautious about *labelling* certain forms of thinking as pathological when they may actually reflect ancient adaptive functions at work. For example, so called 'distorted cognitions' (e.g., fearful or anxious thoughts) may not be errors in the brain as such but may reflect the activation of (previously) adaptive defensive information processing where to over-estimate danger was more adaptive than under-estimating, and fast was more adaptive then slow (Gilbert, 1998). Logical thinking in many domains, especially those related to our social worlds, were not necessarily normative evolutionarily – biases and distortions were often more the norm (Gilbert, Bailey & McGuire, Chapter 1). But again we are not saying that biases cannot spin out of control leading to serious pathologies.

Central role of the client–therapist relationship

Each contributor to this volume emphasizes the central role of the client–therapist relationship in evolutionary psychotherapy. Bailey (Chapter 3) argues that client and therapist usually work most effectively in a kin-like context as opposed to detached professionalism (see also Bailey & Wood, 1998; Wood, 1997). Kriegman (Chapter 4) has strong views about the client–therapist relationship, and he speaks of the power of the relationship as the treatment agent for insight, change and growth. He takes the traditional notions of transference and countertransference a step further and incorporates empathy, kinship, proximate/ultimate motivation, and a number of other evolutionary concepts into his understanding of the 'extraordinarily powerful' and 'intensive analytic relationship'. Liotti (Chapter 11) instructs us on matters of relating appropriately to mal-attached, insecure, and seriously disturbed clients, and Stevens (Chapter 5) contrasts Freud's rational neutrality in therapy with Jung's warm, accepting, and reciprocal alliance between analyst and client. O'Connor (Chapter 13) discusses the phenomenon of 'testing' in therapy where the client reveals pathological beliefs for the purpose of testing the therapist's affection and acceptance, and Bailey (Chapter 3), similarly, refers to situations where clients may act in a challenging manner to test the limits of therapist loyalty and competency.

Evolutionary psychotherapy: The future

The chapters of this book have offered many hints and suggestions about the future directions of evolutionary psychotherapy. Our goal is to stimulate refinement of theory, development of new assessment and diagnostic methods, and the generation of much-needed empirical data in the field. There are four key areas to consider:

Therapeutic relations

First, the dynamics of the client–therapist relationship are central elements of evolutionary psychotherapy. Troisi and McGuire (Chapter 2) introduce the important notion that the quality of the client–therapist relationship exerts a physiological and psychological regulating effect on the client's internal emotional, behavioural and cognitive systems. However true, this declaration raises more questions. Are there a set of necessary and/or desirable client–therapist parameters that go across all (or almost all) helping relationships, or should the relationship be tailored to the particular client's needs? Should the relationship reflect – implicitly or otherwise – a system of ranking with the therapist being more 'dominant', or should the relationships be egalitarian and participatory as advocated by feminist therapists especially (see Hare-Mustin, Maracek, Kaplan & Liss-Levinson, 1979)? Do different clients require different types of relationship according to which strategies and defences are the most problematic? Or should the relationship tend toward the 'professionally neutral' following traditional analysts and behaviourists, or should it reflect kin-like intimacy and sometimes even 'true' psychological kinship (Bailey, Chapter 3), and how should boundaries be maintained – if flexibly rather than rigidly how should we decide? And to what degree should we 'suffer with' our clients as suggested by Kriegman (Chapter 4)? How does the client–therapist relationship vary with mildly disturbed clients to more severely disturbed ones? How do computer-assisted, cognitive-behavioural, self-help programs fit?

We suspect that warm, compassionate, kin-like relations in a more-or-less egalitarian context are most conducive to positive client outcomes in most contexts, but long-term outcome studies will be needed to clarify this and many other relationship issues. Moreover, issues of rank and power are also salient. There is doubt that therapy will progress if clients view their therapists as subordinate to them, emotionally weaker, or unable to contain them or set safe boundaries. The ability to give as well as refuse requests is a mark of power, and feigned efforts to be egalitarian are dishonest and clients often (rightly) see right through them. In so far as some therapists may engage in efforts to re-parent the client, then the power issues in that process need to be explicit and acted on responsibly and not hidden.

A future area that will need careful thought from an evolutionary point of view is that of gender issues in psychotherapy (Rasgon, McGuire & Troisi, Chapter 9). Do same-sex client–therapist relationships operate in similar ways as opposite-sex ones? Is there more danger of same-sex relationships colluding in identifying with gender typical sexual reproductive strategies? Is there more danger of fundamental misunderstanding in opposite-sex client–therapist relationships? Kalman and Moehl (Chapter 8) offer the provocative idea that couples therapy can at times seek to encourage men to adopt strategies that are more in line with female reproductive interests. And men may not fully appreciate the serious damage done to women via sexual harassment and abuse, nor the fear or submissive tendencies that working with a male therapist could ignite. Evolutionary therapists would see gender-matching as a key area for future study.

At the end of the day, we see that relationships heal by providing certain types of signal that are psychobiologically potent and regulating. Just as one cannot expect one drug to work for all folk so its seems obvious that one type of relationship is unlikely to be helpful to all.

Goal-seeking behaviour

Second, the issue of biosocial goal-seeking (and thwarting of such goals) will continue to be a defining feature of evolutionary psychotherapy. Earlier we pointed out that, despite the brain's seemingly infinite capacity for variation, the actual behaviour of human beings tends to revolve around a delimited set of universal themes in the domains of shelter and security, food procurement and nutrition, sexuality and sex roles, mating, parenting, and interaction within and between groups. In applying this logic to therapy, the first question that arises is, 'How do the biosocial goal-seeking efforts of the client intersect with those of the therapist in the client–therapist relationship?' Asked another way, 'How does the personal inclusive fitness system that the client brings to therapy (with its particular impulsions to meet biosocial goals) intersect with the analogous fitness system of the therapist?' (see Bailey, Chapter 3; Kriegman, Chapter 4). These questions reveal that the issues of the client–therapist relationship and client–therapist biosocial goal-seeking are inextricably bound to each other in complex ways. Both considerable theory refinement and therapy process research are sorely needed at this juncture.

For many years, Michael McGuire and colleagues have studied biologically relevant goals as they impact psychopathology (McGuire & Fairbanks, 1977; McGuire & Essock-Vitale, 1981, 1982), and he and Troisi (1998) recently discussed goal/motivation linkages, age and gender aspects of goals, and goal-focused disorder assessments and treatment interventions. Gilbert (1989, 1992; Gilbert, Chapter 6; Gilbert, Bailey & McGuire, Chapter 1) has also discussed the importance of biosocial goals and their role in therapy process and outcome. Despite these efforts, evolutionary psychotherapy has only touched the surface regarding biosocial roles and how they play out in therapy. For example, does failure in pursuing certain goals have greater pathogenic effects than do others, and if so, why? Further, is there some minimal threshold of goal-attainment below which the individual is highly likely to exhibit symptoms of some kind? Are deficient patterns of goal-seeking primarily motivational deficits (see McGuire & Troisi, 1998), or do the affective, behavioural and cognitive systems come significantly into play? Are particular patterns of deficient goal-seeking associated with particular pathological syndromes or psychiatric disorders? Future answers to these and similar questions will greatly aid the evolutionary therapist in making those millisecond-by-millisecond decisions that influence the direction of a particular therapy session.

Specialized processing

Third, theory and research regarding the social brain as a repository of specialized programmes and mentalities subserving a wide range of evolved social strategies (e.g., for in-group:out-group, kinship, reciprocity, deception, deception detection, and so forth) will also be a central theme in the new field. This may well impact on traditional therapies including cognitive ones (see Gilbert, Chapter 6; Allen & Gilbert, Chapter 7, O'Conner, Chapter 13). Some consciously available thoughts and beliefs may be reflections of strategies that are in part the result of defensive processing, and some can be self-deceptive and manipulative. What this means for the actual conduct and focus of therapies like cognitive therapy remains to be investigated. Whether intervention is primarily a mental health treatment, educative or didactic, correctional, or morally exhortative (Orlinsky, 1989), it represents a fundamentally cognitive set of rather abstract messages from the therapist to the client whose intention is to change the client's way of thinking. In fact, 'client change' often means that the client has – over the course of therapy – become more like the therapist in thought and deed (Bailey & Wood, 1998).

Cognitive evolutionists will continue to make finer and finer distinctions about cognitive structures that function adaptively in current environments (e.g., mild fear of strangers), ones that are maladaptively expressed or otherwise dysregulated (e.g., agoraphobia or social anxiety), and those that reflect damage or serious defects in the structure itself (e.g., severe paranoia in schizophrenia or certain dementias). Improved assessment methods supported by empirical research are needed here, because proper classification of type of cognitive dysfunction precedes and, in fact, determines the appropriate range of therapeutic interventions.

Appropriate for the full spectrum of severity

Fourth, the last ten years or so have seen major efforts to apply psychological, psychosocial and therapeutic principles to the severely ill such as those with schizophrenia (Kingdom 1998; Morrison, 1998) and manic depression (Palmer & Gilbert, 1997). As we have stressed many times, evolutionary psychotherapy does not offer another new therapy but seeks an integrative one aided by understanding the evolution of the mind. Given that evolutionary psychotherapy addresses the client at the fundamental levels of human nature, brain structure and function, and biologically relevant goal-seeking, it can therefore utilize research and findings from many other approaches and offer appropriate interventions for the full spectrum of severity of disorder (Troisi & McGuire, Chapter 2). This is because *it is not wedded to a single method*. While an introspective discursive approach, or thought monitoring and challenging approach, or exposure to feared stimuli might suit one person at one time, another may need an active therapy input (an active, powerful ally or parent figure) that helps sort out finances and places to live and offers clear advice and support. One of us (PG), for example, found that a therapy progressed once he had interceded on behalf of the client with a government agency to get her proper benefits. The client said 'it was nice to know there was someone fighting for me for a change rather than against me'. And many clinicians not wedded to therapeutic dogma would probably do likewise. Being seen as a powerful ally can change the emotional relationship between client and therapist, but when should we act this way and when should we encourage the client to act for her or himself? In this sense evolutionary psychotherapy focuses on the needs and signal requirements of clients and not (just) on how to apply a technique or method.

Evolutionary psychotherapists often confront the client's (evolutionary salient) wishes and fears, and like many other therapies, attempt to offer a compassionate understanding of the losses, insecurities, frustrations, and inner conflicts that have been a part of human experience from the beginning. The evolutionary therapist adds, however, a new dimension. Matters of sexual abuse, incest, infidelity, rejection, low self-esteem, repressed anger, depression, addiction, and the like are seen as *species problems as well as individual ones*; this approach not only normalizes the problem in a very subtle way (namely, 'this is not just my personal problem, but most human beings could have this problem in my situation'), but provides a meaningful and scientific frame of reference for making sense of it as well.

Many of the case illustrations in this book involved serious forms of psycho-pathology including depression (Gilbert, Chapter 6; O'Connor, Chapter 13; Sloman, Chapter 12) psychotic depression with possible schizophrenia (Kriegman, Chapter 4), borderline personality disorder (Bailey, Chapter 3; Liotti, Chapter 11), and schizoid personality disorder (Stevens, Chapter 5). In these conditions, the supportive and reparative aspects of the client–therapist interaction are crucial, since, as many authors here point out, anomalies in early attachment and other formative social experiences are often major predisposing factors (see Bailey, Chapter 3; Erickson, Chapter 10; Liotti, Chapter 11; O'Connor; Chapter 13; Sloman, Chapter 12). Anchored to this 'secure base' (Bowlby, 1988), the client and therapist can then venture into the problematic territories of loneliness, self-rejection, disabling social dysfunction and the severely damaged and/or dysregulated emotional/motivational, behavioural, and cognitive systems that characterize some personality disorders, psychosis, and neuropathological syndromes.

In addressing everyday problems, the evolutionary therapist takes a realistic view of human nature, society, and the therapy process as he or she helps the client to construct more health promoting views of the world. However, this is done with the utmost respect and compassion for the human species in general and (like other good therapies) for the client in particular. Human beings can be selfish, narcissistic, deceptive, defensive, xenophobic, sexist, racist, and, indeed, imperfect in all things, but there is grandness and majesty in our ancestral history and cause for optimism in our current state (Tiger, 1979).

Conclusion

This book makes clear that the infant's mind is not a blank sheet, human beings do not act simply at the whim of environment, and, most importantly, human nature – as encoded in the genes over eons of evolutionary time – can no longer be ignored in the affairs of human beings. In the last twenty years attachment theory and research has rightly begun to influence our understanding of psychopathology, and, of course attachment needs are rooted in our evolution. But there is much more to the human mind and its disorders that just disordered attachment systems (Gilbert, 1989, 1992). This book has tried to offer sight of the rich and varied vistas for psychotherapy that lie ahead in approaching the suffering of our species, with an eye for the fact that both client and therapist have one foot in the distant past and one foot in the developmental and contextual environment of modern day.

References

Abrams, G. D. (1986) 'Introduction to general pathology: Mechanisms of disease', in S. Price & L. Wilson (eds), *Pathophysiology: Clinical Concepts of Disease Processes*, (3rd ed.), (pp. 1–116), New York: McGraw-Hill.

Bailey, K.G. (1987) *Human Paleopsychology: Applications to Aggression and Pathological Processes*, Hillsdale, NJ: Lawrence Erlbaum Associates Inc.

Bailey, K.G. (1991) 'Human paleopsychopathology: Implications for the paraphilias', *New Trends in Experimental and Clinical Psychiatry* 7: 5–16.

Bailey, K.G. & Wood, H.E. (1998) 'Evolutionary kinship therapy: Basic principles and treatment implications', *British Journal of Medical Psychology* 71: 509–23.

Barkham, M., Hardy, G.E. & Startup, M (1994) 'The structure, validity and clinical relevance of the Inventory of Interpersonal Problems', *British Journal of Medical Psychology* 67: 171–86

Baron-Cohen, S. (1997) 'How to build a baby who can read minds: Cognitive mechanism in mindreading', in S. Baron-Cohen (ed.), *The Maladapted Mind: Classic Readings in Evolutionary Psychopathology*, (pp. 207–39), Hove, UK: Psychology Press

Beck, A.T. (1987) 'Cognitive models of depression', *Journal of Cognitive Psychotherapy: An International Quarterly* 1: 5–38.

Beck, A.T., Freeman, A. & Associates. (1990) *Cognitive Therapy of Personality Disorders*, New York: Guilford Press.

Bowlby, J. (1988) *A Secure Base: Parent–child Attachment and Healthy Human Development*, New York: Basic Books.

Buss, D.M. (ed.) (1990) 'Biological foundations of personality: Evolution, behavioral genetics, and psychophysiology', [Special Issue], *Journal of Personality* 58: 1–345.

Gilbert, P. (1989) *Human Nature and Suffering*, Hove, UK: Lawrence Erlbaum Associates Ltd.

Gilbert, P. (1992) *Depression: The Evolution of Powerlessness*, Hove, UK: Psychology Press.

Gilbert, P. (1995) 'Biopsychosocial approaches and evolutionary theory as aids to integration in clinical psychology and psychotherapy', *Clinical Psychology and Psychotherapy* 2: 135–56.

Gilbert, P. (1997) 'The biopsychosociology of meaning', in M. Power & C.R. Brewin (eds), *The Transformation of Meaning: Reconciliation Theory and Therapy in Cognitive, Behaviour, and Related Therapies*, (pp. 33–56), New York: Wiley.

Gilbert, P. (1998) 'The evolved basis and adaptive functions of cognitive distortions', *British Journal of Medical Psychology* 71: 447–63.

Hare-Mustin, R., Marecek, J., Kaplan, A. & Liss-Levinson, N. (1979) 'Rights of clients, responsibilities of therapists', *American Psychologist* 34: 3–17.

Herrnstein, R.J. (1977) 'Doing what comes naturally: A reply to Professor Skinner', *American Psychologist* 32: 1013–16.

Horowitz, L.M., Rosenberg, S.E., Baer, B.A., Ureno, G. & Villasenor, V.S. (1988) 'Inventory of interpersonal problems: Psychometric properties and clinical applications', *Journal of Consulting and Clinical Psychology* 56: 885–92.

Kingdom, D. (1998) 'Cognitive behaviour therapy of psychosis: Complexities in engagement and therapy', in N. Tarrier, A. Wells & G. Haddock (eds), *Treating Complex Cases: The Cognitive Behavioural Approach*, (pp. 176–94), Chichester: Wiley.

McGuire, M.T. & Essock-Vitale, S.M. (1981) 'Psychiatric disorders in the context of evolutionary biology: A functional classification of behavior', *Journal of Nervous and Mental Disease* 169: 672–86.

McGuire, M.T. & Essock-Vitale, S.M. (1982) 'Psychiatric disorders in the context of evolutionary biology: The impairment of adaptive behaviors during the exacerbation and remission of psychiatric illnesses', *Journal of Nervous and Mental Disease* 170: 9–20.

McGuire, M.T. & Fairbanks, L.A. (eds) (1997) *Ethological Psychiatry: Psychopathology in the Context of Evolutionary Biology*, New York: Grune & Stratton.

McGuire, M. & Troisi, A. (1998) *Darwinian Psychiatry*, New York: Oxford University Press.

MacLean, P. (1990) *The Triune Brain in Evolution*, New York: Plenum Press.

Morrison. A.P. (1998) 'Cognitive behavioural therapy for psychotic symptom in schizophrenia', in N. Tarrier, A. Wells & G. Haddock (eds), *Treating Complex Cases: The Cognitive Behavioural Approach*, (pp. 195–216), Chichester: Wiley.

Nesse, R.M. (1990) 'Evolutionary explanations of the emotions', *Human Nature* 1: 261–89.

Nesse, R.M. & Williams, G.C. (1995) *Evolution and Healing: The New Science of Darwinian Medicine*, London: Weidenfeld & Nicolson.

Offer, D. & Sabshin, M. (1966) *Normality*, New York: Basic Books.

Offer, D. & Sabshin, M. (1984) *Normality and the Life Cycle*, New York: Basic Books.

Offer, D. & Sabshin, M. (eds) (1991) *The Diversity of Normal Behavior: Further Contributions to Normatology*, New York: Basic Books.

Orlinsky, D.E. (1989) 'Researchers' images of psychotherapy: Their origins and influence on research', *Clinical Psychology Review* 9: 413–41.

Palmer, A. & Gilbert, P. (1977) 'Manic-depression: What psychologists can do to help', in V.P. Varma (eds), *Managing Manic-Depressive Disorder*, (pp. 42–61), London: Kingsley.

Rosenhahn, D. & Seligman, M.E.P. (1995) *Abnormal Psychology*, New York: Norton.

Stevens, A. & Price, J. (2000) *Evolutionary Psychiatry*, (2nd ed.), New York: Routledge.

Tiger, L. (1979) *Optimism: The Biology of Hope*, New York: Simon and Schuster.

Tooby, J. & Cosmides, L. (1990) 'The past explains the present: Emotional adaptations and the structure of ancestral environments', *Ethology and Sociobiology*, 11: 375–424.

Tooby, J. & DeVore, I. (1987) 'The reconstruction of hominid behavioral evolution through strategic modeling', in W.G. Kinzey (ed.), *The Evolution of Human Behavior: Primate Models*, (pp. 183–238), Albany, NY: State University of New York Press.

Wakefield, J.C. (1999) 'Evolutionary Versus Prototype Analysis of the Concept of Disorder', *Journal of Abnormal Psychology* 108: 400–411.

Wilson, D. (1998) 'Evolutionary epidemiology and manic depression', *British Journal of Medical Psychology* 71: 375–96.

Wood, H.E. (1997) *Staying in the Therapy Zone: Kinship and the Art of Therapy Process*. Paper presented at the annual meeting of the ASCAP Society, Tucson, AZ.

AUTHOR INDEX

SUBJECT INDEX